Emotions in the Human Voice

Volume 3: Culture and Perception

Emotions in the Human Voice

Volume 3: Culture and Perception

Edited by
Krzysztof Izdebski

PLURAL
PUBLISHING
INC.

SAN DIEGO
OXFORD
BRISBANE

PLURAL PUBLISHING
INC.

5521 Ruffin Road
San Diego, CA 92123

e-mail: info@pluralpublishing.com
Web site: http://www.pluralpublishing.com

49 Bath Street
Abingdon, Oxfordshire OX14 1EA
United Kingdom

ISBN-13: 978-1-59756-119-8
ISBN-10: 1-59756-119-3

Library of Congress Cataloging-in-Publication Data:

Emotions in the human voice / [edited by] Krzystof Izdebski.
    p. ; cm.
  Includes bibliographical references and index.
  ISBN-13: 978-1-59756-073-3 (v. 1 : alk. paper)
  ISBN-10: 1-59756-073-1 (v. 1 : alk. paper)
  ISBN-13: 978-1-59756-118-1 (v. 2 : alk. paper)
  ISBN-10: 1-59756-118-5 (v. 2 : alk. paper)
  [etc.]
  1. Voice–Psychological aspects. 2. Emotions. I. Izdebski, Krzystof.
  [DNLM: 1. Affect. 2. Verbal Behavior. 3. Auditory Perception. 4. Emotions. 5.
Phonation. 6. Voice Quality. BF 582 E545 2007]
  BF592.V64E44 2007
  153.6–dc22
                                                        2007043352

CONTENTS

FOREWORD

The human voice—what a masterpiece of creation! We laugh with it, we cry with it, we sing with it, we pray with it, we scream with it, we whisper with it—yet, how little do we know about its effect upon the listener. The voice represents our ultimate means of communication from birth to death, yet how little do we know about its impact on human culture and society. While our voice connects us to our fellow humans and other species, we know but little about the mechanics of this transaction.

Even in antiquity, Greek and Roman philosophers were aware that the voice is the mirror of the soul. But it was not until the 20th century and the age of communication that serious investigations were initiated into the relations between the human voice and emotions. Recent research has revealed that the effect of the mother's voice creates a bond with the fetus in utero during the second trimester of pregnancy. With each year of our physical development, the voice and emotions play a more complex role in our adjustment to an ever-more complex world.

The recent Pacific Voice and Speech Foundation Annual Voice Conference on Voice and Emotion held at the Pixar Animation Studios in California represented the first serious attempt to study the complex relations between voice and emotions on a multidisciplinary level. The success of this meeting sparked a global fire of interest to bring together the vast knowledge from various cultures and various specialties, which has not been readily available to interested individuals.

This search extended to academicians and to clinicians, to scientists and to practitioners, to teachers and to writers. In Europe, contributors hail from Scandinavia and Finland in the north; from Italy and Spain in the south; from the United Kingdom, the Netherlands, Belgium, and France in the west; from Russia in the east; and from Germany, Austria, Poland and Switzerland in Central Europe. In the western hemisphere, chapters arrived from the United States, Canada, and Brazil; in the Far East from Japan, and Singapore, and Viet Nam; in the Pacific region from Australia and the Philippines; and in the Middle East from Israel.

The authors represent an equally diverse group of authorities: psychologists, linguists, speech and voice pathologists, physicians, phoniatricians, acousticians, vocal artists and performers, voice coaches, and experts from the fields of radio, computer science, commerce, television, and motion pictures. Over the past several weeks, I have had the opportunity to review this amazing collection of manuscripts, and I am amazed by the wealth and diversity of the submitted information. While the human voice is always one part of the equation, the emotions vary from joy to pain, from sorrow to happiness; from adults to children; from men to women; from spontaneity to stability; from pleasantness to roughness; from health to disease; from the brain to the organs of phonation; from neurology to psychophysiology; from development to recognition; from actor to anime, and—from laughter to love. The information is here and the choice is yours.

All of us share a sincere debt of thanks to the Editor, Dr. Krzysztof Izdebski, an enthusiastic and indefatigable champion of the field of voice, and a dear friend to many of the participating authors. Dr. Izdebski spearheaded the meeting held at the Pixar Studios and has done the lion's share of preparing this book. While all readers will benefit by their study of *Emotions in the Human Voice*, Dr. Izdebski deserves our respect, our admiration, and, above all, our gratitude.

Hans von Leden
Professor of Biocommunications
(Emeritus)
University of Southern California
Los Angeles, California

PREFACE

When my long-standing friend and colleague, Tom Murry of New York City, asked me in April of 2004, while we were munching on some tiny canapés during a coffee break at a voice course in Paris, France, to put into a *book* the experiences of the XV Annual Pacific Voice Conference entitled *Emotions and Voice* held at the Pixar Animation Studio in Emeryville, California, in March of that year, I was not sure if he was still my long-standing friend, had had an episode of hypoglycemia, or suddenly became my newest tormentor. As his then semi-casual request is now coming to a semi-completion, I can truly state that Tom had a vision, which he expressed in that Parisian April milieu with a straight, professorial, but somewhat emotive statement, that simply meant, "KI, you can do it! And I count on you." I am not sure that at the time I heard his voice as a challenge or just a friendly call for a potentially interesting volume collecting conference-related papers. Soon, however, I was to find out.

Upon my return to northern California, I started to reconstruct the taste of the canapés, Tom's voice, and the events of the XV Annual Pacific Voice Conference. My recollections were positive, so I began to look optimistically for the missing links and started to compile a list of potential contributors, who for whatever reasons were absent from our March 2005 happening, but who knew a lot. As soon as I began to put all the materials together and outlined a book, I realized the challenge placed on me by Tom.

This challenge came to me as a big surprise, as I am accustomed to writing, to publishing, to presenting, and to creating year after year new and narrowly focused scientific-clinical content that has made the Annual Pacific Voice Conferences (PVC). PVC is more or less an annual educational activity of the San Francisco based Pacific Voice and Speech Foundation that I chair—a hit among the international crowd of working voice clinicians. What struck me, when I really sat down to chart out this endeavor, was not the vastness of the material on human emotions, but how circumscribed the information was relating to *voice and emotions*. Yes, Diane Bless of Madison, Wisconsin, USA, was correct when we first discussed the program of the conference in the fall of 2004 (no, there was no food involved then, just a phone and her ever-friendly voice and loyal support) in saying that the topic of voice and emotions is terrific and right on time.

Luckily, the faculty of the XV PVC responded, and soon I was able to locate and enjoy the enthusiasm of other emotion researchers who for many reasons were unable to be present at the Emeryville happening, and who agreed to contribute to this volume. Specifically, I felt that I was on the right track after connecting with and experiencing the enthusiasm and dedicated intellectual help on this project of Branka Zei Pollermann of Emotion Research Group in Geneva, Switzerland and a Director of Vox, also in Switzerland. Her contribution to the entire concept was pivotal and fundamental, and I hence dare to nominate Branka for the Honorary Editor.

Looking for further support, I recruited Hans von Leden. Hans is originally from Silesia (a place where I too lived as a child, though long after his departure), and now he is my fellow Californian, though, alas, of southern part, the City of Angels, Los Angeles (where I also lived for a while when attending UCLA). Hans, a cross-cultural erudite, and so aware of our peculiar way of living life, simply told me as he always does, using his measured yet so emotive voice, "Krzysztof, I know you can do it; congratulations and good luck."

More wonderful encouragement came from such professionals as Anne-Maria Laukannen of Tampere, Finland. Now I was sure that this challenge would eventually come to fruition, and after chatting with all the other researchers who so generously embraced the project and promised to deliver in the most collegial and unselfish way, I knew that the book, or the books, would be a reality.

So there was apparently no way for me to retract. With this generous encouragement and upon Tom Murry's continuous insistence, I called S. Singh at Plural Publishing (again, no fancy food around to distract) and presented to him this project as a matter of fact, and after hearing what was cooking, he simply asked, "Krys, do you think anybody will *buy* the book?" He then passed me to a Lauren Duffy of Plural, who proclaimed, "Oh, I love the whole idea, and I am so excited about this book; when can I have it?" It felt safe, as if we found somebody really, really nice to blame if the book fails to sell.

Really, there have been no books or collections on the subject of emotions of the human voice or on emotions in the human voice, and ours was to be first. The book was to be based on the first-ever truly focused international two-day conference on this topic, namely, the XV Annual Pacific Voice Conference commingled with Pixar Studios' interest in voice and cartoon characters. Was this conference instructional enough to the digital art industry on how to make the voices of the brilliant cartoon characters created by Pixar more emotional, more believable, and more scientifically correct, or are they smart enough on their own? When I contacted Pixar with the idea of a joint meeting on voice and emotions, I was placed in the hands of Randy Nelson, Dean of Pixar University, who embraced the project and went with it blindly, as if a gathering of hundreds of people interested in the emotions of the human voice naturally belonged to the studio. Randy, I do feel guilty for all the flack you may have gotten as a result of this conference, but we had a great time, we learned from your faculty and your environment, and you are a generous host who is greatly missed. And just to let you know, the participants ask for a repeat.

The theme of the conference caught the attention of a Pixar activity tracker, a smart local newspaper writer (you do know that Pixar is a big, big business, and big businesses are carefully watched, and I assume you may know that Pixar was just bought by Disney, and this is also big news), who politely accused the organization of "going emotional." Emotions are cardinal no-nos of any big business. And the "accusation" was right on, as in addition to all the fantastic scientific sessions and presentations by Pixar faculty we had an unprecedented opportunity to experience on-line, in real life and in virtual reality, not only a special presentation of the Oscar winning Pixar production of *The Incredibles*, but also to enjoy a 6-hour-long parade of professional voice users (artists) demonstrating vocally coded emotions. This group comprised public speakers, voice-over artists, improvisational actors, stage actors, singers from pop, blues, jazz, country, cabaret, opera, and chorus, storytellers, other performers, cartoon character creators, puppeteers, voice coaches, animators, movie sound creators, and others, all of whom showed their vocally coded emotions in a most remarkable way. Thank you guys, thank you indeed. Pity, then, that the content of these incredible artistic renditions, all focused on highlighting the emotional voice, is missing from this volume.

So what is this book all about? First, it is a *thank you note* to all the contributors, as we all are the editors of equal weight. Next, it is a compilation of the most up-to-date knowledge of what constitutes emotive vocalization *vis-á-vis* currently accepted models of emotions. Obviously, some material is missing and some ideas or results are underrepresented, and obviously, there is room to expand and to improve. Nonetheless, this volume stands alone and provides a solid reference source on the emotions of the human voice in the most comprehensive way presented so far; the collection also unifies all of us into a cross-cultural family of people who believe in the power of vocal emotions.

The choice of the title for the book was a challenge as well, and many versions were possible. I tossed the two words, *emotions* and *voice*, around in

my head for many weeks, and I finally came up with some combinations that meant something to me. So, I asked others to evaluate the power of the final choice of the title. Eventually, *The Emotions in the Human Voice* was selected as the title. Nothing fancy, but these words give a straightforward message and fit among the titles of other publications on the subject of human emotions, e.g., Paul Ekman's 1982 publication entitled, *The Emotions in the Human Face* (I trust you agree with this, Paul).

Though the outline of the March 2005 XV Annual Pacific Voice Conference on Emotions and Voice was organized to flow thematically as if it were a theatrical production, I found myself in a conflict when trying to organize the chapters in a clustered and seemingly logical or sequential fashion. After an honest discussion with Lauren Duffy of Plural (again during a break between our mutual responsibilities while attending a meeting, this time on Coronado Island near San Diego in Southern California, and enjoying ice tea this time rather than French cuisine), we decided on arranging the chapters essentially in alphabetical order by the author's last name. The reasoning was based on the idea that these volumes represent an anthology of interrelated topics, that as such they can be read in any order, and that only upon consuming them all will a reader be ready to utter an emotive vocalization reflective of his or her personal view of the value of this work or specific criticism.

One more thing shall be mentioned that made my efforts in putting this collection together a real pleasure. This was the willingness of Plural to allow me to design the cover and to include nonscientific illustrations. The acceptance by Plural of this idea placed me on a path to search for illustrators and graphic artists who would be willing to produce a cover and the graphic vignettes to be placed on the left page in front of selected chapters.

I admit that I enjoyed the search very, very much. This search took me into the world of art and graphic design that I deeply respect and admire, and it provided me with an emotional break from thinking about the words and the text only. Once I found the artists that I was looking for, it took very little pressure to persuade both of them to contribute on pro-bono bases. Hence, my special thank-you goes to Daniele Coscone of Italy and to Marta Semkowicz of Poland for agreeing to participate. Honestly, it took some emotional work on my part to make this deal, but that is completely another story.

So here we are, ready to indulge in the text placed in front of us. As you come to read these superb contributions, please note that we do vocalize often, in fact daily or nightly, often really freely and spontaneously, and that at times we vocalize on command, and that our vocalizations do carry plenty of emotive content, content that can be truly revealing, even if we do not realize it.

Krzysztof Izdebski

ACKNOWLEDGMENTS

The following people listed here (not in alphabetical order), whose voices I listened to with various intensities at various times in my life, made creating these volumes possible, and for that I am profoundly thankful to all of them. Because all of them transcend all kind of boundaries, professions, systems, religions, age, and all else, I simply ask all of you to accept my humble "thank you," in your native or emotional language and with an appropriate prosodic power. If I missed something, or somebody, please yell at me!

Heather Antonissen, Åsa Abelin, Jean Abitbol, Albert Bandura, Magda Goldberger, Zdenek Hufnagel, Beata Woytowicz, Mara Behlau, Brad Bird, Diane M. Bless, Sylvie Brajtman, Janina Casper, Manuel Pais Clemente, Piero Cosi, Raul M. Cruz, Danielle Coscone, Peter Docter, Maria Dietrich, Carlo Drioli, Steffi Frigo, Anna Paczynska-Izdebski, Grzegorz A W Izdebski, The Singh Family, The Piotr Sokolowski-Enskoog Family, Siri Elliason, Karaminder Ghuman, Isabel Guimarães, Rozalina Gutman, Ioulia Grichkovtsova, Laurie Griffee, The Seshadri Family, The Asenov Family, Anastasia Vavilova, Venislava Georgieva Georgieva, Hristina Djambazova, Brindis Guðmunsdottir, Lucinda Halstead, Sabine Hoffmann, Josef Schlomicher-Their, Anna Maria Hortis-Dzierzbicka, The Deutchman Family, Ellen van der Honert, Mirja Ilves, Julian Konrad Matheus Izdebski, Alexandra Michalina Catherina Izdebski, Kazuhiko Kakehi, Arvid Kapas, Gwen Korovin, Eleanor Park, Jody Kreiman, Marika Kuzma, Anne Maria Laukkanen, Petri Laukka, Heather Lauren, Inneke Mennen, Marilyn C. Izdebski, Norman Boone and The Boones Family, Marilee Monnot, Luiza Renata Motter, Dominique Morsomme, John W. Mullennix, Thomas Murry, Clifford Nass, Randy Nelson, (special thanks for being so PIXAR), Marcos de Sarvat Family, Susana Naidich Family, Kevin Pelphrey, Robert Peterson, Daniela Powsner, Anna Petrini, Jeff Pigeon, Beata Ptaszynski, Raquel M. Ramsey, Ruth Rainero, Lorraine Olson-Ramig, Joe Rauft, Kevin Reher, Brian Rosen, Gary Rydstrom, Lilla-Theresa Sadowski, Annett Schirmer, Marta Semkowicz, Tapio Seppänen, Sumi Shigeno, Julia A. Sidorova, Jennifer Spielman, Andrew Stenton, Claude Steinberg, Kimberly M. Steinhauer, Victoria Stevens, František Šram, The Jüergen Wendler Family, Uyi Thompson Stewart, Rebeca Stockley, Brad Story, Dave Stroud, Veikko Surakka, Marc Swerts, Mihoko Teshigawara, Juhani Toivanen, Miriam van Mersbergen, Ingrid Verduyckt, Jerry Weissman, Willy Wellens, Magda van Opstal, Riitta Ylitalo, Hans von Leden, Herbert H and Sigrid Dedo, Michael Chcial, Jeanelle Mifsud, The Thomas Shipp Family, The Bay Area Italian American Community, The Tonnela Family, Gary Pratt, The Monty Upshaw Family, M.T. Sylvia, Timothy Willcutts, Fred Harris, Kito Gamble, Molly Holm, Michael Grossman, Lydia Hyde, Kathleen

Antonia Tarr, Joel Ben Izzy, Lisa Jenai Hernandez, Lucy Beck, Pam Fry, Karen Mellander-Magoon, Franc D'Ambrosio, Sylvie Sandy Cressman, Kathy Kennedy, Dorota Różańska, Faye Carol, Carolyn Bloom, Martin Stirling, Facing New York, Jacob Johnson, The Schindler Family, The E. David Manace Family, The James E. Kline Family, Trinh Green, Gabriela Heimensen, Kirstem Mott, Rick Sklader, Mieczyslaw Dzierzbicki, Krzysztof and Natalia Izdebscy,

Faculty, staff and management of Pixar and Ex'Pressions, Renata Jaworski, Marianne I. van Zeeland, Mette Fog Pedersen, Stella Rubin "Cognome," Claudia Packman, Annabel Castaldo, Anna Baldi, Ruth Ann Swenson, Misha Didyk, Oksana, Cairo Cocalis, Kevin Beaty, Agata Zubel, Cezary Duchnowski, Lisa Popeil, Alfonso Gianluca Gucciano, Fonta Hadley, Bozena Hammerlink, Luciana Castro, Betty Horwitz, Donald & Angela Bell, Tracy Baldwin, Gerald Berke Family, Jean Zaludek, Florence Blager, Maria Pignati, Ivana Paji-Penavi, Maria Melendez, Branko Stark "Suchy," Michal Broniatowski Family, Roger Crumley Family, Chantal Bianda, Eugenia Chavez, Steven and Hillary Homs, Christopher Homs & Jessica, Adidi Mandpe, Gary Rust, Daniel Hartman, Steven Sloan, Sharon Greeenlin, Viggo Pedersen, Sin-Young Phua, Lisa van der Ploeg, Per-Åke Lindestad, Philippe Dejonkere, Wojtek Chodzko-Zajko, Baśka Oksztel-Matosek, Malgorzata Górecka-Kumek, "Babcia" Michalina Szymanska, "Babcia" Ebska, Halina Heliodora Izdebska, Julian "Julek" W. Izdebski, Jadwiga Mikke, Myron Meyerson, Jorge Pinho, Raymond Hilsinger, Jr., Fred Byl, Santa Večrina Volič, Tin Znaor, Lydija Horvat, Eliott & Sue Bloom, Adria Amenti, Zolza Na-Maxa, Robert Edward Stone Jr., Beata Zrzelska, Ekaterina Osipenko, et al.

And, I also want to thank all my voice patients residing all over the world, representing so many different countries, cultures, languages and ethnic roots, and all the people I met in my life with feminine, masculine, or transgender names and voices, who came to see me because their voice was suffering, and all those other fine people I met in my life, that remain emotional about the way they talk.

CONTRIBUTORS

Toni Badia, Ph.D.
Associate Professor of Computational
    Linguistics
Universitat Pompeu Fabra, Barcelona
Catalunya, Spain
Chapter 12

Janet Baker, M.Sc., Ph.D.
Associate Professor
Course Coordinator Master of Speech
    Pathology
Department of Speech Pathology and
    Audiology
Faculty of Health Science
School of Medicine
Flinders University
Adelaide, Australia
Chapter 7

Mara Behlau, Ph.D.
Director
Centro de Estudos da voz—CEV
Sao Paolo, Brazil
Chapter 16

Steven Connor, D.Phil.
Professor
Modern Literature and Theory
Academic Director
London Consortium Graduate
    Programme
Humanities and Cultural Studies
Birkbeck College
London, United Kingdom
Chapter 18

Piero Cosi, Ph.D.
Researcher
Istituto di Fonetica e Dialettogia
Padova, Italy
Chapter 9

Carlo Drioli, Ph.D.
Allocator
Mathematical, Physical and Natural
    Sciences
Department of Computer Sciences
University of Verona
Verona, Italy
Chapter 9

Gisele Gasparini, Ms.C.
Vice-Director
Centro de Estudos da Voz—CEV
Sao Paolo, Brazil
Chapter 16

Gerardo González, Ph.D.
Professor of Psychology
Department of Psychology
California State University of San
    Marcos
San Marcos, California
Chapter 4

Mirja Ilves, M.A.
Researcher
Research Group for Emotions, Sociality,
    and Computing
Tampere Unit for Computer-Human
    Interaction

Department of Computer Sciences
University of Tampere
Tampere, Finland
Chapter 8

**Krzysztof Izdebski, F.K., M.A.,
Ph.D., CCC-SLP., FASHA**
Chairman: Pacific Voice and Speech
    Foundation
San Francisco, California
And
Associate Clinical Professor
Voice and Swallowing Center
Department of Otolaryngology-Head
    and Neck Surgery
Stanford University, School of Medicine
Stanford, California
Preface, Acknowledgments, Introduction

Kazuhiko Kaheki , Ph.D.
Professor
School of Computer and Cognitive
    Sciences
Chukyo University
Toyota, Japan
Chapter 1

Hideki Kawahara, Ph.D.
Professor
Systems Engineering
Wakayama University
Wakayama, Japan
Chapter 1

Richard D. Lane, M.D., Ph.D.
Professor of Psychiatry, Psychology, and
    Neuroscience
Department of Psychiatry
University of Arizona
Tucson, Arizona
Chapter 7

John W. Mullennix, Ph.D.
Professor
Department of Psychology

University of Pittsburgh at Johnstown
Johnstown, Pennsylvania
Chapter 3

Amy L. Ramos, Ph.D.
Visiting Professor
Chapter 4

Marc Schröder, Ph.D.
DFKI GmbH
Saarbrucken, Germany
Chapter 19

**Juliana Sustento Seneriches, M.D.,
D.A.B.P.N., D.F.A.P.A.**
Visiting Consultant
West Visayas State University
Western Visayas Medical Center
Psychiatry Consortium
Iloilo, Philippines
Chapter 17

Tapio Seppänen, Ph.D.
Professor
Department of Electrical and
    Information Engineering
University of Oulu
Oulu, Finland
Chapter 5

Sumi Shigeno, Ph.D.
Professor
Department of Psychology
Aoyama Gakuin University
Tokyo, Japan
Chapter 11

Julia Sidrova
Ph.D. Student
Moscow State Lomonosov University
Chapter 12

Yuko Sogabe, M.A.
Technical Staff
Riken

Saitama, Japan
Chapter 1

Claude Steinberg, M.A.
Staff Usability Specialist
UserWorks, Inc.
Silver Spring, Maryland
Chapter 6, 14

Osamuyimen Thompson Stewart, Ph.D.
Research Staff
IBM T.J. Watson Research Labs
Yorktown Heights, New York
Fellow
Cambridge Commonwealth Society
Cambridge University
Chapter 2

Veikko Surakka, Ph.D.
Assistant Professor
Head of the Research Group for
   Emotions, Sociality, and Computing
Tampere Unit for Computer-Human
   Interaction
Department of Computer Sciences
University of Tampere
Tampere, Finland
Chapter 8

Kathleen Antonia Tarr, J.D.
Member
American Mensa

Voice-Over Artist
Los Angeles, California
Chapter 13

Mihoko Teshigawara, Ph.D.
Graduate School of Information
   Sciences
Nagoya University
Gifu, Japan
Chapter 10, 15

Juhani Toivanen, Ph.D.
Academy Researcher
Department of Electrical and
   Information Engineering
University of Oulu
Oulu, Finland
Chapter 5

Eero Väyrynen, M.Sc. (EE)
Researcher
Department of Electrical and
   Information Engineering
University of Oulu
Oulu, Finland
Chapter 5

Hans von Leen, M.D.
Professor of Biocommunications
   (Emeritus)
University of Southern California
Los Angeles, California
Foreword

INTRODUCTION

This is one of the shortest introductions the reader of any scientific volume will ever experience. The reason for this brevity is obvious; namely, as the editor of these volumes, I am extremely proud to have been charged with the task of creating this book, yet I clearly recognize that it is not "my book", and that it was created by all of us, all of us who are concerned with the topic of emotions expressed, conveyed, produced, perceived, or generated in the context of the human voice.

The concept that the voice is a carrier of emotions is not a new one. In fact voice, emotions, sexuality, guilt, etc., have been discussed in the Talmud, in the Bible, in Hinduism, in Buddhism, in the Koran, and in many other writings on philosophy or on religious doctrines. Many of the contemporary scholars credited with the development of modern thought and scientific truth about life, or about the evolution of life and of the psychological correlates of life (e.g., Darwin, Freud, Fromm, Jung, etc.), have addressed voice and emotions. So, is there anything we can say about this topic that has not been said before?

These volumes provide the *answer*. We are clearly aware that emotional information is and can be conveyed by a variety of means of human communication. Communication involves content, prosody, gesture, facial expressions, paralinguistic aspects, and cultural know-how. We now know that cross-modality inputs affect the production and perception of another modality. We also know that not all aspects are universal, and that it is OK to be restricted by cultural constraints. With respect to voice and emotions, these modalities are, however, still unclear.

Voice is today a fully acknowledged tool of labor, as so much of our interactions are conducted in the absence or the presence of another person, namely, on the phone or over Internet voice transmission, with the voice signals alone carrying all the clues of our well-being or about our emotional state. Hence, it is not a perplexing question, why we are then ready to make assumptions, judgments, choices, firing and hiring, judicial opinions, criminal recommendations, or purchase choices and other crucial decisions about life based on the emotions we experience regardless of this vocal information?

This volume addresses some topics of vocally coded emotions and certainly neglects many pertinent questions. This book is not a final word in the quest of understanding what constitutes vocally conveyed emotions, but in my opinion, it is a darn good approximation of the current (2008) state of the art on this subject.

Nonetheless, much remains to be discovered and learned. One thing that will become obvious when these volumes are consumed by the reader is the fact that, during the act of acoustically conducted communication, emotional information may be coded and expressed both by the content and by modulation of speech. And although it is almost given that the left brain is in charge of language, emotions are shown to be lateralized to the right part of the brain, and much is to be learned about cross-brain integration.

Moreover, similarities in acoustic profiles, intonation, and emotion flow now permit us to assess the extent of how hemispheric lateralization of speech prosody depends on functional instead of acoustical properties. This brings at least one fundamental question into focus; namely, are there acoustical properties of emotions, and if there are, what are they and how do they differ or influence the functional concepts of emotions? The other fundamental question is that of the discovery of what constitutes an emotion in itself. To trivialize this entire concept, I dare to quote Chomsky and Halle who in the epilogue to their then most fundamental work on English phonology (*The Sound Pattern of English*, 1968) proclaimed that the work they had just published suffers from "fundamental scientific inadequacy." Are these volumes destined to suffer a similar course? So as not to make this an excuse, I will also dare to quote a Latin doctrine, "*Per risum multum debes cognoscere stultum*," rightly or wrongly stating that the perception of voice cues in the laughter of the emotionally disturbed can point to the source of the type of emotional disturbance that produced such a sound. So then, to cover up my own ignorance, I dare to say, "*Nulla aetas ad discendum sera*" or "It is never too late to learn." With this hope I turn the rest to the reader, and I plea for forgiveness of our ignorance of the scope of the subject we so do love.

Krzysztof Izdebski
Oakland/San Francisco, California,
July 9, 2008

To my two special children,
Alexandra Michalina Catherina
and
Julian Konrad Matheus,
whose voices over
their combined 29 years of life
have never failed
to express their emotions—
emotions and voices
I had so many chances
to misinterpret.

Oakland, San Francisco, California, USA,
and all the many places all over the world,
I found myself working on these volumes

CHAPTER 1

Research on Emotional Perception of Voices Based on a Morphing Method

Kazuhiko Kakehi , Yuko Sogabe, and Hideki Kawahara

Abstract

Although a vast amount of information on facial expressions of emotions exists, it is still controversial whether the perception of a facial expression is dimensional or categorical. Moreover, research on perceptions of emotions in speech is scant, as it is difficult to continuously control the level of emotion in utterance in experimental settings. Recently, a new morphing method of emotional voice research has been proposed. This method is based on STRAIGHT, a kind of vocoder technology producing very high quality synthetic speech. In this report we present the results of our experiments on perceptual characteristics of emotional speech using this new method. We varied the stimulus of emotional voice in strength by changing it continuously from one emotional type to another. First, we investigated whether emotional perception of speech was categorical or not, and we found disagreement with the literature. Secondly, we investigated perceptual relationships among the six basic emotional categories of voice using a multidimensional psychological space approach, and then we compared the perceptual characteristics of emotional voice with the results of facial expression for these six emotions. The results indicated that multidimensional characteristics of emotional perception both for emotional voice and facial expression were quite similar. And although we were not able to provide unequivocal perceptual categoricalness of emotional voices, the results parallel those valid for emotional facial expressions.

Introduction

The perceptual characteristics of emotional facial expression have been studied intensively (e.g., Calder, Young, Perrett, Etcoff & Rowland, 1996; De Gelder, Teunisse, & Benson, 1997; Ekman, 1993; Etcoff & Magee, 1992; Morris et al., 1996; Nomura et al., 2003; Shibui & Shigemasu, 2005; Young et al., 1997). However, it is still controversial whether the perception of emotional face expression is categorical or not. Similarly, although a fairly large corpus of studies related to emotional voices exists, almost all involve acoustical features of emotional voices and there are only few studies on the perceptional aspects of emotional voices (e.g., Laukka, 2003; Kakehi & Sogabe, 2005; Matsui & Kawahara, 2003; Sogabe, Kakehi, & Kawahara, 2003).

Although morphing of linear interpolation between two still visual images of facial expressions is rather easy when the corresponding points between two images are determined, the morphed image of emotional face expression can be sufficiently applicable to the perceptual experiment. On the contrary, morphing between two emotional voices is difficult. Despite the existence of several morphing methods for voice, it is rather difficult to obtain high quality morphed voices. This technical problem may introduce degradation of voice quality, which in turn will cause artifacts and affect the perception of emotional voices. To improve on the technology, a new morphing method was proposed recently, based on high quality speech analysis-synthesis technique, called STRAIGHT.

In this chapter, assessments of the quality of morphed voices based on this new method are presented. The main question asked was whether the morphed voice quality was sufficiently natural for perceptual experiments on emotions and voice. The aim was to investigate the degree of categorical perception of emotional voices and to define how multidimensional characteristics in the perception of emotional voices compare to perceptual characteristics of facial expression.

A New Morphing Method

An outline of the high quality morphing method applied to the emotional voice is introduced next. Generally speaking, morphing is a procedure to regenerate a signal from a representation using the shortest possible trajectory between the reference points in an abstract distance space with an appropriate metric distance (e.g., time-frequency space). For speech morphing, reference points are two speech examples. It is crucial to represent these speech examples in terms of perceptually relevant parameters that enable us to define a metric distance, which is isomorphic to our speech perception.

The morphing procedure employed here is based on a speech analysis, modification, and resynthesis system called STRAIGHT. The key concept of STRAIGHT is to represent signals in terms of parameters that embody essential aspects of auditory perception. STRAIGHT decomposes each input speech signal into three components related to physical phenomena: (a) fundamental frequency (F0), (b) smoothed spectrogram, and (c) time-frequency periodicity map. STRAIGHT also provides a sound reconstruction procedure from these three components. In this respect, STRAIGHT is a modern version of a channel vocoder developed in 1939. What makes STRAIGHT different from the classic channel vocoder is a sophisticated design in parameter extraction technology and underlying principles that make a generated signal perceptually relevant to auditory perception. A time-frequency representation that does not suffer from interference caused by impulsive airflow periodically excited by the vocal folds is introduced, to extract smoothed spectrogram.

In the first stage of analysis, F0-adaptive design of a complementary set of time windows is used to effectively eliminate temporal variations in the estimation of power spectrum. Then, a spline function-based F0-adaptive smoothing in the frequency domain is used to eliminate variations due to the harmonic structure of the excitation. Next, it is necessary to introduce an approximation to this general formulation based on an abstract distance metric d_{fx} for enabling practical implementation of the morphing procedure. One such approximation for speech morphing is to define the new distance d_{cp} as a composite operation of a coordinate transformation T and a localized distance metric d_{pp}:

$$d_{fx} \cong d_{cp} = d_{pp}\left(S_{ref}(\omega, \tau), S_{tgt}(T(\omega, \tau))\right)$$

where subscripts "*ref*" and "*tgt*" represent *reference* and *target*, respectively. If the transformation does not have a significant degradation, and if the localized metric distance is Euclidean, the morphing procedure is reduced to a linear interpolation on the reference coordinates.

The procedure used in our morphing method was based on this approximation. This procedure is analogous to visual image morphing when the time-frequency coordinates and the attributes on the coordinate system are replaced by the shape and color (including intensity and texture).

There are several technical issues involved in implementing this procedure. Specifically, the coordinate system and the localized distance must reflect auditory perceptual characteristics, and the transformation must be as simple as possible. Here, the time-frequency plane is used as the coordinate system. The time-frequency coordinate transformation is represented as a piecewise bilinear transformation. It is important to note that the time-frequency coordinate is not isotropic, unlike usual image morphing. Log-frequency scale is used for morphing F0, because the speech F0 dynamics is represented in terms of a linear dynamical equation in the log-frequency domain (Fujisaki, 1998). For the spectral density, morphing is calculated on dB scale representation, because it linearly corresponds well to intensity perception. The time-frequency periodicity index (Kawahara, Katayose, de Cheveigné, & Patterson, 1999; Kawahara & Matsui, 2003 is also transformed by the same mapping function.

In summary, the STRAIGHT-based morphing procedure needs to manipulate following four sets of parameters:

1. Parameters of time-frequency coordinate system
2. Smoothed spectrogram (time-frequency representation)
3. Fundamental frequency trajectory
4. Time-frequency periodicity index

Step-by-Step Illustration of the Morphing Procedure

This section illustrates morphing procedure step by step using a voice example.

1. The first step is to analyze input speech examples using STRAIGHT. Since morphing is a procedure to traverse two examples, it is necessary to prepare a pair of examples. Let's call these two examples *reference* and *target*. In this illustration, we use a Japanese word *hai* (yes in English) spoken in neutral manner and angry manner, respectively.

   The second step is to set anchoring points to define necessary time-frequency coordinate transformation. The goal of this anchoring point selection is to minimize degradations caused by misalignment of two time-frequency representations. There are two types of anchoring points. One

is the temporal anchoring points. To prevent temporal alignment errors, boundaries of phonological elements have to be selected as temporal anchoring points. Initial and final points of voicing, fricatives, and transitions have to be selected first. Also, the initial burst of explosives has to be selected as an anchoring point. The other type of anchoring points is frequency anchoring defined at each temporal anchoring except the beginning and endpoints of the voice. The frequency anchoring points should be placed on formant, because they are spectrally salient and provide dominant energy. It was observed that up to five frequency-anchoring points lower than 5 kHz frequency range are enough to provide natural sounding morphed voices. Figure 1–1 shows selected anchoring points due to this procedure. Note that topological structure of anchoring points on a reference time-frequency space has to be identical to that on a target one in order to conduct the next morphing procedure.

2. The third step is deformation of the time-frequency coordinate of a target example to align to that of a reference example. Figure 1–2 shows how a regular grid structure on the target time-frequency coordinate is deformed into the reference time-frequency coordinate. Note that this deformation of time axis (i.e., mapping from the target temporal axis to the reference temporal axis) is also used for F0 trajectory alignment.

3. The fourth step is interpolation of representing parameters. Assume a hyper parameter

$$\Theta_{mrp}^{(ref)}(r) = \left\{ S_{mrp}^{(ref)}(t,\omega), F0_{mrp}^{(ref)}(t), P_{mrp}^{(ref)}(t,\omega) \right\}$$

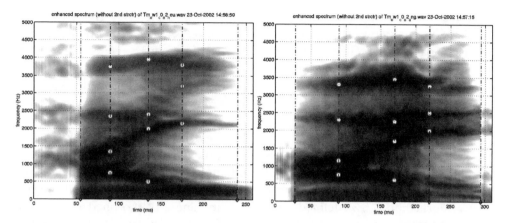

Figure 1–1. Smoothed spectrographic representations of a word *hai* (yes) uttered by a male actor under neutral (*left*) and angry (*right*) emotional conditions. Anchor points on the time-frequency domain are plotted as open circles and temporal anchors are indicated by a vertical interrupted line.

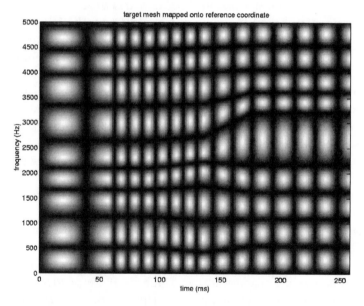

Figure 1–2. Time-frequency grid, which is regular in the target coordinate system, transformed into the reference coordinate system.

which is composed of a set of parameters to represent the morphed voice example on the reference time-frequency coordinate, where represents an index to define the amount of interpolation called *morphing rate*. Then, the morphed hyper parameter $\Theta_{mrp}^{(ref)}(r)$ is calculated using the following linear interpolation equation between the reference hyper parameter $\Theta_{ref}^{(ref)}$ and the target hyper parameter $\Theta_{tgt}^{(ref)}$ using the morphing rate r.

$$\Theta_{mrp}^{(ref)}(r) = r\Theta_{tgt}^{(ref)} + (1 - r)\Theta_{ref}^{(ref)}$$

4. The fifth step is to deform the time-frequency coordinate of the morphed hyper parameter using the inverse transformation $T_{mrp}^{-1}(r)$ defined using the morphing rate r and the inverse mapping T^{-1} of the transformation T from the target coordinate to the reference coordinate. In this implementation, this transformation is calculated using the following linear interpolation of the transformation T and the identity mapping I.

$$T_{mrp}^{-1}(r) = rT^{-1} + (1 - r)I$$

5. Then, by using this transformation, the morphed hyper parameter $\Theta_{mrp}^{(ref)}(r)$ on the reference coordinate is represented as the morphed hyper parameter $\Theta_{mrp}^{(mrp)}(r)$ on the morphed time-frequency coordinate.

6. The final step is to regenerate a speech sample from the morphed hyper parameter $\Theta_{mrp}^{(mrp)}(r)$ using STRAIGHT synthesis procedure.

7. The morphing rate, which is currently defined as a scalar variable, can be generalized to time variable vector function, which enables us to manipulate fundamental frequency F0, STRAIGHT sound spectrogram, time-frequency coordinates, etc., independently. It means that a morphing pathway in the physical multidimensional space can be controlled easily to make a sophisticated stimulus. It is useful for clarifying the characteristics of emotional voices in detail.

Voice Quality by the New Morphing Method

The naturalness of morphed voice quality is very important when conducting an experiment of emotional perception, for the lack of voice naturalness will affect the perceptual dimension of pleasant-unpleasant or positive-negative feelings. There are two aspects with regard to naturalness of morphed voices: one is the naturalness of voice characteristics themselves and the other one is the naturalness of the manner of emotional expression. Both aspects of morphed voices are investigated separately.

Three Japanese words were used: *Kawarazaki-san* (Mr. Kawarazaki), *juuichiji-han* (half past eleven), and *Tokyo* (Tokyo). The meaning of each word is neutral in an emotional sense. The original voice materials were uttered with the emotions of happiness and sadness by a professional male actor (Shigeno, 2003). Participant judges were graduate students (five males and five females) who were asked to evaluate the naturalness of morphed voices in five categories on a 1–5 scale (1 = unnatural and 5 = natural).

The results for naturalness of voice itself and that of the manner of emotional expression are shown in Figure 1–3A and Figure 1–3B, respectively.

The numbers on the horizontal axis indicate the index of morphing level. The interval of the neighbor morphing level is about 0.07 in terms of morphing rate. The points at the left and right ends indicate original voice stimuli uttered by the actor. Morphing level 1 and 15 indicate analysis/synthesis voices using STRAIGHT system (i.e., not morphed). The numbers on the vertical axis indicate the mean opinion score (MOS).

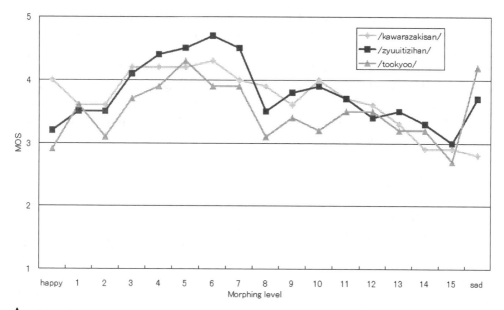

A

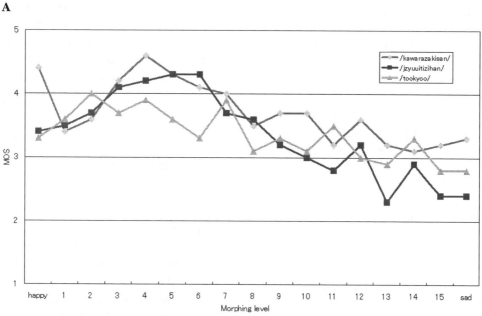

B

Figure 1–3. Naturalness of the morphed voice. (**A**) Voice quality itself. (**B**) The manner of emotional expression.

On the whole, it was found that the naturalness of the morphed voices in terms of voice quality itself was maintained when compared with the original utterances. For the naturalness of the man-ner of emotional expression, there was a tendency of a slight decreasing MOS value from *happy* to *sad*. However, a difference in the naturalness of emotional expression was not found by conditions between original (happy) and morphing level 1, and between original (sad) and morphing level 15. This indicates that the tendency was not due to the effect of the morphing method. The results of the two kinds of naturalness show that the morphed speech could be used in the psychological experiment of emotional perception.

Categorical Perception of Emotional Voices

Using the morphing method, the perceptual characteristics of emotional voice were also investigated. First, forced choice identification tasks were conducted for each series of emotional voices between happy-neutral, sad-neutral, angry-neutral, happy-sad, happy-angry, and sad-angry voices.

Then discrimination tasks were conducted for a pair of morphed voices between two emotional voices in a series as described above.

Identification Task

Method

Participants were 14 undergraduate and graduate students (10 males, 4 females). They were asked to make forced choices with regard to emotional category in response to a vocal stimulus presented through a headset.

Stimuli

A compound word, *Nakamine-san* (Mr. Nakamine), and a nonsense word, *man-amana*, were uttered in seven basic emotions by a male student who was a member of a theatrical club. A pair of original emotional voices was used to produce 13 morphed voices equally spaced physically between two typical emotions. Original and analysis/synthesis (i.e., morphing rate is 0 or 1) voices by STRAIGHT were included in the stimuli.

Results

Three examples of the results are shown in Figure 1–4. The numbers in the vertical line indicate the frequency of the forced choice category. The horizontal line expresses the conditions of morphing level and original voices. The results showed that identification of emotional category changes steeply almost in the middle morphing level (e.g., from 5 to 10 morphing level), thus indicating a clear emotional category boundary between the two typical emotional voices. The results showed a typical pattern of categorical judgment.

Discrimination Test

Method

Participants were the same as in the identification experiment of emotional category. In the discrimination tests, participants were asked to judge whether a pair of stimuli presented through a headset is the same or different in terms of emotional level.

Stimuli

A pair of stimuli was chosen from two adjacent stimuli in a series of morphed voices between two typical emotions, and a morphing level difference of the paired stimuli was selected as three (i.e., the morphing rate difference is 0.21).

Three examples of the experimental results are shown in Figure 1-5. The vertical axis indicates discrimination ratio and the horizontal axis, a pair of morphing level of the paired stimuli (e.g., "2/5" means that the morphing level of stimuli paired were 2 and 5).

The results show that there is no peak of discrimination ratio corresponding to the categorical boundary of two emotions found in the former identification experiment.

Discussion

The degree of categorical perception of emotional voice is judged typically as based on two conditions: one is that there is a clear categorical boundary between two emotional stimuli, which changes continuously from one prototypical category to another, and two: that there is a clear increase of discrimination ratio across the categorical boundary.

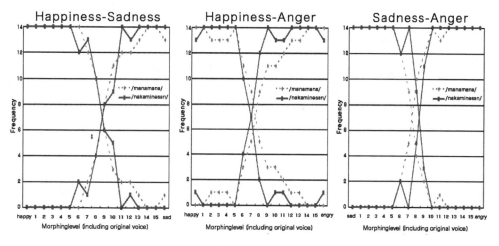

Figure 1–4. Category judgment.

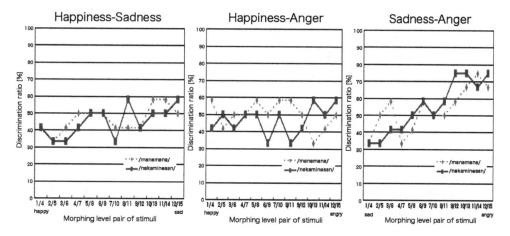

Figure 1–5. Discrimination of a paired morphed voice.

The results of the experiment described here indicate that the first condition of categorical perception was almost satisfied. However, the second condition was not. In the discrimination test, the increase of discrimination ratio for a pair of stimuli, of which morphing level difference was three (e.g., 0.21 morphing rate), was not found in the morphing level region corresponding to a category boundary. In other words, the discrimination ratio of paired stimuli across the categorical boundary did not show the difference compared with that in the same category, though the physical distance of the paired stimuli was the same.

Laukka (2003) reported that both the conditions for categorical perception were satisfied based on the same kind of experiment, and later he concluded that the perception of emotional voices is categorical. There are two main differences between the experiments described in this chapter and those of Laukka's: (a) difference in morphing method of emotional voices, and (b) the type of discrimination test used.

The morphing method used by Laukka was *syllable concatenation method*. In this method, fundamental frequency F0, sound pressure level, and time course feature (duration and so on, though not clearly stated), are linearly interpolated in each syllable included in a stimulus voice. The quality of morphed voices was not described. The effect of morphing method on the experimental results might be caused by the quality of morphed voices or the pathway connecting one typical emotional voice to the other in the physical multidimensional space. Of course, there might be the effects of a speaker, language, and so on.

The type of discrimination test used in our experiment was the AX type, and the one used by Laukka was the ABX type. In the discrimination processing, the representation of the stimulus presented first should be kept in the memory of a subject. The time or form of representation might be different between the AX and ABX methods. However, the cause of the difference in the results obtained cannot be accounted for at this time, and further studies are warranted.

Dimensional Characteristics for the Perception of Emotional Voices

The perceptual characteristics of emotional voices were investigated on a multidimensional psychological space.

Method

Participants were 20 undergraduate students (14 males, 6 females). They were presented a stimulus sequentially under the time course shown in Figure 1–6. They were also asked to assess the emotional level of one of the seven basic emotional categories in six steps (i.e., from 1 = no feeling of the designated emotion to 6 = full feeling of the designated emotion).

Stimuli

Original voices used were the same as those used in the experiment on categorical perception. The series of morphed voices between neutral and the other six basic emotions and those of happiness, sadness, and anger were used.

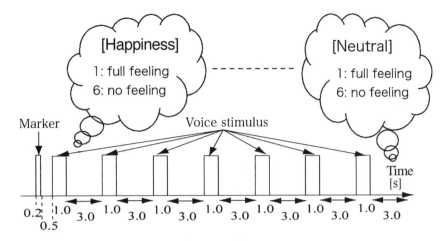

Figure 1–6. Experimental procedure for the data of multidimensional scaling.

Results by MDS Analysis

The results of MDS analysis showed that the experimental stimuli were interpreted in a two-dimensional plane with low distortion. The examples of the MDS analysis are shown in Figure 1-7A. The index attached to a point in the figure indicates the combination of emotion of morphed voices and morphing levels (e.g., AN8: the first two letters show the initials of emotional words; that is, the stimulus was morphed between typical angry voice and neutral; and the morphing level was 8). Though equal morphing level difference means equal distance in a physical space as mentioned before, in middle range of morphing level (e.g., around from 5 to 10), a stimulus point moves rapidly from one emotion to the other in psychological space. This corresponds well to the results of the categorical identification experiment.

The results of the morphing series among anger, sadness, and happiness are shown in Figure 1-7B. The results also match well with those of the identification experiment. And the movement of stimulus point is much more rapid than the case shown in Figure 1-6.

Figure 1-8 shows the same two-dimensional psychological space where the original voices of typical emotions are plotted. The horizontal axis can be interpreted as a pleasant-unpleasant axis and the vertical axis as a high-low axis in activity. Typical emotional voices make a circular structure in the space. However, *neutral* is not in the center of the circle. This means that neutral emotion of voice is not the emotion of mixture or averaged emotional voice.

Perception of Facial Expression and Emotional Voices

Emotional Facial Expression

Two models for the perception of facial expression have been discussed frequently (e.g., Shibui & Shigemasu, 2005): (a) dimensional model, and (b) categorical model. In the dimensional model, it is

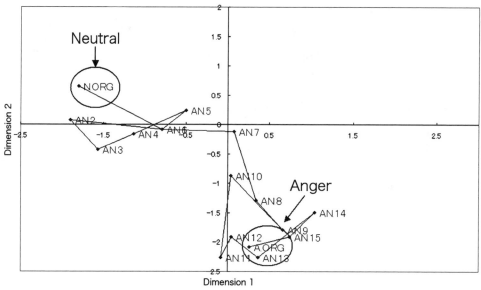

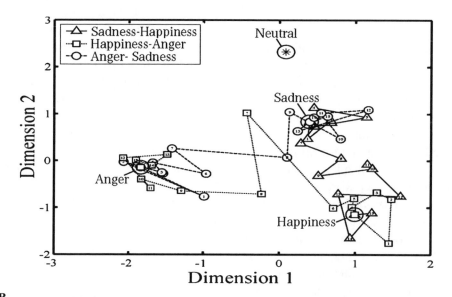

A

B

Figure 1–7. The results of MDS. (**A**) The series of morphed emotional voices between neutral voice as reference and angry voice as target. (**B**) The series of morphed voices among angry, sad, and happy emotional voices.

said that the facial expressions are continuously distributed in a multidimensional space, and that the space is constructed based on the similarity or the dissimilarity between facial expressions. That is, there is no categorical membership in the pro-

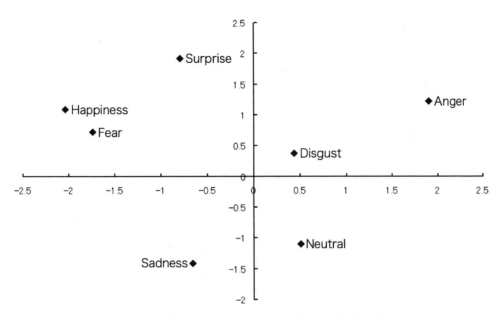

Figure 1–8. The factor space of original emotional voice.

cessing of emotional perception. It means that the facial expression is continuously perceived in the dimensional space.

In the categorical theory, it is said that each category of emotional facial expression exists in isolation without the assumption of mutual dependency among facial expressions. In other words, each emotional facial expression is processed independently. Though there are plenty of studies related to these two models that support either dimensional or categorical models, the issue is still not fully resolved and remains controversial.

Emotional Voice

The apparent lack of a high quality morphing method for voices has prevented progress in the study of perception of emotional voices. Using the new morphing method based on STRAIGHT, the degree of categorical perception and dimensional characteristics of emotional voice were investigated. Though the categoricalness of emotional perception is not yet clearly concluded, results of the dimensional characteristics of emotional voice perception that is similar to that of emotional facial expression were confirmed by the experiment, and the problems of emotional perception for voices were found to parallel findings for facial expression.

Therefore, it is necessary to study further the perception of emotional voice to make a perceptual processing model, as the study presented here is a preliminary one. However, findings suggest a profound relation to many application areas such as speech synthesizers used in human-computer interaction, text-to-speech synthesizers for reading with emotions, and so on.

References

Calder, A. J., Young, A. W., Perrett, D. I., Etcoff, N. L., & Rowland, D. (1996). Categorical perception of morphed facial expressions. *Visual Cognition, 3*, 105-146.

De Gelder, B., Teunisse, J.-P., & Benson, P. J. (1997). Categorical perception of facial expressions: Categorical and their internal structure. *Cognition and Emotion, 11,* 1-23.

Ekman, P. (1993). Facial expression and emotion. *American Psychologist, 48*, 384-392.

Etcoff, N. L., & Magee, J. J. (1992). Categorical perception of facial expressions. *Cognition, 44*, 227-240.

Fujisaki, H, (1998) A note on the physiological and physical basis for the phrase and accent components in the voice fundamental frequency contour. In O. Fujimura (Ed.), *Vocal physiology: Voice production, mechanisms and functions* (pp. 347-355). New York: Raven.

Kakehi, K., & Sogabe, Y. (2005, March). Emotional perception in voices: Is it categorical or not? Paper presented at the XV Annual PVC: PVSF/Pixar Voice Conference: Voice & Emotions, Emeryville, CA.

Kawahara, H., Katayose, H., de Cheveigné, A., & Patterson, R. D. (1999). Fixed-point analysis of frequency to instantaneous frequency mapping for accurate estimation of F0 and periodicity. *Proceedings of Eurospeech 99, 6*, 2781-2784.

Kawahara, H., Masuda-Katsuse, I., & de Cheveigné, A. (1999). Restructuring speech representations using a pitch-adaptive time-frequency smoothing and an instantaneous-frequency-based F0 extraction. *Speech Communication, 27*, 187-207.

Kawahara, H., & Matsui, H. (2003). Auditory morphing based on an elastic perceptual distance metric in an interference-free time-frequency representation. *Proceedings of ICASSP 2003, 1*, 256-259.

Laukka, P. (2003). Categorical perception of emotion in vocal expression. *Annals of the New York Academy of Science, 1000*, 283-287.

Matsui, H., & Kawahara, H. (2003). Investigation of emotionally morphed speech perception and its structure using a high quality speech manipulation system. *Proceedings of the 8th European Conference on Speech Communication & Technology (Eurospeec '03)* Geneva, Switzerland, 2113-2116.

Morris, J. S., Frith, C. D., Perret, D. I., Rowland, D., Young, A. W., Calder, A. J., et al. (1996). A differential neural response in the human amygdala to fearful and happy facial expressions. *Nature, 383*, 812-815.

Nomura, M., Iidaka, T., Kakehi, K., Tsukiura, T., Hasegawa, T., Maeda, Y., et al. (2003). Frontal lobe networks for effective processing of ambiguously expressed emotions in humans. *Neuroscience Letters, 348*, 113-116.

Shibui, S., & Shigemasu, K. (2005). A model of two-dimensional placement of the facial expressions of emotion. *The Japanese Journal of Psychology, 76*, 113-121.

Shigeno, S. (2003). Recognition of emotion transmitted by vocal and facial expression: Comparison between the Japanese and the American. *The AGU Journal of Psychology, 3*, 1-8.

Sogabe, Y., Kakehi, K., & Kawahara, K. (2003). Psychological evaluation of emotional speech using a new morphing method. *Proceedings of the International Conference on Cognitive Science* (pp. 628-633).

Young, A.W., Rowland, D., Calder A.J., Etcoff, N.L., Seth, A. & Perrett, D.J. (1997). Facial expression megamix: Tests of dimensional and category amounts of emotion recognition. *Cognition, 3*, 81-117.

CHAPTER 2

A Paralinguistic Template for Creating Persona in Interactive Voice Response (IVR) Systems

Osamuyimen Thompson Stewart

Abstract

Human-computer interaction via automatic speech recognition (ASR) technology is everywhere around us today. Humans engage in dialogs with machines using speech and machines speak back through prompts. A prompt may be synthesized speech, also called text-to-speech (TTS), or prerecorded audio. For both of these channels, *voice*, *expressiveness*, or *persona* has become significant. The goal of these is to project a natural voice quality that will provide the linguistic and cultural context to get callers to speak with a machine, while having their needs fulfilled. Persona plays an important expressive and social role by signaling the identity of the speaker and providing information about him or her that is of great importance in successful dialog interactions (cf. Lyons, 1977).

Most of the experiments and research on voice and emotions in human-computer interaction have been in the realm of synthesized speech (Cowie et al., 2001; Scherer, 1984a; 1984b; Schroder, Cowie, Douglas-Cowie, Westerdijk, & Gielen, 2001, etc). There is ample description of the motivations and justification for encoding persona in prerecorded prompts

(Cohen, Giangola, & Balogh, 2004; Kotelly, 2003; Nass & Brave, 2005); however, these only offer generic steps on *how to* create a persona's voice, lacking any formalism. Currently, much of persona creation is centered on art and creativity—which are vital—and lacks any shared rigor or systematic process that will make persona scalable, verifiable, and replicable.

Against this background, this paper proposes a paralinguistic template for developing a round persona. A round persona manifests voice modulations and emotional variations tailored to the dialog context. In this regard, the paralinguistic template contains two properties for matching voice with content and emotional context: (a) a specification of the discourse states and their associated discourse content and (b) an array of the paralinguistic features (ASR emotion, speech rate, pitch changes, and articulation) defined for each discourse content.

Introduction

Human-computer interaction via automatic speech recognition (ASR) or interactive voice response (IVR) technology is everywhere around us today—automated banking, pharmaceutical, automotive, cellular phones, and even Barbie dolls—as we engage in dialogs with machines using our voice (speech). With increasing user-adoption of ASR systems, there is now growing concern that dialog interaction is not simply *what* is said (the content), but also, crucially, *how* it is said (voice/cadence). Consider the following sample human-computer dialog using voice:

> Computer: Welcome to the Voice Interactive Game System. Please say the name of the game you would like to play.
>
> User: Talking to Aliens.
>
> Computer: Talking to Aliens. That's a nice selection. All right,

please give me a second to load it and then we can begin . . .

Putting aside the obvious issues regarding how well machines effectively understand human speech, we note that computers speak through what is called *prompts* in voice user interface (VUI) parlance. A prompt is the utterance that a machine or computer system speaks during an interactional exchange. For example, in the illustration above, the machine is queued up to welcome users and then ask for their intent, i.e., the game they would like to play. After users say their game choice, the machine confirms the selection, adds a compliment, and gives instruction regarding what is to happen next.

There is ample evidence (Brave & Nass 2002; Cowie et al., 2001; Schroder et al., 2001, for example) that callers can recognize, and react to the emotive content of speech in spoken dialog systems. The process of encoding emotive properties in prompts is called *persona* (with recorded speech) or *expressiveness* (with TTS). For example, in the sample script above, there are several considerations that must be encoded and projected: if the demography that uses this game system is predominantly the 13–18 age group, then the initial welcome prompt must be perky and happy in order to sustain their attention. Clearly, this voice cannot be boring or dull. Furthermore, note that after the gamer has made a selection, the machine compliments the user with "That's a nice selection." Emotional prompts like these must be spoken by the machine with the right intonation for it to be construed as genuine and natural. In this way, the machine is able to project a natural voice quality that provides the linguistic and cultural context to get users to converse with a machine, while having their needs fulfilled. Abstracting away from the technical details of the ASR software, the relevant question that now arises is, how is the computer able to adapt to the linguistic and cultural context of the dialog?

In order to properly address this question, it is important to distinguish between two formats of speech application prompts: (a) synthesized speech, also called text-to-speech (TTS), where the machine reads back text based on machine-generated speech, and (b) prerecorded speech, where a person who does voice-over work (voice talent) goes to the studio and reads the prepared text, which is digitally recorded and inserted into the speech system in specified situations during dialog interaction.

Typically, the choice of format to be used for a prompt is based on three factors:

1. Commercial or noncommercial systems. Many noncommercial speech systems use TTS to generate prompts, while most commercial systems use prerecorded audio.

2. Static or dynamic messages. Static messages are always the same in the life of the application. For example, a welcome prompt always contains the name of the company. Even if there is a name change, this is not something that happens constantly. Therefore, prompts containing static messages are amenable to prerecording. By contrast, dynamic messages change regularly depending on context or message, for example, status messages that provide up-to-the-minute stock price information or variable dollar amount for an order or service.

3. Usability and customer experience. This is, perhaps, the biggest factor influencing choice of format for prompts. IVR systems are competitively evaluated and benchmarked on a regular basis. User perceptions or reaction to the "voice of the system" is one of the key usability metrics used for measuring customer satisfaction. Because of customer satisfaction consideration, the current reality is that the majority of the prompts in IVR systems are prerecorded, even though many commercial versions of TTS show tremendous promise in producing natural voice quality. In one experiment reported by Boyce (1999), synthesized speech (how it is said) in conjunction with the variations in the length of the prompt (what is said) was most effective at getting users to speak concisely. However, results from the customer satisfaction measures indicated that callers disliked the synthesized speech so much as to offset

any gain in shorter utterances that the TTS offered. Usability evaluation of voice and emotion of an IBM Help Desk system lends empirical credence to this observation regarding user bias. In this application, 98% of the prompts were prerecorded, while only 2% were dynamically generated. The 37 subjects who participated in the survey were requested to make 10 calls each to the system and perform predesigned tasks involving both the TTS prompts and prerecorded audio. At the end of all the calls, they were asked to respond to a usability questionnaire containing eight questions. The analysis of users' response showed that they were able to differentiate overall system persona from the TTS prompts. One hundred percent indicated a strong preference for the persona represented by the prerecorded audio over the TTS. This bias could be reduced very simply to human preference for human voice and emotion with all the attendant paralinguistic cues.

In light of the foregoing, the remainder of the chapter will focus on prerecorded prompts with the understanding that the resulting paralinguistic template can be generalized to TTS prompts.

Motivating Persona in Prerecorded Speech: Overview of Current Approaches

One question that arises from the previous section is, how can we get computer voices to convey comparable human emotions? Most of the experiments and research on voice and emotion in ASR systems have been done within the purview of *emotional synthesis* in TTS (Cowie et al., 2001; Scherer, 1984a; 1984b; Schroder et al., 2001, etc.). This is not the case with prerecorded audio. There is ample description of the motivations and justification for encoding persona with prerecorded prompts (Cohen et al., 2004; Kotelly, 2003; Nass & Brave, 2005); however, these only offer generic steps on *how to* actually create a persona's voice. For example, one suggestion is to write a biographical description of the persona containing details such as type of school attended, kind of car driven, whether single or married, etc. What is crucially missing is how to translate the fine details of a character sketch into the voice of the persona. Why should a voice talent or the voice coach/director care that the persona is a psychology graduate from an ivy-league school? Currently, much of persona creation is centered on art and creativity—which are vital—but there is still a gross lack of shared rigor and systematic process within the IVR community that will make personae scalable, verifiable, and replicable. In other words, what is needed in creating persona is a process showing how all the elegant persona descriptions can be translated into the voice of the application. From a practical voice coaching perspective, these questions are relevant for four reasons.

First, there is a gross simplification of what it takes to project a pleasant voice on the IVR system (For more on the topic of vocal pleasantness consult Chapter 2 in Volume 1: Editor). In most cases, it is assumed that once the prompts have been written and the persona description is done, these are sufficient to guide the voice talent in the recording. This is wrong because it fails to take into consideration the fact that *context* is crucial in projecting the right emotion. Thus, when a script is handed over to a voice talent or a studio coach who knows nothing about the *context* of the specific prompts or entire application, the end result is, inevitably, a disconnect between the voice and the emotional expectations of the IVR system.

Second, it is a matter of fact that not all voice talents are professional actors. Voice-over work or using voice to project a persona is not simply reading a script. In many instances, it requires the voice talent to "perform" and project emotions with controlled cadence and inflections to create a lasting user experience in the mind of the user. Merely reading a script without any expression often results in a boring and unsatisfactory customer experience. The result is that, very often, the persona profile will not match the voice of the application as the voice fails to express a natural range of emotions consistent with sociolinguistic principles of language use. Indeed, actively speaking (in a dialog) is very different from reading a text (as a monolog). The consequence is that users will not choose the voice option and would rather speak to a human agent, further weakening user adoption of IVR systems.

Third, without a systematic process for projecting voice and emotions, the studio sessions are usually unguided. It is quite common to observe sessions where the IVR designer or studio coach engage in prolonged and frustrating interactions with the voice talent. Without any systematic way to translate the persona into the voice, the only metric used is gut instinct. In this situation, there is usually not a whole lot that is mutually agreeable or verifiable in terms of what is acceptable during the recording session. In

fact, one approach has been to attempt to guide the voice talent using intonation cues. For example, in the welcome message stated in the sample dialog in the introduction, the coach might say, "I want it with a high tone," or "Please say it with a low tone." There are two basic drawbacks of this method. One is that using a segmental feature like tonality to project across a sentence is confusing because the voice talent must figure out how to spread the high tone. For one thing, it will be absurd for all the function and content words to come out as high tone. The other drawback is that expectations of "high" and "low" do not always match. One person may be tone deaf while the other is adept at musical notes. In this situation, for example, what the voice talent feels is high may either be too high or even not high enough to the coach. This could very easily lead to frustration that could hold up the session and even upset the voice talent. Such frustration impacts the eventual quality of the output by the voice talent and may unnecessarily increase the number of takes for each prompt during a recording session.

The final and most profound drawback arises when changes are made to a speech application several months or even years after the initial recording. When there is a time interval between recording sessions, an informal process of translating the persona is left open to interpretation, resulting in inconsistencies. The voice and emotion become very difficult to reproduce in a manner that is consistent with the remainder of the application that is unaffected by the change. As a result, many speech application personae start out (in the initial deployment) with high customer satisfaction rates and then very quickly become judged by users as either overenthusiastic (too perky) or overly boring (too flat). This observation speaks to the issue of scalability of IVR persona, raising many unanswered questions. For example, after a speech application has been built how can IVR designers go about modifying or adjusting the persona based on analysis of user interaction data? Also, how do you customize a single persona for multiple clients who share a common application?

To summarize this section, prompting in IVR is not only *what* is said but also *how* it is said. As a result, instead of generic persona descriptions, there should be a systematic process that allows for the translation of the fine details of the character sketch into the voice. Against this background, the next section presents a specific proposal for achieving consistency of personae and the systematic process for their development based on two properties:

1. matching the voice with content
2. matching the voice with the emotional context

These two properties will be motivated and formalized resulting in a paralinguistic template for translating persona into voice in IVR systems.

How to Create a Persona Using a Paralinguistic Template

As suggested in the previous section, IVR persona must be regulated by rounding up the voice to match the content and the emotional context. In other words, it is not enough to simply write a character sketch which says that the persona is a psychology graduate from a prestigious

college. Rather, during a dialog interaction, the social, cultural, and psychological inferences should arise in the mind of the user based on how the voice matches the content as well as how the voice matches each emotional context. Thus, persona takes on a significant expressive and social role by signaling the identity of the speaker and providing sociolinguistic information about the voice of the IVR that is vital for successful dialog interaction.

Matching Voice with Content

The principle of matching voice with content is based on observations of human-human interactions. For example, Reichman (1985) and Sacks, Schegloff, and Jefferson (1974) discuss aspects of the different phases of a human-human conversation (from the introduction through shifting discourse to the conclusion) and the different kinds of linguistic transitions between conversational turns. Adapting their observations to human-machine dialog, specifically toward the goal of matching voice with content, I propose a discourse-pragmatic segmentation of speech application into discourse states.

Discourse State

Discourse state refers to the units (phases) of conversation starting from when callers come into the speech application until they exit. This is based on the assumption that each discourse state is thematically coherent and it deals with a single discourse function or content. Consequently, the following five discourse states (and their subclasses) are proposed for the IVR: welcome, error recovery, partial success, get input, and closing. These are described below respectively.

Welcome State

This is the initial state users come to when they dial a speech application, generally called the main menu. The prompt confirms that users have reached their intended destination (i.e., dialed correct number) and are invited to state the reason for the call. In terms of content, there are three major ways in which the welcome state may vary, each with sub-discourse pragmatic content that must be differentiated:

1. General dialog style
   a. Directed dialog: this is the case where a user is given instructions in terms of what he can say to the system. For example, a user may hear, "For customer service, say 'Agent,' or for account balance, say 'Balance.'"
   b. Open-ended dialog: these are applications where the user is greeted with a prompt that asks, "How may I help you?" and there is no explicit instruction what he can say.
2. Upon initial entry into the application
   a. Novice user: this term applies to those who call the application for the first time or those who have called into the IVR system and have only been able to successfully complete a few tasks.
   b. Expert user: this term refers to repeat callers who have used the application several times before and have been able to successfully complete many tasks.
3. Returning from within application: the IVR must distinguish between:

   a. Callers (novice or expert) who have successfully gone down a path in the speech application and need to "start over" again to initiate a new request.
   b. Callers (novice or expert) who have unsuccessfully gone down a path in the speech application and need to "start over" again either to restate their initial request or ask for a new one.

Error Recovery State

After the welcome, the conversational turn passes on to the user and he is invited to speak his request to the speech application. At this point, we distinguish between two outcomes: (a) cooperative, i.e., when a user speaks his or her request, and (b) uncooperative, i.e., when a user does not speak a request. The nature of cooperativeness and the level of dialog turn in the recovery process affect the content of the next prompt by the system:

1. Confused:
   a. These are callers who say "Hello" instead of stating their request. When this happens, it is usually an indication that they are confused and do not know what to say to the system.
2. Uncooperative: there are several kinds of uncooperative including:
   a. Instances when a caller remains silent instead of stating a request. When this happens, it usually indicates a state of uncooperativeness and unwillingness to speak to the system.
   b. Instances when a caller presses a touch-tone key, e.g., 0, or says "Operator." These actions usually imply he does not want to speak to the machine.

3. Cooperative: a cooperative caller is one who says something that is relevant for moving dialog forward. However, there are occasions when dialog stalls due to limitations of the IVR's understanding. At least, two general situations must be distinguished requiring different discourse content:
   a. When a caller says something that is within grammar but the system fails to properly recognize the request (misrecognition).
   b. When a caller says something that is out of grammar (OOG), which the system has no chance of recognizing.

4. Level of dialog turn: confused, uncooperative, and cooperative situations conversationally require the IVR to offer a thematically coherent and reasonable response. Thus, we must distinguish at least three levels:
   a. First turn: when the caller has stated a request just once.
   b. Second turn: when the caller has to state the request a second time.
   c. Third turn: when the caller is asked to state the request a third time.

Partial Success State

When a user's utterance does not contain sufficient information that the IVR can use to decisively determine the caller's intent, this is referred to as *partial success*. There are three subparts that must be distinguished in terms of content:

1. When a user asks, "What are my options?" The psychology of the user who asks this question must be carefully matched in terms of the content of the response prompt.

2. Disambiguation: very often, users do not speak clearly to the IVR. When the user's utterance is not specific or clearly understood, we must distinguish two kinds of disambiguation strategies:
   a. Ambiguous: this is when a user's utterance could potentially imply two or more choices.
   b. Vague: this is when a user's utterance is semantically generic and too vague to pick out a specific request within the semantic classes of executable actions in the IVR's understanding domain.

3. Confirmation: in this context, a user says something the system understood, but in order to move forward the IVR solicits collaborative concurrence from the user. There are two strategies for realizing this:
   a. Explicit reference: this arises when a user's request is recognized but the system is not "confident" it correctly understood the caller and so it will explicitly ask for clarification. The clarification question explicitly requires a yes or no response from the user.
   b. Implicit reference: this arises when a user's request is recognized with an above average confidence but, due to the nature of business requirements (for example, penalties for inaccurate decisions), the IVR restates what was recognized as part of the process of satisfying the request. An example will help clarify this strategy. If a user says, "I want to see if the $200 I deposited last week has cleared," then, as part of proving the new account balance, the system says "Ok. You want your account balance," prior to provid-

ing the actual account balance. The assumption here is that if what was understood is wrong, by repeating it in the process of satisfying the request the user may interrupt the flow.

Get User Input State

Once a user has passed the welcome state and conversation has started, there are potentially different paths available. For each path, there is always an initial (header) state that attempts to get input from the user. It does so by informing the caller where he is in the IVR (offers a landmark) and provides a list of available options to move dialog along. Also in this phase, we categorize callers that may be returning from within the application after going down an unsuccessful path or that may have successfully completed a task and is ready to begin a new one. The following scenarios may affect the content of this initial (header) state:

1. Get digits or amount.
2. Get name or unique identifier.
3. Get input (non-alpha or -numeric ID).
4. Callers (novice or expert) who have successfully gone down a path in the speech application and need to start over again to initiate a new request.
5. Callers (novice or expert) who have unsuccessfully gone down a path in the speech application and need to start over again either to restate the initial request or ask for a new thing.

Closing (Exit) State

This is when a user is about to leave the IVR. In this situation, depending on whether a task was successfully completed or not and also based on the nature of the

request by the caller, several discourse content options must be distinguished:

1. Announcement: this happens after a user has requested a frequently asked question (FAQ) to which the system provides a canned message. For example, if a user says, "Where do I download the latest Lotus Notes 7.2?" the IVR simply provides the location and process. This may also be a simple database query such as directory assistance where the user says, "I want the phone number for IBM," and the system provides this information to the user.
2. Transfer to agent: this may occur for a variety of reasons including:
   a. After an unsuccessful interaction and call defaults to a level one agent.
   b. After a successful interaction, where the IVR partially collects the user's relevant information and passes the call on to an agent for completion. For example, in a flight reservation system, the IVR collects the confirmation number or flight number from a user who wants to select seats on the flight. The IVR passes the information on to the agent, who completes the request.
3. After a successful task completion and the user says, "I'm done," or "Goodbye," there should be a graceful exit.

These five discourse-pragmatic states are assumed to characterize all speech applications (directed dialog, natural language, or mixed initiative). They indicate the nature of discourse content that both system and caller traverses during a typical interaction. Using these discourse contents, the context of each prompt is specified and this will allow the persona to match voice with content based on the theme of each discourse state, which can be incorporated into the design of prompts. Table 2–1 presents a summary of the characteristics of using discourse content to match voice with content.

The introduction of discourse state offers a systematic basis for producing context-sensitive dialog. Thus, one of the practical uses of this template is that it provides the voice user interface designer an overall picture of the speech application and how to construct prompts that have the right context.

Table 2–1. Summary of discourse state and content for matching voice with content

Discourse State	Categories of Discourse Content
Welcome	Is it directed dialog?
	Is it open-ended dialog?
	Is the user a novice?
	Is the user an expert?
	Is the user returning from within application after success completing a task?
	Is the user returning from within application after unsuccessful attempt to complete a task?
Error Recovery	Did caller say "Hello"?
	Is the user silent?
	Did user press touch-tone keypad or ask for operator?
	Is the phrase in-grammar but not recognized by the system?
	Is the phrase out of grammar?
	What is the level of dialog turn? First, second, or third?
Partial Success	Did user ask "What are my options?"?
	Is request ambiguous?
	What are the levels of ambiguity?
	Is user's request vague?
	Does request need to be confirmed? (implicitly or explicitly)
Get User Input	Get digits or amount?
	Gate name or unique ID?
	Get input (non-alpha or -numeric ID?
	Start over due to failure?
	Start over after successful task?
Closing	Play announcement?
	Transfer to agent after failure?
	Transfer to agent due to partial automation?
	Goodbye after success

Thus far, we have looked at the first step in motivating the paralinguistic template for matching voice with emotion. We have established the notion of discourse state as the formal and systematic basis for writing the content of prompts, and in parallel specifying the emotional content of the words in the prompts. This step is important because, according to Nass and Brave (2005, p. 95), the content that interfaces present to users will also be associated with emotion, no matter how "unemotional" an interface tries to be. This stems from their observation that because the brain tightly integrates the emotion of voice and the emotion of words, therefore, consistency between them is critical.

Matching Voice with Emotional Context

In this section, we examine the other aspect of the paralinguistic template dealing with how to match voice with the emotion. The motivation for matching voice with emotions stems from experiments that have shown that subjects can recognize the emotive content in a speech sample (Banse & Scherer, 1996; Cowie et al., 2001; Pereira, 2000, etc.). For the purpose of creating a template for matching voice with emotional context in the IVR, I propose the notion of *paralinguistic features*. By paralinguistic, I assume certain features of vocal signals such as loudness and what is commonly described as tone of voice, which along with gestures, facial expressions, eye movements, relative distance to the microphone, position (standing or sitting), and so on, play a supporting role in using voice to match the emotional context of speaking.

In general, the functions of paralinguistic phenomena in normal language behavior can be classified based on the modulation of an utterance. According to Lyons (1977), the modulation of an utterance means the superimposing upon the utterance of a particular attitudinal coloring, indicative of the speaker's involvement in what he is saying and his desire to impress or convince the hearer. What is commonly referred to as tone of voice summarizes the most important aspect of the vocal features with a modulating function. Tone of voice involves the recognition of a whole set of variations in the features of voice dynamics: loudness, tempo, pitch fluctuation, continuity, etc. (Abercombie, 1967, pp. 95–110).

In specific reference to the objective of matching voice with emotion, Nass and Brave (2005) observe that *all* voices activate the parts of the brain associated with the measurement of paralinguistic (vocal) cues that mark emotion. Furthermore, Murray and Arnott (1993) provide a detailed account of the vocal effects that are associated with several basic emotions in Table 2-2.

Table 2-2 characterizes human emotions and provides an important foundation for the producing a paralinguistic template for matching voice with emotion for the IVR. In order to adapt Table 2-2 and derive emotional features that pertain to the IVR context, 500 calls were informally analyzed by listening to the interaction between the user and a call routing speech application (which also contained some automated task legs where users can complete their task without an agent's involvement). There were no specific criteria in terms of the male-female requirements or the nature of the call. These 500 calls were picked out randomly to provide a simple basis

Table 2–2. Vocal effects associated with several basic emotions

	Fear	Anger	Sadness	Happiness	Disgust
Speech Rate	Much faster	Slightly faster	Slightly lower	Faster or slower	Very much slower
Pitch Average	Very much higher	Very much higher	Slightly lower	Much higher	Very much lower
Pitch Range	Much wider	Much wider	Slightly narrower	Much wider	Slightly wider
Intensity	Normal	Higher	Lower	Higher	Lower
Voice Quality	Irregular voicing	Breathy chest tone	Resonant	Breathy blaring	Grumbled chest tone
Pitch Changes	Normal	Abrupt on stressed syllables	Downward inflections	Smooth upward inflections	Wide downward terminal inflections
Articulation	Precise	Tense	Slurring	Normal	Normal

for verifying the discourse pragmatic states discussed in the previous section and also to serve as a basis for ascertaining the sort of emotion that might be suitable from Table 2-2.

In general, it was observed from listening to the 500 calls that the IVR should always self-identify with the user by trying to match his emotion (cf. Nass and Brave, 2004). However, of the five basic emotions (fear, anger, sadness, happiness, disgust), anger is the one emotion that did not seem an appropriate emotion to be expressed by the IVR, under any circumstance. This is based on a simple human factors assumption that the IVR should never blame the caller. By extension, the IVR should never raise its voice to the user. Thus, the one lingering question from our adaptation of Table 2-2 is what should the IVR's emotion be when a caller is angry? The proposal is to create two new categories of emotions (sympathy and empathy) based on features and inferences of two existing

basic emotions: sadness and disgust. This would yield the emotions for the IVR shown in Table 2-3.

We turn to the other requirement of the paralinguistic template involving the properties required for the vocal effects. Of the six vocal features proposed (speech rate, pitch average, pitch range, intensity, voice quality, pitch changes, and articulation), only three are included in the current template (speech rate, pitch changes, and articulation). These three are selected because they were easy for the studio coach (and voice talent) to observe and control during preliminary usability trials in five different studio sessions. As previously suggested, the vocal properties of sympathy and empathy are derived from the composition of the vocal features of sadness and disgust. Finally, it was observed that there is the need to acknowledge the special linguistic circumstance surrounding human-computer interaction. This is based on the fact that computers are not humans. And so, there will be conflict situations during dialog interactions where the computer should act like a machine. On this basis, I propose a default vocal feature or quality that is an arch-emotional category labeled as *normal*, i.e., a computer emotion. Table 2–4 presents the resulting chart of vocal effects associated with IVR emotions.

On the basis of the paralinguistic features in Table 2–4, we shall now put it all together by proposing the relevant values (vocal and emotional) for each discourse state (and content) of the IVR.

Emotional Context in IVR: Welcome State

Directed Dialog

The discourse content of the directed dialog is primarily to guide users toward task completion by *directing* them in terms of what they can say in this discourse state. The emotional context should be relaxed, nondistracting, and focused. Three basic emotions are proposed for this state (each depending on the needs and context of the IVR): happiness, neutral, and sadness.

Open-Ended

The discourse content of the open-ended dialog is to encourage the user to engage in a conversation unhindered by choice of words. Like directed dialog, the emotional context should be relaxed, nondistracting, and focused. Three basic emotions are proposed for this state (each depending on the needs and context of the IVR): happiness, neutral, and sadness.

Novice

The discourse content of a novice is based on the profile of a user who has no

Table 2–3. Summary of human emotions and matching IVR emotion

	Basic Emotion				
User Emotion	Fear	Anger	Sadness	Happiness	Disgust
IVR Emotion	Fear	Sympathy; sadness; empathy	Sadness	Happiness	Disgust

Table 2–4. Vocal effects associated with IVR emotions

	Fear	Sympathy	Sadness	Happiness	Empathy	Normal	Disgust
Speech Rate	Much faster	Slower	Slightly slower	Faster or slower	Much slower	Normal	Very much slower
Pitch Changes	Normal	Downward inflections	Downward inflections	Smooth upward inflections	Wide downward terminal inflections	Normal	Wide downward terminal inflections
Articulation	Precise	Normal	Slurring	Normal	Slurring	Normal	Normal

familiarity with the IVR environment and nuances. This user is tentative and unsure. Thus, the emotional context must be simply as neutral (normal) as possible.

Expert

The discourse content of an expert is based on the profile of a user who is familiar with the speech IVR and knows what to do. Thus, the emotional context should be welcoming (happy).

Start Over after Failed Attempt

In this context, there is a problem because task completion has not succeeded. The emotional context is tenuous because the user could very easily become uncooperative and either bail out (ask for operator) or hang up. The voice should convey empathy (sadness).

Start Over after Successful Attempt

In this context, the user has successfully completed a task and could either ask to begin a new one or exit the system. The emotional context should be welcoming (happy).

Table 2-5 presents a summary of the vocal and emotional characteristics of all the discourse content under the welcome discourse state.

Table 2–5. Paralinguistic template for welcome state

Discourse Content	Paralinguistic Features			
	Emotion	Speech Rate	Pitch Changes	Articulation
Directed dialog?	Happy	Faster or slower	Smooth upward inflections	Normal
Directed dialog?	Neutral (normal)	Normal	Normal	Normal
Directed dialog?	Sadness	Slightly slower	Downward inflections	Slurring
Open-ended?	Happy	Faster or slower	Smooth upward inflections	Normal
Open-ended?	Neutral (normal)	Normal	Normal	Normal
Open-ended?	Sadness	Slightly slower	Downward inflections	Slurring
Novice?	Normal (neutral)	Normal	Normal	Normal
Expert?	Happy	Faster or slower	Smooth upward inflections	Normal
From within application. (success)?	Sadness	Slightly slower	Downward inflections	Slurring
From within application. (failure)?	Happy	Faster or slower	Smooth upward inflections	Normal

Emotional Context in IVR: Error Recovery State

Confused Caller: Hello

The discourse content of this state reveals a situation where the caller responds to the IVR's main prompt with a "feeler" phrase like "Hello," or "Are you a computer?" or "Is this a person?" Responses like these suggest that the caller is confused and unsure of what to say. The user sends out a feeler to get a better socio-psychological impression of the discourse participant. The emotional context involves uncertainty or apprehension, which could be mapped into the IVR emotion of fear.

Uncooperative Caller: No Speech

This involves a situation where the caller decides not to participate in a dialog after hearing the voice of the IVR. Users remain silent in the hope that after a few turns, the IVR will give up and transfer the call to a human agent. From an emotional context perspective, this is a stronger form of uncooperativeness because the user will not even respond to verbal stimuli to engage in a dialog. The emotional context may be mapped into the basic human emotion of anger and maps to the corresponding IVR emotion of sadness.

Uncooperative Caller: Request Operator

Typically, this situation arises when the caller does not trust the IVR to satisfy the request. This could stem from a previous experience where the IVR could not understand the user's utterance. The reason for this situation could also simply be based on an advance determination that the problem he is calling about is too complex for the IVR, requiring only human knowledge and assistance. This is a weaker form of uncooperativeness because the user responds to verbal stimuli attempts. The emotional context involves uncertainty or apprehension, which could be mapped into the IVR emotion of fear.

Cooperative: Misrecognition

In this context, the caller says a relevant phrase to the IVR, but due to limitations of the technology the system misrecognizes the user's request. Misrecognition arises due to an error by the system, and so the voice should convey the emotion of disgust.

Cooperative: Out of Grammar

In this context, the caller says a phrase to the IVR; however, due to vocabulary limitations the system fails to understand the user's request. The emotional context involves a weaker form of sadness, which is more accurately captured by the IVR emotion of sympathy.

Dialog Turns

In general, caller frustration increases with each additional dialog turn. Usability experiments have shown that callers do not keep track of time if the user experience is pleasant (Boyce, 1999). Therefore, it is important for the emotional context to map to each level of dialog turn.

1. For the first turn, the basic emotion should be sympathy.
2. The second turn should show sadness.

3. Third turn should show a stronger form of sadness, which corresponds to the IVR emotion of empathy.

The resulting vocal and emotions template for the error recovery discourse state along with the subclasses is summarized in Table 2-6.

Emotional Context in IVR: Partial Success State

User Asks for Other Options

This is a situation where the user's intent is not explicitly covered in the options originally provided by the IVR. A user who requests additional options is cooperative and willing to use the IVR. Therefore, the

emotional context should be mapped into the IVR emotion of happiness.

Ambiguous

Within the semantic domain of the IVR, a single word could refer to multiple entities. When a user produces an ambiguous reference, the emotional state is similar to the first dialog level (under dialog turn) and the voice should convey sympathetic emotion.

Vague

When a caller's speech is semantically appropriate but lacks enough information to be used to precisely determine the user's intent, this is deemed to be a vague situation. Unlike ambiguous, where

Table 2–6. Paralinguistic template for error recovery state

Discourse Content	Paralinguistic Features			
	Emotion	Speech Rate	Pitch Changes	Articulation
Confused caller "Hello"	Fear	Much faster	Normal	Precise
No speech	Sadness	Slightly slower	Downward inflections	Slurring
Request operator	Fear	Much faster	Normal	Precise
Misrecognition	Disgust	Very much slower	Wide downward terminal inflections	Normal
Out of grammar	Sympathy	Slower	Downward inflections	Normal
First dialog turn	Sympathy	Slower	Downward inflections	Normal
Second dialog turn	Sadness	Slightly slower	Downward inflections	Slurring
Third dialog turn	Empathy	Much slower	Wide downward terminal inflections	Slurring

the items within the denotation of the ambiguity are known and can be easily offered to the user, the emotional context in the vague state is different. The IVR will rely on the user's patience to refine the concept until the core semantic area is identified and user intention determined. Typically, this could take between two and three turns to unravel, depending on the level of vagueness. Therefore, this should be mapped to the third dialog level (under dialog turn) and the voice should convey the IVR emotion of empathy.

Implicit Confirmation

In this context, a user's request is correctly recognized and repeated back as part of the process of executing the action requested by the user. The voice should convey the IVR emotion of happiness.

Explicit Confirmation

A user's request is recognized but the IVR is unsure that it has correctly understood the user's intent. The emotional context is similar to the first dialog level (under dialog turn) and the voice should convey the IVR emotion of sympathy.

The resulting vocal and emotions template for the partial success discourse state along with the subclasses is summarized in Table 2-7.

Emotional Context in IVR: Get Input State

The get input state is similar to the welcome state and so the emotional context should be relaxed, nondistracting, and focused. This could translate into one of three kinds of IVR emotions: happiness, normal (neutral), or sadness. Table 2-8 provides a summary of the vocal effects and associated IVR emotions for this state.

Emotional Context in IVR: Closing (Exit) State

In this context, the user has made a request that the IVR has understood.

Table 2–7. Paralinguistic template for partial success state

Discourse Content	Paralinguistic Features			
	Emotion	Speech Rate	Pitch Changes	Articulation
User asks for more options	Happiness	Faster or slower	Smooth upward inflections	Normal
Ambiguous	Sympathy	Slower	Downward inflections	Normal
Vague	Empathy	Much slower	Wide downward terminal inflections	Slurring
Explicit confirmation	Sympathy	Slower	Downward inflections	Normal
Implicit confirmaton	Happiness	Faster or slower	Smooth upward inflections	Normal

Table 2–8. Paralinguistic template for get input state

Discourse Content	Paralinguistic Features			
	Emotion	Speech Rate	Pitch Changes	Articulation
Get input	Happy	Faster or slower	Smooth upward inflections	Normal
Get input	Neutral (normal)	Normal	Normal	Normal
Get input	Sadness	Slightly slower	Downward inflections	Slurring
Novice?	Normal (neutral)	Normal	Normal	Normal
Expert?	Happy	Faster or slower	Smooth upward inflections	Normal
Successful: from within application.	Sadness	Slightly slower	Downward inflections	Slurring
Failure: from within application.	Happy	Faster or slower	Smooth upward inflections	Normal

There are five aspects of a closing state that map to different emotional contexts:

1. When providing a canned message. This arises based on the nature of the request, which could be procedural; for example, a user requests how to get something done, or asks a frequently asked question such as, "What is my account balance?" The nature of the announcement determines the length, but the emotional context should convey the IVR emotion of happiness.

2. When transferring a call to an agent when the request is of a complex type such that it can only be handled by an agent. The IVR emotion should be sympathy.

3. When transferring a call to another IVR, which is set up as an automated function for the requested task. Nass and Brave (2005) observe that users prefer consistency of voice between different computer systems, and since this is typically not the case with most transfers, the IVR emotion expressed should be sympathy.

4. When transferring a call to an agent once the maximum number of tries allowed in that turn has been exceeded (usually, a maximum of three tries is allowed). The IVR emotion should be sadness.

5. When a caller says, "I'm done" or "Good-bye," signaling the end of a conversation and that a transaction is complete. The IVR emotion should be happiness.

Table 2-9 provides a summary of the vocal effects and associated IVR emotions for the closing (exit) state.

Table 2–9. Paralinguistic template for closing (exit) state

Discourse Content	Paralinguistic Features			
	Emotion	**Speech Rate**	**Pitch Changes**	**Articulation**
Announcement	Happiness	Faster or slower	Smooth upward inflections	Normal
Transfer to agent (complex)	Sympathy	Slower	Downward inflections	Normal
Transfer to another IVR	Sympathy	Slower	Downward inflections	Normal
Transfer to agent (failure)	Sadness	Slightly slower	Downward inflections	Slurring
Good-bye	Happiness	Faster or slower	Smooth upward inflections	Normal

Discussion and Conclusion

This template offers a novel approach that provides the formal and systematic way to design the content of an IVR and then to map voice with emotion to yield a round persona. In general, five discourse-pragmatic states are assumed to characterize all speech applications [welcome, error recovery, partial success, get user input, and closing (exit)]. These specify the nature of discourse content that both system and caller traverse during a typical interaction. Using these discourse contents, the context of each prompt is specified and this allows the persona to match voice with content. It highlights the theme of each discourse state, which can be incorporated into the design of prompts, that is, offers a systematic basis for producing context-sensitive dialog. One practical use of this template is that it provides the voice user interface designer an overall picture of the speech application and how to construct prompts that have the right context.

For the purpose of matching voice with emotional context in the speech IVR persona, the notion of *paralinguistic features* is introduced. Paralinguistic features refer to certain features of vocal signals such as loudness and tone of voice. Tone of voice involves the recognition of a whole set of variations in the features of voice dynamics: loudness, tempo, pitch fluctuation, continuity, etc. By adapting the vocal effects and associated basic emotions proposed by Murray and Arnott (1993), seven IVR emotions are proposed for the paralinguistic template: fear, sympathy, sadness, happiness, empathy, normal, and disgust. Consequently, the combination of matching voice with content and voice with emotion yields a consistency in the paralinguistic template through which the IVR's persona and language behavior can be systematically classified.

Finally, the paralinguistic template provides the foundations for a formal and systematic process for creating persona with consistency between voice and emotions. Since the vocal features used in the template have been derived from adopting Murray and Arnott (1993) as well as from an informal evaluation of 500 calls from a call routing application, it is assumed that the discourse states and the associated emotional values are easily verifiable and can be generalized across all speech applications and prompt format (including TTS). These features will need to be formally evaluated.

References

Abercombie, D. (1967). *Elements of phonetics*. Edinburgh, UK: Edinburgh University Press.

Banse, R., & Scherer, K. (1996). Acoustic profiles in vocal emotion expression. *Journal of Personality and Social Psychology*, *70*(3), 614-636.

Boyce, S. J. (1999). Spoken natural dialog systems: User interface issues for the future. In D. Gardner-Bonneau (Ed.), *Human factors and voice interactive systems* (pp. 37-61). Norwell, MA: Kluwer.

Brave, S., & Nass, C. (2002). Emotion in human-computer interaction. In J. Jacko & A. Sears (Eds.), *Handbook of human-computer interaction* (pp. 251-271). New York: Lawrence Erlbaum.

Cohen, M., Giangola, J., & Balogh, J. (2004). *Voice user Interface Design*. Boston: Addison Wesley.

Cowie, R., Douglas-Cowie, E., Tsapastsoulis, N., Votsis, G., Kollias, S., Fellenz, W., et al. (2001). Emotion recognition in human-computer interaction. *IEEE Signal Processing Magazine*, *18*(1), 32-80.

Kotelly, B. (2003). *The art and business of speech recognition: Creating the noble voice*. Boston: Addison-Wesley.

Lyons, J. (1977). *Semantics: 1, 2*. Cambridge, UK: Cambridge University Press.

Murray, I., & Arnott, J. (1993). Towards the simulation of emotion in synthetic speech: A review of the literature on human vocal emotion. *Journal of the Acoustical Society of America*, *93*, 1097-1108.

Nass, C., & Brave, S. (2005). *Wired for speech: How voice activates and advances the human-computer relationship*. Cambridge, MA: MIT Press.

Pereira, C. (2000). Dimensions of emotional meaning in speech. In (Ed.), *Proceedings of the ISCA ITRW on Speech and Emotion: Developing a conceptual framework* (pp. 25-28). Newcastle, Northern Ireland.

Reichman, R. (1985). *Getting computers to talk like you and me*. Cambridge, MA: MIT Press.

Sacks, H., Schegloff, E., & Jefferson, G. (1974). A simplest systematics for the organization of turn-taking for conversation. *Language*, *50*(4), 696-735.

Scherer, K. R. (1984). Emotion as multicomponent process: A model and some cross-cultural data. *Review of Personality and Social Psychology*, *5*, 37-63.

Scherer, K. R. (1984). On the nature and function of emotion: A component process approach. In K. R. Scherer & P. Ekman (Eds.), *Approaches to emotion* (pp. 293-317). Hillsdale, NJ: Erlbaum.

Schroder, M., Cowie, R., Douglas-Cowie, E., Westerdijk, M., & Gielen, S. (2001). Acoustic correlates of emotion dimensions in view of speech synthesis. *Proceedings of Eurospeech*, *1*, 87-90.

CHAPTER 3

Memory for Emotional Tone of Voice

John W. Mullennix

This chapter focuses on how one form of indexical information carried in speech, emotional tone, is processed and represented in human long-term memory. Indexical properties of speech refer to the nonlinguistic aspects of the speech signal that carry personal information about the speaker (Abercrombie, 1967; Ladefoged & Broadbent, 1957; Laver, 1968). The personal characteristics conveyed by voice include physical attributes such as size, physique, sex, and age; psychological attributes related to personality; and social attributes such as regional origin, social status, social values and attitudes, occupation, and group membership (Laver, 1968). When listeners are presented with speech, they tend to make inferences about these personal characteristics based on the acoustic attributes of the speech signal that underlie indexical properties.

Two related questions of interest are examined. The first question is whether the perceptual processing of emotional tone utilizes cognitive resources in the same way that resources are used to process talker voice (Mullennix, 1997). The second question is whether information about emotional tone is stored in episodic representations of speech in long-term memory as a natural byproduct of the linguistic processing of the speech signal.

In recent years, evidence has been accumulating that indexical properties of speech related to talker voice are encoded into memory during speech perception and later affect memory for speech utterances. Much of this research relies upon memory paradigms where the mismatch of indexical properties (e.g., talker voice, speaking rate, voice amplitude) from time of initial presentation to time of later test is manipulated and the effects on memory analyzed. One example of this line of research is a study from Bradlow, Nygaard, and Pisoni (1999), who conducted a recognition memory spoken word experiment. Listeners were presented with lists of spoken words and were later tested with the same words or different words in order to assess recognition memory for the words. Recognition performance was assessed by asking listeners to make judgments about whether the words at time of test were "old" words heard before or "new" words not previously heard. When an old word at time of test was presented in the *same talker voice* or at the *same speaking rate* as the word during initial presentation, recognition memory for the word was better (as compared to words that mismatched in talker voice or speaking rate). However, no such advantage was observed for old words repeated at the same level of sound amplitude as the words presented initially. The memory advantage for an item matching in voice or speaking rate is explained by the availability of this information in memory at time of recognition, with the assumption that the linguistic information and indexical information are tied together in an episodic memory trace for the spoken word. Another result they observed was the absence of a recognition advantage for words repeated at the same amplitude level. This is an important finding, indicating that not all properties of spoken words are automatically encoded and retained in memory, a point which I will return to later on.

It is useful to note that other research using recognition memory paradigms has demonstrated memory advantages for words repeated in the same talker voice (Craik & Kirsner, 1974; Goldinger, 1996; Palmeri, Goldinger, & Pisoni, 1993). As well, studies utilizing voice repetition priming paradigms have shown that talker voice information is encoded into memory and persists (Church & Schacter, 1994; Schacter & Church, 1992). The retention of talker voice in memory has been examined also via memory recall paradigms. For example, when lists of spoken words are presented in different voices, with a long inter-stimulus-interval between words presented on the list, recall from long-term memory (as evidenced by recall of the first few items on the lists) is enhanced (Goldinger, Pisoni, & Logan, 1991; Nygaard, Sommers, & Pisoni, 1995). One explanation for these findings is that, when enough time is available for properly encoding the items into memory, information about each talker voice producing each word item is stored along with the linguistic information corresponding to each spoken word into episodic memory traces.

Nygaard et al. (1995) also tested the effects of variation in speaking rate and amplitude on early memory list item recall. Unlike the results found for talker voice, no memory recall advantage was observed for lists varying in speaking rate or amplitude. This suggested that, at least as evidenced by the use of a serial memory recall paradigm, information about speaking rate and amplitude were not available to assist memory recall for the spoken words. Nygaard et al. (1995) explained the differences in recall as reflecting differences in the way that different sources of variability in speech are handled, with the suggestion that talker voice reflects relatively stable characteristics related to indexical properties of speech, whereas speaking rate is related to more transient aspects of the spoken message. For amplitude, the absence of any effects on memory mirrored the findings of Bradlow et al. (1999) with recognition memory, suggesting that amplitude information is handled quite differently than both talker voice and speaking rate, with no indication that amplitude information is retained in episodic memory.

Thus, at least within the context of the methodological paradigms used in the studies above, there is evidence that talker voice information and, under some conditions, speaking rate information are encoded into episodic memory for speech as a matter of course when speech is perceived. This research adds to the growing idea that episodic representations of speech stored in long-term memory not only contain linguistic information about phonemes, phonology, and lexical structure, but also contain indexical information related to speakers originating the utterances (Goldinger, 1998; Pisoni, 1997). This is referred to as the *non-analytic* view of speech perception and speech representation in long-term memory.

To further ascertain whether this emerging non-analytic view is an appropriate way to characterize how speech is encoded into memory, converging research examining other sources of variation in speech related to indexical properties is warranted. This brings us to the central issue addressed in this chapter, which is whether information about emotional tone of speech is stored in episodic memory for speech utterances. Below, I describe a series of studies conducted in our laboratory that pertain to this issue. In terms of how emotional tone of voice is conveyed, Scherer (2003) classifies vocal utterances that carry emotion into three categories: natural vocal expression (materials recorded in real-life situations where emotion is present), induced emotions (where emotional states are induced into groups of speakers and their speech recorded), and simulated (portrayed) vocal expressions (where actors are asked to produce vocal expressions of emotion based on emotion labels or scenarios). In the studies covered

below, research using simulated vocal expressions is described.

First of all, the work on emotional tone and memory my colleagues and I have carried out was preceded by a study examining the perceptual processing of emotional tone of voice, with special attention to how variation in emotional tone is handled by the perceptual system. Mullennix et al. (2002a) examined whether changes in emotional tone of voice interfered with the perception of linguistic information in speech. In one experiment, the names *Todd* and *Tom* were presented in a male voice or a female voice in one of two emotional tones, either angry or surprised (the emotional tones were produced according to text scenarios and methodology used by Leinonen et al., 1997). Listeners performed a same/different speeded classification task, where the listener indicated whether the two names on each trial were the "same name," e.g., *Todd* and *Todd*, or "different names," e.g., *Todd* and *Tom*. On each trial, the two stimuli were presented in the same voice or in different voices and with the same emotional tone or with different emotional tones. The results showed that when the two stimuli in the pair mismatched in either talker voice or emotional tone, response latencies were slower. An additional experiment replicated this result with two vocal emotions that were more confusable (i.e., angry and commanding). In a second experiment, we presented lists of same-emotion and different-emotion words and asked listeners to perform a phoneme classification task upon the items. We found that for lists where emotional tone varied from word to word, response latencies were slower, compared to lists where emotional tone remained constant. Overall, the results of these experiments showed that stimulus variation in emotional tone results in perceptual interference in much the same way as stimulus variation in talker voice, speech rate, and factors related to consonantal production do (Creelman, 1957; Mullennix, Pisoni, & Martin, 1989; Newman, Clouse, & Burnham, 2001; Peters, 1955; Sommers, Nygaard, & Pisoni, 1994). We concluded that a perceptual mechanism that adjusts to variation in speech utterances is responsible for processing changes in emotional tone, with this mechanism using a measurable amount of cognitive processing resources and time.

Once we established that the perceptual processing of emotional tone resembles the way that perceptual processing of other sources of variation in speech mentioned above occurs, the next step was to examine whether emotional tone is encoded and stored into episodic memory for speech in the same manner as observed in the literature for talker voice and, to some extent, speaking rate. To accomplish this, we embarked on a set of studies utilizing recognition and recall memory paradigms that paralleled the work of Bradlow et al. (1999) and Nygaard et al. (1995). In the first study, we used a recognition memory paradigm to examine emotional tone (Mullennix, Gaston, & Keener, 2000). In the first part of the study, 48 monosyllabic consonant-vowel-consonant (CVC) words were recorded from a male speaker and a female speaker, with the words produced in the emotional tones of angry and surprised. These stimuli were presented to listeners, with listeners instructed to attend to each word and then classify the word as a *noun* or a *verb*. From word to word, the voice of the talker and the emotional tone that the word was spoken in varied in random fashion. This part of the

experiment was designed as a distracter task. The intent was to use the noun/verb task to orient listeners' attention away from the talker voice information and emotional tone information carried on the words. This created a situation where we could examine the "incidental" processing of voice and emotional tone into memory. In the second part of the experiment, a surprise recognition test was performed, with 48 old words and 48 new words presented and listeners deciding whether each word was an old word heard in the first part of the experiment or a new word not heard before. The old words either matched or mismatched in the voice and/or the emotional tone used when initially presented in the first part of the experiment.

The results are shown in Table 3–1, in terms of whether the words at time of test matched the words presented initially in talker voice and/or emotional tone. Across conditions, there was a significant advantage for word recognition in the same-voice/same-emotion condition over all three other mismatch conditions. In other words, recognition was best when talker voice and emotional tone matched the talker voice and emotional tone of the old words presented initially. This result indicated that, even though atten-

Table 3–1. Percent recognition errors for "old" words as a function of talker voice and emotional tone conditions

Condition	% Error
Same-voice/same-emotion	22.2%
Different-voice/same-emotion	38.8%
Same-voice/different-emotion	33.2%
Different-voice/different-emotion	37.2%

tion was drawn away from talker voice and emotional tone when the words were presented initially, some information about both voice and emotional tone were incidentally processed during the noun/verb distracter task, and this information was passed on to episodic memory along with the linguistic representations of the spoken words. The results for talker voice resemble previous research using recognition memory measures (Bradlow et al., 1999; Palmeri et al., 1993), and the results for emotional tone of voice suggest that information about emotional tone is also retained in episodic memory. This result is consistent with theories of episodic memory for speech postulating that indexical information about the talker is stored along with the utterances themselves (Goldinger, 1998; Pisoni, 1997).

To confirm the robustness of this finding, Gaston and Mullennix (2001) conducted another recognition study, the only difference being that the two emotional tones of voice tested were angry and commanding. The results are displayed in Table 3–2. The pattern of results was identical to that observed in the previous study, with recognition memory interfered with by mismatch in both talker voice and emotional tone of voice. Thus, even

Table 3–2. Percent recognition errors for "old" words as a function of talker voice and emotional tone conditions

Condition	% Error
Same-voice/same-emotion	22.0 %
Different-voice/same-emotion	33.5%
Same-voice/different-emotion	33.6%
Different-voice/different-emotion	30.0%

when testing two tones of voice that are acoustically similar, the information is distinctive enough in episodic memory to assist recognition when there is a match of emotional tone from time of initial presentation to time of test.

The next set of studies focused on the recall of information from long-term memory, thus tapping into episodic memory from a slightly different perspective than that observed with the aforementioned recognition memory work. The methodology used was based on the traditional serial recall memory task, a task used in a number of studies examining the encoding of talker voice information into memory (Goldinger et al., 1991; Martin, Mullennix, Pisoni, & Summers, 1989; Nygaard et al., 1995). In this study, we (Mullennix et al., 2002) conducted a serial recall experiment using lists of 10 spoken words. The memory task was a variation of the standard serial recall memory paradigm, where lists of spoken words are presented to listeners who then attempt to remember as many words in each list as possible in their correct order. There were two manipulations. The first manipulation was list type. Three lists were used. The first list was the same-talker/same-emotion (STSE) list, where a male talker voice uttered the words in a neutral "naming" emotional tone of voice. The second list was the same-talker/multiple-emotion (STME) list, where the male talker produced words varying in 10 emotional tones of voice (from Leinonen, Hiltunen, Linnankoski, & Laasko, 1997). The third list was the multiple-talker/same-emotion (MTSE) list, where the words were produced by 10 different talkers (5 male and 5 female) using the naming tone of voice.

First of all, the STSE and MTSE conditions were compared to assess the effect of variation in talker voice on recall. Similar comparisons had been carried out by Mullennix et al. (1989), Goldinger et al. (1991), and Nygaard et al. (1995), who all found that, at fast word presentation rates, memory for words from the primacy region of the serial position curve was worse for MTSE lists compared to STSE lists. Since recall from the primacy region is assumed to reflect access to long-term memory, their results indicated that interference occurs when encoding MTSE words into memory. In other words, when the talker voice changed from word to word, perceptual adjustments to talker voice occurred that utilized cognitive resources otherwise normally allocated to rehearsal and storage processes that transfer words into episodic memory.

The second comparison Mullennix et al. (2002) conducted was between the STSE and STME conditions. This comparison allowed an assessment of whether changes from word to word in the emotional tone of the speaker interfered with encoding words into episodic memory. If primacy recall performance was worse for the STME condition compared to the STSE condition, this would suggest that cognitive resources are used to process changes from word to word in emotional tone of voice, with a resulting negative effect on memory recall.

Mullennix et al. (2002) also manipulated word presentation rate. Others (Goldinger et al., 1991; Nygaard et al., 1995) found that, at relatively slow presentation rates, primacy recall was *better* for multiple-talker lists compared to single-talker lists. Although at first glance this result appears confusing, there is an explanation. The explanation offered is that, when there is a substantial amount of time available for the cognitive system to encode and rehearse the list words,

the additional time is used to store both each word and the talker voice information associated with each word into episodic memory. Then, at the time of recall, both sources of information are accessed and act as retrieval cues, thus enhancing the chances of accurate recall. Given this particular finding with slow word presentation rates, we decided to examine whether a parallel result would be observed with emotional tone of voice. As a result, half the listeners were presented with lists where the words were presented at a 250 ms fast presentation rate and half were presented with words at a 4000 ms slow presentation rate.

The results for the 250 ms condition are shown in Figure 3–1 and the results for the 4000 ms condition are shown in Figure 3–2. For the 250 ms conditions, an analysis of the primacy region of the serial position curve (list positions 1–4) indicated that recall for the STSE condition was better than for both the STME and MTSE conditions. The difference between the two talker conditions (STSE versus MTSE) was readily apparent, while the difference between the two emotional tone conditions (STSE versus STME) was smaller and primarily due to list position 3. For the 4000 ms conditions, recall in the primacy region was significantly better for the STSE condition compared to the STME and MTSE conditions across all primacy list positions 1–4. When examining the data, the difference between the two talker conditions (STSE versus MTSE) was substantial, and the difference between the two emotional tone conditions (STSE versus STME) was substantial.

For the 250 ms fast rate conditions, the superiority of primacy recall for the single-talker conditions over the multiple-talker conditions mirrors the previous work on talker voice and serial recall using

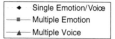

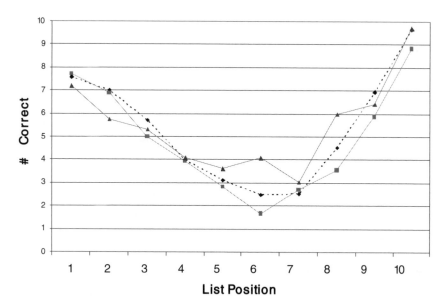

Figure 3–1. Number correct word recall across list position for the single-emotion/single-talker, multiple talker, and multiple emotion conditions at the 250 ms presentation rate.

fast presentation rates (Goldinger et al., 1991; Mullennix et al., 1989; Nygaard et al., 1995). This work suggests that the encoding of spoken words into episodic memory is negatively affected by talker variation from word to word. In addition, and of central interest to us, when examining the effect of emotional tone variation on recall in the 250 ms fast rate condition, there was weak evidence for a similar negative effect of variation in emotional tone on recall.

On the other hand, the results for the 4000 ms condition were somewhat unexpected. The effect of talker variation was identical to what was found at the 250 ms rate, with recall worse in the multiple-talker condition, but this result was contrary to the superiority of recall that Goldinger et al. (1991) and Nygaard et al. (1995) observed for multiple-talker lists at the 4000 ms rate. In addition, we found that primacy recall was worse for multiple-emotion lists in the 4000 ms conditions. Concerned about this contradiction across studies, we decided to retest the 4000 ms conditions in our laboratory using a different stimulus set. The results of this retest replicated our previous finding; thus, we are inclined to believe that our findings were not spurious and were not due to some idiosyncratic aspect of our word lists. At this time, we have no reasonable explanation

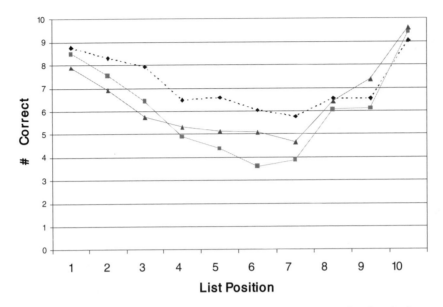

Figure 3–2. Number correct word recall across list position for the single-emotion/single-talker, multiple talker, and multiple emotion conditions at the 4000 ms presentation rate.

for this discrepancy across studies, but the importance of these results merits further investigation. It will be of critical importance to determine whether talker voice and emotional tone are able to be "processed further" when the cognitive system is given more time to encode spoken words into memory, as suggested by the superiority of recall under slow rate conditions reported by Goldinger et al. (1991) and Nygaard et al. (1995).

To summarize the findings from our serial recall memory study, we obtained evidence that, regardless of word presentation rate, primacy recall of spoken word lists suffers when there is variation word to word in emotional tone of voice. This suggests that the perceptual adjustments made to variation in emotional tone of voice require cognitive resources, just as the adjustments made to talker voice do. These resources are drawn away from the resources normally allocated towards processes used to encode, rehearse, and store list items into episodic memory representations of the words. We did not, however, obtain evidence to suggest that when more time is available for the encoding and rehearsal of list items (i.e., under slow presentation rate conditions), emotional tone of voice (and talker voice as well) are stored in a manner that allows the information to become available as additional retrieval cues to help recall the word items.

Conclusion

Overall, the work I have described here coalesces together to form a preliminary picture of how emotional tone of voice is handled by the perceptual system. In terms of perceptual processing, there is clear evidence that cognitive resources are used when adjusting to variation due to emotional tone. This observation has support from other research. Kitayama and colleagues (Ishii, Reyes, & Kitayama, 2003; Kitayama & Ishii, 2002) found Stroop-like perceptual interference due to vocal emotional tone when Japanese and American listeners are attending to word content and vice versa. One could interpret this drawing away of attention from the word items as a mandatory reallocation of attentional resources to process this particular indexical property of the utterance. They also found that the amount of interference was greater for word content for Americans and greater for vocal tone for Japanese, reflecting differences in the importance of tone across the languages. Kitayama (1996) observed that the presence of emotional tone of voice can also affect memory for sentences, with emotional tone having either a facilitating or inhibiting effect depending upon memory load conditions. Kitayama (1996) suggested that, " . . . when a message is delivered in an emotional tone of voice, it captures attention and, further, that the attention thus allocated to the message is divided between the voice and the verbal con-

tent" (p. 304). Our findings also parallel other research showing that resource-intensive perceptual adjustments made in response to variation in talker voice, speech rate, and factors related to consonantal production result in perceptual interference (Creelman, 1957; Mullennix et al., 1989; Newman et al., 2001; Peters, 1955; Sommers et al., 1994).

Thus, it appears that the perceptual processes that operate upon information in the speech signal related to vocal emotion are not "capacity-free." Although the processing of vocal emotion may be *mandatory* and unavoidable, the processing of vocal emotion utilizes measurable attentional/cognitive resources. Furthermore, the use of these resources comes at the expense of processing the linguistic information in the speech utterance and at the expense of encoding and storing the speech information into memory.

Of central interest in this chapter is the issue of whether emotional tone of voice is represented in episodic memory representations of speech utterances. In viewing the research related to this issue, the answer depends upon the experimental paradigm used. In the recognition memory experiments examining variation in emotional tone, we found superior recognition performance for spoken words repeated in the same emotional tone. Emotional tone persisted in memory even when the initial word exposure conditions were designed to focus attention away from this property of the speech utterance. This is consistent with the idea that emotional tone information is automatically encoded into memory along with the spoken words.

However, evidence concerning the encoding of emotional tone into memory obtained with the serial recall paradigm was more equivocal. We found that recall of spoken words from long-term memory was interfered with by variation in emotional tone of voice, suggesting that the cognitive resources used to adjust to this variation are usurped from memory rehearsal and storage processes that place word items into memory. But the results we found at the 4000 ms presentation rate complicate the picture. When more time was available to rehearse each list word and the emotional tone of voice used to produce each word, recall was not facilitated. This result was also found for talker voice, a result which conflicts with previous findings where recall was enhanced when the presentation rate was slower (Goldinger et al., 1991; Nygaard et al., 1995). Thus, the issue of whether emotional tone of voice is automatically encoded into memory along with the linguistic representations of speech utterances has strong support from the recognition memory research, but lukewarm support from the serial recall research. It is clear from this situation that further research needs to be conducted using a variety of memory paradigms in order to provide converging evidence to clarify the situation.

Overall, when examining the role that indexical properties of speech play in speech perception, our findings on emotional tone fit together with the previous work on talker voice, speaking rate, and amplitude to form a more complete picture of how speech is encoded into memory. To summarize where this research stands, we have strong evidence that talker voice is encoded into memory along with linguistic representations of spoken words, and that the talker voice information in episodic memory facilitates memory (Bradlow et al., 1999; Craik & Kirsner, 1974; Goldinger, 1996; Nygaard

et al., 1995; Palmeri et al., 1993). We have some evidence that the speaking rate used to produce words is encoded into memory as well (Bradlow et al., 1999). And finally, we have no evidence that information about amplitude level used to produce words is encoded into memory (Bradlow et al., 1999; Nygaard et al., 1995). When combining these results together with the findings on emotional tone of voice, some ideas emerge regarding the nature of the system responsible for encoding speech into memory representations. Nygaard et al. (1995) suggest that talker characteristics and speaking rate may be encoded into memory somewhat differently and reflect the different roles these two attributes of speech have. They indicate that talker characteristics are relatively permanent and talker voice provides clues about various attributes of the talker, while speaking rate is more transient and is tied into other aspects of the speech signal (Nygaard et al., 1995, p. 998). They also suggest that amplitude information is of low value in terms of distinctive information and is not retained when encoding speech into memory.

When thinking about the possibility that different attributes of speech are handled differently, in terms of whether they are retained in memory as a matter of course of processing speech utterances, it is useful to note that, with respect to vocal emotion, the relationship between the speaker's internal emotional state and the acoustic manifestation of that state is complex. There is no direct one-to-one mapping between the acoustic attributes of the speech signal related to vocal emotion and stored representations of vocal emotions in the listener. The acoustic cues to different vocal emotions are sometimes very similar, and as a result recognition accuracy for identifying vocal emotions is far from perfect. Part of the reason for this situation is due to the fact that we rarely experience vocal emotions in isolation. When engaged in face-to-face conversation, we have a multiplicity of facial and gestural visual cues to assist us in disambiguating vocal emotion. As well, we usually have social context information to draw from to assist the process. Thus, the entire system is built to be redundant, with multiple sources of information to draw upon. Although we know that auditory and visual information are also integrated together to produce speech perceptions (Jones & Callan, 2003; McGurk & MacDonald, 1976), the situation for vocal emotion appears to be even more complex. Thus, it is entirely possible that the encoding of emotional tone of voice unfolds in a very different manner than the encoding of talker voice and the encoding of speaking rate.

Based on the research so far, it is difficult to ascertain exactly how the mental processes work that encode indexical properties of speech into memory with the linguistic representations of speech utterances. In some recent work, McLennan and Luce (2005) suggest that abstract, linguistic aspects of speech are processed separately from specific, indexical properties of speech. It may be that multiple processes operate in parallel to extract both linguistic and indexical aspects of the speech signal, with the processes depositing the information into memory in a way where both aspects of the spoken utterances are tied together so that recall of specific items is enhanced. Given that the effects of indexical properties tend to appear late during the time course of processing (McLennan & Luce, 2005), there may be a process that operates late in the processing cycle that

determines the relevance of the indexical information and whether it gets passed onto episodic memory for longer-term retention. At any rate, any source of variation that alters the spectral/temporal qualities of the speech signal appears to be important (Nygaard et al., 1995), and furthermore appears to be retained in episodic memory for later use. Since emotional tone of voice also alters spectral/temporal qualities of the signal, it is also important and, as we have seen here, appears to be retained in memory as well. Perhaps we will find that it is simply the degree to which a source of variation affects spectral/temporal qualities that determines whether the information composing a given identical property is important enough to be passed on to episodic memory. Or perhaps there are more complex factors responsible for that scenario that we have yet to uncover in the future.

References

Abercrombie, D. (1967). *Elements of general phonetics*. Chicago: University of Chicago Press.

Bradlow, A., Nygaard, L. C., & Pisoni, D. B. (1999). Effects of talker, rate, and amplitude variation in recognition memory for spoken words. *Perception & Psychophysics, 61*, 206–219.

Church, B. A., & Schacter, D. L. (1994). Perceptual specificity of auditory priming: Implicit memory for voice intonation and fundamental frequency. *Journal of Experimental Psychology: Learning, Memory, and Cognition, 20*, 521–533.

Craik, F. I. M., & Kirsner, K. (1974). The effect of speaker's voice on word recognition. *Quarterly Journal of Experimental Psychology, 26*, 274–284.

Creelman, C. D. (1957). Case of the unknown talker. *Journal of the Acoustical Society of America, 29,* 655.

Gaston, J., & Mullennix, J. W. (2001, April). *Variation in voice and emotion and recognition memory.* Paper presented at the 72nd Annual Meeting of the Eastern Psychological Association, Washington, DC.

Goldinger, S. D. (1996). Words and voices: Episodic traces in spoken word identification and recognition memory. *Journal of Experimental Psychology: Learning, Memory, and Cognition, 22,* 1166-1183.

Goldinger, S. D. (1998). Echoes of echoes? An episodic theory of lexical access. *Psychological Review, 105,* 251-279.

Goldinger, S. D., Pisoni, D. B., & Logan, J. (1991). On the nature of talker variability effects on serial recall of spoken word lists. *Journal of Experimental Psychology: Learning, Memory, and Cognition, 17,* 152-162.

Ishii, K., Reyes, J. A., & Kitayama, S. (2003). Spontaneous attention to word content versus emotional tone: Differences among three cultures. *Psychological Science, 14,* 39-46.

Jones, J. A., & Callan, D. E. (2003). Brain activity during audiovisual speech perception: An fMRI study of the McGurk effect. *Neuroreport, 14,* 1129-1133.

Kitayama, S. (1996). Remembrance of emotional speech: Improvement and impairment of incidental verbal memory by emotional voice. *Journal of Experimental Social Psychology, 32,* 289-308.

Kitayama, S., & Ishii, K. (2002). Word and voice: Spontaneous attention to emotional speech in two cultures. *Cognition and Emotion, 16,* 29-59.

Ladefoged, P., & Broadbent, D. E. (1957). Information conveyed by vowels. *Journal of the Acoustical Society of America, 29,* 98-104.

Laver, J. D. M. (1968). Voice quality and indexical information. *British Journal of Disorders of Communication, 3,* 43-54.

Leinonen, L., Hiltunen, T., Linnankoski, I., & Laasko, M. (1997). Expression of emotional-motivational connotations with a one-word utterance. *Journal of the Acoustical Society of America, 102,* 1853-1863.

Martin, C. S, Mullennix, J. W., Pisoni, D. B., & Summers, W. (1989). Effects of talker variability on recall of spoken word lists. *Journal of Experimental Psychology: Learning, Memory, and Cognition, 15,* 676-684.

McGurk, H., & MacDonald, J. (1976). Hearing lips and seeing voices. *Nature, 264,* 746-748.

McLennan, C. T., & Luce, P. A. (2005). Examining the time course of indexical specificity effects in spoken word recognition. *Journal of Experimental Psychology: Learning, Memory, and Cognition, 31,* 306-321.

Mullennix, J. W. (1997). On the nature of perceptual adjustments to voice. In K. A. Johnson & J. W. Mullennix (Eds.), *Talker variability and speech processing* (pp. 67-83). San Diego, CA: Academic Press.

Mullennix, J. W., Bihon, T., Bricklemyer, J., Gaston, J., & Keener, J. (2002). Effects of variation in emotional tone of voice on speech perception. *Language and Speech, 45,* 255-283.

Mullennix, J. W., Gaston, J., & Keener, J. M. (2000, March). *Recognition memory for voice and emotion.* Paper presented at the 71st Annual Meeting of the Eastern Psychological Association, Baltimore, MD.

Mullennix, J. W., Mascilli, M., Moxim, E., Schmadel, J., Spisak, B., & Zatorsky, J. (2002, May). *The encoding of emotional tone of voice into episodic memory for speech.* Paper presented at the Annual Meeting of the Midwestern Psychological Association, Chicago, IL.

Mullennix, J. W., Pisoni, D. B., & Martin, C. S. (1989). Some effects of talker variability on spoken word recognition. *Journal of the Acoustical Society of America, 85,* 365-378.

Newman, R. S., Clouse, S. A., & Burnham, J. L. (2001). The perceptual consequences of within-talker variability in fricative production. *Journal of the Acoustical Society of America*, *109*, 1181-1196.

Nygaard, L. C., Sommers, M. S., & Pisoni, D. B. (1995). Effects of stimulus variability on perception and representation of spoken words in memory. *Perception & Psychophysics*, *57*, 989-1001.

Palmeri, T. J., Goldinger, S. D., & Pisoni, D. B. (1993). Episodic encoding of voice attributes and recognition memory for spoken words. *Journal of Experimental Psychology: Learning, Memory, and Cognition*, *19*, 309-328.

Peters, R. W. (1955). *The relative intelligibility of single-voice and multiple-voice messages under various conditions of noise*. In Joint Project Report No. 56 (U.S. Naval School of Aviation Medicine). Pensacola, FL.

Pisoni, D. B. (1997). Some thoughts on "normalization" in speech perception. In K. Johnson & J. Mullennix (Eds.), *Talker variability in speech processing* (pp. 9-32). San Diego, CA: Academic Press.

Schacter, D. L., & Church, B. A. (1992). Auditory priming: Implicit and explicit memory for words and voices. *Journal of Experimental Psychology: Learning, Memory, and Cognition*, *18*, 915-930.

Scherer, K. R. (2003). Vocal communication of emotion: A review of research paradigms. *Speech Communication*, *40*, 227-256.

Sommers, M. S., Nygaard, L. C., & Pisoni, D. B. (1994). Stimulus variability and spoken word recognition: I. Effects of variability in speaking rate and overall amplitude. *Journal of the Acoustical Society of America*, *96*, 1314-1324.

CHAPTER 4

Assessing Voice Characteristics of Depression among English- and Spanish-Speaking Populations

Gerardo M. González and Amy L. Ramos

Abstract

Here we examine the integration of computerized speech recognition and digital voice analyses (VIDAS) to assess depressed mood and symptoms in English- and Spanish-speaking populations. The findings show VIDAS consistency to administer reliable, valid, and culturally sensitive screening of depression in these populations. VIDAS has been implemented in high volume health care settings that serve diverse patient populations but lack bilingual personnel. VIDAS quickly and unobtrusively collects participant data, scores the data, and generates a report to inform health care staff of the participant's mood and symptoms. As a result, VIDAS assesses many individuals who are unlikely to initially seek out mental health services. However, further study needs to be accomplished in order to enhance and refine the VIDAS interview as a *viable* alternative method of assessment.

The relationship between the gender of the participant and choice of digitized voice showed a preference for a female digitized voice. Several voice characteristics showed significant relationships to depression levels, such as vocal energy and variability; however, the findings have not been consistent across the various VIDAS studies. Shortcomings with the analysis of voice characteristics are discussed and a role of a baseline measurement is stressed as it may be difficult to discriminate between a person who is depressed and one who normally speaks with a monotonic voice, and because psychiatric comorbidity and medications also distort vocal markers for depression. Also gender, age, linguistic, and physical factors that interact with speech characteristics may require developing unique models of vocal emotional properties.

Assessing Voice Characteristics of Depression among English and Spanish Speakers

Depressive disorders afflict 6% to 7% of the general population in the United States (Smith & Weissmann, 1992). Major depressive disorder is the leading cause of disability in the United States and developing countries (World Health Organization, 2001). Many depressed individuals are treated at primary care medical settings, where up to 30% of the patients may be clinically depressed (Broadhead, Clapp-Channing, Finch, & Copeland, 1989). Primary health care settings, however, suffer from deficiencies in screening practices, high patient volume, and enormous time constraints that hinder the adequate assessment of depression. Pérez-Stable, Miranda, Muñoz, & Ying (1990) found that depression was accurately detected in only 36% of primary care medical patients.

Latinos constitute nearly 13% of the U.S. population, comprise the second largest ethnic group in the United States, and are the fastest growing ethnic group in the country (U.S. Census, 2000). Past research suggests that Latinos are at higher risk for depression than non-Latinos. For example, Kessler, McGonagle, Zhao, & Nelson (1994) found that Latinos reported an 8.1% prevalence rate for current affective disorders (7% is the norm). In fact, Mexican Americans reported a higher prevalence for affective disorders than their Mexican-born counterparts (Vega et al., 1998).

Latinos in the United States generally lack accessibility to culturally responsive and linguistically-compatible mental health services (González, 1997). An Epidemiological Catchment Area (ECA) study indicated that only 11% of Mexican Americans (vs. 22% of non-Hispanic Whites), who met the criteria for clinical depression, sought a mental health care provider for treatment (Hough et al., 1987; Shapiro et al., 1984). Latinos underutilize mental health services because of cultural, linguistic, financial, and service delivery barriers (Woodward, Dwinell, & Arons, 1992). Moreover, 40% of the U.S. Latino population primarily speaks Spanish or has limited English proficiency (U.S. Census, 2000).

The absolute number of Latino therapists in the United States (29 for every 100,000 Latinos compared to 173 clinicians per 100,000 non-Hispanic Whites) represents an insufficient number to feasibly meet the present mental health needs of U.S. Latino populations (Center for Mental Health Services, 2000). Clearly, more appropriately trained culturally sensitive bilingual mental health professionals are needed. Yet the growing disparity between the Latino population (estimated to increase over 50% in the next decade) and current pool of Latino clinical psychology doctoral students in the training pipeline (levels static since 1980) makes it unlikely that ample Spanish-speaking professionals will be available to provide necessary services (e.g., Bernal & Castro, 1994). Alternative strategies for delivering culturally responsive mental health assessment services for the detection of depression in Spanish-speaking communities are needed.

Computerized psychological assessment represents several major advantages in the structure, flexibility, and ease of test administration (Kobak, 1996). Structured computerized interviewing improves the quality, quantity, and integrity of clinical data by accurately transcribing, scoring, and storing patient responses, standardizing administration procedures, and minimizing errors attributable to human oversight (Erdman, Klein, & Greist, 1985). For example, a clinician may inadvertently omit up to 35% of clinically meaningful inquiries during an open-ended face-to-face (Climent, Plutchik, & Estrada, 1975). Many depressed patients report a preference for computer interactive interviews over face-to-face interviews, even when patients knew the clinician (e.g., Carr, Ghosh, & Ancill, 1983). One possible explanation for such a prefer-

ence is that computerized interviewing may increase respondent self-disclosure because of discomfort with revealing sensitive issues (e.g., suicidal ideation) to a clinician (Levine, Ancill, & Roberts, 1989). Another appealing aspect of computerized assessment is that it produces a cost savings through the use of more efficient professional time to conduct assessment batteries and treatment (Butcher, 1987). Thus, computerized screening provides a cost-effective and efficient means for assessing depression.

Recent advances in computerized technology offer viable alternative screening methods for populations not reliably assessed with standard paper-and-pencil questionnaires (Starkweather & Muñoz, 1989). For example, illiterates or non-English speakers are less likely to utilize mental services because of written assessment or language barriers. For such populations, computerized technology has the potential to minimize the obstacles that contribute to the underidentification of depression. Among the technologies that have strong potential is computerized speech recognition. A computerized speech recognition application is capable of administering a discrete choice questionnaire by presenting an item (visually on a computer screen or aurally by a prerecorded prompt) and recognizing a spoken response. Based on the capabilities of speech recognition technology and the imminent need for alternative depression screening methods in English- and Spanish-speaking communities, González and colleagues developed bilingual computerized speech recognition applications for screening depression.

Research also indicates that voice analysis may improve the accuracy of detecting depression. Digital analysis of voice characteristics represents a powerful methodology for the objective assessment of depression (Starkweather, 1992). Voice characteristics serve as useful clinical indices for depression symptoms because vocalizations (respiration, articulation, and tension or relaxation of larynx and oral muscles) are mediated by psychomotor disturbance stemming from neurophysiological and subcortical (mesolimbic) dysfunction (Flint, Black, Campbell-Taylor, Gailey, & Levington, 1993; Nilsonne, Sunberg, Ternstrom, & Askenfelt, 1988).

Research demonstrates that several quantitative voice characteristics are good predictors of depression, such as narrow variability in tone (monotone), low fundamental frequency (pitch), and low amplitude or loudness (Hargreaves & Starkweather, 1964; Vanger, Summerfield, Rosen, & Watson, 1992). Multilingual research has generated a model of depressed voice prosody (tempo and rhythm) represented by slower, flatter, and softer voice waves (Darby, Simmons, & Berger, 1984; Kuny & Stassen, 1993; Scherer & Zei, 1988). Cross-cultural studies also suggest that depressed individuals display distinctive speech patterns compared to nondepressed persons, including more pauses and fewer utterances (e.g., Friedman & Sanders, 1992; Stassen, Bomben, & Günther, 1991) and longer vocal response latency (vocal reaction time) to answer a presented item (e.g., Stout, 1981; Talavera, Sáiz-Ruiz, & García-Toro, 1994). Furthermore, changes in speech variables are better predictors of mood change for patients in treatment than psychiatrists' impressions (Siegman, 1987). Thus, voice analysis can help to discern between the acoustic characteristics of depressed and nondepressed persons.

Quantitative acoustic variables include speech rate (number of utterances per time frame), mean pitch (average fundamental frequency of utterances), pitch variability, changes in pitch, and vocal intensity (energy values of an utterance). For example, a sad mood displays identifiable vocal markers (e.g. slow, soft, monotonic speech) that are distinguishable from vocal effects in normal mood and other emotional states. Table 4–1 summarizes the general research findings on vocal characteristics for several emotional states (Murray & Arnott, 1993).

The two most common voice analyses of depression models are the structured speech and free-form speech approaches (Alpert, Pouget, & Silva, 2000). The structured speech approach requires the respondent to repeat a determined sound (please say "A") or to read text (please read the following paragraph). The recorded repetition or text is assessed for mood with short-time, long-time, and spectral analyses. The free-form speech approach involves the assessment of natural open-ended speech. The respondent is asked an open-ended question and the free-form response is recorded and analyzed. Also, it is common to obtain a pretest (baseline) of an individual's voice characteristics and a post-test (after treatment or intervention) to assess change in mood or emotion.

Speech Behavior

Gonzalez and colleagues initiated speech recognition research for investigating speech behavior to increase the detection of depression. Initially, the researchers explored speech behavior, such as vocal

Table 4–1. Summary of the research findings on vocal emotional effects relative to neutral speech

	Sadness	Fear	Disgust	Anger	Happiness
Speech rate	**Slightly slower**	Much faster	Very much slower	Slightly faster	Faster or slower
Pitch average	**Slightly lower**	Very much higher	Very much lower	Very much higher	Much higher
Pitch range	**Slightly narrower**	Much wider	Slightly wider	Much wider	Much wider
Pitch changes	**Downward inflections**	Normal	Wide, downward inflections	Abrupt, on stressed syllables	Smooth, upward inflections
Vocal intensity	**Lower**	Normal	Lower	Higher	Higher
Voice quality	**Resonant**	Irregular voicing	Grumbled, chest tone	Breathy, chest tone	Breathy, blaring
Articulation	**Slurring**	Precise	Normal	Tense	Normal

Note. From "Toward the Simulation of Emotion in Synthetic Speech: A Review of the Literature on Human Vocal Emotion," by I. A. Murray and J. L. Arnott, 1993, *Journal of the Acoustical Society of America*, *93*, pp. 1097–1108.

response latency (VRL) and speech recognition accuracy (SRA), i.e., computer accuracy level for recognizing a participant's utterances. The researchers hypothesized that longer VRL and lower SRA would be related to depressed mood.

The speech recognition applications are based on the Center for Epidemiological Studies-Depression scale (CES-D). The CES-D is a 20-item self-report screening measure developed by the National Institute of Mental Health (NIMH) for assessing the frequency of depressive mood and symptoms during the past week (less than 1 day, 1–2 days, 3–4 days, 5–7 days). In the general population, a cut point score of 16 or greater suggests a high level of depressive symptoms (Radloff, 1977). The CES-D has strong psychometric sensitivity for identifying symptomatic individuals; well established

normative, reliability, and validity data with English- and Spanish-speaking samples; and extensive testing with clinical and nonclinical populations (Mosciki, Locke, Rae, & Boyd, 1989; Myers & Weissman, 1980).

González, Costello, La Tourette, Joyce, & Valenzuela (1997) evaluated a bilingual speaker-dependent cellular telephone-assisted computerized speech recognition CES-D. In a single session counterbalanced design, 32 English (ES) and 23 Spanish speakers (SS) completed randomly ordered computer-telephone (CT) and face-to-face (FF) CES-D methods (0–7 days' response format), the Beck Depression Inventory (BDI) (Beck & Steer, 1993), and the Short Acculturation Scale (SAS). VRL and SRA were measured. The results suggested that the two CES-D methods displayed strong internal consistency estimates (a > .85), good alternate forms reliabilities (> .85), and high correlations to the BDI (r > .80) for both language groups. The two groups rated both methods equally high, but the ES preferred the FF mode because it was more personable. Among SS, the correlation between depression and acculturation was not significant. For the CT method, depression scores directly correlated with VRL (.45) and inversely related to speech recognition accuracy (−.37) across both language groups. Thus, longer VRL and lower SRA (more recognition complications) served as general indices of depression.

González and colleagues conducted two studies with large Spanish- and English-speaking samples and collected retest data on participants in a second session. The purpose of the *two* one-year studies was to develop, test, and evaluate an English and Spanish continuous speaker-independent speech recognition CES-D application for screening depression symptoms by digital cellular telephone. A continuous speaker-independent system is designed to recognize natural continuous speech across multiple independent users. The system does not require template training; thus, interview time is significantly reduced. Also, the system presented the interview using a prerecorded digitized female or male voice selected by the participant. In previous prototypes, only a prerecorded digitized male voice was presented.

Study 1 assessed the psychometric congruence of two speech recognition CES-D methods (0–7 days' choices) for detecting depression levels in ES and SS. A 2 (language) × 2 (method) × 2 (session) repeated measures experimental design was employed. The CES-D was randomly administered to 82 ES and 85 SS in CT or

FF form in two sessions (at least a 2-week interval). Additional measures included a structured demographic interview, the Bidimensional Acculturation Scale (BAS) (Marín & Gamba, 1996), and the BDI. VRL and SRA were also measured. The results suggested that both methods displayed strong psychometric properties. The means for the two methods were generally not significantly different for both ES and SS. The two methods demonstrated high inter-item consistencies (a range .83 to .94) and strong correlations to the BDI (range .68 to .88) for both languages. Test-retest reliabilities were very good (range .84 to .89); however, reliability of the ES CT method was moderate (.47). Although the two language groups rated both methods highly, both groups preferred the FF method. Analyses of the digitized interviewer gender showed that ES chose a female voice significantly more often in the first session while SS selected a female voice more frequently in the second session. FF VRL was positively correlated to depression scores for the ES sample in the first (.29) and second sessions (.46). SRA was negatively correlated with depression scores in the ES first session (−.28) and SS second session (−.45). In other words, depressed persons tended to experience more voice recognition complications during the computer interview requiring more repetitions of the items and more time to complete the interview (González et al., 2000).

Study 2 was a validation study of an English and Spanish telephone-assisted speaker-independent CES-D. The aim of Study 2 was to evaluate the sensitivity (detecting true depressives) and specificity (detecting true nondepressives) of the CES-D for assessing major depression in ES and SS. Presentation of the CES-D (0–7 days' choices) was refined based on the findings of Study 1. The unique features of Study 2 included administering the Composite International Diagnostic Interview (CIDI) (Kessler, Nelson, McGonagle, & Liu, 1996) to identify depressed and nondepressed participants. The relationship of depression scores to the BDI-II, BAS, and VRL were also assessed. Study 2 utilized a $2 \times 2 \times 2$ language $\times$ diagnosis $\times$ session repeated measures (test-retest) design. A total of 160 participants (80 ES and 80 SS) including diagnosis group (depressed and nondepressed) were interviewed.

Data analyses revealed that there were no significant language group differences for the means and variabilities of the CES-D across both sessions. The CES-D displayed strong internal consistency for both language groups in both sessions (a ranged from .88 to .94). Test-retest reliabilities were .85 and .64 for the SS and ES, respectively. There were strong convergent validity coefficients between the CES-D and the BDI-II in both sessions (.69 and .67 for SS and .64 and .87 for ES). CIDI analyses indicated that the CES-D displayed good sensitivity (.76) and specificity (.50) for the first session and similar sensitivity (.77) and specificity (58) in the second session. More than two thirds of all participants selected a female digitized voice for the first session. In the second session, 60% of the participants selected a female voice. Participants positively rated (1 = very uncomfortable to 6 = very comfortable) the CES-D on the first session (both group means over 4.3, no significant differences). VRL and CES-D total scores were positively related in the first session ($r = .14$) but not in the second session (González, 2000).

Digital voice analysis packages (e.g., Avaaz Interactive Voice Analysis System,

IVANS) conduct complex short-time and long-time acoustic analyses for detecting emotion in voice characteristics. Short-time analysis examines a segment of a voice signal, such as a phoneme (basic sound). Long-time spectrum analysis assesses the entire voice signal. Spectral analyses of voice samples generate *spectrograms*, which are two- and three-dimensional visual representations plotted along various acoustic variables (time, frequency, and amplitude). Table 4–2 summarizes the definitions of common acoustic voice measures (Avaaz, 1998). Digital voice analysis was implemented in the next phase of research.

Voice-Interactive Depression Assessment System

Gonzalez and colleagues evaluated the Voice-Interactive Depression Assessment System (VIDAS) to detect depression symptoms (using the CES-D) among English and Spanish speakers. The researchers developed VIDAS using speaker-independent continuous speech recognition technology (Schalkwyk, Colton & Fanty, 1998). The researchers administered VIDAS to the participants using a Pentium laptop computer (Windows XP) with a microphone/speaker handset.

VIDAS presented a discrete choice questionnaire in English or Spanish by playing digitally recorded .wav audio files, recognizing a respondent's spoken answers, scoring the responses, and storing the data. Two bilingual male and female professionals fluent in both English and Spanish recorded the prompts, instructions, and items in a neutral tone to reduce potential biases from participant reactivity. VIDAS randomly ordered

Table 4–2. Definitions of acoustic voice measures

Measure	Definition
Long-Term Average Speech Spectrum (LTASS)	Summary of how energy in an utterance is distributed across frequency, on average, over the duration of the specified signal.
Spectral tilt	Rate at which the energy of the speech signal declines as frequency increases.
Flatness	Represents the flatness of the LTASS. For speech signals that have more noise content ("breathy" signals).
Centroid	A weighted measure that determines the effective fulcrum of the LTASS. For unvoiced sounds, the spectral centroid is usually around 2–3 kHz, while voiced sounds have a lower spectral centroid.
Skewness	Quantifies the spread of the LTASS. For a spectrum that has a Gaussian shape, the skewness is equal to zero. Positive skewness values indicate more energy in the high frequency region, while negative skewness values reflect low frequency spectra.
Kurtosis	Quantifies the shape of the spectrum. Lower kurtosis values indicate flat spectra, while higher values indicate spectra with varying peaks.
Speech Measures	Acoustic measures gathered from running speech.
Tilt	Similar to the spectral tilt parameter, except only the voiced segments of speech are included in the computation of the LTASS.
Harmonic-to-noise ratio	The effect of both pitch and amplitude perturbations. It also accounts for such conditions as the increased noise in the main formant frequency region, increased high frequency noise, and decreased higher harmonics.
Linear prediction signal-to-noise ratio (SNR)	Relies on linear prediction modeling of the input speech sample. The SNR measure is taken as the ratio of the input signal energy and the energy of the residual signal at the output of the linear prediction model. Normal talkers typically have high LP-SNR values, which reflect good linear prediction modeling performance.
Pitch amplitude	The amplitude of the second largest peak of the normalized autocorrelation function of the residual signal.
Spectral flatness ratio (SFR)	A measure of how successfully the LP technique was able to model the input signal. If the LP model is successful, the residual signal is made up of a series of impulses, one at each glottal excitation period.

Note. From *Interactive Voice Analysis System (IVANS) User's Guide*, by Avaaz Innovations Inc., 1998. Reprinted with permission of Avaaz Innovations Inc: London, Ontario, Canada.

the digitized male or female voice to which the participant vocally responded. VIDAS also recorded participant vocal data for subsequent voice analysis using IVANS. Table 4–3 summarizes the basic VIDAS interview sequence.

Table 4–3. Summary of VIDAS interview sequence

---

1. **Introduction**
   a. Interviewer instructs participant (English or Spanish) for completing VIDAS
   b. Interviewer asks participant to choose the gender of digitized interviewer voice (male or female)
   c. Interviewer initiates the VIDAS application
   d. Over the handset, VIDAS greets participant in primary language (English or Spanish) and presents brief instructions for completing a scale (randomized)

2. **Pretest Recording**
   VIDAS instructs participant to repeat a phrase, "This computer responds to my voice."

3. **CES-D Items**
   a. VIDAS presents brief instructions for completing the CES-D items orally
   b. VIDAS begins by presenting an item and waits for the participant's response
   c. Participant verbally responds to the item
   d. VIDAS registers and records the participant's recognized spoken response
   e. VIDAS continues to the next item until all the items are completed
   f. VIDAS proceeds to the conclusion

4. **Post-Test Recording**
   VIDAS instructs participant to repeat a phrase, "This computer responds to my voice."

5. **Conclusion**
   a. VIDAS thanks the participant, requests that the interviewer be advised, and terminates
   b. VIDAS scores and analyzes the responses
   c. VIDAS saves the results in a database
   d. VIDAS generates a brief interpretative report (summary of responses and interpretation)

Study 1 involved the development and *pilot* testing of bilingual telephone and microphone speech recognition VIDAS-1 prototypes. VIDAS-1 was a computer-telephone or computer-microphone (CM) form of the CES-D (0–7 days' choices). Fifty-eight English speakers and 60 Spanish speakers completed a randomly assigned CT or CM method. Other measures included demographics, BAS, the BDI-II, and CIDI.

The results suggested that the CT and CM methods did not significantly differ in total score means and variabilities. VIDAS-1 demonstrated good reliability (a > .80 for CT and CM in both language groups) and strong validity with the BDI-II (*r* range .69 to .73 for CT and CM in both languages). VIDAS-1 demonstrated good sensitivity (.83) and moderate specificity (.38) across language groups and methods. Although ES rated (*M* = 4.5) both VIDAS methods higher than SS (*M* = 3.8), there was no significant language and method interaction. ES and SS were significantly more likely (80%) to select a female digitized voice for the VIDAS interview.

A free-form approach for assessing participants' individual responses to the first two, middle two, and last two CES-D items was utilized. VRL was significantly longer for depressed (M = 5.5 sec) than nondepressed participants (M = 3.3). VRL was also longer for the SS CT group M = 5.5 (SD = 6.3) than the ES CT group M = 3.1, (SD = 1.2) and the SS CM group M = 3.8 (SD = 3.1) than the ES CM group M = 2.1 (SD = .61), respectively. Correlations between CES-D total scores and VRL were examined by VIDAS method and language group. There were no significant correlations between CES-D total scores and VRL for either method or for Spanish speakers. However, a significant correlation was found between CES-D total score and VRL for English speakers, r (26) = .47, p < .05 (Ramos, G. M. González, P. González, Goldwaser, & Preble, 2002).

Study 2 compared VIDAS-1 and VIDAS-2. VIDAS-2 differed from VIDAS-1 in that new depression items (20) and response formats were designed for three subscales: subscale 1 (yes/no), subscale 2 (discrete choices, e.g., "All of the time"), and subscale 3 (open-ended response to questions, e.g., "How was your appetite?"). For the purpose of brevity, only VIDAS-2 subscale 2 data will be summarized. In total, 130 ES and 95 SS participants completed BAS, BDI-II, CIDI, VIDAS-1, and VIDAS-2.

VIDAS-2 demonstrated strong inter-item consistency (ES a .90 and SS a .80) and positive correlations to the BDI-II (ES .65 and SS .53). VIDAS-2 demonstrated strong sensitivity (.82) and moderate specificity (.39) across both language groups. In choosing the gender of digitized voice, 62% of ES and 83% of SS females and 84% of ES and 66% of SS males selected a female voice. Both language groups positively rated VIDAS-2 (scale 1 to 6), but ES had significantly higher levels of comfort (M = 4.4) than SS (M = 4.0). Using a free-form analysis of participant responses to selected sub-

scale 2 items (first two, middle two, and last two), VIDAS-1 depression levels were significantly correlated to measures of voice intensity, such as spectral tilt (−.20) and speech tilt (−.34); thus, depressed individuals displayed less vocal energy. VIDAS-2 did not show significant relationships between voice properties and subscale 2 total scores (Ramos, Shriver, Reza, & González, 2003).

VIDAS-3 was a bilingual computerized speech recognition application for screening depression using two subscales based on CES-D and DSM-IV criteria. In this study, 128 English and 128 Spanish speakers completed a demographic interview, BAS, BDI-II, the CIDI-Short Form, and VIDAS-3. Recordings of participant repetitions of a phrase, "This computer responds to my voice," were obtained before (pretest) and after completion (post-test) of the CES-D.

The results suggested that VIDAS-3 subscales demonstrated high inter-item reliability (.81 to .92), strong criterion validity (.58 to .67), and adequate sensitivity (.64 to .87) and specificity (.44 to .71). Both language groups positively rated VIDAS-3. Male and female participants most often selected a digitized female voice to present VIDAS-3. Long-term average speech spectrum (LTASS) measures (kurtosis, flatness, skewness, and centroid) that assess the tone and pitch of an individual's vocal characteristics were used as the dependent variables in a multivariate analysis of variance (MANOVA).

The results revealed a significant main effect for depression in the participants' pretest recorded phrase across both language groups, [*Pillai's Trace* = .064, F (1, 236) = 6.81; p = .016]. Separate follow-up ANOVAs for each dependent variable showed significant differences in centroid, $F(1, 241) = 9.55$, $p = .002$, skewness, $F(1, 241) = 5.11$, $p = .025$, and kurtosis, $F(1, 241) = 11.60$, $p = .001$. Thus, depressed participants had less vocal energy than nondepressed participants. A MANOVA of LTASS measures revealed a significant main effect for depression in participants' post-test recording [*Pillai's Trace* $= .076$, $F(6, 224) = 3.092$; $p = .006$]. Separate ANOVAs for each dependent variable showed significant differences in flatness, $F(1, 229) = 5.15$, $p = .024$. Depressed participants' vocal responses were flatter than nondepressed participants. As with the pretest results, there were significant differences for centroid, $F(1, 229) = 10.67$, $p = .001$, skewness, $F(1, 229) = 7.18$, $p = .008$, and kurtosis, $F(1, 229) = 12.74$, $p < .0001$.

A MANOVA of speech measures [tilt, voiced tilt, harmonic-to-noise ratio, low pitch-to-signal-to-noise ratio (LP-SNR), pitch amplitude, and signal frequency ratio (SFR)] revealed a significant main effect for depression in participants' pretest recording [*Pillai's Trace* $= .08$, $F(7, 235) = 2.91$; $p = .006$]. Separate ANOVAs for each dependent variable suggested that there were significant differences in harmonic-to-noise ratio, $F(1, 241) = 5.48$, $p = .02$, and pitch amplitude, $F(1, 241) = 7.40$, $p = .007$. Thus, nondepressed participants displayed less noise in their vocal sounds while depressed participants had more hoarse and breathy vocal responses.

Finally, to test for differences across time between depressed and nondepressed participants, dependent *t*-tests were conducted for LTASS and speech measures on variables that were found to show significant differences between depressed and nondepressed participants. There were more significant differences for nondepressed than depressed individuals across time. Specifically, for nondepressed individuals there was a significant difference across time in the skewness $t(171) = -2.43$, $p = .016$, harmonic-to-noise ratio $t(171) = -4.26$, $p < .0001$, and pitch amplitude $t(171) = -4.97$, $p < .0001$. However, for depressed individuals there was only a significant difference in pitch amplitude $t(59) = -2.95$, $p = .005$. In sum, nondepressed participants displayed greater vocal variability in their voice characteristics than depressed participants (González & Shriver, 2004).

Two studies evaluated VIDAS-4 for screening depression and anxiety symptoms in English and Spanish. Study 1 involved 48 ES and 45 SS. Study 2 involved 112 ES and 108 SS. Participants completed a demographic scale, BAS, BDI-II, BAI (Beck & Steer, 1993), CIDI-SF, and VIDAS-4 depression and anxiety subscales. The studies examined the psychometric properties, comfort ratings, and selection of digitized gender for VIDAS-4. Study 2 examined the sensitivity and specificity of VIDAS-4 to detect depression and anxiety levels among comorbid, depressed, anxious, and no-disorder groups. As with VIDAS-3, participant pre- and post-recordings were obtained. The studies found that VIDAS-4 subscales generally demonstrated adequate inter-item reliability (.80–.94), convergent validity (.62–.89), sensitivity (.84–.90), and specificity (.44–.69). Most participants regarded VIDAS-4 as comfortable. Three of four participants selected a female digitized voice. Comorbid participants reported the most severe levels of depression or anxiety.

Participants' pretest and post-test recorded phrases were analyzed using MANOVA to assess differences between the four diagnostic groups by language. Roy's Largest Root was the statistic used instead of more traditional analyses such as Pillai's Trace because Roy's Largest Root is said to be the best statistic for dealing with differences among the groups when the difference is concentrated on the first discriminant function (which was the case, and the test for homogeneity of covariance matrices was positive). The results revealed a significant main effect for LTASS measures among the four diagnostic groups for English-speaking participants [Roy's Largest Root = .11, $F(3, 100)$ = 2.66; p = .037] and Spanish-speaking participants [Roy's Largest Root = .2, $F(3, 81)$ = 3.99; p = .005]. Follow-up analyses did not reveal any significant differences between the four diagnostic groups.

Speech measures assessing the amount of vocal variability and energy between the four diagnostic groups were used as dependent variables in a MANOVA. The results revealed a significant main effect among the four groups, regardless of language [Roy's Largest Root = .094, $F(3,104)$ = 1.97; p = .009]. Follow-up analyses revealed no significant differences between the four diagnostic groups or for each language (Shriver, Ramos, & Gonzalez, 2003).

VIDAS-5 is a computerized speech recognition application for screening depression and anxiety symptoms in English and Spanish. Study 1 was a pilot study of 50 ES and 47 SS. Study 2 involved 108 ES and 109 SS in diverse settings. Participants completed a demographic scale, BAS, BDI-II, BAI, CIDI-SF, and VIDAS-5 (aural or visual methods). The audio portion of VIDAS was the same for the aural and visual methods. The difference between methods involved visual cues for the visual method, such as text and graphical messages to present the items and to reply to a recognized spoken answer. As in VIDAS-3 and -4, pre- and post-test participant recordings were obtained.

Studies 1 and 2 examined the psychometric properties and participant comfort ratings for VIDAS-5. Study 2 also examined psychometric sensitivity and specificity, and participant selection of digitized gender for VIDAS. The studies found that VIDAS-5 generally demonstrated a range of adequate inter-item reliability (.71–.91), convergent validity (.40–.86), sensitivity (.79–.1.0), and specificity (.39–.44). Discriminant validity results demonstrated high overlap between depression and anxiety scales (.31–.79). Several differences were observed in the psychometric properties of VIDAS subscales by language and method, such that the DAS and aural method displayed lower reliability and validity. Participants in both language groups favorably rated the two VIDAS methods but the visual method received higher positive reactions. Participant comfort ratings of digitized voice demonstrated an interaction such that the female *visual* voice and the male *aural* voice were rated more favorably.

In a preliminary analysis of voice characteristics among depressed and nondepressed individuals, correlations were conducted between BDI total scores, CES-D total scores, LTASS measures, and speech measures. Among English-speaking participants, four pretest LTASS measures were significantly correlated with the BDI, including harmonic-to-noise ratio (r = .314, p < .01), signal-to-noise ratio (r = −.267, p < .05), pitch amplitude (r = .262, p <.05), and signal frequency ratio (r = −.245, p < .05). None of the voice variables were significantly correlated with the BDI in Spanish or the CES-D in English or Spanish. Among Spanish-speaking participants, two post-test speech measures were significantly correlated with the BDI, such as tilt (r = -.344, p < .01) and voiced tilt (r = -.348, p < .01). There were no significant correlations between any of the voice variables and the BDI in English or the CES-D in either language. Thus, depressed participants displayed less vocal intensity and variability (Gorzeman, Carter, & González, 2005).

Summary

The research presented here examined the integration of computerized speech recognition and digital voice analyses to assess depressed mood and symptoms in English and Spanish. The findings suggest that VIDAS is a feasible to administer, reliable, valid, positively acceptable, and culturally sensitive application for the screening of depression in English- and Spanish-speaking populations. The relationship between the gender of the participant and choice of digitized interviewer is complex, but most participants more often selected a female digitized voice. The preference for a female therapist has been documented in previous research (Kaplan, Becker, & Tenke, 1991). Most importantly, several voice characteristics demonstrate significant relationships to depression levels, such as vocal energy and variability; however, the findings have not been consistent across the various VIDAS studies.

There are several shortcomings with the analysis of voice characteristics. The literature reports complexities with differentiating between labile and transitional emotional states such as sadness, boredom, and indifference (Scherer, 1986). Moreover, without a baseline measurement, it may be difficult to discriminate between a person who is depressed and one who normally speaks with a monotonic voice. Psychiatric comorbidity also distorts vocal markers for depression. For instance, depressed persons may display mixed voice characteristics that represent both psychomotor retardation and agitation (Mandal, Srivastava, & Singh, 1990). In addition, psychotropic medications alter the vocal expression of depression symptoms, such as change in pitch and voice energy (Standke & Scherer, 1984). There are also gender, age, linguistic, and physical factors that interact with speech characteristics (Scherer, Banse, Wallbott, & Goldbeck, 1991). Differences between male and female voice ranges, age groups (children and geriatric populations), regional pronunciations, and speech impediments may require developing unique models of vocal emotional properties (Scherer, Ladd, & Silverman, 1984). Occasionally, the speech recognition system did not recognize vocal responses accurately. The speaker-independent speech recognition technology used in VIDAS is based on syntax and a phonetic structure. Such systems have limitations with the recognition of variations in vocal utterances. Differences between the respondent's pronunciation and the system's phonetic structure may significantly diminish recognition and affect the interaction between computer and user (Noyes & Frankish, 1994).

Obviously, the limitations of speech recognition and voice analyses need to be addressed. Overall, significant progress has been made toward developing a tool to increase the early and accurate detection of depression cases. VIDAS has been implemented in high volume health care settings that serve diverse patient populations, but lack bilingual personnel. VIDAS quickly and unobtrusively collects participant data, scores the data, and generates a report to inform health care staff of the participant's mood and symptoms.

As a result, VIDAS assesses many individuals who are unlikely to initially seek out mental health services. However, further study needs to be accomplished in order to enhance and refine the VIDAS interview as a *viable* alternative method of assessment.

By and large, past research has focused on standard voice variables, such as pitch, tempo, and speech rate. Acoustic variables that measure fine-grained variations in voice signals, such as shimmer (modulation in amplitude) and jitter (irregularity in vocal vibration), offer new insights into the relationship between mood and voice characteristics (Bachorowski & Owren, 1995). Advancements in experimental methodologies (structured, free-form, and pre-post designs) and digital voice analysis (short-time, long-time, and spectral analyses) can overcome the limitations in the evaluation of speech variables associated with the quality of voice sampling (Murray & Arnott, 1993). State-of-the-art voice analysis software packages that can detect subtle changes in voice properties will aid in evaluating vocal emotion. These new developments offer possibilities to develop a reliable and valid English and Spanish language voice analysis to accurately discern between depression and nondepression.

Acknowledgments. The primary author thanks Colby Carter, Gali Goldwaser, Patricia Gonzalez, Paul Hernandez, Jennifer Reza, Carlos Rodriguez, and Chris Shriver for their efforts in the data collection and data analyses. MBRS grant number MS4567 from the National Institute of General Medical Science (NIGMS) and the LRP program of the National Institutes of Health (NIH) supported the development of this manuscript.

References

Alpert, M., Pouget, E. R., & Silva, R. R. (2000). Reflections of depression in acoustic measures of the patient's speech. *Journal of Affective Disorders, 66,* 59–69.

Avaaz Innovations Inc. (1998). *Interactive Voice Analysis System™ (IVANS) user's guide.* London: Avaaz Innovations.

Bachorowski, J. A., & Owren, M. (1995). Vocal expression of emotion: Acoustic properties of speech are associated with emotional intensity and context. *Psychological Science, 6*(4), 219–224.

Beck, A. T., & Steer, R. A. (1987). *Manual for the revised Beck Depression Inventory.* San Antonio, TX: Psychological Corporation.

Beck, A. T., & Steer, R. A. (1993). *Manual for the revised Beck Anxiety Inventory.* San Antonio, TX: Psychological Corporation.

Bernal, M. A., & Castro, F. G. (1994). Are clinical psychologists prepared for service and research with ethnic minorities? Report of a decade of progress. *American Psychologist, 49,* 797–808.

Broadhead, W., Clapp-Channing, N., Finch, J., & Copeland, J. (1989). Effects of medical illness and somatic symptoms on treatment of depression in a family medicine residency practice. *General Hospital Psychiatry, 11*(3), 194–200.

Butcher, J. (1987). Computerized clinical and personality assessment using the MMPI. In J. Butcher (Ed.), *Computerized psychological assessment: A practitioner's guide* (pp. 161–197). New York: Basic Books.

Carr, A., Ghosh, A., & Ancill, R. (1983). Can a computer take a psychiatric history? *Psychological Medicine, 13*(1), 151–158.

Center for Mental Health Services. (2000). *Cultural competence standards in managed care mental health services: Four underserved/underrepresented racial/ethnic groups.* Retrieved July 26, 2001, from http://www.mentalhealth.org/publications/allpubs/SMA00-3457

Climent, C., Plutchik, R, & Estrada, H. (1975). A comparison of traditional and symptom-checklist-based histories. *American Journal of Psychiatry*, *132*(4), 450–453.

Darby, J. K., Simmons, N., & Berger, P. A. (1984). Speech and voice parameters of depression: A pilot study. *Journal of Communication Disorders*, *14*, 75–85.

Erdman, H., Klein, M., & Greist, J. (1985). Direct patient computer interviewing. *Journal of Consulting & Clinical Psychology*, *53*(6), 760–773.

Flint, A. J., Black, S. E., Campbell-Taylor, I., Gailey, G. F., & Levington, C. (1993). Abnormal speech articulation, psychomotor retardation, and subcortical dysfunction in major depression. *Journal of Psychiatric Research*, *27*, 309–319.

Friedman, E. H., & Sanders, G. G. (1992). Speech timing of mood disorders. In Miller, M. J. (Ed.) *Computer Applications in Mental Health*, 121–142. Haworth Press, Inc.

González, G. M. (1997). The emergence of Chicanos in the 21st century: Implications for mental health counseling, research, and policy. *Journal of Multicultural Counseling and Development*, *25*, 94–106.

González, G. M. (2000, March). *Bilingual telephone-assisted computerized speech recognition interviewing: Automated screening of depression symptoms*. Presentation at the Computers in Psychology 2000 conference, University of York, York, UK.

González, G. M., Costello, C., La Tourette, T., Joyce, L., & Valenzuela, M. (1997). Bilingual telephone-assisted computerized speech-recognition assessment: Is a voice-activated computer program a culturally and linguistically appropriate tool for screening depression in English and Spanish? *Cultural Diversity & Mental Health*, *3*(2), 93–111.

González, G. M., & Shriver, C. (2004). A bilingual computerized voice-interactive system for screening depression symptoms. *Journal of Technology in Human Services*, *22*(4), 1–20.

González, G. M., Winfrey, J., Sertic, M., Salcedo, J., Parker, C., & Mendoza, S. (2000). A bilingual telephone-enabled speech recognition application for screening depression symptoms. *Professional Psychology: Research & Practice*, *31*(4), 398–403.

Gorzeman, A. J., Carter, C. B., & Gonzalez, G. M. (2005, May). *Voice analysis and voice recognition using computerized methods*. Paper presented at the 2005 meeting of the American Psychological Society, Los Angeles, CA.

Hargreaves, W. A., & Starkweather, J. A. (1964). Voice quality changes in depression. *Language and Speech*, *7*, 84–88.

Hough, R. L., Landsverk, J. A., Karno, M., Burnam, M. A., Timbers, D. M., Escobar, J. I., et al. (1987). Utilization of health and mental health services by Los Angeles Mexican Americans and Non-Hispanic Whites. *Archives of General Psychiatry*, *44*, 702–709.

Kaplan, M. S., Becker, J. V., & Tenke, C. E. (1991). Influence of abuse history on male adolescent self-report comfort with interviewer gender. *Journal of Interpersonal Violence*, *6*, 3–11.

Kessler, R. C., McGonagle, K. A., Zhao, S., & Nelson, C. B. (1994). Lifetime and 12-month prevalence of DSM-III—R psychiatric disorders in the United States: Results from the National Comorbidity Study. *Archives of General Psychiatry*, *51*(1), 8–19.

Kessler, R. C., Nelson, C. B., McGonagle, K. A., & Liu, J. (1996). Comorbidity of DSM-III—R major depressive disorder in the general population: Results from the U.S. National Comorbidity Survey. *British Journal of Psychiatry*, *168*(30), 17–30.

Kobak, K. A. (1996). Computer-administered symptom rating scales. *Psychiatric Services*, *47*, 367–369.

Kuny, S., & Stassen, H. H. (1993). Speaking behavior and voice sound characteristics in depressive patients during recovery. *Journal of Psychiatric Research*, *27*, 289–307.

Levine, S., Ancill, R., & Roberts, A. (1989). Assessment of suicide risk by computer-delivered self rating questionnaire: Preliminary findings. *Acta Psychiatrica Scandinavica*, *80*(3), 216–220.

Mandal, M. K., Srivastava, P., & Singh, S. K. (1990). Paralinguistic characteristics of speech in schizophrenics and depressives. *Journal of Psychiatric Research, 24,* 191-196.

Marín, G., & Gamba, R. (1996). A new measurement of acculturation for Hispanics: The Bidimensional Acculturation Scale for Hispanics (BAS). *Hispanic Journal of Behavioral Sciences, 18*(3), 297-316.

Mosciki, E. K., Locke, B. Z., Rae, D. S., & Boyd, J. H. (1989). Depressive symptoms among Mexican Americans: The Hispanic health and nutrition examination survey. *American Journal of Epidemiology, 120,* 348-360.

Murray, I. A., & Arnott, J. L. (1993). Toward the simulation of emotion in synthetic speech: A review of the literature on human vocal emotion. *Journal of the Acoustical Society of America, 93,* 1097-1108.

Myers, J. K., & Weissman, M. M. (1980). Use of a self-report symptom scale to detect depression in a community sample. *American Journal of Psychiatry, 137,* 1081-1084.

Nilsonne, Å., Sunberg, J., Ternstrom, S., & Askenfelt, A. (1988). Measuring rate of change in voice fundamental frequency in fluent speech during mental depression. *Journal of the Acoustical Society of America, 83,* 716-728.

Noyes, J., & Frankish, C. (1994). Errors and error correction in automatic speech recognition systems. *Ergonomics, 37*(11), 1943-1957.

Pérez-Stable, E. J., Miranda, J., Munoz, R. F., & Ying, Y. W. (1990). Depression in medical outpatients: Under recognition and misdiagnosis. *Archives of Internal Medicine, 150,* 1083-1088.

Radloff, L. (1977). The CES-D Scale: A self-report depression scale for research in the general population. *Applied Psychological Measurement, 1*(3), 385-401.

Ramos, A. L., González, G. M., González, P., Goldwaser, G., & Preble, D. (2002, April). *Analysis of voice characteristics using a bilingual computerized speech recognition system.* Presentation at the 82nd Annual Convention of the Western Psychological Association, Irvine, CA.

Ramos, A. L., Shriver, C. L., Reza, J. L., & González, G. M. (2003, May). *A comprehensive review of a bilingual voice-interactive depression assessment system.* Presentation at 2003 American Psychological Society, Atlanta, GA.

Schalkwyk, J., Colton, D., & Fanty, M. (1998). *The CSLU toolkit for automatic speech recognition.* Beaverton, OR: Center for Spoken Language Understanding, Oregon Graduate Institute of Science & Technology.

Scherer, K. R. (1986). Vocal affect expression: A review and a model for future research. *Psychological Bulletin, 99,* 143-165.

Scherer, K. R., Banse, R., Wallbott, H. G., & Goldbeck, T. (1991). Vocal cues in emotion encoding and decoding. *Motivation and Emotion, 15,* 123-148.

Scherer, K. R., Ladd, D. R., & Silverman, K. E. A. (1984). Vocal cues to speaker affect: Testing two models. *Journal of the Acoustical Society of America, 76,* 1346-1356.

Scherer, K. R., & Zei, B. (1988). Vocal indicators of affective disorders. *Psychotherapy & Psychosomatics, 49*(3), 179-186.

Shapiro, S., Skinner, E. A., Kessler, L. G., Von Korff, M., German, P. S., Tischler, G. L., et al. (1984). Utilization of health and mental health services: Three Epidemiologic Catchment Area sites. *Archives of General Psychiatry, 41*(10), 971-978.

Shriver, C. L., Ramos, A. L., & González, G. M. (2003, August). *Bilingual voice-interactive depression assessment system: Psychometric and voice analysis findings.* Presentation at the 110th Annual Convention of the American Psychological Association, Toronto, Canada.

Siegman, A. W. (1987). The pacing of speech in depression. In J. D. Maser (Ed.), *Depression and expressive behavior* (pp. 83-95). Hillsdale, NJ: Erlbaum.

Smith, A. L., & Weissmann, M. M. (1992). Epidemiology. In E. S. Paykel (Ed.), *Handbook of affective disorders* (pp. 111-129). New York: Guilford Press.

Standke, H., & Scherer, K. R. (1984). Vocal indicators of psychoactive drug effects. *Speech Communications, 3,* 245-252.

Starkweather, J. A. (1992). Computer applications in psychiatric interviewing. In K. C. Lun, K. C., Degoulet, P., Piemme, T. E., & Reinhoff, O. I. (Eds.), *Proceedings of the MediInfo 92* (p. 318). Amsterdam: Elsevier Science Ltd.

Starkweather, J. A., & Muñoz, R. F. (1989, May). *Identification of clinical depression among foreign speakers.* Paper presented at the American Association for Medical Systems and Informatics, San Francisco, CA.

Stassen, H. H., Bomben, G., & Günther, E. (1991). Speech characteristics in depression. *Psychopathology, 24,* 88–105.

Stout, R. L. (1981). New approaches to the design of computerized interviewing and testing systems. *Behavior Research Methods, Instruments, & Computers, 13,* 436–442.

Talavera, J. A., Sáiz-Ruiz, J., & García-Toro, M. (1994). Quantitative measurement of depression through speech analysis. *European Psychiatry, 9,* 185–193.

U.S. Census. (2000). *Population projections of the U. S. by age, sex, race, and Hispanic origin: 1995 to 2050.* Washington, DC: U.S. Government Printing Office.

Vanger, P., Summerfield, A. B., Rosen, B. K., & Watson, J. P. (1992). Effects of communication on speech behavior of depressives. *Comprehensive Psychiatry, 33,* 39–41.

Vega, W. A., Kolody, B., Aguilar-Gaxiola, S., Alderate, E., Catalano, R., & Carveo-Anduaga, J. (1998). Lifetime prevalence of DSM-III—R psychiatric disorders among urban and rural Mexican Americans in California. *Archives of General Psychiatry, 55,* 771–778.

Woodward, A. M., Dwinell, A. D., & Arons, B. S. (1992). Barriers to mental health services for Hispanic Americans: A literature review and discussion. *Journal of Mental Health Administration, 19,* 224–236.

World Health Organization. (2001). *Mental health: New understanding, new hope.* Geneva, Switzerland: World Health Organization.

CHAPTER 5

Automatic Discrimination of Emotion from Voice: A Review of Research Paradigms

Juhani Toivanen, Tapio Seppänen, and
Eero Väyrynen

Introduction: Speech, Emotions, and Attitudes

In the phonetic sciences, the relationship between emotions and phonetic/prosodic features of voice or speech has been investigated using various methods since the early 1900s. Electro-acoustic analyses were used by Skinner (1935), for example, while more sophisticated methodologies were introduced in the 1960s, as more accurate instruments were used and the theoretical formulation of emotion-related terminology of speech effects developed rapidly (e.g., Crystal, 1969; Laver, 1968). Also, the term *paralanguage* was introduced, referring to the concept that certain aspects of the speaker's speech are determined by the psychophysiological state of the speaker, and that they are, at least in a genuine emotional speech situation, largely beyond the speaker's volitional control.

By now, a voluminous literature exists on the emotion/prosody interface, and it can be said that the acoustic/prosodic parameters of emotional expression in voice are understood rather thoroughly (see, e.g., Murray & Arnott, 1993; Scherer, 2003). The general view is that pitch (fundamental frequency, F0) is the most important parameter of the vocal expression of emotion (both productively and perceptually); energy (intensity), duration, and speaking rate are the other relevant parameters.

The term *attitude* is widely used both in linguistics and social psychology, and there is clearly some overlap between *attitude* and *emotion*. Linguists (rather than engineers) have studied the prosody of the expression of attitude (rather than that of emotion) for a long time (e.g.,

Kingdon, 1958; O'Connor & Arnold, 1973; Palmer, 1922). Some authors of the "British school" (e.g., O'Connor & Arnold, 1973) propose a vocabulary of hundreds of attitudinal labels, with a corresponding system of pitch contours (i.e., specific intonation patterns such as "rise-fall" or the "level tone"). An implicit distinction is sometimes made between an emotion and an attitude as it is assumed that the expression of attitude (or *stance* in modern terminology) is controlled by the cognitive system that underpins fluent speech in a "normal" communicative situation, while true emotional states are not necessarily subject to such constraints (the speech effects in real emotional situations may be biomechanically determined reactions not fully controlled by the cognitive system). It is, then, possible that attitude and emotion are expressed in speech through at least partly different prosodic cues. However, this distinction is not at all a straightforward one as the theoretical difference between emotion and attitude has not been fully established. Moreover, it seems doubtful why specific intonation patterns (at the clause level) could not be used also to signal purely emotional aspects of speech (we return to this issue at the end of this chapter).

In the present paper, the focus will be on emotions instead of attitudes, and, more specifically, on so-called *basic emotions* to fulfill the aim detailed below. It is commonly assumed that there are a number of emotions which are more basic than others. These include *fear*, *anger*, *happiness*, *sadness*, *surprise,* and *disgust*. Such a classification is based on the hypothesis that these emotions reflect survival-related patterns of responses to events in the constantly changing environment. It is assumed that these emotions are universal as a result of man's

evolutionary history—just consider the importance of, for example, fear in regulating behavior.

Automatic Discrimination of Emotion from Voice: Staking Out the Field

Here we discuss the relationship between voice/speech and emotion from the viewpoint of the automatic classification of emotion from an unknown/unexpected voice signal. This task is highly specific and it represents a real challenge to speech technology. While the basic research on the correlations between affect and prosodic/acoustic features of speech continues, the applied computer speech community is now showing active interest in the specific role of the expression of emotion through voice contained in various speech situations. More specifically, the focus is now on applications centrally involving human-computer interaction with speech as a medium.

New computer speech-based applications are becoming more and more common, forcing unexpected changes in the way in which we interact and store speech information. In the mobile phone context, a very natural and efficient interface is based on speech input as evidenced by hands-free software systems enabling users to speak into a cell phone to define contact information or to surf the Internet. Interactive speech systems can also be utilized in different kinds of customer situations, and the naturalness of the voice quality and prosody is of utmost importance as the customers "talking to a computer" who do not find the synthesized voice acceptable are very likely to hang up or cancel the transaction. Therefore, a more profound understanding of the relationship between voice and emotions must be achieved to improve existing speech recognition and synthesis technology.

A specific area now receiving great attention in the knowledge management industry is the automatic discrimination/ recognition of emotion contained in speech (in this paper *discrimination* and *classification/recognition* are used interchangeably in the context of emotion). While speech-based applications grow fast and show improved quality of speech recognition and synthesis, the next step in the technical evolution may be content-analyzing multimodal applications that are accessible from multiple devices. Therefore, the automatic recognition and classification of affective content of speech may be the next "killer application," sparking new possibilities for speech-based corpus search engines and Internet database technologies if the semantic content of voice signals can be analyzed reliably (Picard, 1997). One example of a relevant concrete application for the end user is a search engine capable of browsing audio files (e.g., radio plays, sound tracks of movies, etc.) also according to their emotional content: such a search engine would mainly utilize prosodic/acoustic information, although vocabulary (such as emotionally charged words) could also be useful.

Parameter Paradigm Utilized in the Automatic Discrimination of Emotion from Voice

As for the automatic discrimination of emotions (also known as sentiment classification), the aim is to map the emo-tional speech samples to discrete basic emotion categories. The procedure is based on an acoustic analysis of the audio data (yielding a number of acoustic parameters) and on the statistical classification of the obtained data (e.g., *k-Nearest-Neighbor*). As was already pointed out, global prosodic features such as pitch, energy, and speaking rate phenomena are relevant to the expression of emotion through speech. Therefore, the same features are used in the automatic discrimination of emotion from the voice signal. The most relevant parameters, classified into appropriate categories representing the process of speech production, are described below.

The *fundamental frequency* (F0) measured in Hertz (Hz) is the rate at which a waveform is repeated per unit in time. The average speaking F0 is usually associated with the *mean F0*, which is the sum of all the frequency measurements divided by the number of all observed glottal periods. The *median F0* is the F0 value which marks the 50th percentile of the distribution (that is, it is the middle F0 value when the F0 values are arranged in order). Finally, the *modal F0* is the F0 value that is the most common value in the speech sample. When the distribution of the F0 values is normal or symmetrical, the mean F0 is the most informative F0 value. If, however, the distribution is clearly skewed, the median F0 is a better parameter describing the average speaking F0.

The highest F0 value and the lowest F0 value are absolute values, and are not often very useful parameters as they may be, in effect, accidental values because they often represent (unintentional) shifts into the falsetto/creak register, respectively. Thus they do not necessarily represent the highest/lowest values "intended" by the speaker. Therefore, a more useful technique is to compute the *5th percentile of F0* (instead of the absolutely lowest F0 value) and the *95th percentile of F0* (instead of the absolutely highest F0 value). If, for example, the 95th percentile is 250 Hz, only 5% of the F0 values are higher than this value.

The highest/lowest F0 values (and corresponding percentiles) naturally give some indication of how dynamic the pitch of the speaker is, but different measures are needed to get a more accurate representation of the liveliness/monotonousness of the speech melody. The *total F0 range* is the absolute difference between the highest observed F0 value and the lowest observed value. This is one way of describing the dynamics of F0 variation in the sample but, again, a better measure is the one based on percentiles (e.g., the *5th–95th percentile range*). Another useful strategy is to quantify F0 variation as an average distance of F0 values from the mean; this measure is the *standard deviation* (SD), that is, the root mean squared deviation (Baken, 1987). The standard deviation can be expressed on the logarithmic *semitone scale* (ST), and then the term *pitch sigma* is used. This is done by using the semitone scale to compare, effectively and in a perceptually relevant way, the F0 ranges produced by different speakers, making intersubject and intergender comparisons meaningful. The effective range is often equaled with the value of 4 SDs in ST (Jassem, 1971).

The liveliness of the speech melody in a speech sample can mean, in addition to the F0 range discussed above, the rate of F0 change. The *slopes of F0 movements* can be expressed in terms of ST per second, for example; the slopes are the rates of F0 change, or angles at which the F0

contours slope. For an entire speech situation, it is possible to compute the average F0 movement size, the maximum/minimum F0 movement size, the average F0 movement rate, and the maximum/minimum F0 movement rate (these parameters can also be determined separately for falls and rises).

In addition to the global F0 features described above, jitter, shimmer, amplitude/intensity, and spectral and temporal features of speech are relevant parameters than can be used in the automatic discrimination of emotion from voice.

Jitter can be defined as the amount of random cycle-to-cycle variation between adjacent pitch periods in vocal fold vibration (Higgins & Saxman, 1989); it is thus a measure of F0 perturbation.

Shimmer is the amount of cycle-to-cycle variation in amplitude between adjacent pitch periods.

Amplitude (or sound pressure) is the magnitude of displacement for a sound wave.

Intensity refers to the amount of energy transmitted per unit of time and area by a sound wave.

Loudness, as a perceptual attribute, is correlated with the physical quality of intensity (sound power) or amplitude (sound pressure). The decibel is a unit of a logarithmic scale of power/energy or intensity. Like the logarithmic semitone scale, the decibel scale is relevant from the viewpoint of perception, approximating the way in which perceived loudness increases as a function of intensity.

In speech production, the supralaryngeal vocal tract is an acoustic filter that acts upon the source of acoustic energy, suppressing the passage of sound energy at certain frequencies and allowing its passage at other frequencies. Those frequencies at which more acoustic energy passes through the supralaryngeal tract are known as *formants*. The average frequencies and bandwidths of formants (especially those of F1, F2, and F3) carry useful acoustic information from the viewpoint of the expression of emotion. The expression of emotion in voice may also be connected with such spectral features as the *distribution of energy at different frequencies in the spectrogram* (a spectrogram is based on measurements of the changing frequency content of a sound over time). It is commonly known, for example, that in angry speech, or when the speaker's voice is very tense (overpressured), there is more energy in the high frequency end of the spectrum: the amount of energy above 1000 Hz increases markedly (the opposite happens in a very lax voice with sorrow or boredom, or in a breathy voice).

Finally, the *tempo of speech* is an emotion-related parameter that can be used in experiments on the automatic discrimination of emotion from voice. Two parameters are crucial, the articulation rate and the speaking rate. *Articulation rate* is defined as the rate at which an utterance is actually produced. Silent pauses are not taken into consideration. *Speaking rate* is the rate of speech for the whole speaking turn. Here, all the speech material within the speaking turn is calculated (thus silent pauses do affect the measurement). The speaking rate can be described in terms of syllables per minute, while the articulation rate can be quantified in terms of syllables per second for the actual speech. Related measures are ratios such as phonation/time, silence/time, etc. Similarly, the average durations of pauses of different kinds can be used as temporal emotion-related parameters.

Statistical Methods Used in the Automatic Discrimination of Emotion from Voice

When the aim is to classify an emotional utterance into one of several predetermined classes, those signal features which best discriminate between the classes must be determined (the problem of feature selection). When using predetermined classes, it is also necessary to access so-called *truth data* (baseline data), that is, information about the *intended* or *interpreted* emotional content of the speech data. The truth data can be defined by asking the producers of the emotional speech data (such as actors) to create certain predetermined vocal emotion portrayals, or a group of listeners can be asked to evaluate the emotional content of speech samples (using forced-choice emotional labeling, for example).

Fisher's linear discriminant (linear discriminant analysis) is typically used as a feature extraction step before classification begins. Fisher's linear discriminant is used for two-class classification: given a vector of observations x, the probability of a binary random class variable c is predicted. Fisher's linear discriminant can be generalized to multiple discriminant analysis: c becomes a categorical variable with N possible states instead of only two. The various acoustic parameters (basically any combination of those described above) are stacked as a multidimensional feature vector and a discriminant analysis is performed in order to find the best feature combination. Fisher's linear discriminant function assumes Gaussian distributions and positions linear decision surfaces in the feature space.

For nonlinear decision surfaces, neural networks such as *Multi-Layer Perceptrons* (MLP) are useful. MLPs are feed-forward neural networks and they are trained with the standard backpropagation algorithm. With one or two hidden layers, MLPs can approximate almost any input-output map, and they apparently approximate the performance of optimal statistical classifiers even in the most difficult problems.

k-Nearest-Neighbor (kNN) is a standard nonparametric method in statistical pattern recognition (Duda, Hart, & Stork, 2001), and it is commonly used in the automatic discrimination of emotion from voice. kNN is a prototype-based method; that is, a set of prototypical feature vectors from each class are stored in the classifier memory. An unknown feature vector is then compared to all prototypes, and k closest (in vector space) vectors are picked up. A majority voting is performed among these to identify the class to which most prototypes belong. The unknown feature vector is assumed to belong to that class. The classifier has one parameter, k, that is set manually by experimentation (usually, k is equal to 1, 3, or 5).

A new classifier of interest within the pattern recognition community is *Support Vector Machine* (SVM), which has its ground in statistical learning theory and is able to cope with very high dimensional feature spaces and small data size. Another potential classification technique is the *Naïve Bayesian Network* (NBN), which is based on probability theory and the assumption of the statistical conditional independence of the descriptors.

In the automatic discrimination of emotion from voice, an important point is that, in practice, an emotional expression may not be performed in its fullest form. In the discrimination procedure, the rel-evant aim may thus be to describe the degree of emotion expressed in speech. This may be especially important for speech corpus search engines in order to get a wider range of hits. Multiple variable regression to emotion degree can be used to combine as much as possible of the pieces of information that parameters provide. Both linear and nonlinear regression can be investigated. MLP is a strong candidate among the nonlinear approaches.

Automatic Discrimination of Emotion from Voice: Research Designs and Results

In the research on the automatic discrimination of emotion from voice, the research designs mainly vary in terms of the following criteria: the spontaneity of the emotional speech material (spontaneous or elicited/acted?), type of truth data (intended or perceived emotional content?), language in which the emotional speech material is produced, acoustic/prosodic parameters used in the classification procedure, and type of classification method employed. Naturally, the size of the material varies (the number of emotional speech samples and the duration of the samples), as do the following parameters: the syntactic/linguistic unit in which emotions are expressed (words, utterances, longer speaking turns, etc.), the number and type of speakers producing the data (linguistically naïve speakers, students, professional actors), and the number and type of listeners evaluating the emotional content of the data (linguistically naïve or non-naïve listeners). An important distinction is between the *speaker-dependent scenario* and the *speaker-independent scenario*: the classification results may be relevant for only a specified speaker (or specified speakers) involved in the emotional speech data production process, or they may be, at least theoretically, generalized to persons (or even a population) not involved in the production of the data. Naturally, significantly better results can be expected for the speaker-dependent scenario; the speaker-independent design is a much more challenging task for the classifier.

Typically, in experiments on the automatic discrimination of emotion from voice, the scenario involves experienced speakers (e.g., actors) reading out words, sentences, or short passages as if they were happy, sad, angry, and so on. Thus, the typical linguistic unit is usually relatively short (long monologs are rarely used), and the speech production procedure is controlled rather strictly. However, recently, more work has been done on spontaneous data (Batliner, Fischer, Huber, Spilker, & Nöth, 2000; 2003; Lee, Narayanan, & Pieraccini, 2001). Below, some relevant studies (research designs and classification results) are reviewed in detail.

Batliner et al. (2000) used a two-class classification task with such emotions as neutral and anger. The experimental scenarios were the following: a speaker-specific setting with data produced by one actor, a speaker-independent setting with data produced by a number of linguistically naïve speakers reading predetermined sentences, and a speaker-independent setting with data produced by linguistically naïve speakers communicating with a malfunctioning automatic speech processing system ("Wizard-of-Oz scenario"). The parameters modeled logarithmic F0, energy, and durational features (e.g., short-term energy maxi-

mum, mean of short-term energy, F0 maximum, F0 minimum, F0 mean, SD of F0, number of voiced regions, number of unvoiced regions, length of longest voiced region, length of longest unvoiced region, and ratio of length of voiced and unvoiced regions). The best classification results were obtained using linear discriminant analysis. The classification result was 89% for the actor scenario, the best feature being length of longest voiced region. The Wizard-of-Oz scenario produced a classification rate of 69%, the best features being the number of voiced regions and the number of unvoiced regions. The read scenario achieved a classification level of 73%; the best features were short-time energy maximum and the mean of short-time energy.

Lee et al. (2001) investigated authentic English human-machine dialogs using linear discriminant classification with Gaussian class-conditional probability distribution and kNN. The emotions were restricted to two classes, *negative* and *non-negative*. The parameters included F0 mean, F0 median, SD of F0, F0 maximum, F0 minimum, energy mean, energy median, SD of energy, energy maximum, and energy range. The classification level for male speakers was 76% (with kNN, k = 3). For the kNN classifier, the following parameters were the most relevant (had the most discriminative power): F0 median, energy mean, energy SD, energy range, energy maximum, and energy median.

Banse and Scherer (1996) investigated the following emotional states: hot anger, cold anger, panic fear, anxiety, desperation, sadness, elation, happiness, interest, boredom, shame, pride, disgust, and contempt. The emotions were simulated by professional actors. Discriminant analysis achieved a discrimination level of 50%; the level was quite comparable to the classification rate achieved by human listeners. The best set of parameters included the following: F0 (mean, SD, 25th percentile, 75th percentile), energy (mean), speech rate (duration of voiced periods), bands in the voiced, long-term average spectrum (125-200 Hz, 200-300 Hz, 500-600 Hz, 1000-1600 Hz, 5000-8000 Hz), Hammarberg index (the measure of the difference of energy maxima in the 0-2 kHz band and the 2-5 kHz band in the voiced part of the utterance), slope of spectral energy above 1000 Hz, proportion of voiced energy up to 1000 Hz, and bands in the unvoiced long-term average spectrum (125-250 Hz, 5000-8000 Hz).

McGilloway et al. (2000) investigated simulated English speech material produced by nonprofessional speakers: emotive sentences (with appropriate lexical content) were used to elicit expressions of anger, happiness, fear, sadness, and neutral. The classification methods were the following: linear discriminant, support vector machines, and generative vector quantization. The best classification level was produced by the linear discriminant methods, approximately 55%. The best parameters included such features as the number of F0 points recovered, median of silence durations, energy below 250 Hz, number of inflections (changes of direction) in F0 contour per tune, and median duration for rises in intensity.

Slaney and McRoberts (1998) attempted to classify three categories of parent-infant communication in English speech: approval, attention, and prohibition. The speech data consisted of more than 500 utterances from adults talking to their infants in a "seminormal" communicative situation (in a room full of toys). The parameters were: F0 slope, mean F0, and mean delta F0 (measured globally over the utterances); additional features were formant information and variance of energy. A Gaussian mixture model was used in the classification, and an average classification level of 57% was obtained for speaker-independent classification. Speaker-dependent classification results varied between 60 and 92%.

Above, mainly speaker-independent emotion classification experiments have been described. In contrast, the speaker-dependent classification of emotion from voice may reach considerably higher performance levels. An example is Oudeyer (2002), who obtained exceptionally high classification levels (92-97%) in a speaker-dependent discrimination between four emotional classes (joy/pleasure, sorrow/sadness/grief, anger, and normal/neutral). The speech data (short Japanese utterances) were produced by professional actors. In the classification procedure, a total of as many as 200 parameters were used. The parameters included mean, maximum, minimum, ranges, percentiles, and inter-percentile ranges of intensity and F0 measurements. A number of algorithms were tested (e.g., RBF neural nets and support vector machines); the best classification results were obtained with AdaBoosted decision trees and rules (AdaBoostM1).

To conclude, it seems that the speaker-independent discrimination rate for four or five basic emotions is not much higher than 60-65%. Summarizing the results of the literature, ten Bosch (2003) suggests that, for *three* (basic) emotions, the automatic speaker-independent classification performance can, at best, reach a level of approximately 70%. Of course, it must be emphasized that the performance level of the classification procedure essentially depends on the nature of the speech data and the research design: generally speaking, higher levels can be expected if the number of emotions is small (and if only basic emotions are tested), with professional speakers producing the speech samples.

Applications and Future Directions

As was described in the introductory section, the automatic discrimination of emotion from voice can have relevant applications in the context of speech corpus search engines and Internet database technologies. Other potential applications can be found in wellness technology. The utilization of the results of the research can have a fascinating new niche applications in (forensic) medicine and vocology. In aviation medicine, methods for automatically recognizing the stress level or emotional state of the pilot are badly needed: there is already some empirical evidence that such voice characteristics as mean F0 and articulation rate can be reliable indicators of the speaker's fatigue state, for example. Similar applications could be useful in crime investigation: voice measurement is a practical and cost-effective tool for determining the probable mental state of an anonymous caller, for instance (given the current safety situation in the world, applications of this kind will probably become very relevant in the not too distant future). In medicine, the automatic classification of emotion could alert a caregiver on duty to signs of emotion that urgently call for attention.

To develop the methods for the automatic discrimination of emotion from voice further, work is needed in a number of areas. First, the classification algorithms should be constantly tested and developed with different kinds of data: basic classification methods (such as linear discriminant analysis) may work well with straightforward data (i.e., with pure emotional speech samples), but the degrees of emotions and emotional variation within a speech sample may require more sophisticated methods. MLP is a promising approach in this respect. Statistical classifier technology may also be applied because the distance of a sample to the decision surface can be computed, which produces a measure of the pureness or mixedness of the expressed emotion.

Second, a more linguistically oriented analysis is needed to investigate the speech melody or intonation of the speech data. As was pointed out earlier, attitude may be expressed in speech through intonational features (through different pitch patterns on semantically important words, typical patterns being *falls* and *fall-rises*, for example). The measures of mean values of F0, intensity, and pause phenomena (routinely used in the automatic discrimination of emotion from voice) do not provide information on the course of pitch at the utterance level, and they do not give any direct information about the linguistically relevant information in pitch. That is, in the automatic classification of emotion from voice, a (large) number of average values of F0, intensity, and temporal and spectral parameters are computed for the whole speech sample, but these values are global parameters: they do not describe F0 features within individual words or clauses. Thus, a linguistic analysis is needed: an obvious taking-off point would be to investigate the relation between syntax and F0, intensity, and so on at the utterance level in the expression of emotion. Unfortunately, this requires lots of manual work—or the development of systems for the automatic prosodic labeling of speech, which is a separate research challenge (Wightman & Ostendorf, 1994). To create systems for automatic prosodic labeling, a language model is needed for describing the legitimate prosodic label sequences, and this model must, of course, be developed separately for each language. To our knowledge, no one has attempted to systematically develop these methods to improve the automatic discrimination of emotion from voice; so far, only the global average parameters have been used. Obviously, this is an area where quantum leaps could be made as regards the development of the methods for the automatic discrimination of emotions from voice.

Third, at some point, it will be necessary to experiment more systematically with authentic emotional speech data. A large part of the existing research has concentrated on speech data that are semiauthentic, at best, but the development of relevant applications (e.g., medical ones) requires that genuinely spontaneous emotional speech data also be on the agenda. Naturally, this approach entails many challenges: it is not easy to have access to databases of authentic emotional material, and ethical considerations are unavoidable here.

Finally, it must be pointed out that experiments on the automatic discrimination of emotion from voice have so far concentrated on major languages, with English as the primary language. The trend may very well continue in the future, and economic considerations naturally play a role here: it is more profitable to develop applications for major languages, and especially if costly language models are built for automatic prosodic labeling,

minority languages are very easily overlooked. However, there are independent research groups working on the automatic discrimination of emotion from voice for small languages (e.g., Toivanen, Väyrynen, & Seppänen, 2004), and it is our hope that this line of research manages to survive in the future.

Conclusion

The automatic discrimination of emotion from voice is an active research area, with important existing applications and very relevant potential future applications. The classification level (also with the speaker-independent scenario) is already relatively high, thus enabling a number of real-life applications. The development of technologies in this area is also rapid; especially classification methods are being developed and refined constantly. The number of acoustic parameters on which the classification procedure is based is very large but it seems that, qualitatively, not so much progress can be made any more with the existing parameter paradigm. Future development requires that linguistic features be utilized more clearly in the classification procedure. The reliable automatic discrimination of authentic emotions from voice is an area where more work is clearly needed—and also where the rewards will be the greatest.

References

Baken, R.J. (1987). *Clinical measurement of speech and voice*. Boston: Taylor.

Banse, R., & Scherer, K. R. (1996). Acoustic profiles in vocal emotion expression. *Jour-*

nal of Personality and Social Psychology, *70*, 614-636.

Batliner, A., Fischer, K., Huber, R., Spilker, J., & Nöth, E. (2000). Desperately seeking emotions: Actors, wizards, and human beings. R. Cowie, E. Douglas-Cowie & M. Schröder (s.), *Proceedings of the ISCA Workshop on Speech and Emotion* (pp. 195-200). Newcastle (Northern Ireland, UK): Queen's University Belfast Press.

Batliner, A., Fischer, K., Huber, R., Spilker, J., & Nöth, E. (2003). How to find trouble in communication. *Speech Communication*, *40*, 117-143.

Crystal, D. (1969). *Prosodic systems and intonation in English*. Cambridge, UK: Cambridge University Press.

Duda, R. O., Hart, P. E., & Stork, D. G. (2001). *Pattern recognition* (2nd ed.). New York: John Wiley & Sons.

Higgins, M. B. & Saxman, J. H. (1989). A comparison of intra-subject variation across sessions of three vocal frequency perturbation indices. *Journal of the Acoustical Society of America*, *86*, 911-916.

Jassem, W. (1971). On the pitch and compass of the speaking voice. *Journal of the International Phonetic Association*, *1*, 59-68.

Kingdon, R. (1958). *The groundwork of English intonation*. London: Longman.

Laver, J. (1968). Voice quality and indexical information. *British Journal of Disorders of Communication*, *3*, 43-54.

Lee, C. M., Narayanan, S., & Pieraccini, R. (2001). Recognition of negative emotions from the speech signal. M. Omologo & A. Acero (Eds.), *Proceedings of Automatic Speech Recognition and Understanding Workshop* (pp. 40-43). Madonna di Campiglio Trento (Italy): IEEE Signal Processing Society.

McGilloway, S., Cowie, R., Douglas-Cowie, E., Gielen, S., Westerdijk, M., & Stroeve, S. (2000). Approaching automatic recognition of emotion from voice: A rough benchmark. R. Cowie, E. Douglas-Cowie & M. Schröder

(Eds.), *Proceedings of the ISCA Workshop on Speech and Emotion* (pp. 207-212). Newcastle (Northern Ireland, UK): Queen's University Belfast Press.

Murray, I. R., & Arnott, J. L. (1993). Toward a simulation of emotion in synthetic speech: A review of the literature on human vocal emotion. *Journal of the Acoustical Society of America*, *93*, 1097-1108.

O'Connor, J. D., & Arnold, G. F. (1973). *Intonation of colloquial English* (2nd ed.). London: Longman.

Oudeyer, P. (2002). Novel useful features and algorithms for the recognition of emotions in human speech. In D. Hirst (Ed.), *Proceedings of the 1st International Conference on Prosody* (pp. 547-550). Aix-en-Provence, France: University of Provence Press.

Palmer, H. E. (1922). *English intonation (with systematic exercises)*. Cambridge, UK: Heffer.

Picard, R. W. (1997). *Affective computing*. Cambridge, MA: MIT Press.

Scherer, K. R. (2003). Vocal communication of emotion: A review of research paradigms. *Speech Communication*, *40*, 227-256.

Skinner, E. R. (1935). A calibrated recording and analysis of the pitch, force and quality of vocal tones expressing happiness and sadness. *Speech Monographs*, *2*, 81-137.

Slaney, M., & McRoberts, G. (1998). Baby ears: A recognition system for affective vocalizations. L. Atlas. Seattle, WA: IEEE Signal Processing Society.

ten Bosch, L. (2003). Emotions, speech and the ASR framework. *Speech Communication*, *40*, 213-225.

Toivanen, J., Väyrynen, E., & Seppänen, T. (2004). Automatic discrimination of emotion from spoken Finnish. *Language and Speech*, *47*, 383-412.

Wightman, C., & Ostendorf, M. (1994). Automatic labeling of prosodic patterns. *IEEE Transactions on Speech and Audio Processing*, *2*(4), 469-481.

CHAPTER 6

Dazed and Confused: Possible Processing Constraints on Emotional Response to Information-Dense Motivational Speech

Claude Steinberg

Introduction

References to vocal expression of emotion apart from speech in nonscientific discourse, whether in the guise of the "call of the wild," the "primordial scream," a "grunt of satisfaction," or a "shriek of terror," suggest that vocal expression may be popularly perceived as a window into what Lazarus (1982, p. 1022) refers to as "irrational and primitive . . . midbrain phenomena,"[1] involving automatic behaviors and purely perceptual responses unmediated by higher cortical functions. Certain scientific perspectives do little to dispel this view, even regarding presumably more refined phenomena like speech inflection. In drawing a distinction between categorical linguistic functions of intonation (like rising question intonation) and gradient *paralinguistic* ones (like wider pitch range or higher pitch for animated anger), Ladd (1996, p. 36) implicitly assumes that linguistic prosody involves learned, language-specific, and

---

[1]By "midbrain," Lazarus presumably means not the corpus callosum connecting the two brain hemispheres, but something akin to what medical anthropologist Clotaire Rapaille would call the "limbic brain," the emotional center midway between the "reptilian brain" and the neocortex (Gladstone, 2004), though common English phrases describing vocalizations suggest they are perceived as having a more reptilian "fight or flight" character.

sometimes arbitrary symbolic relations, whereas emotional vocal expression involves simplistic, universal iconic associations of the sort any sound-producing mammal presumably could imitate. In defending a precognitive account of emotion, Zajonc (1984, p. 119) claims that "emotional features of speech are apparently controlled by the right [brain] hemisphere, whereas semantic and lexical aspects are controlled by the left," a statement that almost suggests Zajonc believes a speaker's vocal expression is in no way determined by the speaker's words. While the evidence on which Zajonc's statement is based[2] demonstrates only that hemispheric differentiation is a prerequisite for producing emotional speech, not necessarily a sufficient condition, statements of this sort perpetuate the unspoken assumption that emotional expression in the voice is somehow independent of cognitive intervention. Without evidence to the contrary, one could jump to the conclusion that listeners' responses to vocal expressions of emotion are no more reliant on higher cortical functions than speakers' expressions of emotion allegedly is, since no great feat of mental processing would seem to be required to decode primitive cries. If listening to presumably unconsciously crafted speech patterns were to involve the complexities of pattern matching and problem solving, that would imply that a speaker wishing to evoke emotion in others, not merely express it, may need to take account of listeners' thought processes. Outside such self-consciously artistic domains as storytelling and theater, the idea that successful

speakers should unconsciously attend—and the less successful fail to attend—to processing constraints on emotion perception, that speakers should in any way be thinking about how to emote, is a premise more likely to provoke hoots of mirth and howls of derision than reasoned discussion. Yet the examples presented herein will suggest just that. Cognitive processing of and emotional response to prosodic features of speech will be shown to be inextricably linked. More significantly, emotional response will be shown to be at times dependent on prior cognitive processing. A listener's failure to resolve semantic incongruities among sound patterns occurring over time or between sound patterns and the semantics of the texts they accompany will be shown to elicit a predictable emotional response, one of uneasiness leading to disengagement, a response that may overpower any other incipient emotion elicited by the component sound patterns or texts.

Auditory analysis of motivational sales-oriented speech will identify vocal behaviors which cause listeners to "zone out," that is, to stop attending to the speaker. It will become apparent that these moments correspond to points where incongruous rhythmic or intonation patterns in the voice make it simultaneously difficult to follow a speaker's argument and difficult to respond emotionally to the speaker other than with frustration or confusion. Yet because listeners generally assume that speakers will make mistakes under pressure and will expect to be forgiven, and because in most situations, it is not crucial that listeners understand

---

[2]" . . . a number of patients with lesions in the right hemisphere . . . produced intelligible speech, but it was speech totally devoid of emotional inflections and other affect-dependent prosodic parameters," (Zajonc, 1984, p. 119).

and respond emotionally to every moment in a speech, most listeners will have neither the justification nor the motivation to become angry with a speaker at these moments or to try to figure out how best to interpret what they are having trouble understanding. Instead, they will become uneasy and uninvolved.

The approach is exploratory and phenomenological, unabashedly so in the belief that insufficient research to date on the emotional connotations of relations among sound patterns across discourse structures in speech precludes the possibility of devising informed hypotheses to test empirically. I played various recordings of professional voice artists from my personal collection and stopped the recordings at points were I either could not determine the speaker's emotional state or where I could not determine how the speaker intended the audience to feel about the subject of the discourse. Somewhat unexpectedly, I found these points to correspond precisely to points at which I became confused about the gist of the speaker's argument. I replayed the passages, sometimes at a slower speed, to identify characteristics of the voice that seemed responsible for my perceptions and that could explain the apparent interrelationship between information processing and emotion perception. Thus, all references to "the listener" should be understood as referring to the researcher himself. Grammatical reference to the first person is avoided not so much to shirk the appearance of self-indulgent musing as because the mental processes described seem to me sufficiently basic and context-independent as to suggest they may be normative and culturally universal rather than idiosyncratic.

It should not be necessary to state, but one of the responsibilities of experimental science is to devise new research methods for testing theories about elusive hypothesized phenomena, be they as hard to see as elementary subatomic particles, as unapproachable as other galaxies, as mysterious as black holes, or as old as the Big Bang. While vocal expression of emotion may be a bit younger, a bit easier to see, a bit less mysterious, and a bit more approachable than some of these physical phenomena, it should not be the job of research on vocal expression of emotion to ignore the dynamic richness of human emotional experience of the voice or reduce it a priori to a set of linear mappings of degrees of vocal behavior to amounts of perfunctory emotional experience supposedly induced in the listener merely because a correlational approach is most convenient for running statistical tests in psychology and speech science labs. If experimental science is to proceed from modeling human behavior and information processing to modeling human experience, a period of field observation and introspection not unlike that which characterized Nicolaus Steno's evolutionary geology, Darwin's evolutionary biology, Louis and Mary Leakey's biological anthropology, and naturalist Jane Goodall's social primatology is not an unreasonable price to pay.

Greek Games— Olympian Emotions

In what has been called the information age, it is becoming a challenge to avoid presenting more information, whether visually or audibly, than an audience can absorb without glazing over and becoming emotionally neutral or hostile. Yet to acknowledge that our perceptual and cognitive apparatus may be incapable of appreciating many subtleties of vocal expression consciously or unconsciously produced by motivational speakers is a dispiriting thought. What speech coach would wish to be in the position of advising an enthusiastic speaker to "cool it" for the sake of the audience? How much better it would be if we could identify a speaker's peccadilloes of omission and commission that prevent or interfere with perception of a message the speaker is otherwise articulating quite well.

A conventional view in social psychology articulated by Miller, Maruyama, Beaber, and Valone (1976) is that listeners assume faster speakers are more competent than slower ones, with the result that faster speakers end up being more persuasive.[3] However, according to Miller et al. (1976), fast speech may be persuasive only because listeners do not have time to think up counterarguments, not because listeners are actually able to process the fast information. In contrast to these researchers, by way of examining the vocal structure of fast speech in infomercials for such products as Prolong Superlubricant and T-Fal Ingenio Fat-free Cookware at the PVSF 2005 Conference on Voice Quality & Emotions, I made the rather audacious claim that as both information density per grammatical unit and words or syllables per second increase, both accuracy of listener comprehension and degree of emotional impact of the message can increase cor-

respondingly, provided that the rhythm and intonation of vocal delivery are structured according to certain rhetorical principles evident in successful infomercials and radio commercials. Compressing extensive lists of product features or offerings into short time spans, these feverish invocations, far from intimidating and alienating audiences with information overload, apparently increase attentiveness and motivate excitement about and interest in a product, else the business model of advertising products exclusively through television infomercials before making them available at retail outlets would not be as profitable a business strategy as it is.

The style of invocation which characterizes minute-long voiceover commercials and what are sometimes referred to as "call to action" segments within 30-minute infomercials sometimes involves the classical figure of *sorites*, or concatenated enthymemes, a chain of product claims containing unstated assumptions, or sometimes simply an enumeration of product features. An example of the latter is provided in Figure 6–1.

The speaker manages to distinguish a series of rapidly articulated, similar sounding items while maintaining the listener's attention and interest through gradual and contextually motivated differentiation of the intonation patterns accompanying each item. The first two items, *baseball bats* and *softball bats*, are contrasted textually and intonationally through different intonation on the initial, stressed syllable. *Baseball bats*, being the standard type for the industry,

---

[3]This applies at least to public speaking. Other research suggests slower rates and dysphonic vocal behavior signaling dysphoric self-deprecation may be somewhat more appreciated in private conversations (Paddock & Nowicki, 1986).

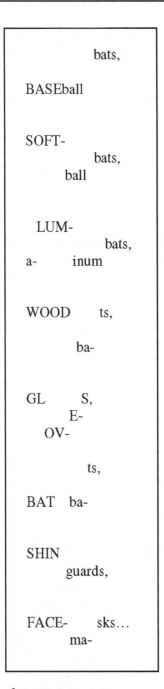

Figure 6–1. Pitch levels in commercial for Aluminumbats.com.

receives initial low tone, while *softball bats*, being an added bonus, receives initial high tone. The intonation assigned to the remaining syllables of each item, like their respective pronunciation, is identical. The contrasting intonation pattern created for *softball bats* is then repeated to highlight the pattern-divergent morphemes within another not necessarily standard product, *aluminum bats*, establishing the expectation for continuation of the pattern for subsequent items in the list. This expectation is partially fulfilled on *wood bats*, but since the word *wood* is a single syllable, the subsequent fall-rise on *bats*, previously assigned to two or three syllables, is compressed to span a single syllable. The compression on *bats* creates a sense of acceleration and invokes subsequent attentiveness, producing the emotional response of anticipation and suspense. This impression is only enhanced when the next item, *gloves*, is presented, since at this point the entire familiar three-tone (high-low-high) pattern is compressed onto a single syllable.[4] Yet despite the increased rate of change in intonation, the textually divergent item *gloves*, which does not contain the either of the morphemes *bats* or *ball*, is easily assimilated and attended to by the listener, in part because the already evoked anticipation of increasing rate of pitch level change has caused the listener to attend more closely to upcoming auditory events, but also in part because the intonation previously assigned to the types of bats is charitably extended to the gloves, thereby symbolically priming a semantic association as well, that these

---

[4]Technically speaking, the intonation on *gloves* actually involves a falling lead-in to a low stressed tone followed by a rise (in Tones and Break Indices notation, H+L*LH%), in contrast to the preceding pattern of high stress followed by a low rise (H*LH%), but this distinction is not necessarily relevant to the elicitation of emotion.

gloves are indeed baseball gloves.[5] A different strategy is subsequently adopted for clearly articulating items for sale that are presumably less strongly semantically associated with bats than gloves are. After an intervening *epanodos*, or return to the low rising pattern that characterized the initial item *baseball bats* when mentioning the equally undistinguished item *bat bats*, the speaker then goes on to assign a new intonation pattern to the items *shin guards* and *facemasks*. This pattern reestablishes the high tone on the initially stressed syllable from before, but departs from previous practice through introducing a down-stepped high tone on the second, unstressed syllable, rather than a low rise. In terms of information processing, the effect is to alert the listener that a new set of items (additional baseball accessories) must be processed on top of the previous set of bats and gloves. In terms of persuasion, the effect is to suggest that the company is taking the customer to a whole new—yet still relatively high—level in terms of product offerings, since now the voice never falls completely, as it did when enumerating types of bats. Since the speaker seems both attentive to the listener's information processing limitations and sensitive to qualitative distinctions among products potentially of interest to the listener, the listener can't help but be impressed that the merchant the speaker represents cares about its customers. Far from being overwhelmed with the great amount of information being presented

per unit time, the listener is more likely to be impressed with the speaker's speed and responsible delivery of his material.

To illustrate the great variety of vocal rhetorical devices practiced in motivationally-oriented speech that is not self-consciously artistic, it may be worth momentarily examining another commercial created by the same company for an exercise costume designed to trap perspiration inside, thereby increasing physical activity and loss of weight (presumably weight in water, despite claims to the contrary). To sell the Real Sauna sauna suit, the company relies on vocal expression to help resolve *enantiosis*, or seemingly paradoxical contrast. Vocal expression is first used to convince the listener that it is quite possible to "DO a LIttle; LOSE a LOT!" when jumping around in a plastic casing. Parallel high-low-high-low intonation is used on each of the two phrases, but whereas pitch changes discontinuously from high to low tone, across syllables, in the sentence, "DO a LIttle," in the sentence "LOSE a LOT" by contrast, a sliding fall from high to low on "LOSE" and "LOT" prolongs these syllables and metaphorically suggests that an extreme reduction in weight (pitch height) can be achieved through small effort (mere manipulation of the vocal tract, a rather effortless physical action).[6] A bit later, another *enantiosis* appears, "MELT unWANTed BOdy FAT aWAY . . . with the SAME aMOUNT of EXerCISE, but with TWICE the reSULTS!"

---

[5]Rhetorically, this is a variant of *anacolutha*, nonreciprocal substitution, to the extent that while bat intonation assigned to gloves can reinforce that the gloves at issue are indeed mitts, thereby relieving the listener of the cognitive burden of momentarily imagining evening gloves, gardening gloves, or snow gloves, the reverse assignment of intonation, from gloves to bats, would not necessarily prime the semantic association between the two pieces of sporting equipment.

[6]In addition to contrasting text-to-tone alignment, another contributor to the emotion-inducing contrast is the fact that the high tone portion of "LOSE" is audibly higher than the high tone portion of the corresponding word in the previous sentence, "DO," producing a relatively more precipitous fall on "LOSE," a fact which

This time, the speaker establishes *isocolon*, or parallel rhythms. Initially the rhythms are trochaic, but after the word "EXerCISE" they change to anapests. The initial four syllables and two stresses per unit time used to describe the effort involved (both before and after use of the sauna suit) give way to three syllables and one stress in perceptually the same unit of time when the speaker describes the final outcome. The shift is a vocal metaphor for the notion that the listener will still be working hard, but with a leaner, more efficient outcome. The effect is to inspire the listener to feel that greater weight loss with no additional effort is indeed possible with this product. As far as emotion goes, the listener can feel more confident about the company's claims because, consciously or not, she has heard the spokesperson himself model the exercise product's possibilities on the smaller yet still physiological scale of articulatory motion.

These examples clearly demonstrate the potential for relations among rhythm and intonation patterns in discourse to elicit emotional response. Even so, there are those who would claim that it is not the apprehension of metaphorical relations among sound patterns that is responsible for emotional response to these examples but rather a confluence of acoustic variables tuned to precise parameters and primitively apprehended as a primordial blueprint for a given emotion. Despite evidence to the contrary from other authors' empirical studies,

studies that suggest it is mimetic gestures, analogues between acoustic or articulatory motions, and situation-relevant or text-appropriate mental or physical processes, that create emotional response (Fónagy, 2001, pp. 87–173), naysayers may insist that a given emotion can be induced in listeners simply by cranking up or turning down dials on a speech synthesizer labeled "pitch height," "pitch range" (extreme endpoints), "pitch register," (average height), "pitch variation" (frequency of change in height), or "speech rate." To show that absolute or relative amounts of such features are not responsible for many emotional responses induced by speech, it seems necessary to provide a different sort of evidence forthwith. These subsequent examples will demonstrate that despite use of wide patch range, significant variation in pitch register and speech rate, a variety of pitch levels within intonation patterns, and variation among intonation patterns and rhythmic patterns, a speaker may nevertheless fail to induce any emotion other than disorientation and alienation through the use of incongruous prosodic relations over time.

The Cart before the Chimera

Another reason to consider instances in which emotional response to speech is compromised rather than enhanced by prosodic structural relations is to put to

---

would be entirely overlooked in a TOBI style phonologically-based transcription system (H* L vs. H*+L) that treats the height of high tones relative to each other as a gradient phenomenon, one perhaps iconic of heightened or subdued emotion but not metaphorically representative of states or behaviors contributing to emotional response. Once again, the important issue is not how high the second sentence's initial high tone is relative to that of the first sentence, but the mere fact that it is noticeably higher, though phonologically parsimonious transcription cannot indicate this. The speaker is not necessarily getting more emotional or conveying more emotion on "LOSE" than he was on "DO." He is using the high tone on "LOSE" to draw a contrast with "DO," to evoke an emotional response through intervening cognitive processing.

rest other experts' claims that departure from canonical prosody per se is the primary impetus for disorientation and alienation among listeners. In his conference paper, "Cadence's Role in Speech: Complete the Arc," corporate speaking coach Jerry Weissman, acclaimed author of *Presenting to Win: The Art of Telling Your Story* and *In the Line of Fire: How to Handle Tough Questions . . . When It Counts,* countered my claims for the comprehensibility and persuasiveness of rapid, uninterrupted, information-dense speech with footage of President George W. Bush addressing the public before and after his having received speech coaching. Weissman's examples purported to demonstrate that information-dense monolog is at great risk of confusing and alienating audiences, of producing the emotion of revulsion in place of whatever the speaker hoped to elicit, unless it presents one idea at a time, each idea separated by a phrase-final fall in pitch followed by a breath-long pause.

However correct Weissman may be, it would be unfortunate if his findings motivated speech coaches to become the elocutionary equivalents of overzealous surgeons, their restrictive admonitions tantamount to excising a patient's vocal folds to correct a minor dysphonia. Given no reason to expect otherwise, listeners may indeed expect speech to conform to Weissman's principles, yet speakers may have good reason to violate these expectations for emotional effect. In a sentence spoken in a stroller commercial (Target Market Advertising Group), "Fabric net storage pouches located in the rear and sides of the stroller cart provide space for purses,

diaper bags, books, or anything else you need," the word *cart* might be expected to receive rising intonation paralleling that of *pouches* to indicate that the phrase it completes, "located in the rear sides of the stroller cart" is a parenthetical appositive, characterizing rather than identifying the "pouches." Instead, the word *cart* is assigned a low tone following a fall, suggesting that the utterance has ended with the word *cart* and that the speaker is speaking in incomplete sentences to detail a list of product features. Yet the sentence continues on immediately thereafter. Consistent with Weissman's recommendations, the excerpt separates two ideas through intervening falling intonation, but contrary to Weissman's recommendation, there is no pause or breath after the fall, hence insufficient cognitive and emotional respite for Weissman's presumably easily overburdened listener. Furthermore, since the fall does not conform to a clause boundary but only to a prepositional phrase boundary, the fall is not typical of conversational speech and hence likely to be unexpected. Yet I would argue that rather than confusing and alienating the listener, this is the sort of speech that simultaneously draws attention and enthralls, speech on which successful advertisers pride themselves. What is actually happening is that the speaker is producing a false ending, a rhetorical move which I suspect may be quite common in commercial voiceover.[7] Variants may include a contextually appropriate ending followed by an unexpected continuation, or something more akin to a device referred to in classical rhetoric as *paraprosdokian*, a premature or pre-

---

[7]Indeed, it can be heard in the Target Market's Winning Edge commercial available on the same Web site.

emptory ending or one inconsistent with the implications of prior context. In either case, the information processing value of such segmentation is in assuring that listeners thoroughly process a complex statement. Whether the pitch fall is expected but not the material that follows it, or whether the longer phrase is expected but not the tonal caesura that interrupts it, processing of the complete proposition is preempted and occurs in stages. The gist of the proposition presented in the material leading up to the false ending (in this case, the placement of the fabric pouches in relation to the stroller cart) is comprehended before subsequent material (in this case, the function of the pouches) is integrated. Whether forced to account for the unexpected divergence or quite expecting to stop early, the listener is not able to suspend apprehension of the sense of the passage until having parsed the syntax of the entire sentence, behavior which might result in comprehension of fewer details, since, as Weissman would argue, greater demands would then be placed on the listener's attention. At the same time, the persuasive value of the technique is in symbolically compelling the listener to realize, through her retrospective reanalysis of the speech pattern either mistakenly presumed to be terminal or unexpectedly introduced, that a valuable product feature that might initially seem quite sufficient in itself (in this case, convenient placement of the pouches) is merely a component of a superset of equally desirable features (which in this case includes an unexpectedly great vari-

ety of uses for the pouches). The concomitant emotional response is one of being overwhelmed, but by the value of the product, not by the amount of auditory information presented. The passage departs significantly from Weissman's prescriptions, yet manages to be both comprehensible and exciting.

Nevertheless, it may not be clear from this successful example of emotional communication how much of its success can be attributed to the more straightforward explanation, its abiding by Weissman's admonition to "complete the arc after each idea," and how much to something as seemingly baroque and recondite as *paraprosdokian*. To better reconcile Weissman's and my perspectives and clarify the contribution of each, it may help to examine instances of information-dense motivational speech that initially appear to conform to rhetorical best practices both I and Weissman outlined at the conference, yet which I suspect are likely to fail to achieve their communicative and emotion-inducing objectives owing to information processing challenges they introduce. It will be trivially apparent that it is not violation of Weissman's putative canonical forms that is responsible for the failure of communication, but rather unmotivated or incongruous parallelism or variation, and it will become implicitly apparent that neither mean nor differential measures of acoustic properties can account for either successful or unsuccessful communication of the emotions discussed, that only categorical acoustic distinctions are involved.[8] At the same time, the

---

[8]This is so even in cases where the behavior responsible for success or failure in communicating emotion involves changes in numbers of rhythmic units or events per unit time. In the first place, as demonstrated in Lehiste (1977) and Couper-Kuhlen (1993), a repeating series of stressed syllables with the same or differing

identification of sources of confusion in the examples of motivational speech presented, followed by an exposition of how each problem might have been avoided, will suggest how speakers attempting to convey a multiplicity of ideas in a concise format may maximize their potential to be simultaneously both comprehensible and exciting.

Raising a Stink: The Perils of Imperfect Parallels

Speech may adhere strongly to one of Weissman's prescriptions, namely, perceptibly long pauses between syntactic units and consistently falling phrase-final intonation, while conforming to a best practice implicit in my analysis of the Aluminumbats.com and stroller cart examples, namely, the exploitation of parallelism and contrast in intonation patterns, yet nevertheless be infelicitous and confusing. This is evident in a passage from a training tape for delicatessen employees selling Swift brand prepared foods, in which listeners are encouraged to become familiar with a variety of cheeses and feature them in a decorative cheese platter. As illustrated in Figure 6–2, the speaker begins by introducing Pasteur, a French cheese, with a high falling tone on the name of the product itself (H* L on the syllable "-TEUR,"), but a more precipitous fall to stressed low tone on its characterization (H+L* L on the word "French").

The faster fall to stressed low tone on *French* suggests that while *Pasteur* itself may be notable, French cheeses in general are heavy and strong, a sentiment reinforced by the text of the subsequent elaboration "like a very strong brick." After a significant pause, the speaker initiates a parallel noun phrase to introduce the next cheese, Danish Jarlsberg. His high falling tones on the characterizations "from DENmark" and "SWISS-type cheese" contrast with the scooped low stress on *French* in the prior noun phrase, reinforcing the weightiness of the French cheese and encouraging the listener to consider national origin to be a determining factor in cheese character. In the third noun phrase, however, something very disturbing happens. The word *French* recurs incongruously, floating along on an unstressed high tone, suggesting it is not particularly heavy. A listener seeking to resolve the incongruity might attribute apparent intonational neglect of the word *French* to the fact that it has been mentioned already in the discourse. However, the stressed high tone fall on the word that immediately follows *French*, the word *cheese*, parallels the intonation

---

numbers of intervening unstressed syllables is only perceptually isochronous—slightly longer and shorter units are mentally stretched or truncated so they sound as if they are of equal duration. Variation across such units also appears to be responded to as a categorically significant approximation of a measurable difference like "as many extra beats as expected ones" or "double time now." Intermediate values and proportions that do not have culturally or experientially salient associations for listeners have no place in this analysis. For example, in the Alumniumbats.com commercial, when the listener hears the acceleration caused by compression of fall-rise to a single syllable on *wood bats*, it is immaterial whether the span of the fall-rise shifted from three syllables (in *aluminum bats*) to one, or from two syllables (in *softball bats*) to one, particularly since the final two unstressed syllables in "aLUMinum" may be heard to occur in the same amount of time as the single unstressed syllable in "SOFTball." What matters is that the speech sounds at one point faster, at another "now even faster," not that it is twice as fast or three times as fast.

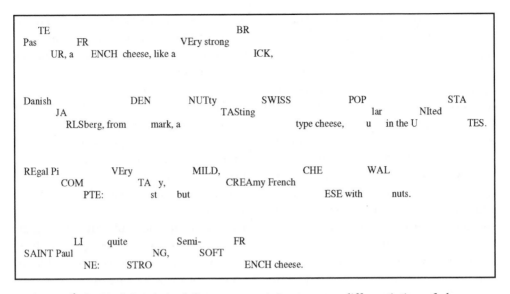

Figure 6–2. Pitch levels in delicatessen training tape on differentiation of cheeses.

of "DENmark" and "SWISS-type," abrogating this pretext by assigning high falling tone to French cheese by association. To make matters worse, the two words that immediately precede the second instance of the word *French* are *mild* and *creamy*. Less and less able to reconcile these contradictions, the listener is then told of a fourth cheese, Saint Pauline. She is told this cheese is "quite strong," a notion which is reinforced with a stressed low tone (L* H H% rising from the word "STRONG"). It too, we learn, is a French cheese, and its strength is reinforced with another fast drop to stressed low tone (H+L* on the word "FRENCH"). In another context, the return of the word *French* with its original intonation pattern might be comforting and reassuring, but here it is disconcerting. Any charitable shift in perspective the listener may have made when hearing about Regale Picompte is now undermined by the contrasting description of Saint Pauline. What is the listener to make of French

cheeses? How is she supposed to feel about them? Are they heavy and strong? Or light and mild? Is national origin even a useful way of distinguishing qualities of cheeses, or did it only seem that way? Perhaps the listener should have been attending to the seemingly contrasting degrees of nuttiness.

The intended audience of deli novices, less likely than their masters to perceive the relative gravity of various fermentation formuli to be a matter of survival, is more likely to dismiss these issues without reflection than equivocate over them. Unable to reconcile the apparent contradictions, employees in training will most likely quit attending to the talk and think about something else. Rather than inspiring confidence in listeners, encouraging them to learn from the speaker and take his advice on what products to feature in their stores, this passage confuses listeners and elicits the emotions of frustration and alienation, and it does so despite its adherence to Weissman's principles for achieving intonational clarity. Yet if a voiceover artist were to attend to how repeated mentions of various referents are intoned in different contexts, he might more clearly convey the attitude he hopes listeners will adopt toward those referents. He could motivate his listeners while presenting a large number of ideas in a small amount of time.

Because the Swift Deli training tapes are half hour lessons designed for captive audiences of employees, who are presumably paid to stay awake and listen to them, the tapes can afford to induce a feeling of monotony through long pauses and repeated phrase-final falling intonation. Such vocal features may also be appropriate for political speeches, the content of which listeners have a vested interest in attending to regardless of whether the presentation is inspiring or insipid. In information-dense motivational speech to uncommitted audiences, however, such as radio commercials and televangelism, Weissman's principles may be considered too time-consuming or energy depleting to be profitably adopted. Speech in these situations as well may confuse listeners and fail to motivate desired emotions, but not necessarily for lack of adherence to Weissman's principles. Both successful and unsuccessful speakers inspire inferences about their topics through similarities and differences in how they articulate parallel and contrasting syntactic constructions and lexical items. Successful speakers have a natural facility for putting these relations in the service of their communicative goals. Less successful speakers may be less sensitive to these relations, but they can learn to modify their utterances through understanding how they are likely to be interpreted.

The perils of intonational parallelism are again evident in Figure 6–3a and Figure 6–3b, contrasting two versions of a golden age radio commercial for Vitalis, a brand of hair tonic.

One version discusses Bob Allison of the Minnesota Twins, the other, Brooks Robinson, at the time the American League's most valuable player. At points, the texts of the two versions are identical except for the name of the celebrity sports hero, but the intonation patterns differ. The first version (Figure 6–3a) begins impressively enough by emphasizing the competitive advantage of the product through a modification contour, a phonological representation of which would be low-high-low-high, with the first high tone generally stressed and the second sometimes stressed as well. More significantly for an analysis of illocutionary affect and social effect, the first high tone of this contour is always higher than the second high tone, iconically connoting something higher than high, or a significant modification to something that is already significant.[9] The modification contour occurs first in the course of four syllables, "to STAY in PLACE," and is then accelerated and compressed to transpire across the two syllables in "withOUT" creating an energetic feeling of rushing toward a destination. That destination is the word "GREASE,"

---

[9]A diametrically opposed meaning may be attributed to use of the same contour in western parts of the UK like Liverpool, as in the phrase "It's ALL the same to ME," in which a lower second high tone on "ME" may serve to modify the higher first high tone on "ALL," suggesting a more restrained, balanced take on a point of contention, but the meaning is still motivated by the iconic relationship between the two high tones.

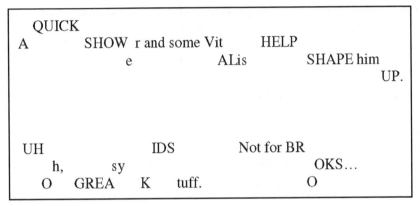

Figure 6–3. a. Pitch levels in confusing television commercial for hair tonic. **b.** Pitch levels in more understandable television commercial for hair tonic.

which is articulated with a precipitous fall, a low tone stress preceded by a momentary scooped down-stepped high tone (!H+L* L L%). The steep fall and emphasis on low tone provides a strong resolution to the sentence. So far so good. We know the product is distinctive in that it achieves its desirable effects without use of a particularly undesirable element.

Afterwards, though, the communication rapidly degenerates. The modification contour recurs on the admonition "LookOUT," which gets our attention,

particularly since it rhymes with and has the same intonation contour as "with-OUT" in the previous sentence, but the phrase that follows, "GREAsy KIDS' stuff," ends with a down-stepped high tone preceding a stressed low (!H+L* L L%), precisely paralleling the ending of previous sentence on the word *grease*. Once again we have a strong resolution in terms of pitch, just as definitive as before, but the words *greasy kids' stuff* seem to belie this. Then we hear "NOT for BOB," which again falls, equally definitively, to a stressed low tone on "BOB."

What are we to make of this? A moment ago we were told this is the product for Bob, and that it wasn't greasy. Now it is equally certain that it's greasy and that Bob doesn't like it. The speaker subsequently resolves the incongruity by clarifying that he has begun speaking about the competitor's product: "Creams and oils plaster hair down, make it look and feel greasy, but Vitalis grooms hair naturally," but by this point it is too late; the listener is too busy absorbing the barrage of words to devote much attention to retrospective reanalysis and error recovery. The listener is less likely to think, "Oh, how clever; I wasn't expecting that surprising shift in focus," than "This guy seems to be chattering on in the same manner without thinking about what he's saying. Why should I even listen?" Given the processing limitations on rapid speech, the listener's emotional response is less likely to be one of amusement

than one of annoyance. The speaker has used intonation patterns in a way that may be rhetorically masterful, but not in a way that can be easily processed in the temporal span of an utterance.

The other version of the commercial, illustrated in Figure 6–3b, is more successful. The phrase, "A quick SHOWer and some ViTALis HELPS SHAPE him UP," reintroduces the product and ends with a resolutely final stressed low tone, but in this version, it is not only the admonition "UH Oh" (analogous to "LookOUT" in the previous example) that features contrastive intonation. Here, in contrast to the concluding low stress on "UP," the final stress in the phrase "GREAsy KIDS' stuff" employs high tone preceded by a momentary scoop upward (L+H* on "KIDS'"). The final word "stuff" receives low tone, but unlike "UP" in the previous utterance, it is not stressed.[10] The difference between the final stressed low tone

---

[10]It is the final pitch accent, or stress-tone alignment, that is most important to and memorable for the listener, not the pitch of the final word in an utterance. In part this is because unstressed syllables—those that are less prolonged—are iconic of reduced import. However, the significance of the stressed syllable may also relate to the fact that while it is possible to have a stressed tone with no unstressed syllables preceding or following it (just silence or another stressed tone), it is not possible to have an unstressed tone with no stressed syllables preceding or following it; in any utterance, some syllable will always be perceived as central and hence stressed. On an implication-realization model of vocal expression, it is possible that stressed syllables generate the expectation that additional pitches on unstressed syllables may follow. The second sentence in the successful Vitalis commercial has what in poetic prosody is referred to as a *feminine* (unstressed) ending ("KIDS' stuff"), the first a *masculine* (stressed) ending ("UP"), but the first sentence may generate the expectation that additional unstressed tones will conclude that sentence, as in " . . . HELP SHAPE him UP a bit . . . " rather than just "HELP SHAPE him UP." Since it is not known with what pitch these final unexpressed syllables might be articulated, it does not make sense to compare the final unstressed syllable in "KIDS' stuff" to any counterpart in the first sentence, but it always make sense to compare the final stressed syllables of two utterances, since there will always be a stress in each utterance.

A generative phonological account of the contrast, one which would posit the existence of unarticulated phantom tones, would reach a similar conclusion through a somewhat different argument. The generativist would say that the low stress on "UP" is actually followed by an unstressed low phrase tone and an unstressed low boundary tone that simply are not heard or phonetically realized since there is only one syllable on which to articulate all the tones. That is, these tones, compressed into the space of a single syllable, exist in the mind, but owing to our physical frailties, not in the voice or the ear. They are not unrealized potential patterns but mental constructs, somewhat like the illusion of an F0 contour that can be reconstituted in a listener's mind by playing its higher formants. These underlying default patterns contrast minimally with final rise to high tone after the low tone stress. The unarticulated unstressed low tones on "UP" would parallel the articulated low tone on unstressed "stuff" in the next sentence, but they would not be distinctive or worthy of comparison with their counterpart in "stuff," since they would constitute more of a predictable default (or "unmarked") pattern than a deliberate (if unconscious) choice on the part of the speaker.

in the preceding utterance and the final stressed high tone in this one provides sufficient contrast to alert the listener to the fact that something different is being discussed now. The topic change is subsequently reinforced by another contrasting pattern at the end of the next phrase, "NOT for BROOKS," which ends with stressed high tone followed by a low tone and a phonetically lower, categorically relatively high tone (or mid tone) at the phrase boundary (H* L H%). Here the listener realizes the speaker can't be talking about the same thing, that Brooks must now have found some unidentified greasy product that is definitely not Vitalis. While there is no amusing incongruity to be resolved here, there is no confusion either. The contrasting stressed high tones on "KIDS" and "BROOKS" alert the listener to watch out for competitors' products and recognize how they differ from that which the speaker is promoting.

In the successful version of the Vitalis commercial, departure from a preestablished intonation pattern prepares the listener for a change of topic, while in the failed version, intonational parallelism prevents the listener from anticipating this change. This suggests that listeners process intonation patterns as a means of structuring and relating arguments in a discourse, not just as a way of disambiguating syntactic structures or expressing speaker attitude. Curiously, during a stint teaching English to foreign speakers as a graduate student, I found that native speakers of East Asian lexical tone languages are often extraordinarily sensitive to intonation, and when learning American English, are generally adept at mastering intonation paradigms for various syntactic patterns and emotional expressions in casual conversation, adopting native-sounding pitch patterns for everything from parenthetical asides to humorous caricatures. Yet it is often extremely difficult for native English speakers to follow these same speakers when they are presenting academic papers aloud in English, quite possibly because the speakers are concentrating on articulating smaller units of speech and have never been coached in how native English speakers employ intonation across larger discourse structures. A native English speaker who fails to recognize a crucial relationship or contrast in an East Asian speaker's presentation may become inattentive, and when the listener's attention returns, first to the speaker's voice and only afterwards to the speaker's actual words, she will have been provided no appropriate preattentive tonal clues to the structure of the argument that can help her to determine how the words she is now hearing fit into the presentation. She may continue to listen politely without comprehension, but if she is truly interested in the topic, she may need to ask for a copy of the paper. Though she may have understood every word she attended to, she will not have been certain of the speaker's main points or how the speaker felt about his topic, and this may cause her to feel that the speaker is uncharismatic and a poor communicator. By attending to intonation patterns across utterances, foreign speakers of a language may become better presenters in languages in which they have already developed a good deal of fluency.

Squozen Out: The Dangers of Unanticipated Departures

While divergence from a preestablished intonation pattern helps the listener anticipate a change of topic in the successful Vitalis commercial, divergence in vocal expression itself can be confusing and alienating if it is not motivated clearly enough for it to be either anticipated or easily reconciled. This may be less of a problem for intonation contours than for metrical sequences, since the latter occupy longer time spans and place correspondingly greater demands on the listener's memory. Figure 6–4 presents a commercial voiceover that on paper would appear to exemplify the masterful manipulation of metrical patterns to achieve rhetorical ends, yet which sounds as if the speaker doesn't know what he's talking about, rattling on without paying much attention to his script.

The phrase, "Four big delicious glassfuls," suffers perhaps in part from inappropriate intonation (e.g., down-step on "big"), but mostly from the fact that in a context where the speaker has been carefully enunciating metrical patterns, it is not immediately apparent to a listener why he should vocally emphasize his main point, that one can obtain four items (four big glasses of orange juice) from a small can of concentrate, by assigning five stresses to the four glasses and additional stresses to the can. If four of the five stresses had been articulated at the same pitch level, or with some regular pattern, and the fifth at a different level, as a culmination, the speaker might then seem to have recognized the unit of four in his voice, but instead each of the five stresses is assigned its own autonomous pitch level: high, down-stepped high, even higher high, low, and middle. Here's a pedantic sounding guy who's supposed to be telling us exactly how many servings we can get out of this

PERCEPTUALLY ISOCHRONOUS UNITS BEFORE PAUSE

0	1	2	3	4	4'	5	6	7
You	WANT your	FAmily to	HAVE the	BEST,	the	NATural	VItamin	C,
The	KIND you	GET from	FRESH,	FROzen		ORange	JUICE from	FLORida,
And	WITH all	THIS,						
It's	SO con-	VENient and	THRIFty:					
	FOUR	BIG de-	LICious	GLASS-		FULS		
from	ONE	LIttle	CAN.					

- Each row represents a pause-delimited utterance.
- Lower rows occur later in time.
- Syllables written in all capital letters are stressed.
- Unit zero ("0") represents an unstressed upbeat to the first stressed perceptually isochronous unit of each pause-delimited utterance.
- Unit 4-prime (shaded) represents a natural subdivision between the first 4 and final 3 stress units in the 7-unit utterances, where a "Strong-weak-Medium-weak pattern" on the first 4 stresses begins to be repeated.
- In the first row, unit 4-prime also signals a momentary pause and upbeat to the fifth stress unit.

Figure 6–4. Perceptually isochronous stress-initiated metrical units in radio commercial for Florida orange juice.

can of orange juice concentrate, but it sounds like he can't even count. What an idiot. Why should we listen to him? Perhaps because his speech is as intricately structured as a piece of 12-tone serial music, the structure of which no one can hear. The passage begins with parallel chains of seven perceptually isochronous units, these chains distinguished from each other by pauses. Because of an additional pause after the first four beats, in the first chain, each seven-beat chain may be heard as containing two sets of four beats, one complete, the other with the final beat missing. The missing fourth beat in each of the three-beat subsets encourages the listener to suspend judgment and attend to the next point. At this point, the patterns become less clear. A somewhat unsettling two-beat chain follows, followed by a somewhat more reassuring three-beat chain. It is possible that what is being presented is a series of increasingly longer chains, each a beat longer than the last, to make the listener feel as if she will continue to derive increasing benefits from drinking Florida orange juice. If so, the listener would expect the next chain to contain four beats, but instead, it contains five (FOUR, BIG-, LIC-, GLASS- and -FULS). In other commercial contexts involving preestablished metrical patterns, the addition of an extra beat may excite the listener, suggesting that more than what one might expect is available in a product, and at the same time permit the speaker to cram more information into a short utterance without losing the listener's attention. Here, however, there is no preestablished metrical pattern against which to evaluate the additional beat. The initial four-beat pattern within the alternating 4-3 seven-beat chain has been aban-doned, and it is not yet clear what has replaced it. The two- and three-beat chains suggest an inchoate 2-3-4 series, but this incipient impression is undermined by the subsequent use of five beats rather than the expected four. Because the listener cannot be sure what is happening metrically, he cannot account for the incongruity between the number of glasses described and the number of stresses used to describe them, and instead of sounding impressive, the orange juice commercial sounds stupid or at least, if not any dumber than most commercials, not worth attending to. The speaker squeezes out an extra beat, but rather than hanging excitedly on his extra words, the listener feels locked out of whatever rhetorical contrivance the speaker has developed.

In information-dense motivational speech, it is neither the challenge of subconsciously identifying and connecting complex patterns of vocal behaviors nor the high density of information per unit time that causes a listener to become dazed and confused where one might expect another emotional response. Rather, it is the fact that at times, variation in vocal expression is so great that it fails to establish expectations for continuations or predictable development of antecedent sound patterns to which subsequently articulated sound patterns can be compared. Without an obvious baseline from which to identify structural correspondences and divergences, the listener cannot react emotionally to vocal developments over time and must base her emotional response on what she hears at the present moment as mediated by stylistic and cultural conventions and corresponding expectations for the development of a discourse genre.[11] As Markman and Gentner (1993) put it, differences must be "alignable," that is, represent divergence from a shared framework, in order to be easily recognizable. Because apples and oranges are both fruits and round objects of similar size, it is much easier to describe how apples differ from oranges than to describe how apples differ from, say, financial advisors. While it is immediately apparent that apples and oranges differ in color and flavor, it requires far more mental resources than are available during preattentive processing of vocal expressions to identify what distinguishes apples from financial advisors.

Sounding Poor— Making Poor Choices

Apples don't have much reason to inspire feelings of security and confidence among those who encounter them, but financial advisors do. They would do well to take some lessons from Suze [sic] Orman of public television fame, best selling author of *The Road to Wealth* and *Nine Steps to Financial Freedom*, and generally highly inspirational televangelist for personal financial planning. But even Suze is capable of some indiscretions when it comes to selecting speech patterns that can best convey her message. For clear communication, it is not sufficient for parallelism to be applied

appropriately and patterns established sufficiently strongly to make divergence recognizable. It is equally crucial that divergent sound patterns be contextually appropriate. As illustrated in Figure 6-5, from a public television fundraising special, Orman conforms to Weissman's best practices, employing a series of nine relatively short phrases separated from each other by breath-long pauses, eight of the nine (all but the penultimate) ending with falling intonation, all at a far slower rate of delivery than is characteristic of the speech in most commercials.

In further conformity with Weissman's requirements for clear communication, though with all due apologies to Ms. Orman, she introduces far fewer new ideas per unit time than is characteristic of much commercial speech. She also conforms to my own best practices, by establishing and repeating a clear pattern of three stresses per utterance to convey simple truths: "So you have GOT to MAKE a STANCE. And you have GOT to UNderSTAND. That TRUTH creATES MONey." After three iterations, the three-stress pattern is obscured somewhat: on the two-beat utterance, "it always HAS, it always WILL," one might expect a third stress on the second "ALways," but this would compromise parallelism with the first unstressed "always." At any rate, the three-beat pattern returns after the next pause: "because the TRUTH makes YOU feel POWerful." The listener by now feels secure and reassured, but when Suze begins to describe what the listener

---

[11]This is not to say that in the absence of predictable temporal patterns, an emotional response cannot be produced by relating sound structures to each other, but these relations are between simultaneous events, for instance, between text and tune at a particular moment, or pitch and rhythm, or cultural expectations brought to bear on the present and actual manifestation (Ferdinand de Saussure's paradigmatic relations), not between temporal patterns developed over the course of a dialog or monolog (Saussure's syntagmatic relations).

PERCEPTUALLY ISOCHRONOUS UNIT BEFORE PAUSE--Analysis 1

0	1	2	3	4	5	6
So you have	GOT to	MAKE a	STANCE			
And you have	GOT to	UNder-	STAND			
That	TRUTH cre-	ATES	MONey.			
It always	HAS, it always	WILL,				
Because the	TRUTH	MAKES you feel	POWerful.			
When you feel	POWerful,					
You	MAKE the	RIGHT de-	CIsions	WITH your	MOney;	
You	KNOW	HOW to	MAKE a de-	CIsion,		
Cuz it's a de-	Cision	BASED out of	POWer			
Which	STEMS from	BEing	TRUTHful	WITH your-	SELF and your	FInances.

PERCEPTUALLY ISOCHRONOUS UNIT BEFORE PAUSE--Analysis 2

0	1	2	3	4	5	6
So you have	GOT to	MAKE a	STANCE			
And you have	GOT to	UNder-	STAND			
That	TRUTH cre-	ATES	MONey.			
It always	HAS, it always	WILL,				
Because the	TRUTH	MAKES you feel	POWerful.			
When you feel	POWerful, you	MAKE the	RIGHT de-	CIsions	WITH your	MOney;
You	KNOW	HOW to	MAKE a de-	Cision,		
Cuz it's a de-	Cision	BASED out of	POWer			
Which	STEMS from	BEing	TRUTHful	WITH your-	SELF and your	FInances.

Each row represents a pause-delimited utterance.
- Lower rows occur later in time.
- Syllables written in all capital letters are stressed.
- Unit zero ("0") represents an unstressed upbeat to the first stressed perceptually isochronous unit of each pause-delimited utterance.
- Shaded cells indicate a point of ambiguity regarding the presence or absence of a pause, since the word "Powerful" differs from the other utterance-final stress units in that pitch does not fall to low tone.

Figure 6–5. Perceptually isochronous stress-initiated metrical units in speech of motivational speaker on personal financial management.

can do with this newfound feeling of power, the stress pattern becomes suddenly quite vague. She pauses slightly after "When you feel POWerful, . . . " and then introduces a series of five stresses: "you MAKE the RIGHT decisions WITH your MONey." Whether the number of stresses per utterance has shifted to five beats or to six, it is certainly no longer three. It suddenly becomes no small challenge to interpret Suze's metrical patterns as guidance for applying one's newfound power to structure one's financial mat-

ters, because one apparently cannot predict the future and cannot plan for what one will hear next. The next utterance, containing as it does four stresses, provides no further clarification. "You KNOW HOW to MAKE a deCIsion," Suze says, but the listener can't really be sure if he does at this point, since he can't figure out why Suze would start arbitrarily varying her metrical patterns at this crucial juncture. The three-stress pattern then returns, but only momentarily, with "'cuz it's a deCIsion BASED out of POWer," the next utterance containing six stresses: "which STEMS from BEing TRUTHful WITH yourSELF and your FInances." No pause or syntactic break appears within this utterance to suggest a division into two sets of three stresses. The strongly established three-beat pattern has proven useless for understanding the complexities of high finance. Desperately grasping at straws, the astute listener whose eyes have not yet glazed over may attempt to match the three-beat pattern reappearing in "'cuz it's a deCIsion BASED out of POWer" to the subsequent six-beat utterance, listening most closely to that utterance's initial three beats and treating the remaining three beats as being extraneous to the pattern and hence of less importance. But doing this only confuses matters. A listener who attempts to align the three-beat metrical pattern of the penultimate utterance with the first three beats of the final utterance and infer a relation between the two hears only "'cuz it's a deCIsion BASED out of POWer, which STEMS from BEing TRUTHful." Given that the listener has already heard that the truth makes you feel powerful, this conclusion, bereft of any further qualification, smacks of rather apple-shaped, tautological reasoning: the fact that P implies Q implies that Q is implied by P. The astute listener is left to wonder what exactly is being said about his financial decisions apart from reiterating their aforementioned etiology in the domain of veracity. By either account, mine or Weissman's, the passage should be a model for communicatively effective prosody, but whatever the value of the financial advice, the passage is instead a brilliantly conceived and flawlessly executed recipe for communicative disaster and psychic ruin. The best choice in terms of retaining the audience's

attention would have been to maintain the three-beat chains of perceptually isochronous units or to vary the voice in a way that would make clear and contextually appropriate reference to them. The worst choice was to veer off in unpredictable directions. It may sound like a platitude when uttered by anyone but Suze, but making poor choices, however well executed, can make you sound poor. Judicious selection of metrical patterns, on the other hand, preserving conformity when appropriate and abandoning it when it accentuates other aspects of your presentation, can make your voice sound rich and can help others to feel equally rich in wisdom, understanding, and concomitant emotional experience.

Two out of Three Experts Agree

The examples of unsuccessful communication presented here illustrate three types of vocal behavior that can compromise a speaker's efforts to influence a listener's emotions. In each case, incongruous relations in vocal expression, rather than surreptitiously supporting the speaker's message, call the listener's attention more to the incongruous manner of speaking than to the message, resulting in a listener's emotional alienation from the speaker and his message. In the first case, vocal parallelism was shown to be inappropriate because of divergence in the message of the text. In the second case, vocal divergence was found to be imperceptible because a base pattern was not clearly established. In the third case, vocal divergence was seen to be perceptible but inappropriate and unmotivated by the text. Contrary to

Weissman's logic, in none of these cases is a particular prosodic paradigm per se (or its absence, like failure to pause between certain intonation units) implicated, but only the ineffective sequential and simultaneous arrangement of these paradigms, that is, a speaker's indiscreet selection of pattern sequences. These sequences either fail to direct the ear's attention to significant relations among prosodic elements and between these and textual elements in a discourse or misdirect the ear's attention to unintended and misleading relations of this sort. However, despite the evident challenges involved in producing effective rapid delivery of information-rich motivational speech, in none of these cases does the nature of the communicative problem preclude a solution involving speech patterns that would require of listeners equally expeditious preattentive perception of relations among vocal expressions, relations as complex as those that characterize the problematic examples themselves.

The key notion arising from this analysis, that it is not complexity per se but failure to take account of (or apparent inattention to) listeners' own expectations for complexity that confuses and alienates listeners, thereby interfering with emotional response, may still seem controversial. Indeed, an empirical study in the area of music psychology would seem to argue to the contrary. In a study of musical information processing by Carlsen (1976), cited in Unyk & Carlsen (1987, p. 6), listeners made the fewest errors transcribing fulfillments of strong melodic expectancies and made the most errors transcribing violations of strong melodic expectancies, with performance on fulfillments and violations of weak expectancies falling in between. This finding seems to suggest that listeners may have difficulty processing departures from culturally or temporally established sound patterns. That is, Carlsen's finding may seem to square better with a prescriptive approach to prosody like Weissman's, in which we are told we must keep things simple in order to be understood. However, violations of strong expectancies must be justified in order to be meaningful, and out of the context of the musical performance in the concert hall, in the psychology lab, listeners may have good reason not to believe what they are hearing. When experimenters butcher tunes for the sole purpose of tripping up unsuspecting listeners, it is no wonder listeners have as much trouble following the melodies as they would assimilating unmotivated prosodic departures. Set the expectancy violations in the context of other musical phrases implicating the need for the violations, and one is likely to find listeners far less likely to censor their initial perceptions, as likely to trust their ears as their upbringing.

More recent research on musical expectancies seems to have taken these objections into account. Schmuckler (1989) recognized that in defining expectancies as continuations which one set of subjects sang when asked to complete a tune, Carlsen's experiments may not have given the singers sufficient context to develop or be able to vocally articulate strong expectancies. Instead of having subjects complete tunes and having a second set of subjects attempt to transcribe the first set of subjects' production or violations thereof, Schmuckler had listeners simply judge the aptness of various musical continuations. He found (p. 122) that familiarity with the passage through repeated hearings led to higher aptness ratings for certain continuations and that certain contour-changing tones were more strongly expected than contour-continuing tones, contrary to the hypothesis that listeners always expect patterns that tend toward simplicity and stasis. He found (pp. 123–125) that tones articulating abstract melodic processes such as gap filling or complementation were actually more strongly expected than tones merely continuing a previously established series. When he compared the relative contributions of superficial melodic contour to abstract melodic relationships in generating expectancies (through regression analysis, p. 125), melodic contour fared miserably, again suggesting listeners attend more to abstract relations. In contrast to Carlsen's flawed experiments, Schmuckler's findings provide empirical support for the idea that listeners more easily perceive (and are thus presumably more easily emotionally influenced by) more complex, abstract sound patterns occurring quickly in time, as long as these patterns are properly structured to take listeners' stylistically and contextually motivated expectations into account. That is to say, those who would like their voices to reach people in the gut should think less of the call of the wild than of call and response. Jones (1987), another music psychologist, assigns the label *dynamic pattern simplicity* to the concept of complex temporal relations that, consistent with Schmuckler's findings, are paradoxically easy to process. "Dynamically simple patterns are ones in which the initial pattern relationships more reliably forecast the 'when' and 'where' of later pitch changes in the pattern . . . Basically this means the simplicity criteria can be based on symmetry properties . . . " (Jones, 1987, p. 629). In other words,

sound patterns are not simple to understand because little is going on; they're simple because you can follow everything that's going on.

A Call to Action

While this paper has provided an introduction to the types of relations among prosodic patterns that can elicit emotional response and those that can inhibit such response, it cannot be said to have provided a complete picture of the types of relations, having focused on certain rhetorical devices evident in a limited set of examples. Furthermore, intonational and metrical sequences have each been discussed separately from each other. By presenting separate sets of examples for intonation and rhythm and separate approaches to diagramming the way rhythm and intonation are perceived, I may have oversimplified a listener's actual experience and may have conveyed the false impression that pitch and metrical patterns constitute entirely separate, unrelated phenomena. Schmuckler (1989) investigated the relative contribution of harmonic vs. melodic expectancies (though not rhythmic ones). He found that they are analyzed independently yet simultaneously by listeners, this despite the fact that melodies imply standard harmonies and that harmonies limit the likelihood of certain melodies. Listeners' ability to attend simultaneously to two patterning systems suggests that metrical and intonational patterns in speech may also be analyzed separately from each other on one level of processing, yet at some level integrated with each other. The possibility of there being additional constraints on processing multiple simultaneous information streams certainly merits more investigation.

Nor does this paper provide a way of predicting exactly when divergence or parallelism among sound patterns will be deemed incongruous, except to the extent that the shape of the sound pattern symbolically contradicts or reinforces the sense of the text it accompanies. Rather than relying on listeners to identify incongruities among patterns, it would be far more helpful both to researchers and professional speakers if one could at some point define incongruous sounding prosodic relations in terms of their formal properties. Some effort in this direction has been undertaken by Jones (1990), who refers to the musical equivalent of intonation or metrical phrase paradigms as *expectancy vectors*, to the musical equivalent of collections of these paradigms as *expectancy schemes*, and to expectancy schemes that are recognizable to listeners and that generate expectancies in listeners as *serial integration regions* or SIRs. She believes that the relation between rhythm and melody is crucial in determining SIR boundaries, and she suggests, with what might initially seem a nod more toward Carlsen than Schmuckler, that these boundaries are defined by certain permissible ratios of pitch change to time change beyond which subsequent sound patterns cannot be easily "integrated" with antecedent patterns but must be "differentiated" from them. However, in defining the constitution of SIRs in terms of pattern simplicity, Jones is not imposing any limits on listeners' ability to relate sound patterns to prior units of sound, to make complex inferences about complex relationships, only on listeners' ability to identify the prior units as single units. She is not saying listeners can't deal with

complexity, only that they must build it with simple blocks. Not only does she provide the beginnings of an operational definition of the size of the blocks, she also makes separate predictions for listener behavior depending on whether a sound pattern diverges from its expected direction within a block or outside a block. She claims (1990, p. 215) that divergence occurring within a serial integration region will be subject to integration by listeners, whereas divergence occurring outside that region will be subject to differentiation. In integration, the listener accepts the observed variant of an expected pattern as a special exception. She exercises her *perceptual* faculties and may experience a bit of brute excitement on the edge of her field of experience. In differentiation, the naïve listener revises her understanding of the expected pattern and develops new, more worldly expectancies. She exercises her *cognitive* albeit unconscious faculties and can experience emotional trauma or delight through unconsciously examining and questioning previously held beliefs. These speculations offer the beginnings of testable hypotheses about emotional response to temporal variation in the voice, though the boundaries of the auditory units will first need to be confirmed through additional experiments with listeners.

Yet once Jones' SIR boundaries have been empirically confirmed, and once her suspected differences in listener responses to within-SIR and between-SIR pattern divergence have been validated or rejected, it will still be necessary to identify bigger boundaries, boundaries in time and complexity of information beyond which coherent relations between patterns can no longer be heard or processed, if we are to predict exactly when speeches containing some of the same patterns as are employed in masterful communications like those of the infomercials will degenerate into confusing, uninspiring drivel. Research employing parametric statistical models to identify how far back in a discourse a listener can recall prosodic patterns as references for imitation or deviation indicative of emotional states, how much detail listeners can recall from these patterns, and how much of an effect various amounts of intervening material may have on memory for the referenced material, would all be welcome complements to research on vocal expression of emotion. However, if this paper has shown anything, it is that neither emotional response to temporal relations among prosodic units nor the variations in the relations themselves is a matter of degree. If a rhythm or intonation pattern is shifted, and a speaker goes from being incredibly exciting to incredibly dull, there is no intervening state where he was somewhat exciting or somewhat dull. Statistical approaches may be appropriate, but only nonparametric methods, involving multiway contingency tables and time series analysis to take account of successive temporal states' influence on each other, can tell us which configurations of temporal relations among sound patterns are most closely associated with various emotional responses.

It should be clear that listeners can be emotionally moved by speech presenting more information in a shorter period of time than they could otherwise process as long as the information is prosodically chunked to indicate textually and contextually appropriate similarities and contrasts among information units. Contra Weissman, pitch falls before and pauses after each unit of information are neither necessary nor sufficient for clear, emotion-laden communication, though these features may be expected by listeners and may be employed or intentionally withheld as commentary on the text. Listeners' apprehension of prosodic similarities and contrasts across information units as mimetic gestures, as vocal illustrations of qualities of the text, evokes various emotional responses analogous to those that can be elicited through watching filmed images accompany a narrative or watching someone dance to music. In order to appreciate the similarities and contrasts, the listener cannot rely entirely on innate or rehearsed conventions for emotional response, as he or she might when, for instance, hearing a series of statements spoken on successively gradually lower pitch levels as rather "mournful" or "lamenting," as opposed to hearing a single statement spoken with a fall of the same range but over a shorter period of time as sounding rather more "definitive" than sad. Because the listener must attend to prosodic change over time, appreciating the similarities and contrasts in speech requires cognitive comparisons to be made extremely rapidly, so there is generally no opportunity for listeners to process prosodic differences on an ordinal, interval, or ratio scale (except when a text explicitly calls attention to numbers, as with the four glassfuls of orange juice). Listeners generally can only listen for and respond to unequivocal similarities and differences. When irregular rhythmic divergence from a preestablished meter is used incongruously, as in Suze Orman's advice (where it accompanies a text message of reassurance but produces the sensation of uncertainty), when metrical parallelism is not established consistently enough to allow the listener to identify divergence from an established meter, as in the orange juice example, or when the number of stressed beats contradicts a number spoken in the text it accompanies, as in the same example, when intonational parallelism is contradicted by contrasting adjectives in the text, as with the cheese lecture, or when apparent contradictions produced through assigning parallel intonation to contrasting elements of text are only resolved later in the discourse, as with the less successful Vitalis hair tonic speech, listeners do not have time to make sense of what they are hearing as they are hearing it. They will lose interest and become emotionally withdrawn.

References

Carlsen, J. (1976). Cross-cultural influences on expectancy in music. A plenary address to the World Congress of the International Society for Research in Music Education. In E. Kraus (Ed.), *International Music Education Yearbook III* (pp. 61-62). Mainz, Germany: Schott.

Couper-Kuhlen, E. (1993). *English speech rhythm: Form and function in everyday verbal interaction.* Amsterdam: John Benjamins.

Fónagy, I. (2001). *Languages within language: An evolutive approach.* Amsterdam: John Benjamins.

Gladstone, B. (2004). The wizard of lizard, *On the Media.* New York: WNYC Radio.

Retrieved May 7, 2004, from http://www.onthemedia.org/transcripts/transcripts_050704_wizard.html

Jones, M. R. (1987). Dynamic pattern structure in music: Recent theory and research. *Perception and Psychophysics, 41*(6), 621-634.

Jones, M. R. (1990). Learning and the development of expectancies: An interactionist approach. *Psychomusicology, 9*(2), 193-227.

Ladd, D. R. (1996). *Intonational phonology.* Cambridge, UK: Cambridge University.

Lazarus, R. S. (1982). Thoughts on the relations between emotion and cognition. *American Psychologist, 37*(9), 1019-1024.

Lehiste, I. (1977). Isochrony reconsidered. *Journal of Phonetics, 5,* 253-263.

Markman, A. B., & Gentner, D. (1993). Splitting the differences: A structural alignment view of similarity. *Journal of Memory and Language, 32*(4), 517-535.

Miller, M., Maruyama, G., Beaber, R. J., & Valone, K. (1976). Speed of speech and persuasion. *Journal of Personality and Social Psychology, 34*(4), 615-624.

Paddock, J. R., & Nowicki, S., Jr. (1986). Paralanguage and the interpersonal impact of dysphoria: It's not what you say but how you say it. *Social Behavior and Personality, 14*(1), 29-44.

Schmuckler, M. A. (1989). Expectation in music: Investigation of melodic and harmonic processes. *Music Perception, 7*(2), 109-150.

Unyk, A. M., & Carlsen, J. (1987). The influence of expectancy on melodic perception. *Psychomusicology, 7*(1), 3-23.

Zajonc, R. B. (1984). On the primacy of affect. *American Psychologist, 39*(2), 117-123.

CHAPTER 7

Emotion Processing Deficits in Functional Voice Disorders

Janet Baker and Richard D. Lane

Abstract

In this chapter we present new findings on the association between functional voice disorders (FVDs) in women and the etiologic role of life stress, coping style, and patterns of emotional expression. New empirical findings reveal that women with FVDs, relative to women with organic voice disorders or healthy controls, had more stressful events, including events that were life-threatening such as strangulation, had more events that involved conflict over speaking out and more powerlessness in the system, had more inhibition or resistance to the expression of emotion, grew up in families with less emotional expression, had more insecure interpersonal attachments, were more likely to have an anxious coping style, and had a greater vulnerability to depression. As such one can discern two distinct themes in these results: one involving a greater amount of emotional distress and negative affect, and one involving some kind of inhibition or alteration in the ability to process that emotional distress that included both more recent as well as more remote, developmental factors.

These findings serve as the springboard for our discussion of how emotional distress, and a relative failure to process it, could result in FVDs. The discussion focuses on the distinction between implicit and explicit emotional processes and their distinct neural substrates. FVDs may arise when emotional distress cannot be adequately processed at the conscious level. This may be associated with an autonomic imbalance favoring sympathetic relative to vagal outflow, resulting in constriction of the intrinsic and extrinsic laryngeal muscles, increased tension in the vocal folds, and an attendant loss of voice. Bringing the emotional distress into conscious awareness in therapy can lead to a top-down modulation of emotional arousal associated with a shift in autonomic balance characterized by an increase in vagal tone and concomitant relaxation of the intrinsic and extrinsic laryngeal muscles. Thus, FVDs may arise when emotional distress is persistent and yet remains largely implicit, whereas treatment of FVDs involves a shift to explicit processing, which itself is associated with an increase in vagal tone. We conclude with suggestions for empirical testing of this etiologic model of emotion processing deficits in FVDs.

Part I: An Investigation into Life Events and Difficulties, Coping Style, and Patterns of Emotional Expression in Women with Functional Voice Disorders

Introduction

Disorders of the voice may be caused by organic conditions. However, many patients presenting to otolaryngologists and speech pathologists are troubled by functional voice disorders. Under this broad label, a diverse terminology has been used reflecting different professional attitudes and beliefs about the very nature of these complex voice disorders and their possible etiologies. The "non-organic" dysphonias have been variously referred to as *hysterical, conversion reactions, hysterical conversion reaction, psycho-* *phonasthenia, war aphonia* or *war neuroses of the larynx, phononeurosis, psychosomatic, mutational falsetto* or *puberphonia* (when occurring in mature adolescents or adult males), *functional, hyperfunctional, muscle misuse or muscle tension disorders, psychogenic,* or *medically unexplained.*

For the purposes of this discussion the non-organic voice disorders will be termed *functional voice disorders* (FVDs). At one end of the spectrum the term *functional* implies an etiological pattern related to psychological processes, where there is sudden or intermittent loss of volitional control over the initiation and maintenance of phonation in the absence of structural or neurological pathology sufficient to account for the voice loss. The loss of voice may be linked to stressful situations where psychological distress can be clearly identified or at least implied, or may develop under seemingly innocuous situations, which may be traced back to traumatic stress experiences that occurred many months, even years prior (Baker, 2003). FVDs in this group are often referred to as *psychogenic voice disorders*, some of which may meet the criteria for a true conversion reaction.

At the other end of the spectrum, the term functional suggests disrupted vocal behaviors that may arise in meeting heavy vocal demands of work or performance, and perhaps in association with upper respiratory infection. Over time this may lead to poor vocal habits, and consequent deterioration in vocal quality, with development of secondary organic changes that are generally amenable to resolution with modification to vocal load and patterns of misuse. These FVDs are referred to as *muscle tension voice disorders*.

As stressed by Aronson (1990) and supported by others (Butcher, Elias, & Raven, 1993; Morrison, Nichol, & Rammage, 1986), "the extrinsic and intrinsic laryngeal muscles are exquisitely sensitive to emotional stress and their hypercontraction is the common denominator in virtually all psychogenic and muscle tension voice disorders" (Aronson, 1990, p. 12). However, it is equally recognized that the relative contribution of psychological factors appears to be the more significant with some dysphonias, and disrupted vocal behavioral patterns the more likely scenario in other cases (Butcher, 1995). In the final analysis, it is the interplay between the psychological and the physical that is fundamental to our understanding of such voice disorders (Aronson, 1990; Baker, 1998; Butcher et al., 1993; Morrison & Rammage, 1994). The broad term *functional voice disorder* will be used in this discussion to incorporate both groups unless specified otherwise.

Background to the Etiological Hypotheses

Much of the early medical and psychiatric literature in relation to etiology of FVDs has been understood against a background of Freud's psychodynamic theory. A clinical picture strongly biased towards a disease model was previously adopted, with FVDs most commonly presenting in females. The underlying etiology was attributed to psychopathology located firmly in the neurotic and hysterical personalities of women, inevitably suffering from unresolved unconscious sexual and/or aggressive urges (Breuer & Freud, 1955).

The subsequent early speech pathology and laryngology literature was rich with anecdotal clinical reports of women with FVD. In such cases it was often referred to as *conversion reaction* or *hysterical aphonia* where the loss of voice was construed as "a transmutation of repressed emotions into some form of bodily expression by blocking the normal functioning of the sensory motor pathways." Such reactions were seen on the one hand to repress the threatening thoughts and feelings from the patient's consciousness but to reflect in a symbolic way by choice of symptoms the nature of that conflict (Viederman, 1983; Ziegler & Imboden, 1962). Such a symptom was assumed to reflect unresolved unconscious psychological conflict within an individual suffering a more serious personality or psychiatric disorder.

By implication many of these women were assumed to have a "hysterical" personality as originally delineated by Briquet (1859). This meant she would be seductive and flirtatious, sometimes hostile and manipulative in her overall disposition, immature in the management of her feelings, especially anger and negative emotions. She denied the presence of emotional distress and was likely to portray *la belle indifference*, one of the hallmark features of the true conversion reaction. She was invariably suggestible, dependent, shallow, theatrical, not to mention an extravert!

During the last 3 decades, there have been a number of studies that have investigated this population more scientifically. These studies have explored gender bias (Baker, 2002; Wilson, Deary, & MacKenzie, 1995), coping style (McHugh-Munier, K. R. Scherer, Lehmann, & U. Scherer, 1997), psychological correlates (Roy, Bless, & Heisey, 2000; Roy et al., 1997), personality structure, and psychiatric disturbance (Friedl, Friedrich, & Egger, 1990; Gerritsma, 1991; House & Andrews, 1987; White, Deary, & Wilson, 1997). In addition, several studies have examined life stresses and circumstances preceding onset of the dysphonia (Andersson & Schalen, 1998; Friedl, Friedrich, & Egger, 1990; House & Andrews, 1988).

A comprehensive review of this literature confirms that FVD does manifest most commonly in women, generally in a ratio of approximately 8:1 females to males (Baker, 2002; Wilson, Deary, & MacKenzie, 1995). Such women, however, do not generally fulfill the criteria of the "hysterical personality profile," nor do they display the characteristic *la belle indifference* as described by Briquet (1859). The more common clinical finding is that most women with FVDs reveal genuine concern about the nature of their voice loss, and are palpably relieved when it returns to normal. It is the clinical experience of the author that they express genuine curiosity about its possible etiology, they are open to the possibility

that their voice disorder may have developed in response to stressful situations, and that the symptoms may reflect upon their emotional state in some way (See Case Example 1).

The studies cited above also show that true conversion reaction as one clinical presentation of FVD is considered to be relatively rare with prevalence figures as low as 4–5% (Akagi & House, 2001; Butcher, 1995; House & Andrews, 1988). Furthermore, the women in these study populations do not exhibit serious psychological disturbance or severe psychiatric disorder with delusional or psychotic thinking (House & Andrews, 1987; Millar, Deary, Wilson, & MacKenzie, 1999; White et al., 1997). On the contrary, they more commonly present with elevated levels of anxiety, emotional maladjustment, and persistent vulnerability to tensional or somatic symptoms, and seem to be more prone to introversion and low levels of clinical depression.

There is some empirical evidence that FVD may follow stressful life events (Andersson & Schalen, 1998; Friedl et al., 1990; Friedl, Friedrich, Egger, & Fitzek, 1993; Gerritsma, 1991; House & Andrews, 1988; Roy & Bless, 2000). Life events related to family and work are among those described, with persistent conflict situations involving close family members or work colleagues as the more likely areas of interpersonal difficulty. In the study reported by Andersson and Schalen (1998), the authors propose "psychogenic voice disorder" should be considered a disturbed capacity for emotional expression" (p. 104).

In perhaps the most comprehensive study to date, FVDs in a group of women followed life events and difficulties that had been operationally defined in terms of

Case Example 1

AB, a 23-year-old female student, developed what appeared to be a viral laryngitis with subsequent loss of voice and whispery aphonia for three weeks. Otolaryngology examination revealed normal vocal fold movement on cough, patterns of muscle tension, and no other laryngeal pathology. Her laryngologist suggested she had a functional dysphonia, possibly due to the viral infection. She was reassured the protective laryngeal constriction would be alleviated by "learning to use her voice properly."

The student attended the first speech pathology session with her mother who was naturally anxious to see if anything could be done to hasten her daughter's recovery. AB was mystified as to the nature of the dysphonia and the long time that it had persisted without any change, and she was keen to know what she could do to "make her voice come back." Following a full psychosocial interview, speech pathology assessment revealed a *psychogenic voice disorder* (PVD), presenting as a whispery aphonia with no modal voice present during any attempts to speak; however, during cough and facilitating exercises designed to trigger vocal fold adduction, normal phonation was readily elicited and quickly consolidated into comfortable conversational speech.

The nature of psychogenic aphonia was explained to the student and her mother by painting a broad picture of the possibilities, such that it would encompass the physical, the functional, and the psychosocial or emotional influences *without any one of these being attributed to the individual*. AB freely explored the ideas with her mother and the clinician, and found that the only pressure of any significance was her ongoing studies. While she was open to the idea that this might have contributed to onset, it did not "fit" for her as a significant stress at that time. She too seemed curious about the possibility that there might be another explanation. She was invited to return for a second interview to ensure that her normal voice had consolidated reliably, and to provide her with the time and space to consider the ideas we had discussed. She left the session very happy with the outcome, but from a therapeutic point of view, the therapist remained troubled and sensed the situation was not fully resolved. Inevitably the presence of the girl's mother had been an issue, and there was a lingering impression that the full story had not been told.

When she returned a week later, this time on her own, her voice was perfectly normal, she appeared happy and calm, and chatted cheerily about her studies. Towards the end of the session, AB quietly asked if it was possible for an event some 4 months previously to have had some bearing on her current symptoms. She reported that after a date with a young man who was well known to her through her course, she was taken to his family home, where his parents were at the far end of the house, and brutally raped by the young man.

She recalled protesting and trying to scream out as he assaulted her, but she was not able to make anyone in the house hear her. He repeatedly told her, "You know you really want it." She felt totally overwhelmed and traumatized, and left feeling guilty and ashamed, wondering if she might have been to blame for leading him on. She chose not to tell her parents, but confided in one friend and saw her local doctor 3 days later due to persisting vaginal bleeding and acute pelvic pain. She was given a referral to the rape crisis center for counseling, which she declined to take up.

AB also chose not to confront the young man, as he was a fellow student, and being supervised by the same academic tutor. She felt afraid that if she spoke out she might be accused of making trouble and that this could reflect on either his or her career. She decided therefore to keep it secret, to accept that this had happened, and resolved to put the experience behind her and move on. At the beginning of the week that she developed the viral laryngitis and subsequent dysphonia, this young man had been assigned to her immediate work environment.

the dimension of *conflict over speaking out* (COSO) (House & Andrews, 1988). Surprisingly, the women in this cohort did not seem to experience severe events and difficulties with high levels of threat or loss as often seen preceding onset of depression in women (Brown, Bifulco, & T. O. Harris, 1987; Brown & T. O. Harris, 1986). However, the less severe events and difficulties were identified as situations in which the person was on the one hand obliged to speak out, and yet in doing so, likely to make things worse.

The dilemma over speaking out often involved the expression of the more negative emotions such as aggression or fear, which if exposed, threatened close relationships and led to loss of face, status, or prestige. These authors reported the women generally exhibited high levels of tension and anxiety in relation to their life circumstances and, while bearing the onus of responsibility in relationships at home and/or work, often felt a sense of futility and powerlessness in speaking out or effecting change.

And so, although there are some differences in emphasis about the etiology of FVDs, there seem to be two promising hypotheses that persist as themes in the literature. The first is that FVDs may develop in response to negative emotions following external life events and difficulties. These may be identified as inherently stressful, or in terms of a qualitative dimension such as conflict over speaking out. The second is that FVDs may represent a struggle with internal psychological conflicts over the expression of unacceptable emotions. This ambivalence may operate in the form of denial, suppression, or repression of the more negative emotions, such as anger, fear, and sadness. The study undertaken, therefore, sought to explore these various areas individually, and then to examine the possible inter-relationship across the different domains of inquiry.

Method

The purpose of the study was to examine the etiology of FVDs in women with either total or partial loss of voice in the absence of organic pathology sufficient to account for the nature and severity of the dysphonia. The main objectives were to examine the patterns of life events and difficulties during the 12 months preceding onset of FVD in women, and to determine whether a number of psychosocial factors intrinsic to the individual may mediate in determining patterns of onset and presentation. These included preferred patterns of emotional expression, personal styles of coping, and nature of attachment in close adult relationships. For the purposes of this publication only selected components of the results will be discussed.

The primary hypotheses were that women with FVDs, in comparison to those with organic voice disorders or non-voice-disordered controls: (a) will differ in their experience of severe life events and major difficulties during the 12 months preceding onset/interview, (b) will differ in their experience of COSO events and difficulties during the 12 months preceding onset/interview, and (c) will differ in their attitudes and behavior regarding the expression of negative emotion.

Study Design

The study was a case-control design. A case by definition was a woman presenting with a voice disorder characterized by perceptual changes to quality, pitch, loudness, or flexibility, sufficient for the voice to be judged as abnormal by an otolaryngologist and speech pathologist in terms of her age, sex, and cultural background. A control was defined as a woman with a perceptually normal voice and no previous history of referral to a speech pathologist or otolaryngologist for voice disorder requiring medical, surgical, or therapeutic intervention.

Source of Participants

Research participants were recruited from both the public and private sectors in order to obtain a cohort that is representative of the population currently seeking help for voice disorders in South Australia, which is largely a "community-based" rather than a "hospital-based" population. Recruitment from the public sector took place from the voice analysis clinics of the three major teaching hospitals serving different geographical regions in South Australia, and from the private sector, drawing on referrals from the practices of eight speech pathologists, including the investigator. This represented 89% of those speech pathologists specializing in voice in South Australia.

Selection of Cases

Participants were women 18–80 years of age, presenting with a voice disorder diagnosed by both an otolaryngologist and speech pathologist, ideally no more than 6 months previously. Potential participants were excluded if they presented with a neurological voice disorder causing a dysarthrophonia affecting the muscles of respiration, phonation, articulation, and resonance. This may have occurred in association with a progressive neurological condition such as motor neuron disease.

Differential Diagnosis

Differential diagnosis was based upon data from the medical letters of referral, the diagnostic assessment and clinical reports of the attending speech pathologists and otolaryngologists, and the investigator's own clinical evaluation with reference to the Diagnostic Classification System for Voice Disorders (DCSVD) (Baker, Ben-Tovim, Butcher, Esterman & McLaughlin, 2007), designed specifically for the project. Women were given a primary diagnosis of either functional voice disorder or organic voice disorder.

Selection of Control Group

The non-voice-disordered control group comprised a community sample of women 18–80 years of age drawn from colleagues, friends, or acquaintances of the research subjects, or individuals approached by the investigator. The investigator assessed the controls at the time of recruitment as having a perceptually normal voice. They were not required to undergo laryngoscopic examination as this was considered an unnecessarily invasive procedure; however, they were excluded if they had a previous history of referral to a speech pathologist or otolaryngologist for voice disorder.

Matching of Controls

Control group women were matched for 10-year age band, and on the basis of known vocal demands associated with their identified occupations and levels of involvement with people. For instance, if a case woman aged 33 years taught physical education in a state primary school, a control was sought between the ages of 30 and 39 years who taught a comparable subject with primary school-aged children and from a school in a similar geographical location. Matching of controls was on an approximate 1:1 ratio, and was closer for the FVD group than the OVD group, as this was the cohort of primary interest.

Materials and Behavioral Instruments

Data were gathered via five standardized self-report questionnaires that target coping styles and personality traits related to patterns of emotional expression and an extensive semistructured interview that included demographic and clinical voice data and material relating to the life events and difficulties experienced by women during the 12 months preceding onset of the voice disorder/interview and overall attachment style.

Questionnaires Related to Personality Traits and Emotional Expression

The self-report questionnaires were: the Self Assessment Questionnaire—Nijmegen (SAQ-N) (Van der Ploeg, 1989), the Ambivalence over Emotional Expression (AEQ) (King & Emmons, 1990), and the Family of Origin Expressive Atmosphere Scale (FOEAS) (Yelsma, Hovestadt, Anderson, & Nilsson, 2000). The Manifest Anxiety Scale Short Form (BMAS) (Bendig, 1956) with the Marlowe-Crowne Social Desirability Scale (MC) (Crowne & Marlowe, 1960) were used together to establish Repressive Coping Style.

The Self Assessment Questionnaire —Nijmegen (SAQ-N). The English version of this 98-item questionnaire was used to explore a range of personality traits, dispositions, and patterns of emotional expressiveness. The Dutch version of the SAQ-N was developed as the basis for several large studies in the Netherlands looking into psychosocial factors and the development of breast cancer in women (Bleiker & Van der Ploeg, 1997; Van der Ploeg, 1989). It is made up of 11 scales, most of which have been recognized internationally as valid and reliable measures. Traits of general importance in studying personality and disease are included such as anxiety, anger, depression, and the experience of social support. In addition, there are several scales that distinguish between emotional expression-in, emotional expression-out, and emotional control.

Ambivalence over Emotional Expression (AEQ). The Ambivalence over Emotional Expression Question-

naire (AEQ) was used as the measure to determine the participants' self-reported attitudes to the expression of positive and/or negative emotions. The scale is a 28-item self-report questionnaire and is one of two developed by King and Emmons (1990) in relation to emotional expression and its possible contribution to psychological and physical well-being.

The AEQ assesses the construct of conflict or ambivalence over emotional expression, and is distinct from the nonexpression of emotion.

The Family of Origin Expressive Atmosphere Scale (FOEAS). The Family of Origin Expressive Atmosphere Scale (FOEAS) was used to obtain an assessment of the participant's perceived expressiveness in family of origin. The FOEAS is a 22-item self-report questionnaire derived from the original 40-item Family of Origin Scale (FOS) where participants are asked to respond to statements pertaining to the level of expressive atmosphere in his or her family of origin.

Repressive Coping Style. Based on the seminal work of Weinberger et al. (1979), *repressors* have been defined as individuals who score low on self-report measures of trait anxiety, but high on self-report measures of defensiveness. These two measures together have been widely used in the health psychology research to identify four coping styles: *repressor* (low anxiety–high defensiveness), *low anxious* (low anxiety–low defensiveness), *high anxious* (high anxiety–low defensiveness), and *defensive high anxious* (high anxiety–high defensiveness). The Manifest Anxiety Scale Short Form (BMAS) (Bendig, 1956) was used as the measure to establish trait anxiety for the repressive coping style dimension, and the Marlowe-Crowne Social Desirability Scale (MC) (Crowne & Marlowe, 1960) as the measure of repressive defensiveness. In order to identify the repressor and nonrepressor groups the BMAS and MC total scores were dichotomized at their median values. These were then combined to create a new variable with four categories to express coping styles: *repressive coping* (MC ≥ 19 and BMAS < 6), *low anxious* (MC < 19 and BMAS < 6), *high anxious* (MC < 19 and BMAS ≥ 6), and *defensive high anxious* (MC ≥ 19 and BMAS ≥ 6).

Semistructured Interview

Life Events and Difficulties Schedule (LEDS). The full version of the Life Events and Difficulties Schedule (LEDS) (Brown & T. O. Harris, 1978) was used for an exploration of the life circumstances of case women in the 12 months prior to onset of the voice disorder, and in the 12 months prior to hypothetical onset at time of interview for the control group.

Over the last 35 years numerous studies using the LEDS have consistently shown strong associations between severe life events and difficulties and the development of clinical depression and anxiety disorders in the general population (Brown & T. O. Harris, 1978; Brown, T. O. Harris, & Hepworth, 1995; Finlay-Jones, 1989). The interview has also been used to investigate the relationship between events and difficulties preceding onset of physical health conditions such as amenorrhea (T. O. Harris & Brown, 1989) and breast cancer in women (Chen et al., 1995; Protheroe et al., 1999) and several functional health conditions such as digestive problems (Craig, 1989), pain in association with appendectomy (Creed,

Craig, & Farmer, 1988), globus pharyngis (M. B. Harris, Deary, & Wilson, 1996), chronic fatigue syndrome (Hatcher & House, 2003), and functional voice disorders (House & Andrews, 1988). A recent critical review of research studies investigating the relationship between life events and a range of psychosocial variables for breast cancer in women found the LEDS to be the most thorough and reliable approach to this complex area of investigation (Butow et al., 2000).

The LEDS is a semi-structured investigator-based interview. The instrument clearly defines the basic units of study in terms of discrete events, which culminates in their impact 10–14 days after the start of the event, and chronic difficulties that are ongoing for 4 weeks or more. Events and difficulties are explored across 10 main areas of inquiry such as work, reproduction, housing, health, marital and partner relationships, and other relationships including children and so on. There is a formal training process, and there are strict guidelines for inclusion criteria for events and difficulties, assessment of contextual and reported threat, independence of the incident from the research condition, and ratings of severity of threat. Severe events, the only ones repeatedly found to be of etiological significance in the onset of depression in women, are defined by ratings of 1 = marked or 2 = moderate on the long-term contextual threat, and must also be focused on the individual, either alone or jointly with close ties (Brown & T. O. Harris, 1978). However, in the pursuit of completeness in other health areas where established data have not yet been gathered, moderate and non-severe may also be included for analysis. All severe, moderate, and non-severe events were included for analysis in this study.

Difficulties, which must be ongoing for at least 4 weeks, are rated on a seven-point scale for up to 2 years prior to onset, with tracking of changes over the 12-month period of investigation. Although only major difficulties have been found to be of etiological significance in previous studies on depression in women (Brown & T. O. Harris, 1986), marked, moderate, and mild difficulties may also be examined for the same reasons outlined above.

In addition to the traditional measures, the LEDS enables emphasis on specific qualitative classes of events and difficulties relevant to the specific research area of inquiry. The COSO dimension developed by House and Andrews (1988) in collaboration with the LEDS team was of particular interest to our investigation, and the operational definition includes two essential features:

■ The situation or event under consideration is one in which the subject has some definite and strong commitment, for example as a caregiver, a good employee, or a maintainer of family cohesion.
■ A conflict arises in which the subject is under pressure to say something as a way of continuing to cope with that commitment, and yet is constrained not to do so by the strong possibility that anything that might be said could well make matters worse (House & Andrews, 1988, p. 312).

All events and difficulties included in the analysis were also rated for COSO.

A final qualitative aspect to the COSO dimension, which we termed *powerless in the system* (PITS), was introduced for this study. This was based upon the finding that in so many cases where women were in conflict over speaking out—whether they spoke out or not—they were often required to persevere with little hope of resolution to their adverse situation. This feature was particularly evident with the many school teachers and women in service industries to the public. Their ongoing situation mirrored the observations made by House and Andrews (1988) and Pat Barker in her Regeneration Trilogy (1991) regarding men in time of war who developed war neurosis of the larynx or conversion reaction aphonia. This happened, not so much when they were facing combat, but when defeat was inevitable, and where they were required to "soldier on in the face of futility." In consultation with one of the senior authors of the LEDS team, this new dimension of PITS was added to all COSO events and difficulties in the analysis and was rated as present or not.

Attachment Style and Social Support

Attachment Style Interview (ASI). The Attachment Style Interview (ASI) (Bifulco, Lillie, Ball, & Moran, 1998) was used to provide an indication of attachment style and patterns of social support in current adult relationships. This interview may be conducted independently or in association with the LEDS interview, as was done for this study.

The ASI is an investigator-based instrument, and therefore the researcher forms the judgments in rating the features of attachment style and support. Rating thresholds are determined by a 2-day training in London with members of the team and with reference to a "manual of precedent benchmarked examples" (Bifulco et al., 1998). The ASI gives a measure of overall attachment style, with five differentiated attachment profiles and degrees of insecurity of attachment. The global measure is based on the researcher's judgment of the respondent's ability to form and maintain intimate relationships with partner and close support figures. The scoring of features of attachment style and social support is based upon the information derived from the full interview, drawing upon both attitudinal and behavioral material.

Procedures

The procedures included the formal training in the administration of the LEDS and the ASI, then recruitment of research and control participants, and finally the collection and analysis of the data.

Demographic information was gathered immediately after participants had been recruited for the study and had given their written and informed consent. Biographical material included details in relation to age, cultural background, current marital status and the number and ages of any children, family of origin constellation, whether or not parents were alive or deceased (including the age of women when either parent died, if applicable), number of siblings, and participant's order in the family. Any evidence of self-reported experience of violence, strangulation, or sexual abuse in their lifetime was collected during the personal interview and transcribed onto the demographic data form. Details were also recorded regarding highest level of education achieved, current occupation and employment status, and socioeconomic status. The self-report questionnaires related to personality traits and patterns of emotional expression were then given to all case and control participants. Women were asked to return the questionnaires at the research interview; however, none of the respondents' answers to the questionnaires were known to the investigator prior to the interview.

The research interview involved an exploration of the life events and difficulties during the 12 months preceding onset of the voice disorder for the case women, and in the 12 months prior to hypothetical onset at time of interview for the control group and then attitudes and behaviors related to social support and overall attachment style. Integral to this process was the assessment of tapes of the early interview ratings to meet the requirements of the LEDS and ASI training requirements, an inter-rater reliability assessment of ratings for the LEDS and ASI interviews with the LEDS team in London, and consensus meetings with the senior author of the LEDS team again in London, after all interviews had been rated, to ensure independent scrutiny of COSO and PITS events and difficulties. Only selected results related to the demographic details, self-report questionnaires, and interview data from the LEDS and ASI are presented for this publication.

Data Entry and Management

Questionnaire scoring for the SAQ-N, AEQ, FOEAS, BMAS, and MC was conducted using Stata 9.0, as specified by each instrument. The Attachment Style Interview data were scored for ability to make and maintain relationships (standard or non-standard), overall attachment style, and number of social supports according to criteria specified for the instrument. The final scores for the ASI were included with the questionnaire data relating to personality and psychological traits.

The LEDS interview data were scored according to Brown and T. O. Harris (1989) for severe, moderate, and non-severe events, and then major, marked, moderate, and mild difficulties experienced in the 12 months prior to onset/interview. The total number of both events and difficulties was calculated for each woman, as was the number of women who experienced at least one severe, moderate, or non-severe event and at least one major marked, moderate, or mild difficulty. The COSO dimension was included as a qualitative measure for all events and difficulties with ratings for both severe COSO (1–2) and mild COSO (3). The feature of PITS for all COSO incidents was rated as present or absent.

Statistical Analysis

All data analyses were conducted using SPSS 11.5.0 for Windows. Demographics, traits, and the LEDS data were reported and compared between the three study groups: functional voice disorder, organic voice disorder, and control. Categorical variables were reported as frequencies and percentages and compared between study groups using chi-squared tests, with Fisher-Freeman-Halton test where appropriate. Continuous normally distributed variables were reported as means and standard deviations and compared between study groups using one-way analysis of variance (ANOVA), with Sheffe post hoc test. Skewed continuous variables were expressed as medians and inter-quartile range and compared between study groups using a Kruskal-Wallis test. P-values were reported, with those ≤ 0.05 considered statistically significant. Factor analysis was used to reduce the trait data for multivariate analysis.

Logistic regression was used to determine whether the number and severity of life events and difficulties and psychological traits predicted voice disorder status. Models were tested for potential confounders, including age, socioeconomic status, employment status, education, and any experience of violence, strangulation, or sexual abuse. Odds ratios (OR) and 95% confidence intervals (CI) were reported for regression models.

Results

Over the study period 73 women with FVDs, 55 women with OVDs, and 66 control women were interviewed. For the purposes of this publication, we will be presenting only selected data from this study.

Demographic Data

Comparison of study groups showed similarities across age, marital status, and number of children in their current family. In family of origin, there were no significant differences between study groups in family order, whether or not the participant's parents were deceased, and the age of women at parental death, if applicable. The OVD group had lower levels of education, employment, and socio-economic status compared with FVD and control groups (Table 7–1). More women in the FVD and OVD groups reported experience of violence, strangulation, or sexual abuse in their lifetime (Table 7–1). More women in the FVD group had experienced strangulation at some time in their life ($n = 10$, 14%), compared with the OVD women ($n = 4$, 7%) and control group women ($n = 1$, 1%), ($p = 0.025$).

Table 7–1. Selected demographics of participant women

	FVD n = 73		OVD n = 55		Control n = 66		
	Mean	SD	Mean	SD	Mean	SD	Sig.
Age (years)	47.2	10.9	48.4	14.5	46.6	13.9	$p = 0.737$
	n	%	*n*	%	*n*	%	
Australian born	52	71.2	44	80.0	55	83.3	$p = 0.265$
Education							
Secondary	22	30.1	29	52.7	16	24.2	$p = 0.016$
TAFE/trade school	11	15.1	4	7.3	10	15.2	
CAE/university	40	54.8	22	40.0	40	60.6	
Employment							
Employed	63	86.3	33	60.0	53	80.3	$p = 0.010$
Unemployed	4	5.5	10	18.2	5	7.6	
Retired	6	8.2	12	21.8	8	12.1	
Socioeconomic status #	1043.3	105.4	997.1	103.5	1082.4	67.7	$p < 0.001$
Experience of sexual abuse, violence, or strangulation	36	49.3	18	32.7	14	21.2	$p = 0.002$

Note: SD: standard deviation, # median and inter-quartile range; FVD: functional voice disorder; OVD: organic voice disorder; Sig: significance; CAE: college of advanced education; socioeconomic status: socioeconomic index of disadvantage for areas (SEIFA) (Trewin, 2001).

Managerial, professional, or supervisory occupations were common among study participants. Overall, 69% (*n* = 50) of FVD women, 65% (*n* = 43) of control women, and 42% (*n* = 24) of OVD women were occupied in these roles. Within professional occupations, FVD and control women were more likely to be educational or health professionals (FVD: *n* = 30, 41%; control: *n* = 25, 38%), compared with the OVD group (*n* = 16, 29%). These figures highlight that matching on the basis of occupation with known vocal demands and involvement with people was closer between the FVD and control group than the OVD and control group.

Questionnaire Data Related to Personality and Psychological Traits

Women in the FVD group were more anxious ($p < 0.001$), angry ($p = 0.021$), and prone to depression ($p < 0.001$), with a tendency for emotional expression-in ($p = 0.048$), fewer social supports ($p < 0.001$), and lower levels of optimism ($p = 0.004$) than the OVD or control group, as determined by the SAQ-N. There were no significant differences between groups on the rationality, understanding, anti-emotionality, emotional expression-out, or emotional-control subscales. Women in the FVD group were more likely to have a *nonstandard or insecure* attachment style ($n = 29$, 40%), compared with the OVD ($n = 13$, 23%) and control ($n = 8$, 12%) groups as assessed by the ASI. Women in the FVD group were more likely to exhibit a *markedly or moderately fearful* overall attachment style ($n = 15$, 21%), compared with women in the OVD ($n = 7$, 13%) and control group ($n = 3$, 4.5%). Relatively few women in the FVD group

($n = 15$, 20%) were judged to have a *clearly standard* overall attachment style, compared with the OVD ($n = 19$, 34%) and control ($n = 30$, 45%) groups.

Table 7-2 summarizes the results of those questionnaires, tapping specifically into repression or ambivalence over emotional expression (AEQ, FOEAS, repressive coping). Women with FVD reported higher levels of ambivalence over emotional expression than OVD or control women. Similarly, FVD women reported lower levels of emotional expressiveness in their family of origin than the OVD and control women. As highlighted in Table 7-2, women in the FVD group were less likely to report a repressive coping

Table 7–2. Psychological traits reflecting ambivalence over emotional expression

	FVD n = 73		OVD n = 55		Control n = 66		
	Mean	SD	Mean	SD	Mean	SD	Sig.
AEQ	83.9	21.7	71.7	20.8	73.9	19.6	$p = 0.002$
FOEAS	68.8	21.1	74.8	19.8	78.3	17.8	$p = 0.017$
	n	%	*n*	%	*n*	%	
Coping Styles							
Repressive coping	14	19.2	19	34.5	24	36.4	$p < 0.001$
Low anxious	6	8.2	10	18.2	16	24.2	
High anxious	37	50.7	12	21.8	14	21.2	
Defensive high anxious	16	21.9	14	25.5	12	18.2	
	73	100.0	55	100.0	66	100.0	

Note: FVD: functional voice disorder; OVD: organic voice disorder; Sig.: significance; SD: standard deviation; AEQ: Ambivalence over Emotional Expression (King & Emmons, 1990); FOEAS: Family of Origin Expressive Atmosphere Scale (Yelsma, Hovestadt, Anderson, & Nilsson, 2000); Coping styles: Marlowe-Crowne Social Desirability Scale (MC) (Crowne & Marlowe, 1960) and Taylor's Manifest Anxiety Scale–Short Form (BMAS) (Bendig, 1956). In order to identify the repressor and nonrepressor groups the BMAS and MC total scores were dichotomized at their median values. These were then combined to create a new variable with four categories to express coping styles: *repressive coping* (MC $\geq$ 19 and BMAS < 6), *low anxious* (MC < 19 and BMAS < 6), *high anxious* (MC < 19 and BMAS $\geq$ 6), and *defensive high anxious* (MC $\geq$ 19 and BMAS $\geq$ 6).

style and generally more likely to report higher anxiety than the OVD and control group women.

Life Events and Difficulties Data

Women in the FVD group, as compared to the OVD and control groups, were more likely to have experienced at least one severe event, and at least one major, marked, or moderate difficulty in the preceding 12 months (Table 7-3). Women in the FVD group experienced a greater number of severe events ($p < 0.001$), major difficulties ($p = 0.045$), marked difficulties ($p < 0.001$), and moderate difficulties ($p < 0.001$) than women in the OVD or control groups. There was no significant difference between groups for the total numbers of moderate and non-severe events or mild difficulties.

Conflict over Speaking Out and Powerless in the System Data

Women in the FVD group compared with the OVD and control groups were more likely to have experienced at least one COSO event, COSO difficulty, or COSO difficulty also rated as PITS in the 12 months preceding onset/interview (Table 7-4). Similarly, FVD group women experienced a greater number of COSO events ($p < 0.001$), COSO difficulties ($p < 0.001$), and COSO difficulties also rated as PITS ($p < 0.001$).

Multivariate Analysis

Principal components factor analysis was used to reduce the trait questionnaire data for logistic regression analysis. Four factors were retained, Factor 1—anxiety

Table 7–3. Number of women who experienced at least one life event or difficulty in the 12 months prior to voice disorder onset or interview (controls)

	FVD $n = 73$		OVD $n = 55$		Control $n = 66$		
	n	%	n	%	n	%	Sig.
Events							
At least one severe	54	74.0	12	21.8	9	13.6	$p < 0.001$
At least one moderate	15	20.5	6	10.9	6	9.1	$p = 0.112$
At least one nonsevere	64	87.7	46	83.6	60	90.9	$p = 0.481$
Difficulties							
At least one major	17	23.3	6	10.9	3	4.5	$p = 0.004$
At least one marked	32	43.8	7	12.7	6	9.1	$p < 0.001$
At least one moderate	63	86.3	38	69.1	33	50.0	$p < 0.001$
At least one mild	29	39.7	22	40.0	26	39.4	$p = 0.998$

Note: FVD: functional voice disorder; OVD: organic voice disorder; Sig.: significance. Severe event = severity rating of 1–2 focused on self or jointly with close tie; moderate event = severity rating of 2 focused on a close tie or confidante, possession, or pet; nonsevere event = severity rating of 3–4 and focused on self, other, possessions, or pet; major difficulty = severity rating 1–3 for 2 years or more and not involving a purely health difficulty; marked difficulty = severity rating 1–3 for at least 6 months and not involving a purely health difficulty; moderate difficulty = severity rating of 4; mild difficulty = severity rating of 5–6.

Table 7–4. Number of women who experienced at least one conflict over speaking out (COSO) event, COSO difficulty, or COSO difficulty with powerless in the system (PITS) in the 12 months prior to onset of voice disorder or before interview for controls

	FVD n = 73		OVD n = 55		Control n = 66		
	n	%	*n*	%	*n*	%	Sig.
At least one COSO event	40	54.8	5	9.1	6	9.1	p < 0.001
At least one COSO difficulty	38	52.1	5	9.1	6	9.1	p < 0.001
At least one COSO difficulty with PITS	26	35.6	2	3.6	4	6.1	p < 0.001

Note: FVD: functional voice disorder; OVD: organic voice disorder; Sig.: significance; COSO: conflict over speaking out; PITS: powerless in the system.

and insecure attachment style; Factor 2—ambivalence over emotional expression; Factor 3—anger and anxiety; and Factor 4—rationality and understanding.

Logistic regression was used to determine whether the number and severity of life events and difficulties in the 12 months preceding onset/interview (including COSO) and psychological traits predicted voice disorder status. Three models were fitted: (1) FVD versus control, (2) FVD versus OVD, and (3) OVD versus control. Model 1, which compared FVD and control group women, had four major components that accounted for 84.9% of the variance. The number of severe events (OR = 7.95, 95% CI 3.03-20.85), moderate events (OR = 6.06, 95% CI 1.69-21.75), COSO difficulties (OR = 5.04, 95% CI 1.71-14.81), and mild COSO difficulties (OR = 9.03, 95% CI 2.363-34-509) were associated with an increased likelihood of FVD. Model 2, which compared FVD and OVD group women, had three main components, which accounted for 80.5% of the variance. The number of severe events (OR

= 2.12, 95% CI 1.24-3.62), COSO difficulties (OR = 3.86, 95% CI 1.57-9.45), and mild COSO difficulties (OR = 5.235, 95% CI 1.66-16.45) were associated with an increased likelihood of FVD versus OVD. For Model 3, comparing OVD and control group women revealed that neither life events nor difficulties were predictive of study group status.

Discussion

This case-control study was the first in Australia to explore etiology of FVD in women and to focus specifically on the possible interrelationship between life events and difficulties, attachment style, coping style, and patterns of emotional expression. The study demonstrated that women with FVD were more likely to have experienced severe events and major difficulties in the 12 months preceding onset of dysphonia than the OVD and control groups. This finding differed from the study previously reported by House and Andrews (1988), who also used the Life Events and Difficulties Schedule, and who reported women with FVD were no more likely to experience severe events and difficulties than controls, rather more moderate and nonsevere events. The severe events and difficulties have been traditionally associated with high levels of threat in relation to loss, whether it be of another person, role, or a cherished idea, and have been seen as provoking situations for depressive illness (Brown et al., 1987; Brown & T. O. Harris, 1978; 1986). Our findings therefore suggested some differences in our total population from that of House and Andrews (1988), which might be related to the fact that the majority of women were in family situations and employed in professions, many of whom were in teaching, health, or supervisory roles where vocal demands and responsibility for others were very high.

In addition, we found that the women with FVD experienced more conflict over speaking out events and difficulties than OVD or control women. These situations occurred primarily across the domains of work, marital relationships, and other relationships, including children. This was the first time this COSO dimension has been tested out with another voice disordered population, and it confirmed the findings of the original study (House & Andrews, 1988). Furthermore, we demonstrated that the new dimension to the COSO rating of powerlessness in the system (PITS), especially for long-term difficulties, was an additional factor likely to predict voice disorder status. This was evident in difficulties across the domains of work content and work relationships, especially for school teachers, where a woman often had to persevere, despite protest, and without recourse for resolution. This may have implications for the very high number of teachers seeking worker's compensation for work-related voice injury in Australia, the United States, and Europe. In our population of women, it often seemed to be as much related to ambivalence over coping with the nature of the job, as it was to work load or vocal demands. See Case Example 2.

The self-report questionnaire data confirmed previous studies that have shown women with FVD in comparison with OVD and controls tend to be more highly anxious. They were more likely to experience anxiety and knew they were prone to anxious feelings and that this affected their behavior in relation to seeking support or confiding in others. Many women judged to have an anxious overall attachment style commented spontaneously throughout the interview that had they been asked the same questions at a different time, that is, prior to their current marriage, job, or situation with family of origin, they may well have responded differently. These interesting comments raise the question as to whether or not overall attachment style in adult relationships in is fact sufficiently stable to be thought of only as a trait, and that maybe it can also be considered in terms of a state, contingent upon current relationships and interpersonal experiences.

Contrary to one of the original hypotheses regarding women with FVD being more likely to exhibit a repressive coping style, the results did not support this contention. In fact, the control group women were the more repressive, which raises interesting issues about whether or not a repressive coping style is necessarily unhealthy. It suggests that to a degree, many women may seem to function very effectively in their professional roles and relationships—either despite using a repressive coping style, or possibly because

Case Example 2

CD, a 57-year-old woman, lived alone, having divorced some 20 years previously. She was in regular contact with her three grown up children, one of whom had been suffering serious health difficulties, but was now in remission. Her daughter had been having serious marital difficulties, and CD had moved house twice during the research period. Questionnaire data revealed a defensive high anxious coping style, high levels of ambivalence over the expression of negative emotion and low expressiveness of emotion in family of origin—"my mother stayed emotionally neutral; if I actually raised my voice in anger, that would have been written in blood in my mother's memory—engraved and never forgiven."

CD was a high school teacher accustomed to teaching Year 11 and 12 English with advanced students, and she described events and chronic difficulties related to her job that reflected both a COSO and PITS scenario. During the 4 years immediately prior to onset, CD had been employed as a PAT teacher with the education department. This meant she had no permanent position and that she was required to move to any school at short notice, and teach in any subject area with any age group of students. In these schools the students had low motivation to learn, were less academically able, and were prone to serious behavioral problems. "I was effectively being deskilled each year and when you're a PAT teacher, you tend to get the dregs when you go into a school—all they wanted to do was stamp around and pretend to be Jerry Springer—you know that level of academic aptitude." She regularly asked for more suitable classes but was told if she wanted to keep her job, she had to accept what was offered. After teachers in the education department in SA have had 10 years permanent placement in any one school they are obliged to accept this PAT status.

In the second week of term, again teaching outside her subject area with students who were "noisy, non-academic and with lots of behavioral problems," CD lost control of the class—and then her voice completely. "I was not able to cope—couldn't get them to listen—to make myself heard." She described feelings of frustration and distress at the humiliation of not being in control. CD was then off work on sick leave for 3 months on the basis of "a vocal disorder related to muscle tension in the neck, upper back, and throat muscles," and a subsequent depression in relation to her vocal disorder.

When the speech pathology evaluation and research interview were conducted 3 months after onset, CD was still dysphonic, with a high-pitched soft and whispery voice produced in falsetto mode. Her intonation pattern was unusually young and childlike for someone of her age and with such sophisticated command of language, also flat and monotonous, with an overall affect that was listless and apathetic. She was diagnosed with a psychogenic voice disorder, and her presentation was typical of a true conversion reaction. After the LEDS had been conducted, CD was asked if she was sure there was nothing else she wished to say about the classroom situation that had precipitated the muscular tension. CD then described in extremely graphic language "flashes of an unspoken desire to violently silence a particular student by bashing his head against the wall or desk." CD reported that these flashes had continued throughout the 3-month period of her being on sick leave and that this was the first time she had articulated these violent images either to herself or another person. CD was able to recover normal voice after this revelation, and therapy over the ensuing months helped her to put words to the nature of the COSO and PITS situations facing her and how ambivalence of emotional expression learned early in her life may have shaped her responses to such challenging situations.

it is expedient to do so. These questions perhaps deserve further investigation.

The women in the FVD group in comparison to the OVF and control women were more inclined to be ambivalent about the expression of both positive and negative emotion and to recall coming from families where they reported lower levels of expressiveness of emotion in general. These findings are particularly interesting when integrated with the life events and difficulties data, which so often involved COSO situations as a major component of the incident.

In conclusion, FVDs in this cohort of women seemed to develop as an expression of tension or anxiety following stressful life events. These events often involved conflict over speaking out in situations in which defeat seemed inevitable and a sense of futility often prevailed. These etiological findings have likely implications for therapeutic interventions with FVDs. From a clinical point of view it is important to understand what processes may be operating when a FVD resolves spontaneously, or during therapeutic intervention that is either successful or unsuccessful in helping to restore voice. At a physiological level it is important to understand how strong negative emotions may effectively block the sensorimotor pathways responsible for voluntary and involuntary vocalizations, and then how a different emotional experience mediated by language and understanding may restore phonation to normal. With these issues in mind, we now turn to a discussion that attempts to address etiology, treatment, and physiology within a common framework.

Part II: Emotion Processing Deficits in FVDs: Psychological and Neuroanatomical Perspectives

Introduction

This empirical study showed that women with FVDs, relative to women with OVDs or healthy controls, had more stressful events, including events that were life-threatening (such as strangulation), had more events that involved conflict over speaking out and more powerlessness in the system, had more inhibition or resistance to the expression of emotion, grew up in families with less emotional expression, had more insecure interpersonal attachments, and were more likely to have an anxious coping style and a greater vulnerability to depression. These new findings provide a solid foundation for considering how emotion may be contributing to the etiology of FVDs.

One can discern two distinct themes in these results. One theme is that FVDs are associated with a greater amount of emotional distress and negative affect. The other is that there is some kind of inhibition or alteration in the ability to process emotional distress that includes both more recent, as well as more remote, developmental factors. The latter are suggested by the observations that patients with FVDs often grew up in families with less emotional expression and had more insecure interpersonal attachments. The question then becomes how to under-

stand the nature of the problem in processing emotion that has a developmental origin.

One important observation from this study is that these female patients were deeply concerned about their voice disorders and were relieved when their problem improved. This profile is very different from the classic Freudian conceptualization of hysteria that includes *la belle indifference*. Indeed, as noted above, empirical studies have failed to support many of the claims that Freud made about hysteria. Although the Freudian concept that conversion involves "a transmutation of repressed emotions into some form of bodily expression" may on its face to have some appeal, a closer examination of this idea reveals its limitations. Is the problem in FVD really one of "repressed" emotions? What is the nature of this transmutation of emotion? Why should repression lead to bodily expression? Although Freud could not answer these questions, subsequent developments within the psychoanalytic tradition have proposed alternatives to these original formulations that have in turn created the opportunity for a more modern approach to the problem.

The observation that patients with FVDs experienced stressful life events that were at times life threatening provides a point of departure. Case Example 1 involved a woman who was raped but could not tell her parents or press charges against her assailant. She did, however, tell a friend and a local doctor shortly after the incident. Case Example 2 involved a woman who was consciously aware of violent fantasies but had never discussed these fantasies with anyone. Thus, the story is not one of repression and later catharsis during treatment, and the data involving assessment of the repressive coping style bear this out. Although she had a clear recollection of the event, the processing of the emotions associated with the trauma was somehow limited. How is this to be understood?

The concept of "unformulated experience" is especially helpful in this context. Donnel Stern (1983) proposed that when trauma occurs, patients often have difficulty describing what happened and what they felt. Contrary to classic Freudian theory, the emotions are not fully formed and differentiated, lying in the unconscious waiting to be uncovered by overcoming defenses. Rather, the emotions and memories have not been previously brought to the light of conscious scrutiny and remain undifferentiated until consciously processed. Thus, severely stressful experiences are associated with relatively undifferentiated negative affect that is persistent. It is only when the emotions are discussed with another person and formulated with that person that the traumatic experience can be metabolized and experienced fully *for the first time*.

Part of the reason this conceptualization is useful is that, contrary to Freudian theory, the contents of the unconscious are themselves now thought to be unformulated and undifferentiated. In a 1975 paper entitled "A Critical Re-examination of Freud's Concept of Unconscious Mental Representation," Schimek (1975) demonstrates how Freud's concept of unconscious fantasies and their motivational properties are based upon a conception of perception, memory, and thought that is inconsistent with modern understanding within academic psychology of how these processes work. For example, instead of mental contents lying in the unconscious fully formed waiting to be unveiled at the point when the forces of

repression are overcome, they are undifferentiated, sensorimotor schemes that are not yet represented symbolically. Schimek places particular emphasis on the importance of updating psychoanalytic concepts using Piagetian principles. Thus, a Piagetian conceptualization of emotion may be particularly applicable to the problem of FVDs.

Levels of Emotional Awareness

In 1987 Lane and Schwartz (1987) developed a model called *levels of emotional awareness*. This model holds that an individual's ability to recognize and describe emotion in oneself and others is a cognitive skill that undergoes a developmental process similar to that which Piaget described for cognition in general. A fundamental tenet of this model is that individual differences in emotional awareness reflect variations in the degree of differentiation and integration of the schemata (elementary knowledge structures) used to process emotional information, whether that information comes from the external world or the internal world through introspection. People at the low end of the developmental continuum experience emotions in an undifferentiated, somatic way. According to this model, patients with FVDs are struggling with emotions that are undifferentiated and situated at a somatic level of expression. It should be noted that patients with FVDs may well be functioning at a different level of emotional awareness in areas of their lives unrelated to the stressful or traumatic events.

The five levels of emotional awareness in ascending order are awareness of physical sensations, action tendencies, single emotions, blends of emotions, and blends of blends of emotional experience (the capacity to appreciate complexity in the experiences of self and others). The five levels therefore describe the cognitive organization of emotional experience. They describe traits, although they may also be used to describe states. The levels are hierarchically related in that functioning at each level adds to and modifies the function of previous levels but does not eliminate them. A given emotional response can be thought of as a construction consisting of each of the levels of awareness up to and including the highest level attained. Thus, the feeling of fear is part of an emotional response that consists of the combination of physical sensations associated with visceral arousal, an action tendency such as the desire to escape, and the feeling of fear itself.

In this regard, it is important to consider that a fear response can occur without the feeling of fear. For example, patients with chest pain who do not have structural heart disease may be diagnosed as having "panic without fear" (Fleet, Martel, Lavoie, Dupuis, & Beitman, 2000). The physiological substrate of the fear response is present and is fully experienced in consciousness, but the feeling of fear is somehow dissociated from the bodily sensations, and the latter constitute the basis for the medical attention being sought. This is an illustration of what might be described as *implicit aspects of emotion*. Implicit aspects of emotion consist of physiology and behavior in the absence of the feeling that is characteristic of a given emotion. We use the term *explicit aspects of emotion* to refer to the conscious experience of emotional feelings such as fear, sadness, or happiness.

The five levels of emotional awareness can in fact be mapped onto the distinction between implicit and explicit processes. Level 1 (physical sensations) and 2 (action tendencies) phenomena, viewed in isolation, would not typically be considered indicators of emotion, but when emotional responses occur these are fundamental components. The peripheral physiological arousal and action tendencies associated with emotion are implicit in the sense that they occur automatically and do not require conscious processing in order to be executed efficiently. Levels 3, 4, and 5 consist of conscious emotional feelings at different levels of complexity. These conscious feelings constitute explicit aspects of emotion in the sense that (a) they are conscious and (b) they have the requisite qualitative characteristic needed to unequivocally classify these experiences as emotional feelings. The levels of emotional awareness framework therefore put implicit and explicit processes on the same continuum, and at the same time distinguish between types of implicit (Level 1 vs. Level 2) and explicit (Level 3 vs. Level 4 vs. Level 5) processes.

Thus, when a traumatized individual develops a FVD, the emotions associated with the trauma are unformulated and undifferentiated, and are expressed primarily in the physiological domain (Level 1). Somehow this physiological expression contributes to the development of a FVD. To understand how this may occur, we now turn to a consideration of the neural substrates of emotional awareness.

Neural Substrates of Emotional Awareness

A rudimentary neuroanatomical model of emotional awareness that distinguishes between implicit and explicit processes has been formulated (Lane, 2000). Parallels between the corresponding neuroanatomical and psychological models are schematically depicted in Figure 7–1. The evidentiary basis for this model can be found in other publications (Lane, 2000; Lane & McRae, 2004: Lane & Garfield, 2005). Both models are hierarchical and show a similar architecture of concentric shells. The concentric architecture means that each new level subsumes and modulates that of previous levels. Although both the psychological and neuroanatomical models designate five levels, we do not intend to suggest a direct correspondence between a given level in one model and that of the other model. In general, implicit functions at Levels 1 and 2 in the psychological model correspond to Levels 1–3 in the neuroanatomical model, and explicit functions at Levels 3–5 in the psychological model correspond to Levels 4 and 5 in the neuroanatomical model.

Levels 1 and 2 in the psychological model involve implicit processes that are automatic, modular, and cognitively impenetrable. Subcortical structures participate in the automatic generation of emotional responses associated with absent or diffusely undifferentiated awareness. It may be speculated that the neural substrates of Level 1 in the psychological model include the thalamus and hypothalamus (diencephalon) and brainstem. At Level 2 in the psychological model, the sensorimotor enactive level, crude distinctions between globally positive and globally negative states can be made. The amygdala appears to be preferentially activated in association with aversive stimuli (Zald, 2003), and the ventral striatum, including the nucleus accumbens, is preferentially activated by appetitive or reward stimuli (Koob & Goeders, 1989). The outputs from this stage of processing are widespread. Emotions at this level are represented in actions such as gestures and other movements that have an either/or quality. Much evidence suggests that the basal ganglia participate in the automatic behavioral displays of

Neuroanatomical   Psychological

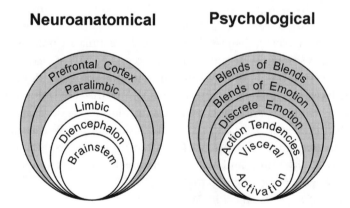

Figure 7–1. Parallels in the hierarchical organization of emotional experience and its neural substrates. The shell structure is intended to convey that each succeeding level adds to and modulates lower levels but does not replace them. Although each model contains five levels, a one-to-one correspondence between each level in the psychological and neuroanatomical models is not intended. Lower levels with white background correspond to implicit processes. Higher levels with gray background correspond to explicit processes.

emotional gestures and expression (Gray, 1995; Rolls, 1990). They likely participate in mediating emotional procedures. A key tenet of this model is that structures at this level, such as the amygdala (Cahill & McGaugh, 1998; LeDoux, 1996), are essential for implicit processing and contribute to but are not sufficient for the explicit experience of discrete emotions.

Levels 3–5 in the psychological model involve explicit processes that are influenced by higher cognitive processes, including prior explicit knowledge. The on-line experience of Levels 3–5 constitutes phenomenal awareness, which is mediated by the addition of paralimbic structures to the network of structures that mediate implicit aspects of emotion. Paralimbic structures include the anterior cingulate cortex, insula, temporal pole, and orbitofrontal cortex. Orbitofrontal cortex activity appears to be associated with the perception of somatic sensations in context, biasing behavior either toward or away from a stimulus (Damasio, 1994), overriding automatic processes in the amygdala, and participating in extinction, among other functions (Emery & Amaral, 2000).

Phenomenal awareness can be differentiated into background feelings and feelings that are the focus of attention. When focal attention is directed to the experience of emotion, the dorsal anterior cingulate is activated and interacts with the other structures at this level and below (area 2 in Figure 7–2). Background feelings can be thought of as that type of conscious emotional experience that is not associated with attention to it or reflection upon it. Ventromedial prefrontal cortex (area 1 in Figure 7–2), somatosensory cortex, right parietal cortex, the insula, and the temporal pole are associated with background emotions.

The highest level of the neuroanatomical model is prefrontal cortex. The paracingulate region of medial prefrontal cortex (area 3 in Figure 7–2) is necessary for reflective awareness. Frith and Frith (1999) addressed the function of this area (also called the paracingulate sulcus). They hypothesize that this area subserves the ability to mentalize, i.e., identifying the mental states of others. This function evolved from the action system for the purpose of identifying the intensions of conspecifics and anticipating their future

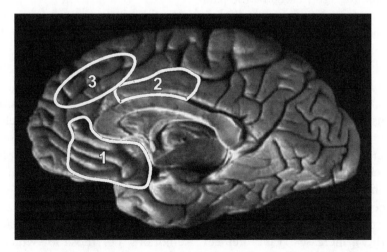

Figure 7–2. Structures on the medial surface of the frontal lobe that participate in (**1**) background feelings, (**2**) attention to feelings and (**3**) reflective awareness of feelings.

actions. It is reasonable to conclude, then, that the paracingulate sulcus is a substructure within the prefrontal cortex that participates in mediating the representations of mental states (including emotional states) of both self and others. Indeed, recent evidence indicates that this is the case (Ochsner et al., 2004).

The anatomical relationship between key structures in the model is depicted in Figure 7–2. As noted, there are three types of conscious emotional experience that are addressed: (a) background feelings; (b) focal attention to feelings; and (c) reflection upon feelings. Background feelings are subserved by a variety of structures in the ventral medial frontal lobe (labeled "1") including orbitofrontal cortex, ventromedial prefrontal cortex, and ventral and pregenual anterior cingulate cortex, as well as insula, temporal pole, and right parietal lobe structures involved in mapping of somatic states. Focal attention to feelings is subserved by dorsal anterior cingulate cortex (labeled "2") and the structures to which it is connected. The establishment of a representation of mental state that can be used for purposes of reflection and future planning is subserved by the paracingulate region of the dorsomedial prefrontal cortex (labeled "3"). The function of all of these structures in mediating different aspects of conscious experience is dependent upon the generation of emotional responses in limbic, diencephalic, and brainstem structures.

Recent imaging studies of emotional arousal indicate that as activity in the anterior cingulate cortex (just between areas 1 and 3 in Figure 7–2) increases, vagal tone, as measured by the high frequency component of heart rate variability (HRV), increases (Lane, Reiman, Ahern, & Thayer, 2001). The correlation between HRV and anterior cingulate cortex activity supports the hypothesis that routing emotional information from subcortical structures to these phylogenetically more advanced cortical areas has the effect of modulating the visceral expression of emotion. Thus, as summarized by the "neurovisceral integration" model of Thayer and Lane (2000), becoming consciously aware of emotions involves a bottom-up transfer of information from subcortical to cortical structures. If one has an accepting attitude and one experiences the feelings, this is associated with cortical and paralimbic processing that in turn leads to a top-down inhibition or modulation of subcortical activation mediated by vagal activation. Thus, conscious processing has a dampening effect on emotional arousal associated with increased vagal tone. If the emotions are not consciously processed or are consciously processed in a limited way, vagal tone will be lower and the dampening effect will occur to a lesser extent.

Application to FVDs

The levels of emotional awareness model provides a way of understanding how both strong negative affect and some interference with the conscious processing of it could lead to physiological changes that could contribute to the emergence of FVDs. The developmental model is consistent with those observations that suggest that the problem that patients with FVDs have in emotion processing arose earlier in life. It is also consistent with the observation that patients with FVDs struggle with unacceptable emotions, i.e., those for which there is difficulty with the conscious acceptance and processing of the painful emotions associated with life stress or trauma.

In patients with FVDs, constriction of the extrinsic and intrinsic laryngeal muscles is observed that in turn induces excessive tension in the vocal folds. Heightened sympathetic arousal, attenuated vagal stimulation, or the combination of the two can induce these changes (Demmink-Geertman & Dejonckere, 2002; Rosen & Sataloff, 1997). Thus, the neurovisceral integration model can account for the chain of events that appears to lead to FVDs: stressful life experiences under certain circumstances induce emotions that are difficult or impossible to consciously process that in turn lead to a deficit in vagal tone. This deficit in vagal tone contributes to a heightening in constriction of the extrinsic and intrinsic laryngeal muscles that then leads to excessive vocal fold tension and FVDs.

It is noteworthy that improvement in FVDs can be achieved through stimulation of involuntary vocalizations such as coughing. One of the therapeutic principles that follows from the Piagetian perspective is that one must meet the patient at the level where they are (Lane & Pollerman, 2002). Stimulation of involuntary vocalizations can be construed as an intervention at the implicit level. It may be that coughing itself is associated with a change in autonomic input to the vocal folds. Coughing is a vagus-mediated protective reflex (Delacourt, 2001) that may increase vagal tone.

Our level of understanding is not advanced enough to say why it is that one person gets FVD whereas another person has a myocardial infarction and a third person gets an ulcer. We also cannot account for the sex difference in FVDs given our current level of understanding of how men and women compare in the neural processing of emotion. However, the general framework proposed above generates new hypotheses to be tested and offers a way forward to investigate the neural substrates of FVDs.

For example, in future research it would be important to examine whether there is evidence of a deficit in emotional awareness in women with FVDs. This deficit may pertain to the trauma itself rather than a more pervasive trait-like deficit in these patients. One would also predict that vagal tone as indexed by respiratory sinus arrhythmia would be diminished in patients with FVDs and would increase with successful treatment. One would also predict that in an imaging context recall of traumatic experiences would be associated with deficits in anterior cingulate cortex functioning during the symptomatic phase of FVDs (Shin et al., 2004) and that with recovery of vocal function one would observe a reversal of this deficit accompanied by an increase in vagal tone. One would also predict that with successful treatment of the voice disorder the ability to describe the emotions associated with the stressful life experiences would improve by becoming more complex and differentiated. If confirmed, such findings would be useful in making the diagnosis of FVDs and tracking the recovery process during treatment.

Acknowledgements. The case-control study described in part in this chapter represents original work toward my doctoral thesis, which was completed in 2006. I wish to acknowledge the assistance from the Departments of Psychiatry and Speech Pathology and Audiology at Flinders University and Flinders Medical Centre of South Australia, and my supervisors Professor David Ben Tovim,

Director of Clinical Epidemiology Unit, Flinders Medical Centre, Professor Andrew Butcher, Speech Pathology, Flinders University, Professor Adrian Esterman, Biostatistics, University of South Australia, and the invaluable assistance of Dr. Kristin McLaughlin. In addition I would like to acknowledge Dr. Tirril Harris from the Sociomedical Research Group Department of Social Psychiatry, HSRD Institute of Psychiatry St Thomas's, London, UK. Dr. Harris provided my original training for the LEDS and ASI, and has provided ongoing support throughout the project both with informal queries and the formal inter-rater reliability studies.

References

Akagi, H., & House, A. (2001). Epidemiology of conversion hysteria. In P. W. Halligan, C. Bass, & J. Marshall (Eds.), *Contemporary approaches to the study of hysteria* (pp.73–87). Oxford, UK: Oxford University Press.

Andersson, K., & Schalen, L. (1998). Etiology and treatment of psychogenic voice disorder: Results of a follow-up study of thirty patients. *Journal of Voice, 12*(1), 96–106.

Aronson, A. E. (1990). *Clinical voice disorders: An interdisciplinary approach* (3rd ed.) New York: Thieme.

Baker, J. (1998). Psychogenic dysphonia: Peeling back the layers. *Journal of Voice, 12*(4), 527–535.

Baker, J. (2002). Psychogenic voice disorders —Heroes or hysterics? A brief overview with questions and discussion. *Logopedics, Phonology, Vocology, 27*, 84–91.

Baker, J. (2003). Psychogenic voice disorders and traumatic stress experience: A discussion paper with two case reports. *Journal of Voice, 17*(3), 308–318.

Baker, J., Ben-Tovim, D.I., Butcher, A., Esterman, A., & McLaughlin, K. (2007) Development of a modified diagnostic classification system for voice disorders with inter-rater reliability study. *Logopedics, Phonology, Vocology, 32* (3), 99-112.

Barker, P. (1991). *Regeneration.* London: Viking Press.

Bendig, A. W. (1956). The development of a Short Form of the Manifest Anxiety Scale. *Journal of Consulting Psychology, 20*(5), 384.

Bifulco, A., Lillie, A., Ball, C., & Moran, P. (1998). *Attachment Style Interview (ASI). Training manual.* London: Royal Holloway.

Bleiker, E. M. A., & Van der Ploeg, H. M. (1997). The role of (non) expression of emotions in the development of cancer. In A. J. J. M. Vingerhoets, F. Van Bussel, & J. Boelhouwer (Eds.), *The (non) expression of emotions in health and disease* (pp. 221–236). Tilburg, Netherlands: Tilburg University Press.

Breuer, J., & Freud, S. (1955). Studies on hysteria. In J. Strachey (Ed.), *The standard edition of the complete works of Sigmund Freud.* London: Hogarth Press.

Briquet, P. (1859). *Clinical and therapeutic treatise on hysteria.* Paris: Balliere.

Brown, G. W., Bifulco, A., & Harris, T. O. (1987). Life events, vulnerability and onset of depression: Some refinements. *British Journal of Psychiatry, 150*, 30–42.

Brown, G. W., & Harris, T. O. (1978). *Social origins of depression.* London: Tavistock.

Brown, G. W., & Harris, T. O. (1986). Establishing causal links: The Bedford College studies of depression. In H. Katsching (Ed.), *Life events and psychiatric disorders* (pp. 107–183). Cambridge, UK: Cambridge University Press.

Brown, G. W., & Harris, T. O. (1989). *Life events and illness.* London: The Guilford Press.

Brown, G. W., Harris, T. O., & Hepworth, C. (1995). Loss, humiliation and entrapment among women developing depression: A patient and non-patient comparison. *Psychological Medicine, 25*(1), 7–22.

Butcher, P. (1995). Psychological processes in psychogenic voice disorder. *European*

Journal of Disorders of Communication, 30, 467-474.

Butcher, P., Elias, A., & Raven, R. (1993). *Psychogenic voice disorders and cognitive behaviour therapy.* San Diego, CA: Singular.

Butow, P. N., Hiller, J. E., Price, M. A., Thackway, S. V., Kricker, A., & Tennant, C. C. (2000). Epidemiological evidence for a relationship between life events, coping style, and personality factors in the development of breast cancer. *Journal of Psychosomatic Research, 49*, 169-181.

Cahill, L., & McGaugh, J. L. (1998). Mechanisms of emotional arousal and lasting declarative memory. *Trends in Neurosciences, 21*(7), 294-299.

Chen, C. C., David, A. S., Nunnerly, H., Michell, M., Dawson, J. L., Berry, H., et al. (1995). Adverse life events and breast cancer: Case-control study. *British Medical Journal, 311*, 1527-1530.

Craig, T. K. J. (1989). Abdominal pain. In G. W. Brown & T. O. Harris (Eds.), *Life events and illness* (pp. 233-259). New York: Guilford Press.

Creed, F., Craig, T., & Farmer, R. (1988). Functional abdominal pain, psychiatric illness, and life events. *Gut, 29*, 235-242.

Crowne, D. P., & Marlowe, D. (1960). A new scale of social desirability independent of psychopathology. *Journal of Consulting Psychology, 24*(4), 349-354.

Damasio, A. R. (1994). *Descartes' error: Emotion, reason, and the human brain.* New York: G. P. Putnam's Sons.

Delacourt, C. (2001). Physiopathology of the cough. *Archives de Pediatrie, 8*(Suppl. 3), 600-602.

Demmink-Geertman, L., & Dejonckere, P. (2002). Nonorganic habitual dysphonia and autonomic dysfunction. *Journal of Voice, 16*(4), 549-559.

Emery, N. J., & Amaral, D. G. (2000). The role of the amygdala in social cognition. In R. Lane, L. Nadel, G. Ahern, J. Allen, A. Kaszniak, S. Rapscak, et al. (Eds.), *Cognitive neuroscience of emotion* (pp.156-191). New York: Oxford University Press.

Finlay-Jones, R. (1989). Anxiety. In G. W. Brown & T. O. Harris (Eds.), *Life events and illness* (pp. 95-112). London: The Guilford Press.

Fleet, R. P., Martel, J. P., Lavoie, K. L., Dupuis, G., & Beitman, B. D. (2000). Non-fearful panic disorder: A variant of panic in medical patients? *Psychosomatics, 41*(4), 311-320.

Friedl, W., Friedrich, G., & Egger, J. (1990). Personality and coping with stress in patients suffering from functional dysphonia. *Folia Phoniatrica, 42*, 13-20.

Friedl, W., Friedrich, G., Egger, J., & Fitzek, T. (1993). Zur psychogenese funktioneller dysphonia. *Folia Phoniatrica, 45*, 10-13.

Frith, C. D., & Frith, U. (1999). Interacting minds —A biological basis. *Science, 286*(5445), 1692-1695.

Gerritsma, E. J. (1991). An investigation into some personality characteristics of patients with psychogenic aphonia and dysphonia. *Folia Phoniatrica, 43*, 13-20.

Gray, J. A. (1995). A model of the limbic system and basal ganglia: Applications to anxiety and schizophrenia. In M. S. Gazzaniga (Ed.), *The cognitive neurosciences* (pp. 1165-1176). Cambridge, MA: MIT Press.

Harris, M. B., Deary, I. J., & Wilson, J. A. (1996). Life events and difficulties in relation to the onset of globus pharyngis. *Journal of Psychosomatic Research, 40*, 603-615.

Harris, T. O., & Brown, G. W. (1989). The LEDS findings in the context of other research: An overview. In G. W. Brown & T. O. Harris (Eds.), *Life events and illness* (pp. 385-437). London: The Guilford Press.

Hatcher, S., & House, A. (2003). Life events, difficulties and dilemmas in the onset of chronic fatigue syndrome: A case-control study. *Psychological Medicine, 33*, 1185-1192.

House, A., & Andrews, H. B. (1987). The psychiatric and social characteristics of patients with functional dysphonia. *Journal of Psychosomatic Research, 31*, 483-490.

House, A., & Andrews, H. B. (1988). Life events and difficulties preceding the onset of functional dysphonia. *Journal of Psychosomatic Research, 32*(3), 311-319.

King, L. A., & Emmons, R. A. (1990). Conflict over emotional expression: Psychological and physical correlates. *Journal of Personality and Social Psychology, 58*(5), 864–877.

Koob, G. F., & Goeders, N. E. (1989). Neuroanatomical substrates of drug self-administration. In J. M. Liebman & S. J. Cooper (Eds.), *Neuropharmacological basis of reward* (pp. 214–263). New York: Oxford University Press.

Lane, R. (2000). Neural correlates of conscious emotional experience. In R. Lane, L. Nadel, G. Ahern, J. Allen, A. Kaszniak, S. Rapcsak, et al. (Eds.), *Cognitive neuroscience of emotion* (pp. 345–370). New York: Oxford University Press.

Lane, R., & Garfield, D. (2005). Becoming aware of feelings: Integration of cognitive-developmental, neuroscientific and psychoanalytic perspectives. *Neuropsychoanalysis, 7*, 5–30. [A Target Article, published with 27 pages of peer commentary, by Galatzer-Levy, Greenberg, Modell, Panksepp, & Posner].

Lane, R., & McRae, K. (2004). Neural substrates of conscious emotional experience: A cognitive neuroscientific perspective. In M. Beauregard (Ed.), *Consciousness, emotional self-regulation and the brain* (pp. 87–122). Amsterdam: John Benjamins.

Lane, R., & Pollerman. B. (2002). Complexity of emotion representations. In L. Feldman Barrett & P. Salovey (Eds.), *The wisdom in feelings* (pp. 271–293). New York: Guilford.

Lane, R., Reiman, E., Ahern, G., & Thayer, J. (2001). Activity in medial prefrontal cortex correlates with vagal component of heart rate variability during emotion. *Brain and Cognition, 47*, 97–100.

Lane, R. D., & Schwartz, G. E. (1987). Levels of emotional awareness: A cognitive-developmental theory and its application to psychopathology. *American Journal of Psychiatry, 144*, 133–143.

LeDoux, J. E. (1996). *The emotional brain: The mysterious underpinnings of emotional life.* New York: Simon & Schuster.

McHugh-Munier, C., Scherer, K. R., Lehmann, W., & Scherer, U. (1997). Coping strategies, personality, and voice quality in patients with vocal fold nodules and polyps. *Journal of Voice, 11*(4), 452–461.

Millar, A., Deary, I. J., Wilson, J. A., & MacKenzie, K. (1999). Is an organic/functional distinction psychologically meaningful in patients with dysphonia? *Journal of Psychosomatic Research, 46*(6), 497–505.

Morrison, M. D., Nichol, H., & Rammage, L. A. (1986). Diagnostic criteria in functional dysphonia. *Laryngoscope, 94*, 1–8.

Morrison, M. D., & Rammage, L. A. (1994). *The management of voice disorders.* San Diego, CA: Singular.

Ochsner, K. N., Knierim, K., Ludlow, D. H., Hanelin, J., Ramachandran, T., Glover, G., et al. (2004). Reflecting upon feelings: An fMRI study of neural systems supporting the attribution of emotion to self and other. *Journal of Cognitive Neuroscience, 16*(10), 1746–1772.

Protheroe, D., Turvey, K., Horgan, K., Benson, E., Bowers, D., & House, A. (1999). Stressful life events and difficulties and onset of breast cancer: Case-control study. *British Medical Journal, 319*, (1027–1030).

Rolls, E. T. (1990). A theory of emotion, and its application to understanding the neural basis of emotion. *Cognition and Emotion, 4*(3), 161–190.

Rosen, D. C., & Sataloff, R. Y. (1997). *Psychology of voice disorders.* San Diego, CA: Singular.

Roy, N., & Bless, D. M. (2000). Personality traits and psychological factors in voice pathology: A foundation for future research. *Journal of Speech, Language, and Hearing Research, 43*, 737–748.

Roy, N., Bless, D. M., & Heisey, D. (2000). Personality and voice disorders: A superfactor trait analysis. *Journal of Speech, Language, and Hearing Research, 43*, 749–768.

Roy, N., McGory, J. J., Tasko, S. M., Bless, D. M., Heisey, D., & Ford, C. (1997). Psychological correlates of functional dysphonia: An investigation using the Minnesota Multiphasic Personality Inventory. *Journal of Voice, 11*(4), 443–451.

Schimek, J. G. (1975). A critical re-examination of Freud's concept of unconscious mental representation. *International Review of Psycho-Analysis, 2*, 171–187.

Shin, L. M., Orr, S. P., Carson, M. A., Rauch, S. L., Macklin, M. L., Lasko, N. B., et al. (2004). Regional cerebral blood flow in the amygdala and medial prefrontal cortex during traumatic imagery in male and female Vietnam veterans with PTSD. *Archives of General Psychiatry, 61*(2), 168–176.

Stern, D. B. (1983). Unformulated experience: From familiar chaos to creative disorder. *Contemporary Psychoanalysis, 19*(1), 71–99.

Thayer, J. F., & Lane, R. (2000). A model of neurovisceral integration in emotional regulation and dysregulation. *Journal of Affective Disorders, 61*, 201–216.

Trewin, D. (2001). *Information paper: Census of population and housing: Socioeconomic indexes for areas, Australia 2001: Australian Bureau of Statistics.* Canberra: Australian Bureau of Statistics.

Van der Ploeg, H. M. (1989). *Self-Assessment Questionnaire—Nijmegen (SAQ-N).* Lisse, Netherlands: Swets and Zeitlinger.

Viederman, M. (1983). The psychodynamic life narrative: A psychotherapeutic intervention useful in crisis situations. *Psychiatry, 46*, 236–246.

Weinberger, D., Schwartz, D., & Davidson, R. (1979). Low-anxious, high-anxious, and repressive coping styles: Psychometric patterns and behavioural and physiological responses to stress. *Journal of Abnormal Psychology, 88*(4), 369–380.

White, A., Deary, I. J., & Wilson, J. A. (1997). Psychiatric disturbance and personality traits in dysphonic patients. *European Journal of Disorders of Communication, 32*, 307–314.

Wilson, J. A., Deary, I. J., & MacKenzie, K. (1995). Functional dysphonia. Not 'hysterical' but seen mainly in women. *British Medical Journal, 311*, 1039–1040.

Yelsma, P., Hovestadt, A. J., Anderson, W., & Nilsson, J. (2000). Family-of-origin expressiveness: Measurement, meaning, and relationship to alexithymia. *Journal of Marital and Family Therapy, 26*(3), 353–363.

Zald, D. H. (2003). The human amygdala and the emotional evaluation of sensory stimuli. *Brain Research, 41*, 88–123.

Ziegler, F. J., & Imboden, J. B. (1962). Contemporary conversion reactions 11: A conceptual model. *Archives of General Psychiatry, 6*, 279–287.

CHAPTER 8

Emotions, Anthropomorphism of Speech Synthesis, and Psychophysiology

Mirja Ilves and Veikko Surakka

Abstract

Affective computing is a relatively new research area in the field of human-computer interaction (HCI), which aims to integrate emotions into human-computer interaction. Recent scientific findings have shown that emotions have a central and important role in human behavior, and for this reason, bringing emotions into HCI is important. Emotions can be communicated in HCI, for example, by computer agents that are capable of humanlike behavior, such as speech, facial expressions, gestures, and head movements. Addition of these humanlike qualities to computers means that they become more anthropomorphic.

Currently, relatively few studies exist on the effects of anthropomorphism, and the previous research has also mainly concentrated on the effects of animated computer agents. However, the voice of an agent is at least as important as its visual appearance. In addition, users' emotional responses to anthropomorphism are also mainly unexplored. The studies which have explored users' subjective experiences have used questionnaires, but when studying the affective states of the users' self-reports they have some limitations. Thus, we propose that developing anthropomorphic features for HCI physiological recordings should be used in addition to the behavioral methods. In this chapter we provide a brief overview of the previous research concerning the emotions and anthropomorphism in HCI. We also report one of our recent experiments that investigated the effects of two different speech synthesizers on subjects' psychological experience and pupil size variation. The findings of our study suggest that more anthropomorphic synthesizers had significant effects on users' reactions on both psychological and physiological levels. The findings also show that psychophysiological measurements can be advantageous when evaluating anthropomorphic features.

Keywords used in this chapter are anthropomorphism, emotion, pupil size, synthesized speech.

Introduction

Affective computing is a research area in the field of human-computer interaction (HCI), which aims to integrate emotions into HCI. Emotions have a central and important role in human behavior, and for this reason, bringing emotions into HCI is important. Recent scientific findings have shown that emotions have a central role in human cognitive processes (Damasio, 1994). For example, Picard (1997) has summarized that emotions significantly affect human perception, rational decision making, learning, and other cognitive functions. In addition, researchers of human-human interaction have shown that emotions significantly influence social communication, such as quality of interaction or willingness to continue interaction (Surakka & Hietanen, 1998; Zajonc, 1980). Furthermore, it has been suggested that people react socially also to computers, and tend to use similar interaction rules in HCI as in human-

human interaction. Thus, it has been suggested that humans treat computers as another social entity, and this means also that people experience computers, at least partly, as an anthropomorphic creature (Nass, Steuer, & Tauber, 1994).

There are basically two theoretical views of emotions. Discrete emotion theory derives from the idea that there is a set of distinctive prototypical emotions like sadness, anger, surprise, joy, disgust, and fear (Ekman, 1994; Ekman et al., 1987). The other way of defining emotions has been the dimensional view. This theory defines emotions via sets of bipolar dimensions. The most frequently used dimensions are valence and arousal. The valence dimension reflects the pleasantness of an emotional response from negative pole to positive pole. The arousal dimension reflects the level of experienced arousal from low arousal or even relaxing pole to highly excited pole during emotional stimulations and reactions (Bradley & Lang, 1994; Lang, Greenwald, Bradley, & Hamm, 1993).

Emotions are known to produce changes in the physiology, for example, both in neuromuscular activity and autonomic nervous system activity (ANS), and also in the subjective experiences. For this reason it is generally agreed that when studying emotions it is important (even imperative) to make multimethod measurements in order to validate the results (Frijda, 1986; Lang et al., 1993). One widely used measurement has been the analysis of electromyographic (EMG) activity of facial muscles during emotionally provoking stimulation (Larsen, Norris, & Cacioppo, 2003). Several studies have shown that pleasant stimuli elicit greater activity in zygomaticus major (activated when smiling) and unpleasant stimuli elicit grater activity in corrugator supercilii (activated when frowning) (e.g., Bradley & Lang, 1994 Dimberg et al., 2000). One indicator of ANS activity is the variation of pupil size. The pupil reacts to changes in illumination. Previous studies have also shown that pupil dilation is positively associated with increased cognitive load (Hyönä, Tommola, & Alaja, 1995; Kahneman & Beatty, 1966; Schluroff, 1982). In addition, during emotionally arousing conditions, whether pleasant or unpleasant, pupils have been shown to dilate as compared to emotionally neutral stimulation (Janisse, 1974; Partala & Surakka, 2003). One advantage of pupil size measurements is that pupil size cannot be voluntarily controlled, and thus it reflects well spontaneous physiological activity.

Humanizing the computer interfaces has long been one of the major goals of researchers in the field of HCI (Walker, Sproull, & Subramani, 2004). Previously the computer systems were regarded only as tools, but nowadays the interfaces are more often designed to mimic the way humans communicate with each other (Qvartfordt, Jönssön, & Dahlbäck, 2003; Schaumburg, 2001). One way to humanize computers is to include computer agents as a part of human-computer interface. Agents communicate with users and, for example, help people to accomplish tasks carried out at the computer (e.g., Cassell, 2000; Churchill, Cook, Hodgson, Prevost, & Sullivan, 2000; Lester, Towns, Calloway, & FitzGerald, 2000).

Adding humanlike qualities to computers means that they become more anthropomorphic. Humanlike characteristics that can be used to increase the anthropomorphism include, for example, facial expressions, body posture, gaze direction, gestures, personality, and voice (Breazeal, 2003; Heckman & Wobbrock, 2000). The level of anthropomorphism of synthesized voice, for example, can be increased by better modeling of human voice. There are relatively few existing studies that have investigated the pros and cons of anthropomorphism (Schaumburg, 2001), and the results of these studies have been somewhat controversial. There are, for example, findings that support the importance of humanlike features in visual and audio components. It has been suggested, for example, that emotional expressions are crucial in order to make interaction with social agents more enjoyable (Lester, Towns, & FitzGerald, 1999). In addition, we (Ilves & Surakka, 2004) found recently that only the more humanlike voice evoked emotion-specific facial muscle responses when the subjects listened to sentences with different emotional content spoken by two different speech synthesizers. In our study subjects listened to synthesized emotionally negative, neutral, and positive sentences while their facial EMG activity from two muscles, corrugator supercilii and zygomaticus major, was measured. The results showed that the corrugator activity decreased significantly more during and after the positive sentences than during and after the neutral sentences spoken by the more human-like speech synthesizer. On the other hand, it has also been suggested that humanlike features in the computer may evoke false mental models of the interfaces and mislead the users into thinking that computer is more capable than it really is (Dehn & van Mulken, 2000; Shneiderman & Maes, 1997; Xiao, 2001). Further, in the study of Power et al. (2002) the abstract characters were rated as significantly more friendly and pleasant than the realistic-looking characters. So it cannot be taken for granted that adding humanlike features to computers always leads to more pleasant interaction between human and computer.

Because anthropomorphism means that the computer has features that give it humanlike qualities, integrating emotions into HCI can also be seen as an important component in enhancing anthropomorphism of computers. There is promising evidence that integrating emotions into HCI has positive effects on users. It has been found, for example, that emotionally positive feedback and intervention given by speech synthesis facilitates cognitive performance and helps recovery from autonomic arousal during computerized problem-solving tasks (Aula & Surakka, 2002; Partala & Surakka, 2004).

There are several ways for communicating emotions in human-human interaction, and of course these should be carefully considered when implementing emotions for anthropomorphic computer agents. Emotions are communicated frequently by nonverbal cues such as facial expressions and gestures (Ekman & Friesen, 1976 Surakka & Hietanen, 1998). Emotions can also be communicated, for example, by using speech as a communication tool. Speech is unique to humans, and it is also a very natural way of communication. It is known from the previous research that in vocal communication the basic discrete emotions (e.g., happiness and anger) can be communicated via and recognized from both the emotion-related prosodic cues and the content of the spoken messages. Emotions can also be communicated and recognized by the combination of both the content and the prosodic cues (Hietanen, Surakka, & Linnankoski, 1998; Scherer, Ladd, & Silverman, 1984). The emotion-related prosodic features that have been found to differentiate emotions are, for example, speech rate, loudness, and pitch level (Murray & Arnott, 1993). Emotions can be recognized quite accurately from vocal cues. Scherer (1989) has reported that the average recognition accuracy across the different studies has been 60%, when an average expected recognition by chance is about 12%.

There is also good evidence that using only the verbal content of the spoken message without prosodic variation evokes subjects' emotional reactions. Recent studies that have used synthesized speech with emotional content in the context of dimensional emotion theory clearly indicate that emotionally positive and negative emotional messages have significantly different consequences for the emotional responses and cognitive operations of a computer user (Aula & Surakka, 2002; Partala & Surakka, 2003). Based on this recent evidence speech synthesis seems to offer a promising alternative, for example, for giving emotional feedback to the user. Using speech in HCI has also the advantage that, because users are frequently overloaded with visual information by current interfaces, visually delivered emotional messages can be lost in the flood of the other visual information or distract the user from his or her current task. Further, the use of synthesized speech has important benefits when we want to study the effects of spoken emotional messages in HCI. By speech synthesizer it is possible to produce emotional messages by using either the content of the speech alone or by combining it with carefully controlled prosodic changes.

The development of speech synthesis has advanced quite fast during the last decades, and today there are several methods to produce synthetic speech. All of these have some benefits and some drawbacks. Perhaps the simplest and most popular way to produce natural sounding synthetic speech is the concatenative method, which uses prerecorded samples of speech with different lengths for digitizing. One of the important aspects in concatenative synthesis method is to find a correct length for the digitized unit. As the length of the unit increases also the naturalness of the speech improves, but at the same time the amount of required units and memory is increased (Lemmetty, 1999). Two speech synthesizers were used in the present study, Mikropuhe and Suopuhe. These two speech synthesizers are concatenative synthesizers, but they are based on different sample lengths. Suopuhe uses longer sample units, and thus the voice of Suopuhe sounds more natural than the voice of Mikropuhe. By using these two Finnish speech synthesizers it is possible to relatively easily explore the effects

of varying levels of anthropomorphism (i.e., more vs. less anthropomorphism) from subjects' emotional reactions.

The most frequently used approach to study peoples' subjective reactions to anthropomorphic features is to use questionnaires (Dehn & van Mulken, 2000; Prendinger, Mori, & Ishizuka, 2005). However, these kinds of self-reports have some disadvantages, for example, when studying the emotional responses of subjects. People may answer in a way that is socially desirable, and people may also be insensitive to the faint changes of their affects (Larsen et al., 2003). It is known that emotional reactions and processing of emotional information can be very fast. Even subliminal emotional stimulations are frequently found to significantly affect both minute physiological responses and more holistic subjective ratings (Whalen et al., 1998; Zajonc, 1980). In fact, Rosenberg and Ekman (1997) pointed out that, although facial expressions and physiological responses can be monitored continuously, there is no way to do this for subjective experiences. This means that physiological measurements can have some advantages over subjective rating scales and questionnaires. These two types of measurements can also be complementary to each other. Thus, in addition to questionnaires, another possibility for studying the effects of anthropomorphism is to use psychophysiological measurements. However, due to the complex nature of emotional reactions, the most reliable way is to use multiple methods concurrently.

The present aim was to study the effects of synthetic speech on subjects' physiology (pupil size variation) and psychological experiences by varying the emotional content of the messages and the level of anthropomorphism. Emotionally negative, neutral, and positive stimulus sentences were delivered to the subjects by the two above-mentioned speech synthesizers: Mikropuhe and Suopuhe. The prosodic features of both synthesizers were set to zero in order to keep the prosodic cues of the voices as neutral as possible. This made it possible to compare if these synthesizers (or in other words different levels of anthropomorphism) would evoke different emotion-related reactions.

Methods

Subjects

Twenty-six voluntary subjects (15 females, 11 males, mean age of 26.0, range 19–45 years) were studied. The subjects had normal or corrected to normal vision and normal hearing by their own report. They were unaware of the purpose of the experiment.

Equipment

The stimulus presentation was controlled by the E-Prime program (Schneider, Eschman, & Zuccolotto, 2002) running on a Pentium II PC computer. The stimuli were delivered via loudspeakers at a constant comfortable volume level. The pupil size was recorded from subjects' right eye with the Applied Science Laboratories (ASL) series 4000 eye-tracker with a sampling rate of 50 Hz. The speech synthesizers were Mikropuhe version 4.2 and Suopuhe (see http://phon.joensuu. fi/suopuhe/). Both synthesizers are con-

catenative Finnish-speaking synthesizers, and the sound of Suopuhe is based on longer sample units than Mikropuhe.

Stimuli

Twelve different sentences with emotional content, four negative, four neutral, and four positive sentences, were used (Table 8–1). Emotional sentences were produced using both the male voice of Mikropuhe speech synthesizer and the male voice of Suopuhe speech synthesizer. The length of each stimulus was approximately the same, 2.2 seconds. Fundamental frequency of both synthesizers' voices was set to 100 Hz. The speed of the synthesizers was set at the same rate, and the volume was nor-

Table 8–1. Stimulus sentences used in the experiment (translated from Finnish)

Stimulus Category	Object of the Sentence	
	Computer	**User**
Negative	I am angry.	You look angry.
	I am in a bad mood today.	You seem to be in a bad mood today.
Neutral	I feel normal.	You look normal.
	I feel ordinary today.	You seem ordinary today.
Positive	I am happy.	You look happy.
	I am in a good mood today.	You seem to be in a good mood today.

malized at 60 dB using Cool Edit 2000 program. Prosodic features of the voices were set to zero to keep the prosody of the voices as neutral as possible.

Experimental Procedure

The laboratory was introduced to the subjects, and they were told a cover story that the purpose of the experiment was to measure their involuntary eye movements during auditory information processing. The subjects were seated in a comfortable chair, and an adjustable neck rest was used to keep the eyes at a distance of 90 cm from the center of the computer screen. The subjects were told that the experiment would last about 10 minutes and they were instructed to carefully listen to the sentences spoken by a speech synthesizer.

Before the experimental phase speech synthesizers gave the instructions to the experiment so that subjects had time to get accustomed to the synthesized speech. After the instructions the eye tracker was calibrated and the experimental phase began. During the experiment the subject was instructed to look at a fixation cross at the center of the screen. Ten seconds from the onset of the fixation point the first stimulus was delivered. The fixation point disappeared 5 seconds after the offset of the stimulus, which indicated that the subject could move her or his eyes to prevent eye fatigue. Five seconds later the subject heard a beep and the fixation cross reappeared to signal the end of the resting period. Next stimulus was delivered after 5 seconds from the onset of the fixation point.

Finally, the subjects rated the stimuli on two dimensions, valence and arousal, with two nine-point bipolar scales. On the valence scale, the lower end of the scale represented a negative emotional experience, and the upper end represented a positive emotional experience. On the arousal scale, the lower end represented calm and the upper end highly aroused emotional experience. In both scales the center of the scale represented a neutral experience (see Bradley & Lang, 1994).

The stimuli were presented randomly and the ratings were automatically recorded by E-Prime 1.0 program. First, the subjects heard a stimulus and gave a valence rating. Then the stimulus was repeated and subjects gave an arousal rating. After each rating a beep indicated that the rating had been registered. The rating scales were presented in the computer screen and the subjects used a keyboard to give the ratings. Before the actual stimulus ratings, there were two exercise stimuli in order to make sure that subject was comfortable with giving the ratings. Before leaving the laboratory, the subjects were interviewed and debriefed about the purpose of the study.

Data Analysis

The pupil data were analyzed as follows. First, the eye blinks and artifacts were removed from the data. Sudden brief increases and decreases of at least 0.375 mm within a 20 ms time interval were judged as artifacts (Partala & Surakka, 2003). After removing the blinks and artifacts, the data were baseline corrected using a 500 ms prestimulus baseline. Then the data were categorized according to the synthesizers and the stimulus categories to two sets of data: data during the stimuli and data 3 seconds following the stimulus offset.

The statistical analysis was as follows. First, trend analyses were conducted separately for the data spoken by Suopuhe and those spoken by Mikropuhe using one-way repeated measures analysis of variance (ANOVA). Post hoc comparisons were made with Bonferroni corrected pairwise t-tests when needed, that is, when more than two pair-wise comparisons were made. Finally, the data spoken by different synthesizers were compared using paired samples t-test.

Results

Subjective Ratings

Figure 8–1 presents the averaged valence ratings. A one-way ANOVA for the data spoken by Suopuhe revealed a significant linear relationship between the emotion categories, $F(1, 25) = 50.0$, $p < 0.001$. Pair-wise comparisons showed that the ratings of valence were significantly lower for the negative sentences as compared to the neutral, $t = 3.1$, $df = 25$, $p < 0.05$, and the positive sentences, $t = 7.1$, $df = 25$, $p < 0.001$. The ratings of valence for the neutral sentences were significantly lower than for the positive sentences, $t = 6.7$, $df = 25$, $p < 0.001$. A one-way ANOVA for the data spoken by Mikropuhe also revealed a significant linear relationship between the emotion categories, $F(1, 25) = 27.2$, $p < 0.001$. Pair-wise comparisons showed that the ratings of valence were significantly lower for the negative sentences as compared to the neutral, $t = 2.6$, $df = 25$, $p < 0.05$, and the positive sentences, $t = 5.2$, $df = 25$, $p < 0.001$. The ratings of valence for the neutral sentences were significantly lower than for the positive sentences, $t = 4.8$, $df = 25$, $p < 0.001$. Pair-wise comparisons between the emo-

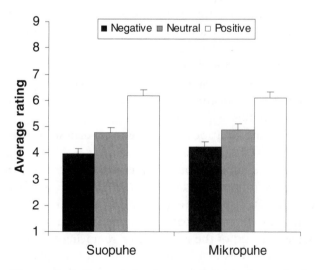

Figure 8–1. Averaged valence ratings and standard error of the mean (SEM) of the stimulus categories spoken by Suopuhe and Mikropuhe.

tion categories spoken by different synthesizers did not show any significant differences.

The averaged arousal ratings of the data spoken by Suopuhe and the data spoken by Mikropuhe are presented in Figure 8-2.

A one-way ANOVA for the data spoken by Suopuhe revealed a significant quadratic relationship between the emotion categories, $F(1, 25) = 8.1, p < 0.01$. Pairwise comparisons showed that the negative sentences were experienced as more arousing than the neutral sentences, $t = 2.1, df = 25, p < 0.05$. Also the difference between the neutral and positive sentences approached statistical significance, $t = 2.0, df = 25, p < 0.06$. The one-way ANOVA for the data spoken by Mikropuhe did not show significant effect of emotion category.

Pair-wise comparisons between the synthesizers showed that the negative sentences were rated as more arousing when the sentences were spoken by Suopuhe as

compared to the negative sentences spoken by Mikropuhe, $t = 2.7, df = 25, p < 0.05$. The differences between the neutral and positive sentences were not significant.

Pupil Diameter

Figure 8-3 and Figure 8-4 indicate that the effects of the emotion categories were somewhat different for the data spoken by Suopuhe and for the data spoken by Mikropuhe.

One-way ANOVAs for the data during the stimulus did not show significant effect of the emotion category for either the data spoken by Suopuhe or the data spoken by Mikropuhe. A one-way ANOVA for the data after the sentences spoken by Suopuhe revealed a significant quadratic relationship between the emotion categories, $F(1, 25) = 9.7, p < 0.01$. Pairwise comparisons showed that pupil dilation after the negative stimuli ($t = 2.5, df = 25, p < 0.05$) and the positive stimuli

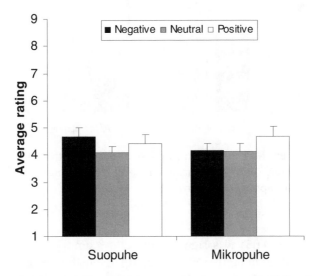

Figure 8–2. Averaged arousal ratings (and SEM) of the stimulus categories spoken by Suopuhe and Mikropuhe.

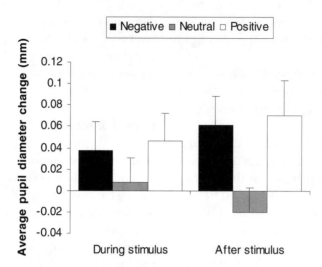

Figure 8–3. Averaged pupil size variations from the baseline (and SEM) during and after the stimulus categories spoken by Suopuhe.

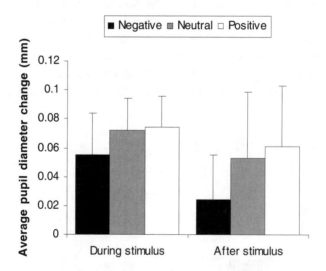

Figure 8–4. Averaged pupil size variations from the baseline (and SEM) during and after the stimulus categories spoken by Mikropuhe.

($t = 2.7$, $df = 25$, $p < 0.05$) was significantly larger than after neutral stimuli. The one-way ANOVA for the data spoken by Mikropuhe did not show a significant effect of emotion category. Pair-wise comparisons between the emotion categories spoken by different synthesizers did not show any significant differences.

Discussion

The present results showed that the sentences spoken by both speech synthesizers evoked changes in subjects' physiology and psychological experiences. However, the results revealed that the sentences spoken by Suopuhe, the more humanlike synthesizer, caused more variation in both the subjects' physiology and subjective experiences than the sentences spoken by Mikropuhe. The significant curvilinear association between the negative, neutral, and positive sentences was found for the pupil data after the sentences spoken by Suopuhe. Further analysis (i.e., 3 seconds from the stimulus offset) showed that pupil dilation was significantly larger after the negative and the positive sentences than after the neutral sentences when the sentences were spoken by Suopuhe. There were no significant differences between the stimulus categories when the sentences were spoken by Mikropuhe. In addition, the analysis of arousal ratings revealed significant results only for the data spoken by Suopuhe. There was a significant quadratic relationship between the sentences spoken by Suopuhe.

The analysis of valence ratings showed that the sentences spoken by both synthesizers were experienced as we expected. The positive sentences were rated as more positive than the negative or neutral sentences, and the negative sentences were experienced as more negative than the neutral or positive sentences.

Our pupil findings are in line with previous results and support the findings that pupils dilate to affective stimuli (Partala & Surakka, 2003). The association between the valence dimension and pupil dilation was curvilinear, as suggested earlier by Janisse (1974). According to the present results the arousing features of the stimulus are especially crucial. The pupils dilated after the negative and the positive sentences more than during the neutral sentences. The positive and the negative sentences were also rated as more arousing than the neutral sentences. These significant differences between the emotion categories were found only for the data spoken by Suopuhe. In contrast, the arousal ratings of the different sentence categories spoken by Mikropuhe did not differ. Further, there were no significant differences in pupil size variation when the sentences were spoken by Mikropuhe. Thus, our results are also in line with the findings, which emphasize the importance of anthropomorphic features (e.g., Ilves & Surakka, 2004; Lester et al., 1999).

Although the valence ratings of the negative sentences were lower than the valence ratings of the neutral and positive sentences, they were also quite high. This suggests that the sentences were experienced as quite pleasant in spite of the content of the messages. This is in line with some earlier findings that have found that even negatively worded feedback can have some positive consequences on subjects. For example, in the study of Partala and Surakka (2004) subjects were exposed to preprogrammed mouse delays in an interactive problem-solving task, and following the delays positively and negatively worded interventions were given via speech synthesizer. They found that frowning activity attenuated after both the negative and positive interventions. The smiling activity was largest during the positive interventions, but it increased also during the negative interventions. It has been previously suggested that people like to obtain feedback, or they even seek feedback because it is reassuring (see Ashford & Cummings, 1983; Kluger & DeNisi, 1996). Thus, in spite of the content of the feedback, it may have positive effects to the subjects' behavior.

One important factor in evoking emotions may be the relevance of the content of the stimuli for a person. For example, Cacioppo et al. (1985) have found earlier that facial EMG activity is sensitive only to personally relevant information processing. In our study more anthropomorphic emotionally negatively and positively charged sentences evoked stronger pupil and arousal responses than the neutral sentences. The neutral information can be seen as information that does not provide personally meaningful knowledge to the subjects, and for this reason, it may be ignored. Thus, feedback given by speech synthesizers can be used to regulate users' emotional state, as long as it is personally arousing.

As said, previous studies have found that positive intervention and feedback delivered through synthesized speech during human-computer interaction have positive effects on the user (Aula & Surakka, 2002: Partala & Surakka, 2004). In these studies only one synthesizer was used. In our study two speech synthesizers were used, without any interaction context between subject and computer. The results showed that in addition to the emotional content of the spoken message, the features of the voice had a significant effect. Thus, our results point out that when designing components of speech synthesizers and interfaces, the anthropomorphic features, at least in audio components, need to be taken into careful consideration, at least in the

cases we want to evoke and get in touch with users' emotional reactions.

In the present study the prosodic cues were kept as neutral as possible, and in spite of that significant changes in the subjects' physiology and subjective ratings were found. Previous findings have stated that emotions can be recognized from the content of the speech or the prosodic features of the voices. So, it is conceivable that adding prosody to the speech would produce even stronger effects than was the case for the present findings. The ratings of arousal of the stimulus were quite low, and it is probable that more arousing stimuli would cause stronger effects. Possibly speech prosody and the level of arousal a synthesizer is evoking in the user are positively associated. Thus, adding the prosodic cues may result in higher arousal experiences.

Although there is growing interest in developing anthropomorphic computer agents, little data exist to verify their impacts on users. Thus, our results offer important knowledge for the development of computer agents. Dehn and van Mulken (2000) also brought up the need for more systematic and fine-grained study. They conclude that several existing studies have, for example, manipulated various variables between the control and experimental condition, so the interpretation of the results is difficult. Further, it does not appear to be appropriate to ask whether the anthropomorphic agent improves human-computer interaction or not, but the questions must be more detailed (e.g., What kind of animated agent used in what kind of domain influences what aspects of the user's attitudes or performance?). The present study aimed to avoid these problems by focusing on comparing the emotional effects of two different speech synthesizers with carefully controlled experimental design. The previous research has also mainly concentrated on the effects of animated computer agents (e.g., Power, Wills, & Hall, 2002; Rickenberg & Reeves, 2000). However, the voice of an agent is at least as important as the appearance, but there exist only few studies investigating how people respond to agents' voices.

Users' emotional responses to anthropomorphism are also mainly unexplored. Besides the observation of human behavior and measuring performance when interacting with animated agents, users' subjective experiences have been measured with questionnaires. When studying the affective states of the users, self-reports have some limitations. Occasionally the changes in emotional states are so slight that people may be insensitive to them. Emotions are evoked quickly and their offset is typically within a time frame of few seconds. Although the subjective experience is an essential part of an emotional reaction, by using only self-reports, the faint and momentary changes in affects cannot be reached. Instead, by psychophysiological measurements these kinds of temporal changes are possible to study. We argue that in developing anthropomorphic features for HCI both physiological and behavioral recordings should be used. Using only behavioral methods (questionnaires and rating scales) may dramatically fail to tap the important subtle differences that are perceived from the communication of speech synthesizers. Our results, for example, revealed significantly different pupil reactions to two synthesizers, though the subjective valence ratings between synthesizers did not differ. Thus, our study showed that psychophysiological research orientation offers an objective and a complementary way to study emotional reactions to the computer agents, and more specifically, for example, to the different levels of anthropomorphism.

The most interesting finding in our study is the different emotional reactions to two different speech synthesizers. In the future, the comparison between natural and synthesized speech might be interesting. It could be one way to study on the issue of required realism to elicit emotional reaction. However, controlling the prosodic features of human voice is quite difficult, while the prosodic features of synthesized voice can be controlled carefully. This means that the effects of realism and naturalness can be studied reliably also by varying carefully the prosodic cues of synthetic voice. Thus, the focus of our future research is to study how carefully controlled changes in speech prosody affect changes in human psychophysiology.

In sum, our findings suggest that increasing the level of anthropomorphism in computer agents (like in an intervening speech synthesizer during problem situations) evokes stronger emotion-related psychological and physiological effects. In general, this can be considered as a desired goal because emotions are known to have a significantly modulating role for the quality of communication (Zajonc, 1980). Thus, anthropomorphism is important to take into account, for example, when designing social-emotional agents capable of establishing good rapport with the user. In addition, difficult questions related to anthropomorphism can be objectively studied by psychophysiological measurements.

Acknowledgements. We thank all the voluntary test subjects. This study was supported by the Academy of Finland (Project no. 177857).

References

Ashford, S. J., & Cummings, L. L. (1983). Feedback as an individual resource: Personal strategies of creating information. *Organizational Behavior and Human Performance*, *32*, 370-398.

Aula, A., & Surakka, V. (2002). Auditory emotional feedback facilitates human-computer interaction. In X. Faulkner, J. Finlay, & F. Détienne (Eds.), *Proceedings of HCI 2002* (pp. 337-349). London: Springer-Verlag.

Bradley, M. M., & Lang, P. J. (1994). Measuring emotions: The self-assessment manikin and the semantic differential. *Journal of Behavioral Therapy and Experimental Psychiatry*, *25*(1), 49-59.

Breazeal, C. (2003). Emotion and sociable humanoid robots. *International Journal of Human-Computer Studies*, *59*(1-2), 119-155.

Cacioppo, J. T., Petty, J. R., & Morris, K. J. (1985). Semantic, evaluative, and self-referent processing: Memory, cognitive effort, and somatovisceral activity. *Psychophysiology*, *22*(4), 371-384.

Cassell, J. (2000). Embodied conversational interface agents. *Communications of the ACM*, *43*(4), 70-78.

Churchill, E. F., Cook, L., Hodgson, P., Prevost, S., & Sullivan, J. W. (2000). May I help you? Designing embodied conversational agent allies. In J. Cassell, J. Sullivan, S. Prevost, & E. Churchill (Eds.), *Embodied conversational agents* (pp. 64-94). Cambridge, MA: MIT Press.

Damasio, A. (1994). *Descartes' error: Emotion, reason, and the human brain*. New York: Putnam.

Dehn, D. M., & van Mulken, S. (2000). The impact of animated interface agents: A review of empirical research. *International Journal of Human-Computer Studies*, *52*(1), 1-22.

Dimberg, U., Thunberg, M., & Elmehed, K. (2000). Unconscious facial reactions to emotional facial expressions. *Psychological Science*, *11*(1), 86-89.

Ekman, P. (1994). Strong evidence for universals in facial expressions: A reply to Russell's mistaken critique. *Psychological Bulletin*, *115*(2), 268-287.

Ekman, P., Friesen, W. V., O'Sullivan, M., Chan, A., Diacoyanni-Tarlatzis, I., Heider, K., et al. (1987). Universals and cultural differences in the judgments of facial expressions of emotion. *Journal of Personality and Social Psychology*, *53*(4), 712-717.

Ekman, P., & Friesen, W.V. (1976). *Pictures of facial affect*. Palo Alto. CA.: Consulting Psychologists Press.

Frijda, N. H. (1986). *The emotions*. New York: Cambridge University Press.

Heckman, C. E. & Wobbrock, J. O. (2000). Put your best face forward: Anthropomorphic agents, e-commerce consumers, and the law. In C. Sierra, M. Gini, & J. S. Rosenschein (Eds.), *Proceedings of Autonomous Agents 2000* (pp. 435-442). Barcelona, Spain: ACM Press.

Hietanen, J. K., Surakka, V., & Linnankoski, I. (1998). Facial electromyographic responses to vocal affect expressions. *Psychophysiology*, *35*, 530-536.

Hyönä, J., Tommola, J., & Alaja, A.-M. (1995). Pupil dilation as a measure of processing load in simultaneous interpretation and other language tasks. *Quarterly Journal of Experimental Psychology: Human Experimental Psychology*, *48A*(3), 598-612.

Ilves, M., & Surakka, V. (2004). Subjective and physiological responses to emotional content of synthesized speech. In N. Magnanet-Thalmann, C. Joslin, & H. Kim (Eds.), *Proceedings of CASA 2004* (pp. 19-29). Geneva, Switzerland: Computer Graphics Society (CGS).

Janisse, M. P. (1974). Pupil size, affect and exposure frequency. *Social Behavior & Personality*, *2*(2), 125-146.

Kahneman, D., & Beatty, J. (1966). Pupil diameter and load on memory. *Science*, *154*, 1583-1585.

Kluger, A. N., & DeNisi, A. (1996). The effects of feedback interventions on performance: A historical review, a meta-analysis, and a preliminary feedback intervention theory. *Psychological Bulletin, 119*(2), 254-284.

Lang, P. J., Greenwald, M. K., Bradley, M. M., & Hamm, A. O. (1993). Looking at pictures: Affective, facial, visceral, and behavioral reactions. *Psychophysiology, 30,* 261-273.

Larsen, J. T., Norris, C. J., & Cacioppo, J. T. (2003). Effects of positive and negative affect on electromyographic activity over zygomaticus major and corrugator supercilii. *Psychophysiology, 40,* 776-785.

Lemmetty, S. (1999). *Review of speech synthesis technology.* Unpublished master's thesis, Helsinki University of Technology, Finland. Retrieved November 3, 2007, from http://www.acoustics.hut.fi/~slemmett/dippa/thesis.pdf

Lester, J., Towns, S., Calloway, C., & FitzGerald, P. (2000). Deictic and emotive communication in animated pedagogical agents. In J. Cassell, J. Sullivan, S. Prevost, & E. Churchill (Eds.), *Embodied conversational agents* (pp. 123-154). Cambridge, MA: MIT Press.

Lester, J. C., Towns, S. G., & FitzGerald, P. J. (1999). Achieving affective impact: Visual emotive communication in lifelike pedagogical agents. *International Journal of AI in Education, 10*(3-4), 278-291.

Murray, I. A., & Arnott, J. L. (1993). Toward the simulation of emotion in synthetic speech: A review of the literature on human vocal emotion. *Journal of the Acoustical Society of America, 93*(2), 1097-1108.

Nass, C., Steuer, J., & Tauber, E. R. (1994). Computers are social actors. In B. Adelson, S. T. Dumais, & J. S. Olson (Eds.) *Proceedings of CHI 1994* (pp. 72-78). Boston: ACM Press.

Partala, T., & Surakka, V. (2003). Pupil size variation as an indication of affective processing. *International Journal of Human-Computer Studies, 59,* 185-198.

Partala, T., & Surakka, V. (2004). The effects of affective interventions in human-computer interaction. *Interacting with Computers, 16*(2), 295-309.

Picard, R. (1997). *Affective computing.* Cambridge, MA: MIT Press.

Power, G., Wills, G., & Hall, W. (2002). User perception of anthropomorphic characters with varying levels of interaction. In X. Faulkner, J. Finlay, & F. Détienne (Eds.), *Proceedings of HCI 2002* (pp. 37-52). London: Springer-Verlag.

Prendinger, H., Mori, J., & Ishizuka, M. (2005). Using human physiology to evaluate subtle expressivity of a virtual quizmaster in a mathematical game. *International Journal of Human-Computer Studies, 62*(2), 231-245.

Qvartfordt, P., Jönssön, A., & Dahlbäck, N. (2003). The role of spoken feedback in experiencing multimodal interfaces as human-like. In S. L. Oviatt, T. Darrell, M. T. Mayburt, & W. Wahslter (Eds.), *Proceedings of ICMI 2003* (pp. 250-257). Vancouver, Canada: ACM Press.

Rickenberg, R., & Reeves, B. (2000). The effects of animated characters on anxiety, task performance, and evaluations of user interfaces. In T. Turner, G. Szwillus, M. Czerwinski, F. Peterno, & S. Pemberton (Eds.), *Proceedings of CHI 2000: Human factors in computing systems* (pp. 49-56) Hague, Netherlands: ACM Press.

Rosenberg, E. L., & Ekman, P. (1997). Coherence between expressive and experiential systems in emotion. In P. Ekman & E. L. Rosenberg (Eds.), *What the face reveals: Basic and applied studies of spontaneous expression using the facial action coding system (FACS)* (pp. 63-85). Oxford, UK: Oxford University Press.

Schaumburg, H. (2001). Computers as tools or as social actors? The users' perspective on anthropomorphic agents. *International Journal of Cooperative Information Systems, 10*(1-2), 217-234.

Scherer, K. R. (1989). Vocal measurement of emotion. In R. Plutchik & H. Kellerman (Eds.), *Emotion—Theory, research, and experience* (Vol. 4, pp. 233-259). San Diego, CA: Academic Press.

Scherer, K. R., Ladd, D. R., & Silverman, K. E. A. (1984). Vocal cues to speaker affect: Testing two models. *Journal of the Acoustical Society of America*, 76, 1346-1356.

Schluroff, M. (1982). Pupil responses to grammatical complexity of sentences. *Brain & Language*, 17(1), 133-145.

Schneider, W., Eschman, A., & Zuccolotto, A. (2002). *E-Prime user's guide*. Pittsburgh, PA: Psychology Software Tools.

Shneiderman, B., & Maes, P. (1997). Direct manipulation vs. interface agents. *Interactions*, 4(6), 42-61.

Suopuhe. (2004). Retrieved April 19, 2004, from http://phon.joensuu.fi/suopuhe/. University of Helsinki, & University of Joensuu.

Surakka, V., & Hietanen, J. K. (1998). Facial and emotional reactions to Duchenne and non-Duchenne smiles. *International Journal of Psychophysiology*, 29, 23-33.

Walker, J. H., Sproull, L., & Subramani, R. (2004). Using a human face in an interface. In E. Dykstra-Erickson, & M. Tscheligi (Eds.), *Proceedings of CHI 2004* (pp. 85-91). Vienna: ACM Press.

Whalen, P. J., Rauch, S. L., Etcoff, N. L., McInerney, S. C., Lee, M. B., & Jenike, M. A. (1998). Masked presentations of emotional facial expressions modulate amygdala activity without explicit knowledge. *The Journal of Neuroscience*, 18, 411-418.

Xiao, J. (2001). Understanding the use and utility of anthropomorphic interface agents. In J. Jacko & A. Sears (Eds.), *Exended Abstracts CHI 2001* (pp. 409-410). Seattle, WA: ACM Press.

Zajonc, R. B. (1980). Feeling and thinking: Preferences need no inferences. *American Psychologist*, 35, 151-175.

CHAPTER 9

LUCIA, a New Emotive/Expressive Italian Talking Head

Piero Cosi and Carlo Drioli

Summary

In this chapter we present a study on audiovisual speech analysis and synthesis, for the creation of natural and expressive talking heads. The framework for the modeling of facial and lip movements, and the visual design of an animated MPEG-4 talking face, are first discussed. Then, the design of the voice synthesis modules aimed at producing expressive/emotive speech synthesis is described. The resulting audiovisual synthesis system integrates voice synthesis, facial animation, and a markup language-based interface that allows production of synchronized and emotionally coherent audio and video outputs from tagged text.

Introduction

" . . . Human communication technologies have matured to the point where it is now possible to conceptualize, develop and investigate computer systems that interact with people much like people interact with each other . . . " (OGI CSLU Reading Tutor Project[1]), and a new generation of intelligent and embodied animated virtual agents that engage users in natural face-to-face conversational interaction is not a futuristic flight of the imagination anymore (Cole et al., 2003). An intelligent virtual agent (IVA) is one that mimics the actions of real humans and behaves intelligently in the context of a specific application. A complete IVA

---

[1]OGI CSLU—Reading Tutor Project: http://cslr.colorado.edu/beginweb/reading/reading.html

must simultaneously interpret the user's auditory and visible speech, eye movements, facial expressions, and gestures to detect for example agreement, distress, trouble, confusion, desire to interrupt, and so on, and must also produce natural and expressive auditory and visible speech with facial expressions and gestures appropriate to the physical nature of language production, the context of the dialogue, and the goals of the task. In other words, an IVA will mimic the actions of real persons and behave intelligently and appropriately in the context of specific task domains.

The research in this field is relevant to a wide number of applications, in which human-computer interaction is characterized by natural face-to-face conversation: from dialog systems for information access and e-commerce services, to e-learning tutoring for teaching speech and language skills to children, to animation of avatars and characters in virtual environments and computer games.

The final goal of our work is to develop an Italian female IVA we named LUCIA (Cosi, Fusaro, & Tisato, 2003) that would be able to engage adults and children in face-to-face conversational interaction.

At this stage of LUCIA's development, only her expressive talking head capabilities have been taken into consideration. LUCIA is, in fact, a three-dimensional animated MPEG-4 (http://www.chiariglione.org/mpeg) computer talking head that produces emotive/expressive natural speech produced by an emotive/expressive version (Tesser, Cosi, Drioli, & Tisato, 2005) of the Italian Festival TTS (Cosi, Tesser, Gretter, & Avesani, 2001), as illustrated in the block diagram shown in Figure 9–1, and a wide variety of facial expressions and emotions.

LUCIA's Animation Engine

The knowledge that both acoustic and visual signal simultaneously convey linguistic, extralinguistic, and paralinguistic information is well accepted in the speech communication community, and this knowledge constitutes the basis for the work presented here.

Instead of imposing ad hoc expert rules, a data-driven procedure was utilized to build LUCIA both from an acoustic and a

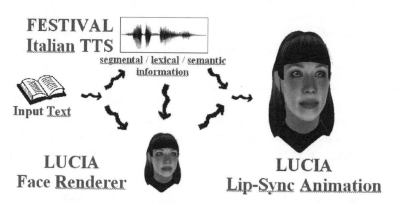

Figure 9–1. LUCIA's functional block diagram.

visual point of view. Our Italian talking head has been in fact directly driven by various style- and emotion-specific speech corpora together with their emotional visual counterparts, in the form of labial movements and facial expressions.

Visual Framework

Visual data are physically extracted by an automatic optotracking movement analyzer for 3D kinematics data acquisition called ELITE (Ferrigno & Pedotti, 1995). ELITE provides 3D coordinate reconstruction starting from 2D perspective projections by means of a stereophotogrammetric procedure, which allows a free positioning of the TV cameras. The 3D data coordinates of 28 reflecting mark-

ers positioned on the model subject face are then used to create a lips articulatory model and to drive directly, copying human facial movements, our expressive and emotive talking face (Figure 9-2).

All the movements of the 28 markers are recorded and collected, together with their velocity and acceleration, simultaneously with the coproduced speech, which is usually segmented and analyzed by means of PRAAT (http://www.fon.hum.uva.nl/praat) (Boersma, 1996), that computes also intensity, duration, spectrograms, formants, pitch synchronous F0, and various voice quality (VQ) parameters that are quite significant in characterizing emotive/expressive speech (Drioli, Tisato, Cosi, & Tesser, 2003; Magno Caldognetto, Cosi, Drioli, Tisato, & Cavicchio, 2003).

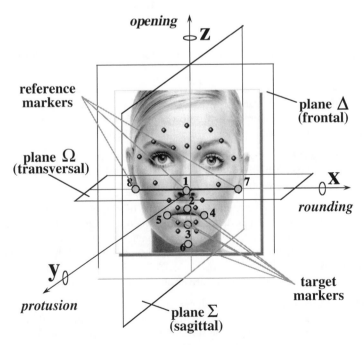

Figure 9–2. Position of reflecting markers and reference planes for the articulatory movement data collection on a real face.

Lips Articulation Model

The most common parameters selected to quantify the labial configuration modifications used in the analysis of the labial movements are listed in Table 9-1.

The parameter estimation procedure for LUCIA's lips articulation model is based on a least squared phoneme-oriented error minimization scheme with a strong convergence property, between real articulatory data Y(n) and modeled curves F(n) for the whole set of R stimuli belonging to the same phoneme set:

$$e = \sum_{r=1}^{R} \left(\sum_{n=1}^{N} \left(Y_r(n) - F_r(n) \right)^2 \right) \quad (1)$$

where F(n) is generated by a modified version of the Cohen-Massaro coarticulation model (Cohen & Massaro, 1993) as introduced in Pelachaud et al. (2001) and Cosi et al. (2002a). This model imple-

ments Löfqvist's gestural theory of speech production (Löfqvist, 1990), and it is profoundly inspired by Browman and Goldstein's work on articulatory phonology (Browman & Goldstein, 1986). Each phoneme is specified in terms of speech control parameters (e.g., lip rounding, upper and lower lip displacement, lip protrusion) characterized by a target value and a dominance function.

Dominance functions of consecutive phonemes overlap in time and specify the degree of influence that a speech segment has over articulators in the production of preceding or following segments. The final articulatory trajectory of a specific parameter is the weighted average of the sum of all dominances scaled by the magnitude of the associated targets.

The values of the coefficients of the model have been determined starting from a corpus of real labial movements

Table 9–1. Meaning of some of the most commonly chosen articulatory parameters

Lip opening (LO), calculated as the distance between markers placed on the central points of the upper and lower lip vermillion borders [d(m2,m3)]; this parameter correlates with the *high-low* phonetic dimension.

Lip rounding (LR), corresponding to the distance between the left and right corners of the lips [d(m4,m5)], which correlates with the *rounded-unrounded* phonetic dimension: negative values correspond to the lip spreading.

Anterior/posterior movements (protrusion) of upper lip and lower lip (ULP and LLP), calculated as the distance between the marker placed on the central points of either the upper and lower lip and the frontal plane Δ containing the line crossing the markers placed on the lobes of the ears and perpendicular to Δ plane [d(m2, Δ), d(m3, Δ)]. These parameters correlate with the feature *protruded-retracted*: negative values quantify the lip retraction.

Upper and lower lip vertical displacements (UL, LL), calculated as a distance between the markers placed on the central point of either upper and lower lip and the transversal plane Ω passing through the tip of the nose and the markers on the ear lobes [d(m2, Ω), d(m3, Ω)]. Hence, positive values correspond to a reduction of the displacement of the markers from the Ω plane. As told before, these parameters are normalized in relation to the lip resting position.

of an Italian speaker pronouncing VCV symmetrical stimuli, where V is one of the vowels /a/ /i/ or /u/, and C is one of the Italian consonant phonemes. The corpus represents spatio-temporal trajectories of labial parameters such as those specified in Table 9-1, and even if the number of parameters to be optimized is rather high, the size of the corpus is large enough to allow a meaningful estimation. However, due to the presence of several local minima, the optimization process has to be manually controlled in order to assist the algorithm convergence.

The mean total error between real and simulated trajectories for the whole set of parameters is lower than 0.3 mm in the case of bilabial and labiodental consonants in the /a/ and /i/ contexts (Perin, 2000, p. 63).

MPEG-4 Animation

LUCIA is able to generate a 3D mesh polygonal model by directly importing its structure from a VRML file (Hartman & Wernecke, 1996) and to build its animation in real time.

LUCIA emulates the functionalities of the mimic muscles, by the use of specific *displacement functions* and of their following action on the skin of the face. The activation of such functions is determined by specific parameters that encode small muscular actions acting on the face, and these actions can be modified in time in order to generate the wished animation. Such parameters, in MPEG-4, take the name of *facial animation parameters,* and their role is fundamental for achieving a natural movement. Moreover, the muscular action is made explicit by means of the deformation of a polygonal reticule built around some particular key points

called *facial definition parameters* (FDP) that correspond to the junction on the skin of the mimic muscles.

LUCIA is a graphic MPEG-4 compatible facial animation engine implementing a decoder compatible with the *predictable facial animation object profile*. FDPs define the shape of the model while FAPs define the facial actions and, given the shape of the model, the animation is obtained by specifying the FAP stream that is for each frame the values of FAPs (Figure 9-3). In a FAP stream, each frame has two lines of parameters. In the first line the activation of a particular marker is indicated (0, 1), while in the second, the target values are stored in terms of differences from the previous ones.

Moving only the FDPs is not sufficient to smoothly move the whole 3D model; thus, each *feature point* is related to a particular *influence zone* constituted by an ellipses that represents a zone of the reticule where the movement of the vertexes is strictly connected. Finally, after having established the relationship for the whole set of FDPs and the whole set of vertexes, all the points of the 3D model can be simultaneously moved with a graded strength following a raised-cosine function rule associated to each FDP.

Each feature point follows MPEG-4 specifications where a FAP corresponds to a minimal facial action. When a FAP is activated (i.e., when its intensity is not null) the feature point on which the FAP acts is moved in the direction signaled by the FAP itself (up, down, left, right, etc). Using the pseudomuscular approach, the facial model's points within the region of this particular feature point get deformed. A facial expression is characterized, not only by the muscular contraction that gives rise to it, but also by an intensity and a duration. The intensity factor is

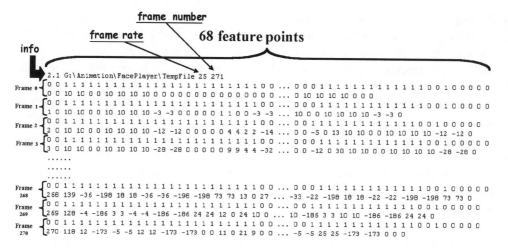

Figure 9–3. The FAP stream.

rendered by specifying an intensity for every FAP. The temporal factor is modeled by three parameters: onset, apex, and offset (Ekman & Friesen, 1978).

The FAP stream needed to animate a *facial animation engine* (FAE) could be completely synthesized by using a specific animation model, such as the lips coarticulation one used in LUCIA, or it could be reconstructed on the basis of real data captured by an optotracking hardware, such as ELITE.

At the current stage of development, as illustrated in Figure 9-4, LUCIA is a textured young female 3D face model built with 25,423 polygons: 14,116 belong to the skin, 4616 to the hair, 2688 × 2 to the eyes, 236 to the tongue, and 1029 to the teeth, respectively.

Currently the model is divided in two subsets of fundamental polygons: the skin on one hand and the inner articulators, such as the tongue and the teeth, or the facial elements such as the eyes and the hair, on the other. This subdivision is quite useful when animation is running, because only the reticule of polygons corresponding to the skin is directly driven by the pseudomuscles, and it constitutes a continuous and unitary element, while the other anatomical components move themselves independently and in a rigid way, following translations and rotations (for example, the eyes rotate around their center). According to this strategy the polygons are distributed in such a way that the resulting visual effect is quite smooth with no rigid "jumps" over the entire 3D model.

Visual Emotions

Different from lip movements, at the present time, emotional visual configurations are not learned by specific model built on real data, such as the lips, but are designed and refined by means of visual inspection of real data. Emotional configurations are then superimposed to the lips' movement. As already underlined in the above section, in MPEG-4 animations, FDPs define the shape of the model while FAPs define the facial actions. The intensity and the duration of an emotive expression are driven by an intensity factor that is rendered by specifying an intensity for every FAP, and by a tempo-

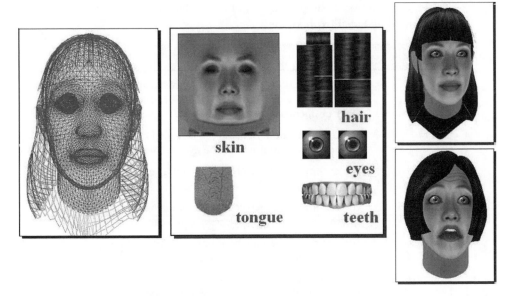

Figure 9–4. Lucia's wireframe, textures, and renderings.

ral factor which is modeled by onset, apex, and offset parameters, as explained in Ekman and Friesen (1978).

The onset and offset represent, respectively, the time the expression takes to appear and to disappear; the apex corresponds to the duration for which the facial expression is at its peak intensity value. These parameters are fundamental to convey the proper meaning of the facial expressions. In our system, every facial expression is characterized by a set of FAPs. Every set of FAPs allows for example the creation of the six facial expressions corresponding to the six basic primary emotions of Ekman's set (Table 9–2), chosen here for the sake of simplicity, and for every expression only three levels of intensity (low, medium, high) have been simulated.

As for LUCIA, "emotion basis" *EB(t)* and "emotion display" *ED(t),* both functions of the time *t,* are distinguished. An *EB(t)* involves a specific zone of the face such as the eyebrow, mouth, jaw, eyelid, and so on. *EB(t)* includes also facial move-

ments such as nodding, shaking, turning the head, and movement of the eyes. Each *EB(t)* is defined as a set of MPEG-4 compliant FAP parameters:

$$EB(t) = \{ fap3 = v_1(t);$$
$$\ldots\ldots\ldots\ldots; fap68 = v_k(t)\}$$

where $v_1(t),\ldots,v_k(t)$ specify the FAPs' function intensity value created by the user. An *EB(t)* can also be defined as a combination of *EB'(t)* by using the '+' operator in this way:

$$EB'(t) = EB_1'(t) + EB_2'(t)$$

The emotion display is finally obtained by a linear scaling:

$$ED'(t) = EB(t)*c = \{ fap3 = v_1(t)*c;$$
$$\ldots\ldots\ldots\ldots; fap68 = v_k(t)*c)\}$$

where *EB* is a *facial basis* and *c* a constant. The operator * multiplies each of the FAPs constituting the *EB* by the constant *c*. The onset, offset, and apex (i.e., the

Table 9–2. The six basic primary emotions of Ekman's set with corresponding facial expressions

Expression	Description
Anger	The inner eyebrows are pulled downward and together. The eyes are wide open. The lips are pressed against each other or opened to expose the teeth.
Fear	The eyebrows are raised and pulled together. The inner eyebrows are bent upward. The eyes are tense and alert.
Disgust	The eyebrows and eyelids are relaxed. The upper lip is raised and curled, often asymmetrically.
Happiness	The eyebrows are relaxed. The mouth is open and the mouth corners pulled back toward the ears.
Sadness	The inner eyebrows are bent upward. The eyes are slightly closed. The mouth is relaxed.
Surprise	The eyebrows are raised. The upper eyelids are wide open, the lower relaxed. The jaw is opened.

duration of the expression) of emotion is determined by the weighed sum of the functions $v_k(t)$ ($k = 3,...,68$) created by mouse actions. In Figure 9–5, two simple emotional examples for fear and happiness are illustrated.

LUCIA's Voice: Emotive Text-to-Speech Synthesis

LUCIA's voice relies on an emotive text-to-speech synthesis aimed at producing emotionally adequate speech starting from a tagged text. Emotive speech synthesis has recently gained much attention, as new expressive/emotive human-machine interfaces are being studied that try to simulate the human behavior while reproducing man-machine dialogs, and various attempts to incorporate the expression of emotions into synthetic speech have been made (Murray & Arnott, 1993; Schröder, 2001).

The speech characterization of a certain emotion must be defined by the measure of its associated acoustic correlates, which directly derive from the physiologic constraints. For example, when feeling fear or happiness, the heart beats, bloody pressure increases, mouth becomes dry and there are occasional muscle tremors, the voice increases in loudness and speech rate, and the spectrum becomes richer in high frequency components (Cahn, 1990). Many researches on the vocal expression of emotion have demonstrated that many features may be involved. They tended to be focused on prosody correlates such as pitch variables, especially F0 level and range, but also on the pitch contour and on the amount of jitter[2] or shimmer,[3] pausing

---

[2]Jitter is perceptual cycle-to-cycle pitch variations.

[3]Shimmer is the perceptual cycle-to-cycle amplitude variation.

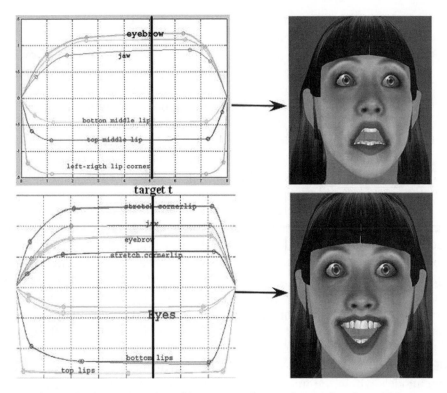

Figure 9–5. Fear (top) and happiness (bottom) emotional examples.

structure, speech rate, and intensity differences (Gobl & Chasaide, 2003). These parameters are relatively easy to measure and control (Scherer, 1986). However, other fundamental speech correlates of the emotions are based on the spectral and voice/speech quality[4] analysis.

The voice engine of LUCIA is based on the Festival text-to-speech synthesis framework developed at CSTR (Taylor, Black, & Caley, 1988), and on the MBROLA diphone concatenation acoustic back-end (Dutoit & Leich, 1993). In the following, two components that are particularly relevant to emotive speech synthesis will be discussed, that is, the prosodic control module and the voice quality control module.

The task of a prosodic module in a TTS synthesizer is that of computing the values of a set of prosodic variables, starting from the linguistic information contained in the text that has to be synthesized. In up-to-date TTS technologies, synthesis control has been mainly focusing on phoneme duration and pitch, which are the two main parameters conveying the prosodic information. Recently, data-driven machine learning techniques, such as CARTs (classification and regression trees; Breiman, Friedman, Olshen, & Stone, 1984), have proven to be effective for prosody modeling, and for providing substantial improvements over previously known rule-based approaches. Trees are

---

[4]Voice quality distinguishes the modality of the glottal signal production (tense voice, creaky voice, modal voice, breathy voice, harsh voice, whispery voice).

constructed by a data-driven training process, and are made of a set of yes/no or if/then questions relating to the structural linguistic data in order to predict the dependent prosodic variable.

Results on the use of simple phoneme duration and F0-based CARTs for learning different speaking styles for Italian have been reported in Cosi et al. (2002b) and Tesser et al. (2004), and the learning of emotive prosody is addressed in Tesser et al. (2005). This approach to the modeling of prosodic correlates of emotional speech will be discussed in the following.

Today, the speech synthesis community is also showing an increasing interest in the control of a broader class of voice characteristics. As an example, voice quality is known to play an important role in emotive speech, and some recent studies have addressed the exploitation of source models within the framework of articulatory synthesis to control the characteristics of voice phonation (d'Alessandro & Doval, 1998; Gobl & Chasaide, 2003). Intensity, for example, intended as the acoustical correlate of loudness, can in principle be roughly controlled by changing a gain factor uniformly across the spectrum. However, it is recognized that the result of such processing is not perceived as natural due to the lack of spectral balance modifications correlated to vocal effort variations that occur in real speech (Campbell, 1995; Sluijter, van Heuven, & Pacilly, 1997). Other voice quality cues are important as well in the characterization of nonmodal phonatory styles observed in emotive speech, and the control of the related acoustic cues in a diphone concatenation framework is required to embed a set of ad hoc signal processing techniques to modify

the original timbre characteristics of recorded diphones.

Various approaches are known that can be used to convert the timbre of a neutral voice into that of an emotional one. A possible choice is to use voice conversion algorithms (Kain & Macon, 2001; Stylianou, Cappé, & Moulines, 1998), usually based on Gaussian mixture models, which are used to transform the spectral characteristics of the voice of a speaker into that of another one. Some experiments have been done with this regard (Drioli et al., 2003) but only for a small corpus of VCV[5] sequence such as "aba" /'aba/ and "ava" /'ava/ uttered with different emotions. Another possible technique is based on the study and analysis of the acoustic correlates of the emotions, aimed at providing simple signal processing manipulations (e.g., changing the spectral tilt, adding aspiration noise, or changing the shimmer and jitter), which will allow switching from a neutral timbre to an emotional one. Here we will discuss this last approach in combination with the CART-based prosodic modeling.

Analysis of Emotive Speech: Emotional Database

The best speech material suited for studying emotions would be that produced spontaneously during naturally occurring emotional events. However, quite serious methodological problems arise when collecting these data. Emotional voice samples obtained in natural situations are generally rare, very brief, and not infrequently suffering from bad recording quality (Scherer, 2003). In addition, there

---

[5]VCV means vowel-consonant-vowel.

are often severe labeling problems in determining the precise nature of the underlying emotion. Moreover, for training TTS prosodic models a large emotional corpus is required. For all these reasons, the simulated (portrayed) vocal expressions approach was chosen here. Professional actors were asked to produce vocal expressions of emotion (often using standard verbal content) as based on emotion labels and/or typical scenarios (Scherer, 2003). Using this method, as pointed out by Scherer (1986), it cannot be excluded that actors overemphasize the expression of emotion, and that emotions reflect socio-cultural norms or expectations more than the psychophysiological effects on the voice as they occur under natural conditions. Nevertheless, unlike for the emotional ASR framework, TTS synthesis is a field in which several applications oriented towards the traditional emotion archetypes exist (Douglas-Cowie, Cowie, & Campbell, 2003).

The Emotional-CARINI (E-Carini) database has been recorded for this study. It contains the recording of the novel *Il Colombre* by Dino Buzzati read and acted by C. Carini, a professional Italian actor, in different elicited emotions. According to Ekman's theory (Ekman, 1992) six basic emotions plus the neutral (narrative-style) one have been taken into consideration: anger, disgust, fear, happiness, sadness, and surprise. The duration of the database is about 15 minutes for each emotion.

Emotional Prosodic Data-Driven Modeling: A Differential Approach

A wide number of studies on speech and emotions investigate the differences of emotional states with respect to a "neutral" state (Anolli & Ciceri, 1997; Huang, Hon, & Acero, 2001; Murray & Arnott 1993), and the transformation of a neutral utterance (real or synthetic) into an emotional one has been attempted with various techniques. Here a CART data-driven approach will be used to design an emotional prosodic module that learns the differences between the neutral prosody and the emotional one. For each prosodic parameter x (i.e., F0 and duration), the parameter difference is given by $\Delta x = x_E - x_N$, where x_E is the emotional value for parameter x, as given by the acoustic analysis of the emotional database, and x_N is the neutral one, as predicted by a prosodic module trained on a neutral database. In the synthesis stage, the emotional data will be obtained using the simple superimposing model $x_E = x_N + \Delta x$. To be able to separate the macro-prosody factors from the micro-segmental prosody ones, and to reduce data sparseness, various solutions were adopted, including the use of z-scores, normalization with respect to value ranges, and the use of parametric models for intonation curve (Tesser, 2005; Tesser et al., 2005).

The training of differential CARTs was preferred over the training of emotion-specific CARTs, because this approach allowed us to use smaller databases for the different emotions (15 minutes each in our case, whereas the neutral one had a duration of about 50 minutes). Moreover, with this approach it is straightforward to implement smooth transitions from neutral to emotional speech for each emotion.

Duration E-Model

The macro-prosodic differences on duration are represented in Table 9–3, where the average statistics of the duration of

Table 9–3. Phoneme duration means (μ) and standard deviations (σ) calculated on the E-Carini database for different emotions

Emotion	μ (s)	σ (s)	μ_Δ (s)	σ_Δ (s)
Neutral	0.094	0.045	—	—
Anger	0.077	0.034	−0.017	−0.010
Disgust	0.103	0.055	0.009	0.011
Fear	0.078	0.036	−0.016	−0.009
Joy	0.076	0.032	−0.018	−0.013
Sadness	0.104	0.052	0.010	0.007
Surprise	0.076	0.033	−0.018	−0.012

Note. The columns μ_Δ and σ_Δ represent the mean and the standard deviation of the differences between the emotional durations that and neutral ones.

phones in the different emotions are shown.

Looking at the differences between the emotive durations and the neutral ones (μ_Δ), it can be observed that the emotions with a negative σ_Δ might have a faster rhythm in comparison with the neutral one, while those with a positive value might be slowed down. This is only a broad analysis, but it is useful to have a general picture of the various rhythms used in the emotions. Details on the procedures for the training of the statistical model are given in Tesser et al. (2005). Using this approach the emotive duration prediction can be separate into a macro- and a segmental prosodic part. The macro-prosodic part is implemented by a table of the means and standard deviations for each phoneme and emotion, and the segmental prosodic part it is implemented by the differential CARTs.

Intonation E-Model

The macro-prosodic component of the intonation is the F0 mean and range val-ues. Table 9–4 shows the average statistics of the pitch mean, lower bounds (LB) and upper bounds (UB), the pitch range (R = UB − LB), and the differences with the neutral for each emotions in the E-Carini database.

Also in the intonation case for effective comparison between neutral and emotional values it is necessary to find a good representation of the data. A valuable representation for intonation curves is the PaIntE (Parametric Representation of Intonation Events) model (Cosi et al., 2002c; Möhler, 1998; Möhler & Conkie, 1998). A pitch range normalization was performed in order to get rid of the influence of different pitch range levels in the different emotions. This normalization was done using the LB and UB values of Table 9–4. If we call PN_{Ereal} the real normalized PaIntE parameter vector in the emotional case and PN_{Npred} the predicted normalized PaIntE vector in the neutral case, the difference is given by ?PN = PN_{Ereal} − PN_{Npred}. The whole procedure for the design of the emotional intonation module is given in Tesser et al.

Table 9–4. Pitch boundaries and means for the different emotions in the E-Carini data-base

Emotion	LB (Hz)	μ (Hz)	UB (Hz)	R (Hz)	LB_Δ (Hz)	μ_Δ (Hz)	UB_Δ (Hz)	R_Δ (Hz)
Neutral	62	105	213	169	—	—	—	—
Anger	66	122	258	192	4	17	45	23
Disgust	53	81	238	185	−9	−24	25	16
Fear	66	114	223	157	4	9	10	−12
Joy	63	129	308	245	1	24	95	76
Sadness	53	89	208	155	−9	−16	−5	−14
Surprise	66	136	250	184	4	31	37	15

Note. The LB column represents the lower boundary, UB the upper boundary, and R the pitch range. The columns with the subscript symbol Δ represents the same entity calculated on the differences between the emotional F0 and the neutral one.

(2005). Using this approach the emotive intonation prediction can be separate in a macro-prosodic part and a segmental one. The macro-prosodic part is implemented by Table 9-4 of the UB and LB means of each emotion and the segmental prosodic part is implemented by the differential CART.

Intensity E-Model

Due to the current state of art diphone synthesizer, the segmental intensity model does not have a great perceptual relevance. Nevertheless, if we examine the intensity means of different emotions (Table 9-5), we can notice the differences in the average statistics of the intensity evaluated for nonsilence speech.

Joy (72.7 dB) and anger (71.9 dB) are characterized by a high intensity mean, which is a characteristic of emotions with a high degree of physiological activation. By contrast, there are sadness (62.2 dB) and disgust (68.5 dB) with a low intensity mean, while for surprise and neutral we have a medium intensity

Table 9–5. Intensity means (μ) for different emotions in the E-Carini database

Emotion	μ (dB)	μ_Δ (dB)
Neutral	70.1	—
Anger	71.9	1.8
Disgust	68.5	−1.6
Fear	70.1	0
Joy	72.7	2.6
Sadness	62.2	−7.9
Surprise	70.1	0

Note. The column with Δ represent the differences between the emotional intensity and the neutral ones.

(70.1 dB). For fear, the intensity mean values collected from the E-Carini database lie around the same values obtained for neutral and surprise (70.1 dB). This is in contrast with what can be found in other studies (Anolli & Ciceri, 1997), and is due principally to the choice of considering the intensity only at the macro-prosodic level using a simple perceptual energy filter on the whole phrase.

Voice Quality (VQ) E-Model

In order to be able to control voice quality in diphone concatenative synthesis, it is necessary to embed opportune signal processing routines into the synthesis framework. The Festival-MBROLA speech synthesizer, which originally provides controls only for pitch and phoneme duration, has been further extended to allow for control of a set of low level acoustic parameters that can be combined to produce the desired voice quality effects. Time evolution of the parameters can be controlled over the single phoneme by instantaneous control curves. Here we give a rough description of the implementation of some of the low level acoustic controls:

- Spectral tilt ("SpTilt"): the spectral balance is changed by a reshaping function in the frequency domain that enhances or attenuates the low and mid-frequency regions, thus changing the overall spectral tilt;
- F0 flutter ("F0Flut"): random low frequency fluctuations of the pitch; the low frequency fluctuations are obtained by random noise band-pass filtering, the second order band-pass filter being tuned in the 4 Hz–10 Hz range;

- Spectral warping ("SpWarp"): the rising or lowering of upper formants is obtained by warping the frequency axis of the spectrum (through a bilinear transformation), and by interpolation of the resulting spectrum magnitude with respect to the DFT frequency bins.

A three-level hierarchic model was designed, in which the affective high level attributes (e.g., <anger>, <joy>, <fear>, etc.) are described in terms of medium level voice quality attributes defining the phonation type (e.g., <modal>, <soft>, <pressed>, etc.). These medium level attributes are in turn described by a set of low level acoustic attributes defining the perceptual correlates of the sound (e.g., <spectral tilt>, <shimmer >, <jitter>, etc.). The low level acoustic attributes correspond to the acoustic controls that the extended MBROLA synthesizer can render through the sound processing procedures described above. In Figure 9-6, an example of a qualitative description of high level attributes through medium and low level attributes is shown.

Given the hierarchical structure of the acoustic description of emotive voice, we performed preliminary experiments

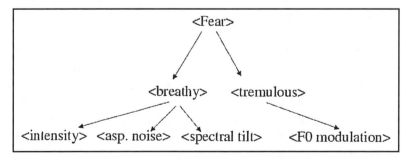

Figure 9–6. Qualitative description of voice quality for fear in terms of acoustic features.

focused on the definition of speaker-independent rules to control voice quality within a text-to-speech synthesizer. Different sets of rules describing the high and medium level attributes in terms of low level acoustic cues where designed, based on acoustic analysis of the E-Carini database and on previous studies (Drioli et al., 2003). Table 9–6 shows an example of the mapping between emotions, voice quality, and low level acoustic parameters that was implemented and adopted in our experiments. Values are in the range [0,1], and have different meanings for the different parameters. For example, SpTilt = 0 means maximal deemphasis of higher frequency range, whereas SpTilt = 0 means maximal emphasis; AspNoise = 0 means absence of noise component, whereas AspNoise = 1 means absence of voiced component, thus letting aspiration noise component alone; for F0Flut, Shimmer, and Jitter, value = 0 means effect is off, whereas value = 1 means effect is maximal; SpWarp = 0 means maximal spectrum shrinking, and SpWarp = 1 means maximal spectrum stretching.

Anger is characterized by a loud, harsh voice implemented by an attenuation of the low-mid frequency (SpTilt = 0.3) and a lowering of upper formants (SpWarp = -0.4). To realize the fear voice quality (tremulous and breathy) a random F0 fluctuation is added (F0Flut = 0.7). Joy and surprise (loud and breathy) are realized by a high attenuation of the low-mid frequency (SpTilt = 0.4). Disgust has a harsh voice quality that has been realized by an attenuation of the low-mid frequency (SpTilt = 0.3) and a raising of upper formants (SpWarp = 0.35). The breathy voice quality of sadness is implemented by a substantial lowering of upper formants (SpWarp = -0.5).

Emotional Festival TTS

A general overview of the Festival-MBROLA architecture framework for emotional TTS synthesis in shown in Figure 9–7: for a given emotion and a given input text, the Natural Language Processing (NLP) module operates to produce a phonetic-linguistic representation of the text.

These data are used by the prosodic modules to predict the emotive prosody. Both the duration and intonation modules use the differential approach: the internal data are used by both the neutral

Table 9–6. Voice quality modifications and low- level acoustic parameters implementation for different emotions

Emotion	Voice quality	Low-level acoustic parameters
Anger	loud and harsh	SpTilt = 0.3, SpWarp = 0.4
Disgust	harsh	SpTilt = 0.3, = SpWarp = 0.35
Fear	tremulous and breathy	SpTilt = 0.3, F0Flut = 0.7, SpWarp = 0.4
Joy	loud and breathy	SpTilt = −0.4
Sadness	breathy	SpWarp = −0.5
Surprise	loud and breathy	SpTilt = 0.4

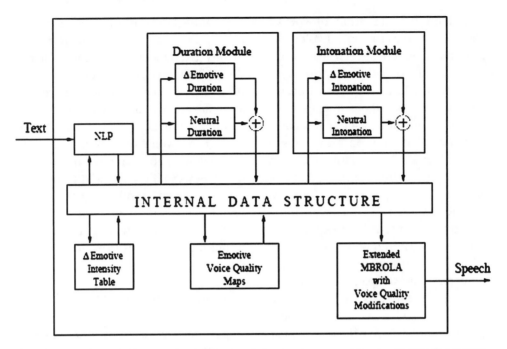

Figure 9–7. Overall functional diagram of the implemented Festival-MBROLA E-TTS.

module and emotional differential one and subsequently summed to provide the emotional prosody pattern.

Evaluation

The prosody prediction models were assessed both with an objective and a subjective evaluation. Moreover, prosody prediction and voice quality modifications were assessed together and separately with a subjective evaluation.

Objective Evaluation

An objective evaluation of the prosodic modules was performed by splitting both the Carini and E-Carini database in a training set (90%) and a test set (10%), and measuring the differences between the synthetic prosody and the actual

prosody in the test set. An indication of the performance can be given by the RMSE and correlation ρ between the original prosodic signal and the predicted one, and by the absolute error $|e|$ between the two prosody patterns. Table 9–7 shows the RMSE and the correlation ρ between the original and the predicted values computed by the duration module for the different emotions. The mean and the variance of the absolute error $|e|$ are also given. The values on the first three columns are expressed in z-score units, while the values on the last three columns are expressed in seconds.

In prosody prediction the most significant values are the RMSE and the correlation: looking at the z-score RMSE and correlation columns the best performance is obtained by the neutral duration module (lowest RMSE 0.88 and highest correlation 0.64). This can be due to

Table 9–7. Duration prediction results for the different emotions

Emotion	RMSE	$\mu_{|e|}$	$\sigma_{|e|}$	ρ	RMSE(s)	$\mu_{|e|}(s)$	$\sigma_{|e|}(s)$
Neutral	0.88	0.66	0.58	0.64	0.039	0.039	0.026
Anger	1.20	0.79	0.90	0.46	0.041	0.027	0.031
Disgust	0.99	0.65	0.74	0.50	0.054	0.035	0.041
Fear	1.03	0.70	0.75	0.56	0.037	0.025	0.027
Joy	0.88	0.62	0.63	0.61	0.028	0.020	0.020
Sadness	0.89	0.60	0.66	0.59	0.046	0.031	0.034
Surprise	0.93	0.65	0.66	0.62	0.030	0.022	0.022

the fact that the emotional database is smaller than the neutral one, and to the fact that the errors in the emotional modules are the sum of the errors on the neutral module and on the differential one. The worst result has been obtained by anger, with a resulting very simple differential CART, and best results were obtained for the surprise and joy modules, with more complex corresponding CARTs.

Looking again at the z-score RMSE column, sadness has a good performance too (0.89), and surprise (0.93), disgust (0.99), and fear (1.03) have mid-low scores. As for the correlation coefficient, the duration module of disgust, fear, and sadness have mid values (all above 0.5). Looking at the values expressed in seconds it can be noticed that joy and surprise have the best performance, but it is necessary to underline that these values are intrinsically correlated with the speech rate of the given emotion, and then joy and surprise that have the highest speech rate will have the lowest values of RMSE

if express in seconds. However, these values can be useful to having a dimensional idea of the prediction errors.

Intonation. Table 9–8 shows the results for the different emotions in the objective evaluation test for the intonation module. The values on the first three columns are expressed in pitch normalized units,[6] while the values on the last three columns are expressed in Hz.

Also in the intonation case the best performance has been obtained by the neutral intonation module (lowest RMSE 0.13 and highest correlation 0.43). Making a comparison with the correlation values for the durations on Table 9-7, it can be noticed that the correlation values are much lower in the intonation case. This is due to different aspects that make the intonation prediction more difficult than the duration one. Moreover there is a difference between the correlation coefficients of the neutral intonation module (0.43) and the emotive ones (0.28, 0.22, 0.16, 0.23, 0.19, 0.22) and

---

[6]In pitch normalized scale 0 and 1 correspond respectively to the lower bound and the upper bound of F0 in the given emotion.

Table 9–8. Intonation prediction results for the different emotions on the test set

Emotion	RMSE	$\mu_{|e|}$	$\sigma_{|e|}$	ρ	RMSE(Hz)	$\mu_{|e|}$(Hz)	$\sigma_{|e|}$(Hz)
Neutral	0.13	0.09	0.07	0.43	29	20	15
Anger	0.20	0.16	0.12	0.28	38	30	24
Disgust	0.15	0.11	0.10	0.22	28	21	19
Fear	1.25	0.18	0.17	0.16	39	28	26
Joy	0.22	0.18	0.13	0.23	54	43	32
Sadness	0.20	0.14	0.14	0.19	31	22	22
Surprise	0.27	0.21	0.17	0.22	49	39	30

this is probably due also to the decreasing size of the data available for learning the emotional intonation with respect to the neutral case.

As for the emotions looking at the pitch normalized RMSE values, the best performances are obtained by the disgust (0.15). As the opposite, the worst result has been obtained by surprise (0.27), due to the fact this emotion is characterized by a large pitch variability. The Hz RMSE values are obviously influenced by the pitch range of the given emotion; the worst score is obtained by joy (54 Hz) and the best by the low degree of physiological activation emotions: disgust (28 Hz) and sadness (31 Hz). Also in this case the significance of these scores is doubtful, but these values can be useful for having a dimensional idea of the prediction errors.

Subjective Evaluation

The effectiveness of the prosodic modules and of the voice quality modifications was also assessed with perceptual tests aimed at evaluating: (a) the single contribution on the emotional expressiveness carried out separately by the emotional prosodic modules and the emotive voice quality modifications, and (b) the synergistic contribution given by the union of these two correlates of the emotive speech. Four types of test sentences were generated:

(A) *neutral* prosody *without* emotive *VQ* modifications;

(B) *emotive* prosody *without* emotive *VQ* modifications;

(C) *neutral* prosody *with* emotive *VQ* modifications;

(D) *emotive* prosody *with* emotive *VQ* modifications.

For each emotion and for each of these four conditions, two utterances were produced by the new emotional TTS system for a total of 48 sentences, which were presented in a randomized order to 40 listeners, who judged, knowing the target emotion and the level of acceptability of the emotional synthesis, within a MOS scale (5 = excellent, 4 = good, 3 = fair, 2 = poor, 1 = bad). Results are summarized in Figure 9–8. Cases B, C, and D had always better results than those obtained for case A, signifying that emo-

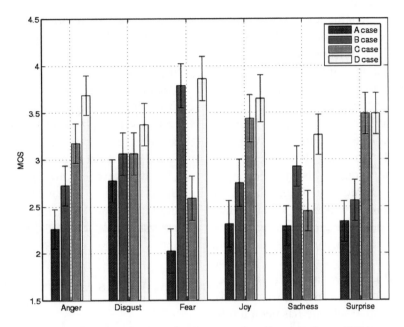

Figure 9–8. Subjective evaluation results (for A,B,C, and D; see text).

tive modules were quite successful. Case D always shows better MOS values and this is an indication that the created emotive prosodic modules quite improve the acceptability of the emotional TTS. Emotive VQ modifications alone were superior to the neutral case, except for fear and sadness. This can be the consequence of the fact that the contribution of prosody and voice quality might differ between different emotions, or might indicate that the chosen VQ acoustic processing should be modified for these emotions.

It is immediately evident that in B, C, and D cases the results are always better than those obtained in the A case, and this indicates that emotive modules were quite successful. D case always shows better MOS values and this gives an indication that the created emotive prosodic modules quite improve the acceptability of the emotional TTS. Emotive VQ modi-

fications alone were superior to the neutral case apart from the fear and sadness case, indicating that with these emotional moods the chosen VQ acoustic modification should be modified.

Emotion Audiovisual Markup Language

The affective presentation markup language (APML) for behavior specification allows one to specify how to mark up the verbal part of a dialog so as to add to it the "meanings" that the visual and the speech generation components of an animated agent need to produce the required expressions (De Carolis et al., 2004). So far, the language defines the components that may be useful to drive a face animation through the facial animation parameters and facial display functions. A scheme for the extension of a previously developed APML has been studied. The extension of such language is intended to support voice-specific controls. An extended version of the APML has been included in the Festival speech synthesis environment, allowing the automatic generation of the MBROLA control file from an APML tagged text with emotive tags. This module implements the three-level hierarchy introduced before, in which the affective high level attributes (e.g., <anger>, <joy>, <fear>) are described in terms of medium level voice quality attributes (phonation type), and low level acoustic attributes (the perceptual correlates of sound). This descriptive scheme has been implemented within Festival as a set of mappings between high level and low level descriptors. This APML extension allows the generation of emotive facial animation and speech synthesis, starting from tagged text such as:

> <performative type = "inform">
>
> <voqual type = "modal" level = "1.0'>This is my modal voice. </voqual><voqual type = "tremulous" level = "1.0">This is my tremulous voice.</voqual>
>
> </performative>.

LUCIA's System Architecture

FAP stream generation components and the audio synthesis components have been integrated into a unique system able to produce the facial animation, including emotive audio and video cues, from tagged text. The facial animation framework relies on previous studies for the realization of Italian talking heads (Cosi et al., 2003; Magno Caldognetto et al., 2004). A schematic view of the whole system is shown in Figure 9-9.

The modules used to produce the FAP control stream (AVENGINE), and the speech synthesis phonetic control stream (Festival), are synchronized through the phoneme duration information. The output control streams are in turn used to drive the audio and video rendering engines (i.e., the MBROLA speech synthesizer and the face model player).

Conclusions and Future Work

In this chapter, we discussed audio/visual speech analysis and synthesis issues, for the creation of natural and expressive talking heads. An automatic optotracking 3D movement analyzer was implemented, in order to build up the animation engine based on the Cohen-Massaro coarticulation model, and also to create the correct WAV and FAP files needed for the animation of LUCIA, an animated MPEG-4 talking face.

LUCIA's voice is based on an Italian version of Festival-MBROLA speech synthesis environment, modified for expressive/emotive synthesis. A data-driven method for the design of emotive prosodic modules was illustrated, as well as a rule-based Festival-MBROLA voice quality modification module, designed for control of temporal and spectral characteristics of the synthesis.

Even if emotional synthesis still remains an attractive open issue, our preliminary evaluation results underline the effectiveness of the proposed solutions. From the results of perceptual tests, it can be concluded that adequate emotional

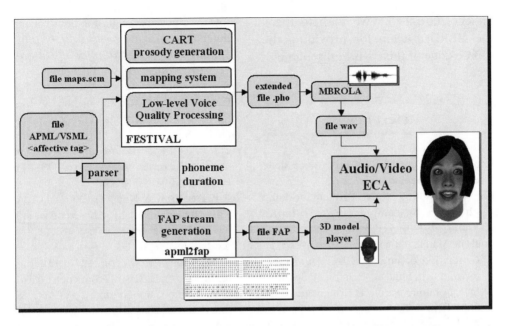

Figure 9–9. Block scheme of the system designed to produce the facial animation with emotive audio and video cues from tagged text.

speech can be obtained within a diphone-based approach, and that emotional prosodic modeling based on data-driven approaches produces appreciable results. Moreover, subjective tests demonstrated that voice quality processing increases the quality of the perceived emotion.

Finally, an interface to the speech synthesizer was described that gives the user the possibility of specifying a desired emotion for the text through a markup language. The audiovisual synthesis system driven by the tagged text integrates voice synthesis and facial animation, so to provide a speech synthesis control stream (PHO file) and a facial animation control stream (FAP file), which are used in turn to produce synchronized and emotionally coherent audio and video outputs.

For the future, improvements are foreseen for some specific aspects, such as the modeling of smooth transition from one emotion to the other, both on the visual and on the acoustic side. Refinements on the evaluation procedures will be conducted such as, for example, perceptual tests for comparing human movements and talking head animations, thus giving us the possibility to gain insights about where and how the animation engine could be improved. Similarly, the modeling of prosody and of voice quality will be improved through the use of more advanced signal processing techniques and specifically designed perceptual tests.

Acknowledgements. Part of this work has been sponsored by PF-STAR (Preparing Future multiSensorial inTerAction Research, European Project IST- 2001-37599, http://pfstar.itc.it), and TICCA (Tecnologie cognitive per l'interazione e la cooperazione con agenti artificiali, joint "CNR - Provincia Autonoma Trentina"

Project 2001–2003). We wish to thank the MBROLA team for providing the source code of their synthesis engine.

References

Anolli, L., & Ciceri, R. (1997). La voce delle emozioni. *Franco Angeli s.r.l,.*

Boersma, P. (1996). PRAAT, a system for doing phonetics by computer. *Glot International, 5*(9/10), 341–345.

Boula de Mareil, P., Clrier, P., & Toen, J. (2002). Generation of emotions by a morphing technique in English, French and Spanish. In Laboratoire Parole et Language (UMR 6057 CNRS) (Ed.), *Proceedings of Speech & Prosody Workshop 2002*, [CD-ROM]. Antony, France: Extor.

Breiman, L., Friedman, J. H., Olshen, R. A., & Stone, C. J. (1984). *Classification and regression trees.* Wadsworth and Brooks/Cole, Pacific Grove, CA: Advanced Books & Software.

Browman, C. P., & Goldstein, L. (1986). Towards an articulatory phonology. *Phonology Yearbook, 3*, 219–252.

Cahn, J. E. (1990). The generation of affect in synthesized speech. *Journal of the American Voice I/O Society, 8*, 1–19.

Campbell, N., & Isard, S. (1991). Segment durations in a syllable frame. *Journal of Phonetics(19)*, 37–47.

Campbell, W. (1995). Loudness, spectral tilt, and perceived prominence in dialogues. In (Ed.), *Proceedings of ICPhS* (pp. 676–679).

Cohen, M., & Massaro, D. (1993). Modeling coarticulation in synthetic visual speech. In N. Magne-nat-Thalmann & D. Thalmann (Eds.), *Models and techniques in computer animation* (pp. 139–156). Tokyo: Springer-Verlag.

Cole, R., van Vuuren, S., Pellom, B., Hacioglu, K., Ma, J., Movellan, J., et al. (2003). Perceptive animated interfaces: First steps toward a new paradigm for human computer interaction. *Proceedings of the IEEE: Special Issue on Multimodal Human Computer Interface, 91,* 1391–1405.

Cosi, P., Avesani, C., Tesser, F., Gretter, R., & Pianesi, F. (2002). On the use of cart-tree for prosodic predictions in the Italian Festival TTS. In P. Cosi, E. Magno, & A. Zamboni (Eds.), *Voce, canto, parlato-studi in onore di Franco Ferrero* (pp. 73–81). Padova, Italy: UNIPRESS.

Cosi, P., Fusaro, A., & Tisato, G. (2003). LUCIA, a new Italian talking-head based on a modified Cohen-Massaro's labial coarticulation model. In ISCA (Ed.), *Proceedings of EUROSPEECH 2003* (pp. 127–132). Rundle mall, Australia: Casual Production Pty Ltd.

Cosi, P., Magno Caldognetto, E., Perin, G., & Zmarich, C. (2002). Labial coarticulation modeling for realistic facial animation. In IEEE (Ed.), *Proceedings of 4th IEEE International Conference on Multimodal Interfaces ICMI 2002* (pp. 505–510). Piscataway, NJ: IEEE, IEEE Service Center.

Cosi, P., Tesser, F., Gretter, R., & Avesani, C. (2001). Festival speaks Italian! In Dalsgaard, P., Lindberg, B., Benner, H. & Tan, Z. H. (Eds.), *Proceedings of EUROSPEECH 2001* (pp. 509–512). Aalbor, Denmark: Kommunick Grafiske Løsinger A/S.

Cosi, P., Tesser, F., Gretter, R., & Pianesi, F. (2002). A modified "PaIntE Model" for Italian TTS. In (Ed.), *Proceedings of IEEE Workshop on Speech Synthesis*. [CD-ROM]. Piscataway, NJ: IEEE, IEEE Service Center.

d'Alessandro, C., & Doval, B. (1998). Experiments in voice quality modification of natural speech signals: The spectral approach. In ISCA, Proceedings of 3rd ESCA/COCOSDA Workshop on Speech Synthesis (Ed.), *Proceedings of 3rd ESCA Workshop on Speech Synthesis* (pp. 277–282).

De Carolis, B., Pelachaud, C., Poggi I., & Steedman, M. (2004). APML, a Mark-up Language for Believable Behavior Generation. In Prendinger H., Ishizuka M. (Eds.), *Life-Like Characters, Springer,* 65–85.

Douglas-Cowie, E., Cowie, R., & Campbell, N. (2003). Speech and emotion. *Speech Communication, 40*(1-2), 1-3.

Drioli, C., Tisato, G., Cosi, P., & Tesser, F. (2003). Emotions and voice quality: Experiments with sinusoidal modelling. In ISCA, (Ed.), *Proceedings of VOQUAL ESCA/ Workshop* (pp. 127-132). Cédex, France: LIMSI-CNRS.

Dutoit, T., & Leich, H. (1993). MBR-PSOLA: Text-to-speech synthesis based on an MBE re-synthesis of the segments database. *Speech Communication, 13*(3-4), 167-184.

Ekman, P. (1992). An argument for basic emotions. In N. L. Stein, & K. Oatley (Eds.), *Basic emotions* (pp. 169-200). Hove, UK: Lawrence Erlbaum.

Ekman, P., & Friesen, W. (1978). *Facial Action Coding System*. Palo Alto, CA: Consulting Psychologist Press.

Ferrigno, G., & Pedotti, A. (1985). ELITE: A digital dedicated hardware system for movement analysis via real-time TV signal processing. In IEEE (Ed.), *IEEE Transactions on Biomedical Engineering, BME-32* (pp. 943-950). Piscataway, NJ: IEEE Service Center.

Gobl, C., & Chasaide, A..N. (2003), The role of the voice quality in communicating emotions, mood and attitude. *Speech Communication, 40*, 189-212.

Hartman, J., & Wernecke, J. (1996). *The VRML handbook*. Addison Wessley.

Huang, X., Hon, H. W., & Acero, A. (2001). *Spoken language processing: A guide to theory, algorithm, and system development*. Upper Saddle River, NJ: Prentice Hall.

Kain, A., & Macon. M. W. (2001). Design and evaluation of a voice conversion algorithm based on spectral envelope mapping and residual prediction. In (Ed.), *Proceedings of ICASSP 2001* (Vol. 2, pp. 813-816).

Löfqvist, A. (1990). Speech as audible gestures. In W. J. Hardcastle & A. Marchal (Eds.), *Speech production and speech modeling* (pp. 289-322). Dordrecht, Netherlands: Kluwer Academic.

Magno Caldognetto, E., Cosi, P., Drioli, C., Tisato, G., & Cavicchio, F. (2003). Coproduction of speech and emotions: Visual and acoustic modifications of some phonetic labial targets. In Schwartz, J. L., Berthommier, F., Cathiard, M. A. & Sodoyer, D. (Eds.), *Proceedings of AVSP 2003, ISCA/Workshop* (pp. 209-214). Standhal, France: Institute de la Communication Parlee, CNRS UMR 5009, INP Grenoble, Université

Möhler, G. (1988). Describing intonation with a parametric model. In (Ed.), *Proceedings of ICSLP 1988* (pp. 2581-2584).

Möhler, G., & Conkie, A. (1998). Parametric modeling of intonation using vector quantization. In (Ed.), *Proceedings of Third International Workshop on Speech Synthesis*.

Murray, I..R., & Arnott, J. L. (1993). Toward the simulation of emotion in synthetic speech: A review of literature on human vocal emotion. *Journal of the Acoustical Society of America, 93*(2), 1097-1108.

Pelachaud, C., Magno Caldognetto, E., Zmarich, C., & Cosi. P. (2001). Modelling an Italian talking head. In Massaro, D. W., Light, J., & Geraci, K. (Ed.), *Proceedings of AVSP 2001, ISCA/Workshop* (pp. 72-77). Santa Cruz, CA: Perceptual Science Laboratory, University of California.

Perin, G. (2000). *Facce parlanti: sviluppo di un modello coarticolatorio labiale per un sistema di sintesi bimodale*. Master's thesis, University of Padova, Italy.

Scherer, K. R. (1986). Vocal affect expression: A review and a model for future research. *Psychological Bullettin, 99*, 143-165.

Scherer, K. R. (2003). Vocal communication of emotions: A review of research paradigms. *Speech Communication, 40*(2-3), 227-256.

Schröder, M. (2001). Emotional speech synthesis: A review. In (Ed.), *Proceedings of EUROSPEECH 2001* (Vol. 1, pp. 561-564).

Sluijter, A., van Heuven, V., & Pacilly, J. (1997). Spectral balance as a cue in the perception of linguistic stress. *Journal of the Acoustical Society of America, 101*(1), 503–513.

Stylianou, Y., Cappé, O., & Moulines, E. (1998). Continuous probabilistic transform for voice conversion. *IEEE Transactions on Speech and Audio Processing, 6*(2), 131–142.

Taylor, P., Black, A., & Caley, R. (1988). The architecture of the Festival speech synthesis system. In (Ed.), *Proceedings of 3rd ESCA Workshop on Speech Synthesis* (pp. 147–151).

Tesser, F. (2005). *Emotional speech synthesis: From theory to applications.* Doctoral dissertation, DIT—University of Trento, Trento, Italy.

Tesser, F., Cosi, P., Drioli, C., & Tisato, G. (2004). Prosodic data driver modelling of a narrative style in Festival TTS. In (Ed.), *Proceedings of 5th ISCA Speech Synthesis Workshop* [CD-ROM].

Tesser, F., Cosi, P., Drioli, C., & Tisato, G. (2005). Emotional FESTIVAL-MBROLA TTS synthesis. In (Ed.), *Proceedings of INTERSPEECH 2005.* [CD-ROM].

CHAPTER 10

Perceptions of Japanese *Anime* Voices by Hebrew Speakers

*Mihoko Teshigawara, Noam Amir, Ofer Amir,
Edna Milano Wlosko, and Meital Avivi*

Introduction

In this paper, we report on some preliminary results of an ongoing international collaborative investigation of how cartoon voices from one culture are perceived by people from other cultures. Our objective is to identify universal and culturally-specific aspects of the perception of vocal stereotypes of personality and emotion. We have a special interest in voice quality, particularly in voice qualities that involve a change in the shape of the supraglottic area (i.e., constricting the supraglottic area or expanding it by lowering the larynx), in addition to other phonetic properties that can be investigated in relation to impression formation.

In Chapter 15[1], Teshigawara reports on a perceptual experiment that used content-masked Japanese *anime* voice excerpts as stimuli (see also Teshigawara, 2003; 2004). The results of the perceptual study showed that supraglottic states (laryngeal constriction and larynx lowering) played an important role in Japanese listeners' impressions of personality traits and emotional states. We replicated this experiment in Israel to determine whether this finding could be extended to listeners from a very different cultural and linguistic background. To our knowledge, Hebrew vocal stereotypes have not yet been systematically studied. This study, therefore, is a good starting point for phonetic research into Hebrew vocal stereotypes.

To date, very few cross-cultural studies on vocal stereotyping have been conducted (Lee & Boster, 1992; van Bezooijen, 1988). Van Bezooijen correlated phonetic

---

[1]Readers are advised to refer to Chapter 16 to complement the experiment details not discussed in the present chapter.

measures, including voice quality, with personality trait ratings by participants from the Netherlands and other countries. The results of her study suggest the importance of voice quality in impression formation across cultures: the correlations between the trait ratings and the voice quality measures were in the same direction across participant groups regardless of the culture or language of the listeners, suggesting that there may be universal factors involved in the perception of voices. Since Japan, along with two Western countries and one African country, was included in van Bezooijen's (1988) study, we may predict that Japanese, Western, and African listeners would attribute similar personality traits to Japanese *anime* voices as well. However, in van Bezooijen's study, the phonetic correlates of the factor *voice quality* are not very clear. For example, *harsh* and *laryngeal tension* are negatively correlated with *creak*, which is somewhat counter-intuitive. In our study, we will investigate the relationship between trait ratings by Hebrew listeners and a select set of voice quality settings (supraglottic states and phonatory states), as was investigated for Japanese listeners, as reported in Chapter 15 and Teshigawara (2003; 2004).

Scherer, Banse, and Wallbott. (2001) conducted a decoding experiment using vocal portrayals of four emotions and an emotionally neutral state. While they do not discuss their results in relation to the phonetic correlates of emotional speech, they report that there is some universality in the perception of emotional speech, based on the judgments of listeners from nine countries. Since vocal cues to emotion are likely connected to vocal stereotypes of good and bad characters (as discussed in Chapter 15, the connection to

vocal stereotypes of bad characters may be particularly strong), the results of Scherer et al. (2001) provide further support for the assumption that there may be some universality in the perception of vocal stereotypes.

To summarize, the present study addresses the following two research questions:

> *Question 1:* Do native Hebrew speakers perceive Japanese *anime* voices similarly to Japanese listeners?

> *Question 2:* Do supraglottic states play an important role in Hebrew speakers' perceptions?

Method

Since this study aimed to replicate as closely as possible the experiment conducted with Japanese participants, the same methods and stimuli described in Chapter 15 and Teshigawara (2003; 2004) were used, that is, 27 content-masked cartoon voice excerpts (see Chapter 15 for more details). The original Japanese questionnaire was translated into Hebrew by a native Japanese speaker who is an expert in Hebrew literature. Then, native Hebrew speakers (the coauthors of this chapter) compared the Hebrew translation with the English translation provided by the first author.

The participants were 21 female undergraduate students (average age 23.02 years old) from the Communication Disorders Department at Tel Aviv University. All participants were native Hebrew speakers with no knowledge of Japanese.

The experiment was run in small groups of four to six people in a sound-attenuated room. This experiment was the first of two experiments on the cross-cultural perception of voice quality using the random-splicing technique (see Chapter 15, Stimuli, p. 266). In the other experiment, participants listened to a version of the same stimuli that was not random-spliced. Teshigawara et al. (2007) compared the results of the two experiments in order to examine whether or not the results of the first experiment were artifacts of the random-splicing technique. It was reported that in general the participants rated the stimuli comparably in the two experiments. Below, we discuss only the results of the experiment with the random-spliced stimuli.

Results and Discussion

Prior to the conversion of trait ratings into z-scores, we examined the consistency of participants' trait ratings by calculating Pearson's correlations for each participant relative to the average ratings of all participants. We retained the results of the participant with the fewest significant correlations with the average ratings (11 out of 21 items; $p < .05$), since removing this participant's results affected the resulting correlation coefficients between trait ratings and phonetic measures only slightly.

Trait ratings were converted into z-scores within each participant, across stimuli, for each trait item; and were averaged across participants for each stimulus. In order to examine the relationships among the 19 adjective trait items, Pearson's correlations were calculated for these

items separately for characters played by male and female voice actors. The resulting correlation patterns were generally similar to those obtained from the Japanese listeners, in that it appeared that favorable traits were correlated with one another and comprised a single group. However, the constituents of the group were slightly different from those in the results from the Japanese listeners. In the ratings for female voice actors, almost all items appeared to be moderately to strongly correlated with one another, except for the items *strong* and *loud*—thus, the Hebrew listeners' ratings were structurally simpler than those of the Japanese listeners. The following items showed more pronounced differences between the two cultures: *big*, *perseverant*, *curious*, *positive emotion*, and *relaxed*.

Next, to investigate the relationship between the experimental results and the phonetic correlates, we calculated Pearson's correlations between trait ratings and the selected phonetic measures separately for the two sexes (see Table 10-1). (For the remainder of this section, please refer to Table 15-1 in Chapter 15 for the results of the correlation analysis obtained from Japanese speakers/listeners.)

As was the case with correlations across trait items, the overall correlation patterns were similar between the two cultures: degrees of laryngeal constriction were significantly correlated with a number of positive trait items (e.g., *loyal*, *conscientious*), whereas degrees of larynx lowering and acoustic measures (i.e., F0 SD and mean F2 for /a/) were correlated with smaller numbers of items. However, the fact that the strength of the correlations was weaker for female voice actors than for male voice actors in both cultures possibly reflects the properties

Table 10–1. Correlations between perceptual experiment items and phonetic measures

| | Auditory Measures | | | | | | Acoustic Measures | | | | | |
| | Supraglt const. | | Larynx lower. | | Breathy | | Mean F0 | | F0 SD | | F2 for /a/ | |
Trait items	M	F	M	F	M	F	M	F	M	F	M	F
Physical char.												
Big	-.34	.19	.60	.32	-.06	-.27	-.21	-.63**	-.64	.24	-.92**	-.61**
Good-looking	-.82**	-.67**	.17	-.19	.33	.61**	-.74*	.52*	-.44	-.18	-.27	.28
Personality												
Brave	-.51	-.51*	.56	-.06	.00	.41	-.41	-.06	-.82**	-.05	-.88**	-.15
Selfless	-.83**	-.75**	.32	.08	.15	.68**	-.72*	.24	-.70*	-.30	-.58	-.12
Loyal	-.90**	-.79**	.25	.07	.22	.62**	-.70*	.39	-.71*	-.28	-.48	.14
Perseverant	-.16	-.65**	.63	.11	-.12	.50*	-.37	.24	-.65	-.37	-.78*	.18
Intelligent	-.85**	-.73**	.29	-.27	.29	.65**	-.83**	.38	-.64	-.27	-.43	.36
Strong	-.33	.02	.76*	.12	-.25	-.07	-.38	-.48*	-.61	.13	-.89***	-.45
Sociable	-.86**	-.62**	-.01	-.26	.41	.63**	-.70*	.35	-.53	-.11	-.20	.23
Calm	-.82**	-.43	.26	-.33	.29	.75**	-.84**	-.16	-.51	.00	-.34	.02
Curious	-.51	-.29	.21	-.30	.15	.30	-.71*	.55*	-.05	-.14	.04	.48*
Conscientious	-.90**	-.77**	.08	-.08	.39	.61**	-.71*	.40	-.64	-.38	-.35	.20
Sympathetic	-.87**	-.70**	-.01	-.12	.39	.64**	-.66	.29	-.55	-.24	-.22	.21
Emotion												
Positive	-.78*	-.57*	.19	-.32	.22	.74**	-.78*	.20	-.49	-.08	-.34	.30
Vocal char.												
High-pitched	.54	-.44	-.76*	-.26	-.14	.17	.66	.81**	.67*	-.08	.74*	.60**
Loud	.70*	.35	.07	-.08	-.56	-.73**	.66	.19	.29	.20	-.22	-.03
Relaxed	-.82**	-.30	.24	-.36	.27	.74**	-.85**	-.11	-.43	.06	-.20	.17
Pleasant	-.86**	-.66**	.15	-.23	.33	.76**	-.80**	.29	-.54	-.13	-.28	.23
Attractive	-.85**	-.55*	.19	-.31	.34	.65**	-.82**	.44	-.53	-.10	-.32	.34

Note. M (males): *n* = 9, except mean F0 and F0 SD, where *n* = 8. F (females): *n* = 18. * *p* < .05. ** *p* < .01.

180

of the stimuli. That is, the distribution of voice types, and therefore of articulatory characteristics, differed between the two sexes; this factor, rather than cross-cultural similarity, may account for these results. (For instance, only a few voices were identified as Hero Type II among voices played by female voice actors). Below, we elaborate on the similarities and differences in the patterns of correlation between the two cultures.

First, we focus on the similarities in the correlation patterns between phonetic measures and trait ratings. Degrees of laryngeal constriction had the largest number of significant correlations with trait items in the case of male voice actors (13 items), and the second largest for female voice actors (12 items); these results are comparable to those obtained from Japanese listeners. As with the Japanese listeners, the direction of correlations was negative, suggesting that the greater the degree of laryngeal constriction, the lower the ratings for favorable traits (e.g., *good-looking*, *loyal*). Therefore, we may say that the degree of laryngeal constriction played an important role in Hebrew listeners' perceptions of the voices of heroes and villains, as was the case in the Japanese listeners' perceptions.

Other general patterns of correlation with trait items that were similar to those obtained for Japanese listeners included the degrees of breathiness in female voice actors; and to a lesser extent, degrees of larynx lowering and mean F2 for /a/ in male voice actors. As with the Japanese listeners, for females, the direction of the correlation for breathiness was opposite to that found for laryngeal constriction, suggesting that increased breathiness led to higher ratings for favorable traits. The

number of significant correlations with trait items was the largest (14) for this measure in female voice actors. As for degrees of larynx lowering in male voice actors, while the magnitude of the correlations was slightly lower compared to what was seen for the Japanese listeners, we found positive correlations with the physical characteristic *big* (the correlation was not significant) and the personality trait *strong*, as well as a negative correlation with *high-pitched*. In other words, as with the Japanese listeners, we can say that larynx lowering, a supraglottic state, played a role in the Hebrew listeners' perceptions, at least for voices played by male voice actors. The mean F2 for /a/ was negatively correlated with a similar set of traits to those positively correlated with degrees of larynx lowering, including *big*, *brave*, *strong*, and *high-pitched*.

In summary, the general correlation patterns between phonetic measures and trait items were similar across the two cultures, suggesting underlying perceptual similarities. In addition, supraglottic states, especially laryngeal constriction, correlated well with participants' ratings of favorable trait items, suggesting the importance of these articulatory characteristics in the perceptions of both Hebrew and Japanese listeners. Therefore, the answers to our two research questions were both "yes."

Now, we turn to differences in the correlations between phonetic measures and trait ratings between the two cultures. The items that were correlated with different phonetic measures between the two cultures included *big*, *perseverant*, *sociable*, *curious*, *positive emotion*, and *(vocally) relaxed*. Among these items, the differences in *perseverant*, *sociable*,

positive emotion, and *relaxed* were strik-
ing because these traits showed significant positive correlations with breathiness for female voice actors, a pattern
not seen in the Japanese listeners' data.
These traits were negatively correlated
with laryngeal constriction for both
sexes and with mean F0 for male voice
actors, although not all of these correlations were significant.

Among the Japanese listeners, the correlation between *positive emotion* and
laryngeal constriction was negligible (a
moderate negative correlation with lowered larynx for females); and for female
voice actors, *sociable* was only moderately negatively correlated with laryngeal
constriction and positively correlated
with mean F0. In other words, for the
Japanese listeners, these traits did not
pattern with the items that correlated
with laryngeal constriction. By contrast,
for the Hebrew listeners, these traits were
rated in a similar way to other favorable
traits such as *good-looking* and *loyal.* If
we were to perform a factor analysis of
the Hebrew listeners' data, these items
might be incorporated into the same factor with the other trait items that correlated with laryngeal constriction, making
the overall factor structure simpler than
that obtained from the Japanese listeners' ratings. (Milano Wlosko and Avivi,
2005, report that a fewer number of factors were extracted from Hebrew listeners' ratings than from Japanese listeners'
ratings, using a subset of trait items.)
However, in order to investigate whether
these contrasts are attributable to cultural or linguistic differences between
the two countries, we would need to
increase the number of stimuli and provide sufficient variation in degrees of
laryngeal constriction, larynx lowering,
and other phonetic measures.

Thus far, we have not discussed in
detail the phonetic measure of mean F0,
despite the fact that it showed a number
of correlations with trait items. In some
ways, the correlation patterns of mean F0
with trait items were somewhat similar
between the two cultures, in that mean
F0 could be associated with degrees of
laryngeal constriction for male voice
actors. However, compared to the Japanese listeners, for the Hebrew listeners
this measure seemed to play a larger role
in the perception of male voice actors and
a diminished role in that of female voice
actors. For males, mean F0 was significantly negatively correlated with a larger
number of favorable trait items (12 items
versus 6 for the Japanese listeners, exclud-
ing *high-pitched*, which was positively
correlated). Thus, we may say that the
preference for low-pitched male voices
was more pronounced in the Hebrew listeners' ratings. By contrast, for females,
the number of significant correlations
between mean F0 and trait items was half
that for Japanese listeners (5 items for
the Hebrew listeners versus 10 for the
Japanese listeners). In addition, with the
exception of the two items *good-looking*
and *high-pitched*, the same items were
not correlated with mean F0 in the two
groups of listeners. We may say that mean
F0 in female voices contributed to favorable ratings by Japanese listeners to a
much greater extent than for Hebrew listeners. The fourth and fifth authors, who
conducted the experiment in Israel, noted
participants' comments that the pitches
in the experimental stimuli sounded too
high, especially for the male speakers.

According to Teshigawara (2003, p. 74),
the mean F0 of adult male heroes (including those not included in the experimental stimuli) was roughly 1.4 to 1.6 times
higher than the average Japanese male

voice in real life, while the mean F0 of adult female heroes was 1.3 to 1.5 times higher than the average Japanese female voice. Although these pitch levels are conventional in Japanese *anime*, the pitch of male characters' voices may generally be lower in Hebrew cartoons. If this is the case, Hebrew listeners may have perceived the stimuli as unnaturally high-pitched, possibly influencing their ratings. To support this hypothesis, it would be necessary to measure the F0 used by Hebrew cartoon characters.

To summarize the differences between the two cultures thus far, Hebrew listeners tended to perceive the stimuli in simpler ways than the Japanese listeners, as reflected in the correlation patterns between such phonetic measures as laryngeal constriction, breathiness, and mean F0, and the trait ratings. Possible explanations for the prima facie perceptual simplification seemingly performed by Hebrew listeners include: Hebrew listeners were unfamiliar with the vocal conventions of Japanese *anime*; the present stimuli lacked perceptual cues that were important for Hebrew listeners to differentiate vocal stereotypes more finely; and Japanese speakers/listeners make finer distinctions in vocal stereotypes than Hebrew listeners. Japanese listeners were more sensitive to vocal emotions than American listeners. However, we should also note that all the Hebrew listeners in our study were female, whereas the Japanese listeners included both sexes, a factor which may have affected our results. Again, further research is necessary to examine the effects of listener sex on trait ratings in this type of experimental setting.

Finally, in order to investigate how individual speakers were rated by listeners from the two cultures, we averaged within each speaker, for each culture, the z-scores for the following eight items correlating with laryngeal constriction: *good-looking, selfless, loyal, intelligent, calm, sympathetic, pleasant,* and *attractive*. We excluded items that were noted to differ substantially between the two cultures or between the two sexes in the Japanese listeners' ratings (Chapter 15, Results section). As shown in Figure 10–1, most speakers scatter around the dotted diagonal line that connects equal rating scores between the two cultures, suggesting that individuals were rated more or less similarly across the two cultures. In addition, the speakers with the same markers are placed more or less close to one another, indicating that speakers of the same voice type were rated similarly to one another in the two cultures. There were seven speakers whose average ratings differed more than 0.4 points between the two cultures. Of these speakers, three received higher ratings from the Japanese listeners, while four were rated higher by the Hebrew listeners. Although further investigation is necessary to determine the basis of these differences, we discuss two interesting cases below.

The first case is a villainous supporting role (1S in Figure 10–1), exhibiting laryngeal constriction (i.e., identified as a Villain Type I voice; see Teshigawara, 2003, p. 56 and 124). Japanese listeners perceived this character similarly to villains with laryngeal constriction, whereas Hebrew listeners perceived the character much more positively, increasing the average z-score by approximately 1 point over the Japanese listeners' ratings. The difference between this voice and the other voices exhibiting laryngeal constriction lies in the degree of harshness; while this voice

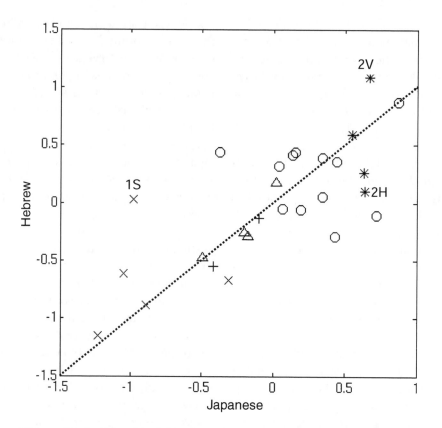

Figure 10–1. Plot of individual speakers using average z-score ratings by Japanese and Hebrew listeners. *Note.* ✳ Hero Type I (female), ○ Hero Type I (male), △ Hero Type II, ✕ Villain Type I, + Villain Type II. 1S: a child male supporting role; 2H: an adult male hero; 2V: an adult male villain. See the text for details.

sounds constricted, it is not harsh. Therefore, it is possible that, for Hebrew listeners, degree of harshness may perform a different role in trait attribution than was the case for Japanese listeners. Future research with experimental stimuli differing in degrees of harshness would be necessary to investigate the relationship between this variable and trait ratings.

The second case involves a pair of voices in the *anime Sailor Moon*, both of which were identified as Hero Type I

voices (with a slight degree of larynx lowering and no laryngeal constriction; (see Chapter 15, p. 268). In fact, one of these voices is used to portray a hero (2H), while the other is used to portray a villain (2V). While Japanese listeners rated these two voices favorably, Hebrew listeners rated the villain higher than the hero by approximately 1 point. Although more data would be needed to support our hypothesis, we speculate that the differences in the Hebrew ratings may stem from the breathiness in the hero's voice, since otherwise the two voices were quite similar.

In this chapter, we do not discuss the two questionnaire items that involved choosing appropriate categories for the speakers, namely, age (female or male) and age group (0–10; 11–18; 19–35; 36–60; over 61). A preliminary analysis of these items revealed that two middle-aged to elderly female characters with extreme harshness were almost invariably judged by the Hebrew listeners to be male and in the same age range (slightly younger for one that was higher-pitched and not diplophonic). It is possible that middle-aged female characters with harsh voice are rare in Hebrew cartoons. Although this type of voice does not generally occur among older Japanese women in real life, female villains and tricksters often exhibit these vocal characteristics in *anime*, reflecting the use of vocal stereotypes.

Conclusion and Future Research

In this chapter, we discuss the results of an experiment in which we used Japanese cartoon voices to compare Hebrew listeners' perceptions of vocal stereotypes with those previously identified for Japanese listeners (see Chapter 16). We found that despite the significant differences in culture and language in Israel and Japan, the overall tendencies in trait ratings were similar between the two cultures. Speakers exhibiting laryngeal constriction were rated unfavorably for positive traits. However, our findings also

suggested that there may be fine differences in vocal attunement between the two cultures. For instance, a low-pitched male voice might be more favored by Hebrew listeners, whereas a high-pitched female voice might be more favored by Japanese listeners.

In future research, it would be necessary to conduct an auditory and acoustic analysis of the voices of Hebrew cartoon characters in order to test our hypotheses about the pitch of male characters' voices and the voice quality of older female characters, and to be able to compare Japanese and Hebrew cultures in these respects. As mentioned in Chapter 16, it would also be important to increase the number of stimuli in order to obtain more reliable and generalizable results. A cross-experiment using original Hebrew and random-spliced stimuli would also further corroborate the present findings and Teshigawara et al. (2007). Finally, we would like to extend our cross-cultural experiments to other cultures/languages. We are now preparing an experiment in Austria, and we continue to seek international collaborators in order to increase the number of participating cultures/languages and obtain more generalizable results.[2]

References

Lee, H. O., & Boster, F. J. (1992). Collectivism-individualism in perceptions of speech rate: A cross-cultural comparison. *Journal of Cross-Cultural Psychology, 23,* 377–388.

---

[2]We would like to recruit new collaborators from other cultures/languages. Correspondence concerning the cross-cultural experiment should be addressed to Mihoko Teshigawara, E-mail: mteshi@alumni.uvic.ca

Milano Wlosko, E., & Avivi, M. (2005). *Social stereotypes and their influence on interpersonal impression of voice quality: A comparison between Japanese and Hebrew speaking listeners* [Hebrew]. Undergraduate seminar report at Communication Disorders Department, Tel Aviv University.

Scherer, K. R., Banse, R., & Wallbott, H. G. (2001). Emotion inferences from vocal expression correlate across languages and cultures. *Journal of Cross-Cultural Psychology, 32*, 76-92.

Teshigawara, M. (2003). Voices in Japanese animation: A phonetic study of vocal stereotypes of heroes and villains in Japanese culture. Doctoral dissertation at University of Victoria, Canada. [retrievable from http://web.uvic.ca/ling/students/graduate/Dissertation_Teshigawara.pdf]

Teshigawara, M. (2004). Vocally expressed emotions and stereotypes in Japanese animation: Voice qualities of the bad guys compared to those of the good guys. *Journal of the Phonetic Society of Japan, 8*(1), 60-76.

Teshigawara, M., Amir, N., Amir, O., Milano Wlosko, E., Avivi M. (2007). Effects of random splicing on listeners' perceptions. In J. Trouvain & W. J. Barry (Eds.), *Proceedings of the ICPhS 2007* (pp. 2101-2104). Saarbrücken, Germany: Universität des Saarlandes.

Van Bezooijen, R. (1988). The relative importance of pronunciation, prosody, and voice quality for the attribution of social status and personality characteristics. In R. van Hout & U. Knops (Eds.), *Language attitudes in the Dutch language area* (pp. 85-103). Dordrecht, Netherlands: Foris.

CHAPTER 11

Recognition of Vocal and Facial Emotions: Comparison between Japanese and North Americans

Sumi Shigeno

Abstract

Three experiments were conducted to investigate cultural differences between the Japanese (J) and the North Americans (NA) in the recognition of the six basic vocal and visual representations of emotions using a congruent and incongruent experimental paradigm. In the first experiment, the recognition by J and NA participants of facial emotions expressed by J and NA actors was compared. In the second experiment, the recognition of vocal emotions was compared. In the third experiment, the audiovisual stimuli were made with voices used in the second experiment that were dubbed onto typical emotions expressed on the faces used in the first experiment, and congruent and incongruent emotions expressed by face and voice were compared. In every experiment, 11 Japanese and 11 North Americans (10 Americans and 1 Canadian) participated. The materials were five words or short sentences spoken in Japanese and in American English expressing six basic emotions: happiness, surprise, anger, disgust, fear, and sadness. The results indicate that (a) participants can easily recognize the vocal or the facial emotional expression of a speaker who belongs to the same culture as that of the participants, (b) Japanese participants are not good at recognizing fear in both facial and vocal emotional expressions, and (c) both Japanese and North American participants identify an incongruence between audio and visual emotional expressions more often by means of the facial emotion than the vocal emotion. These results suggest that identifying the emotion of a speaker from a different culture is difficult and that people will predominantly use visual rather than vocal information to identify emotion.

Introduction

When we recognize a speaker's emotion, the display rules of a culture to which the perceiver and the speaker belong define the recognition of emotion. The investigation of cultural similarities and differences in the recognition of emotion has mainly focused on facial expression. For example, the findings of Ekman and Friesen (1971), using photographs of emotional faces, provided evidence for cultural agreement about the universal facial expression of six basic emotions: happiness, surprise, anger, disgust, fear, and sadness. Ekman and Friesen (1975) further reported that among these six basic emotions there was high agreement for some emotions (e.g., happiness) and low agreement for other emotions (e.g., fear).

Meanwhile, those who are brought up in a culture where the expression of emotion is parsimonious are not good at perceiving emotions of others or at expressing their own emotion. Japanese express their emotion on their faces to a lesser extent than the North Americans,

but they can usually communicate with partners without difficulty. Thus, one possibility is that the Japanese use other signals, such as voice, to express their emotions (Shigeno, 1998). The first purpose of the research reported here was to examine the cultural similarities and differences between Japanese and North Americans in the recognition of facial and vocal expressions of the six basic emotions.

As noted by Ekman and Friesen (1975) we often fail to observe the speaker's face even in a face-to-face situation, and instead, we use the vocal (auditory-only) or both vocal and facial (audiovisual) expression of emotion more often than facial (visual-only) expression alone to recognize the speaker's intended expression of emotions. Nonetheless, this area of research has been mostly neglected (Ekman, 1985; Murray & Arnott, 1993; Shigeno, 2000a; 2000b). Therefore, the second purpose of this chapter was to conduct an experiment that would address this area; hence, we report here on our findings on performances of Japanese and North Americans in the recognition of audiovisual expression of emotion.

Furthermore, in day-to-day communication, the true emotions of a speaker are often covered with other vocal or facial emotions. This is illustrated in Figure 11–1 (Shigeno, 2005).

The question to be asked is, what happens if one dissimulates his or her true emotion with the facial or vocal expression of other emotions? This question becomes even more intriguing in the cross-cultural context; hence, we asked a next question, namely, are there any differences between Japanese and North Americans in perceiving or guessing the actual emotion? Consequently, the third purpose of this research reported here was to explore the recognition of dissimulated emotion through the study of incongruent emotional expressions and to compare that recognition between the Japanese and the North Americans. Results from the stimulus presentation similar to this discrepancy between audition and vision are known as the McGurk effect in speech perception. McGurk and MacDonald (1976) found that observers presented with audiovisual stimuli constructed by dubbing an utterance of a CV syllable onto lip movements of the same speaker uttering a different CV syllable believed that a speaker said, for example, "da," when the speaker had actually uttered /ba/ while /ga/ was presented visually. Based on the results from these three experiments, cultural similarities and differences between Japanese and North Americans are discussed.

Experiment 1

The purpose of Experiment 1 was to compare Japanese and North American participants on the recognition of emotions expressed only by facial movements performed by Japanese and North American actors.

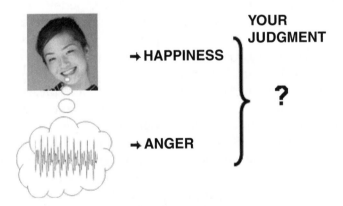

Figure 11–1. In communication in our daily life, we sometimes express an emotion that is different from our actual emotion. The girl smiling in this figure is in fact angry. What is your judgment of her true emotion? Is she happy or angry?

Method

Participants

There were two groups of participants: one group consisted of 11 Japanese (J-participants) and the other consisted of 10 Americans and one Canadian (NA-participants). They were graduate and undergraduate students without hearing or vision deficits. They had never lived outside of their home countries for more than one year, as the NA-participants were overseas exchange students who had been studying in Japan but for less than one school year.

Visual Stimuli

Visual stimuli were videotaped emotional faces without sound. Two adult male actors in their 30s served as speakers. One of the actors was Japanese (33 years old) and the other was American (39 years old). The Japanese and the North American actors uttered five words or short sentences in Japanese and in American English, respectively. These were *to-o-kyo-o* (Tokyo), *ju-u-i-chi-ji-ha-n* (eleven-thirty), *ka-wa-ra-za-ki-sa-n* (Mr. Kawarazaki), *sa-yo-o-na-ra* (good-bye), and *so-o-de-su-ka* (Is that so?) in Japanese, and *New York*, *Rio de Janeiro*, *Margaret*, *Saturday*, and *Is that so?* in American English. These words were selected as by themselves they do not represent any emotions, but may be used in our daily conversations with or without emotional content.

While acting, they were only permitted to use such expressions as intonation, pitch of voice, and/or impersonation and they were instructed not to use such expressions as laughing, crying, and/or clicking with their tongues. Stimuli se-lected for the experimental viewing were chosen by two judges, including this experimenter, on the best facial emotional expression among several samples obtained from each actor.

Speakers' faces were recorded by a beta-cam recorder (Sony, BVW-35). The recordings were edited to appear in a random order and dubbed onto S-VHS videotapes. The duration of each visual stimulus was 1693–2254 ms in Japanese and 1858–2650 ms in American English. There were video recordings of 30 utterances—6 emotions × 5 items. The views of each face occurred twice in a random order. The final presentation videotape thus included 60 stimuli per speaker. A 200-ms pure-tone warning signal was presented 1.5 s ahead of the visual stimulus. The warning signal was given to enhance experimental performance.

Procedure

Participants were instructed to watch the speaker's face (no sound) carefully and to judge the emotion just from facial movements. The experimenter always sat next to a participant to check that the participant watched the monitor carefully. Viewers did not need to identify the word or short sentences that were spoken. The stimuli were presented on a 29-in. TV monitor (Victor, AV-29F2) positioned comfortably at eye level.

Half of the J- or the NA-participants were presented the video of the J-speaker first and the rest were presented the video of the NA-speaker first. Ten responses were obtained per participant, so in total 110 responses (10 × 11 participants) were obtained for each of the six emotions from either J-speakers or NA-speakers. The judgment duration was 3-s.

Results and Discussion

When an emotion was identified as that which the speaker intended to express, the response was judged to be correct. The average percentage of correct responses of the Japanese and the North American speakers for each of the six emotions was obtained from all 11 participants. Although the percentages of correct identification were high in every condition, the emotion of the NA-speaker was more correctly identified than that of the J-speaker by both J- and NA-participants (see Figure 11-2).

The results were confirmed statistically by conducting a 2 × 2 ANOVA—speaker (Japanese versus North American) × participant (Japanese versus North American). Neither the interaction nor the effect of the participant was at a statistically significant level, but the main effect of the speaker was statistically significant [$F(1, 20) = 10.20$, $p < .005$].

The percentages of correct identification of the six emotions expressed by the J- and the NA-speaker are compared between the J- and the NA-participants, as shown in Table 11-1.

Note that the percentage of correct identification of each emotion was high for both the J- and the NA-speaker. However, the correct identification of fear expressed by the J-speaker when observed by the J-participants (62%) was lower than the correct identification of any other emotions ($p < .005$). This is in agreement with the literature and supports the notion that recognition of fear using photographs of emotional expression is very difficult to identify in every culture (e.g., Ekman, Friesen, & Ellsworth, 1972). The present results using video recordings also make it clear that fear is identified at a lower rate than that of other emotions. Expressional movements of a face might have more information than photographs, but the present results

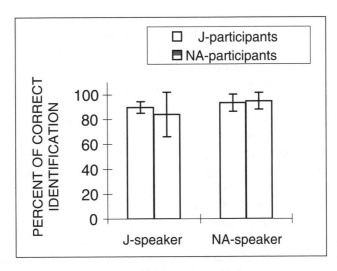

Figure 11–2. Mean percentages of correct responses obtained from visual-only presentation.

Table 11–1. Percentages of correct identification in visual-only condition

Participants	Happiness	Surprise	Anger	Disgust	Fear	Sadness
J-speaker						
J	100	90	99	92	62	96
NA	91	83	92	74	79	86
NA-speaker						
J	100	100	94	85	86	97
NA	92	98	93	95	95	97

indicate that the accuracy of recognition of emotion is not significantly improved even if using video recordings of faces.

The six basic emotions were plotted in two-dimensional psychological spaces calculated by multidimensional scaling (MDS) to further examine cultural similarities and differences between the Japanese and the North Americans in recognizing speakers' emotions. The positions of the six basic emotions are represented in Figure 11–3.

There are four cases, Figures 11–3a through 11–3d, of cultural relationship between speaker and participant. Two cases are the same-culture relationship: J-J (J-speaker and J-participant) and NA-NA (NA-speaker and NA-participant), Figures 11–3a and 11–3d, respectively. The other two cases are the different-culture relationship: J-NA (J-speaker and NA-participant) and NA-J (NA-speaker and J-participant), Figures 11–3b and 11–3c, respectively. The positions of the six emotions in the graphs were very similar among the four cases except those of surprise and sadness. The results suggest that emotional facial movements would be recognized in a similar manner despite cultural differences.

Experiment 2

The purpose of Experiment 2 was to compare the recognition by J- and NA-participants of vocal emotion expressed by Japanese and North American actors.

Method

Participants

Eleven Japanese and 11 North American participants took part in this experiment. All had also participated in Experiment 1.

Vocal Stimuli

The vocal stimuli used in Experiment 2 were the emotional voices without visual presentation, which were recorded in Experiment 1. One voice was that of the Japanese speaker and the other was of the North American actor. As in the first experiment, two people selected the best vocal expression for each item that conveyed the six basic emotions.

Emotional voices expressed by the actors were recorded on a beta-cam

(a) J-J condition

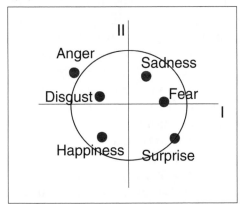

(b) J-NA condition

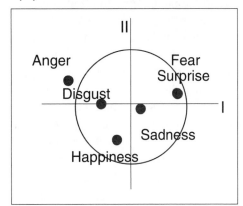

(c) NA-J condition

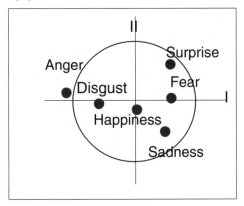

(d) NA-NA condition

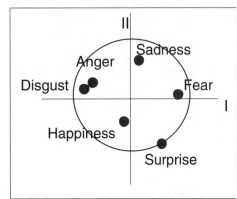

Figure 11–3. Two-dimensional psychological spaces in visual-only experiment.

recorder and were edited so that each voice appeared twice in a random order. The five words or short sentences in Japanese and in American English were the same as those used in Experiment 1. Thirty voices— 6 emotions × 5 items— were used as stimuli. The final audiotape then included 60 trials per speaker. A 200-ms pure-tone warning signal was presented 1.5 s prior to each auditory stimulus.

Procedure

All vocal stimuli were played through a loudspeaker at about 68–75 dB (A scale) in a soundproof room. Participants were instructed to listen carefully to what the speaker was saying and to judge his emotion from the voice sample. They did not need to identify what was said. The duration of each auditory stimulus was 693–1254 ms for the Japanese sound and

858–1650 ms for the American English sound. The judgment duration was 3 s.

Half of the J- and the NA-participants were presented the voices of the J-speaker first and the rest were presented the voices of the NA-speaker first. Each participant judged 10 times for each of the six emotions, so in total 110 responses were obtained from the 11 participants, who were either J- or NA-participants. The other procedure was the same as that in the Experiment 1.

Results and Discussion

When the vocal emotion was identified as that which the speaker intended to express, the response was judged to be correct. The averaged correct percentages for each of the six emotions expressed by the J- and the NA- speakers were obtained from the 11 participants. The performance of J-participants was better than that of NA-participants in the case of the J-speaker, while that of NA-participants was better in the case of the NA-speaker, as indicated in Figure 11–4. This means that participants identify the vocal emotion of the speaker belonging to their culture better than that of the speaker belonging to a different culture.

To confirm the result, a 2 × 2 ANOVA —speaker (Japanese versus North American) × participant (Japanese versus North American) was conducted. As a result, the interaction was statistically significant [$F(1, 20) = 58.24$, $p < .000001$]. In the case of the J-speaker, the performance of J-participants was better than that of NA-participants [$F(1, 20) = 22.03$, $p < .0005$], while in the case of the NA-speaker, the performance of NA-participants was better than that of J-participants [$F(1, 20) = 4.48$, $p < .05$].

The identifications of six emotions expressed by the J- and the NA-speaker as determined by the J- and the NA-participants are compared in Table 11–2.

The percentages of correct identifications were generally lower than those

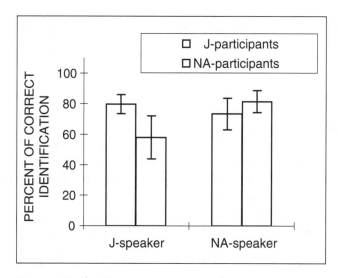

Figure 11–4. Mean percentages of correct responses obtained from auditory-only presentation.

Table 11–2. Percentages of correct identification in auditory-only condition

Participants	Happiness	Surprise	Anger	Disgust	Fear	Sadness
			J-speaker			
J	89	81	92	85	42	90
NA	46	68	68	48	64	54
			NA-speaker			
J	67	74	80	74	49	97
NA	70	83	95	78	79	85

of recognized facial emotion in Experiment 1 (see Figure 11-2). The percentage of correct identification of fear expressed by the J-speaker as recognized by the J-participants (42%) was lower than the correct identification of any other emotion ($p < .0005$). The results as a whole were similar to those obtained for facial movement in Experiment 1.

The six emotions were plotted in a two-dimensional space calculated by MDS to examine the cultural similarities and differences between Japanese and North American participants in recognizing speakers' emotion. The positions of the six basic emotions are shown in Figure 11-5.

The positions of the six emotions in the graph were very similar among the four cases of cultural relationships, like those described in Experiment 1, although in the cases of the North American speaker, Figures 11-5c and 11-5d, both the Japanese and the North American participants categorized the six emotions into three categories. The three categories are happiness and surprise, anger and disgust, and fear and sadness. The results suggest that the emotional voice of the North American speaker was not as delicate as that of the Japanese speaker.

Experiment 3

The purpose of Experiment 3 was to explore if the expression of vocal and facial emotions are different from each other, how the participants recognize them, and how the cultural similarities and differences influence recognition performance.

Method

Participants

Eleven Japanese and 11 North American participants took part in Experiment 3. All had also participated in Experiments 1 and 2.

Mixed Stimuli

The mixed stimuli were the audiovisual material of the facial movements and voices used in Experiments 1 and 2, respectively. To make the audiovisual stimuli, the voices were dubbed onto the faces. The duration of audiovisual stimuli was the same as that of the visual-only stimuli.

(a) J-J condition

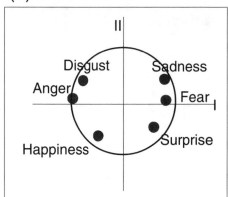

(b) J-NA condition

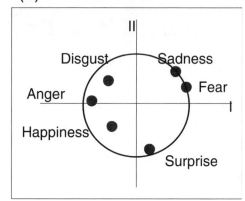

(c) NA-J condition

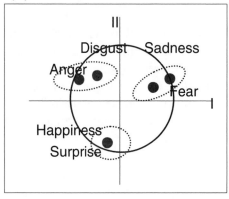

(d) NA-NA condition

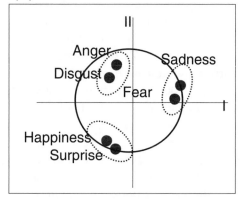

Figure 11–5. Two-dimensional psychological spaces in auditory-only experiment.

There were two stimuli conditions. One condition is called the *congruent condition*, where facial and vocal emotions are the same, such as a happy face with a happy voice. The other condition is called the *incongruent condition*, where facial and vocal emotions are different, such as a happy face with a sad voice.

Each audiovisual stimulus appeared once in a random order with a 3-s interval. In total 180 audiovisual stimuli—6 facial emotions × 6 vocal emotions × 5 items—were used.

Procedure

Audiovisual stimuli were presented in Experiment 3. Participants were instructed to listen to and watch carefully what the speaker said and only to judge his emotion from both his voice and face. They did not need to identify what he said. The other procedure was the same as that in Experiments 1 and 2. Five responses were obtained per participant for each emotion pair of audiovisual stimuli, so 55 responses were obtained from either

11 Japanese participants or 11 North American participants for each of the 36 audiovisual stimuli.

Results and Discussion

The results from the congruent condition and the incongruent condition were analyzed separately.

Congruent Condition

When the emotion was identified as that which the speaker intended to express, the response was judged to be correct. The averaged percentages of correct responses were high and no differences were recognized between the identifications made by the J- and the NA-participants of the J- and the NA-speakers, as shown in Figure 11-6.

The percentages of correct identification of six emotions expressed by the J-

and the NA-speaker as identified by the J- and the NA-participants are compared in Table 11-3.

It was found that fear was very difficult for the J-participants to identify even using both facial and vocal information. The percentage (57%) was lower than that of any other emotion ($p < .0005$).

Incongruent Condition

The results from the audiovisually incongruent condition in which vocal and facial expressions are different from each other are represented in Figure 11-7. The percentages of the selection of vocal/facial/other emotion are given. In the abscissa of Figure 11-7, vocal means that the vocal emotion was selected, facial means that the facial emotion was selected, and other means that an emotion other than vocal or facial emotion was selected. For example, when there is a happy face with a sad voice, if the judgment is that

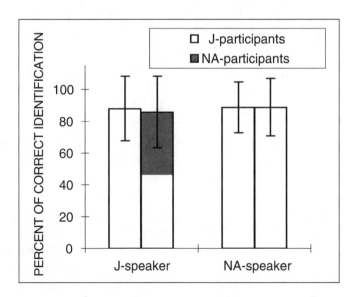

Figure 11–6. Mean percentages of correct responses in congruent condition obtained from audiovisual presentation.

Table 11–3. Percentages of correct identification of emotion expressed by J- and NA-speakers obtained from J- and NA-participants in congruent condition

Participants	Happiness	Surprise	Anger	Disgust	Fear	Sadness
J-speaker						
J	95	88	97	94	57	98
NA	93	85	93	83	76	86
NA-speaker						
J	92	96	88	89	74	93
NA	75	95	93	94	88	89

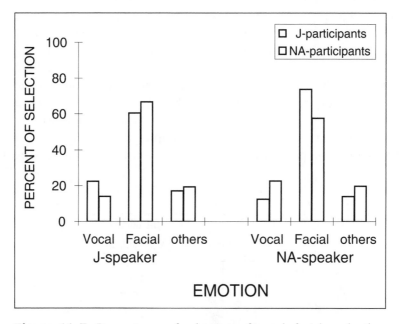

Figure 11–7. Percentages of selection of vocal, facial, and other emotions for audiovisually incongruent expression of emotion.

he is happy (the facial emotion), it is counted to be facial. Figure 11-7 indicates that the J- and the NA-participants identify the audiovisually incongruent stimuli more often by the facial rather than by vocal emotion. The results suggest that when we are required to identify the audiovisually incongruent emotion, visual information would be more available than auditory information.

The identifications of emotion expressed by the J- and the NA-speaker as determined by the J- and the NA-participants are shown in Table 11-4.

Table 11–4. Percentages of correct identification for each pair of incongruent audiovisual emotions in (a) J-J, (b) J-NA, (c) NA-J, and (d) NA-NA conditions

(a) J-J (Japanese speaker-Japanese participants) condition

Presentation		Response (%)					
Audition	Vision	Happiness	Surprise	Anger	Disgust	Fear	Sadness
Happiness	Surprise	11	79		4	6	
	Anger			94	4		2
	Disgust	2	2	8	76	2	10
	Fear		45	6	5	40	4
	Sadness	5		4	5	6	80
Surprise	Happiness	92	8				
	Anger		16	81	3		
	Disgust		12	8	58	7	15
	Fear		46	1		50	3
	Sadness		6	10	2	6	76
Anger	Happiness	91	6		3		
	Surprise	4	75	16	4	1	
	Disgust		4	49	45	1	1
	Fear		23	49	3	25	
	Sadness		2	26	12	11	49
Disgust	Happiness	55	6	4	35		
	Surprise		27	8	58	5	2
	Anger			59	41		
	Fear		11	11	39	36	3
	Sadness			4	42	18	36
Fear	Happiness	89	6				5
	Surprise	4	77			16	3
	Anger		9	45	3	10	33
	Disgust		3	6	36	13	42
	Sadness					4	96
Sadness	Happiness	90	4				6
	Surprise	3	56			23	18
	Anger			30	5	8	57
	Disgust			2	40	8	50
	Fear		18			43	39

continues

Table 11–4. *continued*

(b) J-NA (Japanese speaker-North American participants) condition

Presentation		Response (%)					
Audition	Vision	Happiness	Surprise	Anger	Disgust	Fear	Sadness
Happiness	Surprise	7	*81*	3		9	
	Anger		5	*86*	7		2
	Disgust	*1*	4	16	75	1	3
	Fear	*1*	46	3	1	*48*	1
	Sadness		8	5	8	5	74
Surprise	Happiness	*91*	9				
	Anger		6	*83*	10	1	
	Disgust		9	15	73		3
	Fear	2	36	4	6	*52*	
	Sadness		*10*	14	5	7	64
Anger	Happiness	88	7	*3*	2		
	Surprise	5	*61*	16	5	11	2
	Disgust		4	42	54		
	Fear		32	28	5	35	
	Sadness		5	36	7	2	50
Disgust	Happiness	*94*	2	2	*2*		
	Surprise	6	69	1	*9*	14	1
	Anger		2	*66*	29	3	
	Fear		35	6	6	*52*	1
	Sadness		3	6	*14*	3	74
Fear	Happiness	*90*	6	2			2
	Surprise	3	*56*		4	*37*	
	Anger	2	5	*67*	16	5	5
	Disgust		7	10	*55*	8	20
	Sadness			3	5	*14*	78
Sadness	Happiness	*90*	5		3	2	
	Surprise	4	*52*	5	1	23	*15*
	Anger	2	7	*52*	14		25
	Disgust		2	8	*52*	6	32
	Fear		16	2	3	*61*	18

Table 11–4. *continued*

(c) NA-J (North American speaker-Japanese participants) condition

Presentation		Response (%)					
Audition	**Vision**	**Happiness**	**Surprise**	**Anger**	**Disgust**	**Fear**	**Sadness**
Happiness	Surprise	*1*	97			1	1
	Anger		25	*65*	7		3
	Disgust		2	16	*80*		2
	Fear		26	2		*66*	6
	Sadness			4	7	7	*82*
Surprise	Happiness	*92*	8				
	Anger		*4*	87	5	3	1
	Disgust		7	17	*74*		2
	Fear		*30*			67	3
	Sadness	3	*4*	4	7	6	76
Anger	Happiness	*88*	3	*9*			
	Surprise	3	83	*14*			
	Disgust			*39*	61		
	Fear	2	16	*21*		54	7
	Sadness			*26*	11	7	56
Disgust	Happiness	*80*	6	8	*6*		
	Surprise		*81*	10	*6*	3	
	Anger			88	*12*		
	Fear	1	7	8	*6*	73	5
	Sadness			3	*12*	8	77
Fear	Happiness	*86*	10				4
	Surprise		*89*			7	4
	Anger			78	3	*5*	14
	Disgust		3	21	43	*10*	23
	Sadness	4				*11*	85
Sadness	Happiness	*84*	4				12
	Surprise		65			17	*18*
	Anger			58	6	4	*32*
	Disgust			8	43	4	*45*
	Fear		4			70	*26*

continues

Table 11–4. *continued*

(d) NA-NA (North American speaker-North American participants) condition

Presentation		Response (%)					
Audition	Vision	Happiness	Surprise	Anger	Disgust	Fear	Sadness
Happiness	Surprise	4	96				
	Anger	3	13	66	18		
	Disgust		15	5	80		
	Fear	3	45	1	1	49	1
	Sadness	1	13	5	26	10	45
Surprise	Happiness	69	27	4			
	Anger	3	16	60	19	2	
	Disgust		17	7	74	2	
	Fear	2	36			62	
	Sadness	1	26	1	15	13	44
Anger	Happiness	53	13	22	12		
	Surprise	5	61	25	8	1	
	Disgust			34	66		
	Fear		13	28	11	48	
	Sadness			37	36	3	24
Disgust	Happiness	60	9	6	25		
	Surprise	3	63	7	22	5	
	Anger			64	36		
	Fear		14	6	24	53	3
	Sadness			7	49	5	39
Fear	Happiness	57	19		4	14	6
	Surprise	3	63		1	32	1
	Anger			59	23	12	6
	Disgust		3	8	64	18	7
	Sadness		2	2	4	35	57
Sadness	Happiness	54	9		4	5	28
	Surprise	5	43		2	25	25
	Anger		3	51	21	3	22
	Disgust				55	7	38
	Fear				3	77	20

Different tendencies are recognized in the selection of vocal emotion between the J- and the NA-participants in several audiovisually incongruent emotions. For example, in the case of the J-speaker, the judgment by the Japanese participants of a happy face with a disgusted voice was 55% happy and 35% disgusted. However, for the NA-participants, 92% judged it as happy and only 3% as disgusted. This difference may be caused by cultural differences, and recognizing vocal emotion in an incongruent condition would be very difficult, especially in the case where a speaker belongs to a different culture from that of the observer.

General Discussion

Facial emotions were selected more than vocal emotions in incongruent cases where both were expressed by the speaker. This tendency is recognized more clearly when the speaker belongs to a different culture than that of the participants. For example, if the speaker is a North American and an incongruent face and voice stimuli are presented, the percentages of correct selection of his facial emotion are greater for the J-participants than that for the NA-participants, and vice versa. However, in general, the J-participants are more sensitive to vocal emotions than the NA-participants.

From the present experiments, several important points regarding the influence of recognition of emotion were obtained. First, the performances of visual-only and audiovisual presentations are almost equal, thus suggesting that we may mainly use facial information to identify the emotion of others in face-to-face communication in our daily lives. Second, the performances

in recognizing the emotion of auditory-only presentation are not as high as those of visual-only or audiovisual presentation in both the J- and the NA-participants. This gap is a significant factor in missing or misinterpreting the emotional information when conversing over the phone or when not attending to a face in a face-to-face setting. If this indeed is proven to be a universal, the implications are profound not only for cross-cultural settings but within a culture as well.

In the audiovisually incongruent condition, however, the cultural differences between the J-participants and the NA-participants seem to influence the identification of emotions. Participants correctly identified the emotion of a speaker belonging to their culture more easily than that of a speaker belonging to a different culture. Furthermore, even in the incongruent condition, the J-participants identify vocal emotion more accurately than the NA-participants. The study again points out that cultural similarities and differences are very important, especially in identifying incongruent expressions of emotions. Again, the implications are far reaching and can be profound.

References

Ekman, P. (1985). *Telling lies*. New York: Norton.

Ekman, P., & Friesen, W. V. (1971). Constants across cultures in the face and emotion. *Journal of Personality and Social Psychology, 17*, 124–129.

Ekman, P., & Friesen, W. V. (1975). *Unmasking the face*. Englewood Cliffs, NJ: Prentice-Hall.

Ekman, P., Friesen, W. V., & Ellsworth, P. (1972). *Emotion in the human face: Guidelines for research and an integration of findings*. New York: Pergamon Press.

McGurk, H., & MacDonald, J. (1976). Hearing lips and seeing voices. *Nature*, *264*, 746–748.

Murray, I. R., & Arnott, J. L. (1993). Toward the simulation of emotion in synthetic speech: A review of the literature on human vocal emotion. *Journal of the Acoustical Society of America*, *93*, 1097–1108.

Shigeno, S. (1998). Cultural similarities and differences in the recognition of audio-visual speech stimuli. *Proceedings of International Congress on Spoken Language Processing* (Vol. 2, pp. 281–284). Sydney, Australia:

Shigeno, S. (2000). Emotional perception of speech sounds under audio-visual presentation. In Doré, F. Y. (Ed.), *Abstracts of the XXVII International Congress of Psychology* (p. 53). Stockholm, Sweden:.

Shigeno, S. (2000). Perception of the pretended emotion under audio-visual presentation. In (Ed.), *Proceedings of International Conference on Development of Mind* (p. 134). Tokyo.

Shigeno, S. (2005, March). *Recognition of vocal and facial emotions: Comparison between the Japanese and the American*. Paper presented at the XV Annual Pacific Voice Conference: PVSF/Pixar Voice Conference: Voice & Emotions, Emeryville, California.

CHAPTER 12

Automatic Recognition of Emotive Voice and Speech

Julia Sidorova, John McDonough, and Toni Badia

Abstract

It is important to know a user's emotional state for a number of applications, such as in human robotic interfaces, call centers, and spoken tutoring systems. An aim of a speech emotion recognition (SER) engine is to take a speech fragment as an input and to produce as an output an estimate of the antecedent emotional state the speaker. In other words, SER maps a speech fragment into one of the label(s) denoting specific emotional state(s). As we will show in this chapter, this challenge has been the subject of a great deal of recent research effort.

SER is rooted in the observation that acoustic parameters correlate with speaker's emotional state, and earlier studies were devoted to this correlations (Williams and Stevens, 1972). The main acoustic parameters studied typically were pitch (F0), energy, articulation, rate and spectral shape. For instance, it was generally accepted that the emotions connoting joy, anger, or fear showed higher mean pitch and amplitude, with greater F0 and amplitude variations, than neutral speech. Sadness displayed the opposite effect on F0 and amplitude than anger, joy, and fear, as sadness was characterized by low mean F0 and signal amplitude. Speech rate was also noted to vary with various emotions. For example, the fastest speech rate was noted for angry speech and the slowest rate for sad speech.

The early SER studies aimed at revealing general acoustic correlation of emotion assumed to be contained in the speech signal, rather than building an efficient automatic recognition device. Since then and despite significant advances, many problems remain unsolved before constructing truly effective SER systems.

This chapter begins with a discussion of which emotions a SER system should be capable of recognizing. We then present general issues pertaining to the design of SER experiments. In Section "Mathematical models of classifiers," we present three classifiers that find frequent applications in SER, namely (1) the k-nearest neighbor (k-NN) classifier, (2) the multilayer perceptron, and (3) the hidden Markov model. We also review recent publications, wherein each classifier was applied to the SER task. Finally, we present a notion of a single "combined" classifier, which is specifically tailored for the SER problem.

Language and Psychological Issues

Which Set of Emotions Needs to Be Recognized?

A fundamental question in SER research is the question of which emotions should be recognized. Currently literature is however unclear in providing universally accepted and a uniform definition of emotion or of a generally accepted set of "basic" emotions. (To read more about current concepts please consult Chapters 3, 11 and 13 in Volume 1 of this publication and Chapters 5, 8 and 19 in Volume 3 of these series) Moreover, standard speech corpora whose utterances have been tagged with emotion labels have only recently are being collected and are becoming publicly available (see http://emotion-research.net). These two factors make it difficult to compare the performance of the different SER systems. In practice, the emotions defined in the MPEG-4[1] are often used. This set of emotions comprises anger, joy, disgust, fear, sadness, surprise, and neutral affect. Using the MPEG-4 emotions outline provides for the possibility of comparing and relating the experimental work with previously described results. Therefore, the MPEG-4 set of emotions is a reasonable choice for testing a new classifier or when SER is tried on a previously untested natural language.

---

[1]MPEG-4 is the global multimedia standard defined by the Motion Pictures Experts Group 4, working within the International Organization for Standardization (ISO).

However, when SER is to be conducted with a particular application in mind, a different emotion set may be required. For example, in the work on SER Petrushin (2000), focused on SER application to a call center, with recognition between two states was aimed at *agitation* and *calmness*.

For tasks related to human-to-computer interfaces MPEG-4 emotions appear to be too dramatic, because they relate to stereotyped performing emotions, as they are constructed in characterized performances (as in films). In tasks related to human-to-computer interfaces the aim is to be sensitive to everyday emotional states, and therefore the "blended emotions" are preferred. For example, in such contexts, the following sets of emotions are considered: excitement, boredom, irritation, enthusiasm, stress, satisfaction, and amusement as in (Karpouzis & Kollias, 2005) or anger, fear, excuse, satisfaction, and neutral as in (Devillers, Vidrascu, & Lamel, 2005).

Use of Non-Acoustic Information to Determine Emotion

To increase recognition accuracy and success, current tendency in SER research is to use some other information apart from speech acoustics, specifically the information derived from a spoken content (Lee & Narayanan, 2005), including facial expression and physiological data are incorporated. For example, when emotion recognition is executed by using a combination of acoustic (72.2%) and semantic (59.6%) analysis, the overall recognition rate increases to 92% (Müller, Schuller, & Rigoll, 2004). Similarly, combined audiovisual emotion recognition leads to better recognition rates (approximately 84%) than acoustic (approximately 67%) or video (approximately 68%) alone (Song, Bu, Chen, & Li, 2004). Other studies have also substantiated the power of combining various data to achieve improved automatic recognition of emotions (Kim, André, Rehm, Vogt, & Wagner, 2005). These authors report that user-dependent and -independent emotion recognition can be improved substantially when fusing physiological and voice data.

Authentic Speech Emotions vs. Actor Imitations

In practice, two types of speech corpora are used: (a) the authentic speech emotions produced in ad hoc situations and (b) the imitations of emotions produced by actors. The authentic emotions are much harder to collect, but are available at, for example, call centers and some live TV programs. Considering the acted corpora when building an emotion recognizer for spontaneous emotions may not be reasonable because it has been shown that the results of artificial data transfer poorly to the real data (Devillers, Vidrascu, & Lamel, 2005). Moreover, the report of Vogt and André (2005) suggests that feature sets for acted and authentic emotions are only capable of intersecting, and are far from equal. These authors demonstrated that the important features for acted emotions include basic pitch and pauses (when describing sadness), while the important features for realistically capturing emotional expressions are the mel frequency cepstral coefficients (MFCCs) (mainly low coefficients and first derivatives) and the extrema of pitch and energy.

Language Units

Another important question is which language unit must be chosen to recognize emotions. Emotion recognition is usually performed on whole spoken utterances,[2] although estimation of emotion is possible from smaller units (e.g., an isolated word or even one syllable), or on bigger ones (a whole speaker turn). Theoretically emotion can change along the length of the utterance. Therefore it may be convenient to begin to recognize an emotion already within the word boundaries as opposed to the phrase length (Aina, Hartmann, & Strothotte, 2003).

Low Level Features[3]

Low level features are understood as either long- or short-time ones. Long-time features are determined from the entire utterance or from the entire recording of a speech sample. The typical measures that are used to describe the text are the means, medians, standard deviations, and percentiles, all estimated over the entire utterance length. Short-time features are determined in a smaller time window (usually 20 to 100 msec). Contemporary research approach favors the long-time features (Li & Zhao, 1998) because the long-time features identify emotions better than short-time ones. Nonetheless, using long-time features has drawbacks. Essentially, longer samples tend to ignore

the temporal structure of speech. For instance, interrogative sentences usually imply a wider pitch contour than affirmative ones, so that the pitch standard deviation in the interrogative phrase is usually larger. But since this deviation is only a reflex of the syntax of the sentence and has nothing to do with the emotional style, it interferes with the emotion recognizer that takes such long features into account (Nogueiras, Moreno, Bonafonte, & Marino, 2001).

Not all features are equally relevant. Some features are important in combination with others, and some might be noisy (McGilloway, Cowie, Douglas-Cowie, Gielen, Westerdijk, Stroeve, 2000). Irrelevant features and high dimensionality of data can hurt performance of memory-based methods (like k-NN). To solve this problem, a feature selection procedure is needed, and there are various algorithms for reducing feature dimensionality.[4] Feature selection improves the quality of object description in the database.

Speech Emotion "Typology"

Scherer (2000) elaborated on the hypothesis of the universality of the emotion effects on vocal production (versus language variability). This is of practical importance specifically for the development and marketing of speech technology products, as little customization of the respective algorithms would be necessary,

---

[2]An utterance is a prosodically complete speech fragment, and can be bigger or smaller than a written sentence.

[3]A useful, free voice statistics tool can be found in http://www.praat.org. The present authors were able to extract observation vectors for SER experiments consisting of 116 individual features.

[4]A useful, free data-mining software is found at http://www.cs.waikato.ac.nz/~ml/weka/

if emotion effects on the voice were universal, whereas culturally or linguistically relative emotional effects would require special adaptations for specific languages or countries. The results of perception experiments support a mild version of the universality hypothesis. The experiment in question deals with languages of three families: Germanic (Dutch and English), Romance (Italian, French, and Spanish), and non-Indo-European languages spoken in Indonesia. According to the experiment, belonging to a language family seems to correlate with emotion coding too: meaning being similar in languages (e.g., in grammar and basic vocabulary) implies similarity in speech emotion coding (by means of pitch, energy, time-related parameters, etc.).

In phonetics, acoustic parameters are traditionally divided into two classes: prosodic parameters (pitch, intensity, and duration) and segmental ones (spectrum and energy). Some vocally transmitted emotions are better described (and recognized) via prosodic parameters, and are therefore sometimes referred to as "prosodic" emotions, while other emotions are more easily identified with segmental parameters, and are consequently called "segmental" emotions. Languages however tend to differ in the way they encode vocally transmitted emotions. For example, in Spanish sadness and surprise are expressed with prosodic elements, while happiness and cold anger are represented by segmental features (Montero, Gutierrez-Arriola, Cordoba, Enriquez, & Pardo, 1998). On the contrary, in Japanese anger, surprise, and sorrow are prosodic, while joy and fear are segmental (Moriyama & Ozawa,1999).

Mathematical Models of Classifiers

In this section, principles of three of the most widely used classifiers in SER, namely, k-Nearest Neighbor (k-NN), Multiplayer Perceptron (MLP), and the Hidden Markov Model (HMM), are outlined. In addition, we present a new experimental classifier based on both syntactic and statistical machine learning techniques. The k-NN is a clustering method of classification, based on the minimum distance from the query instance to the training samples. The MLP is an artificial neural network that learns nonlinear function mappings. The HMM is a finite-state machine, which is often used also as a classifier.[5] These are by no means the only classifiers which have been applied to the SER problem; for a more exhaustive list, see (Oudeyer, 2002).

Selecting the optimal algorithm for a given classification task is not always straightforward. Given that no algorithm is uniformly optimum for all tasks, choosing a classifier typically involves many empirical trials on large representative data bases. Some are more efficient with certain types of class distributions, and some are better at dealing with many irrelevant features or with structured feature sets. Such testing in speaker-dependent

---

[5]For more detailed studies and descriptions of k-NN and MLP, the interested readers should consult a detailed tutorial on classifier theory and classifier ensembles published by Kuncheva (2004). For continuous density HMMs, readers should consult the textbook by Deller, Proakis, & Hansen, (1993).

and -independent conditions is illustrated in Table 12-1 and Table 12-2.

Preliminaries

A classifier assigns class labels to objects. Objects are described by a set of measurements called attributes or features. For SER the objects are the speech fragments. The set of features are the low level features extracted from the utterance. Classes correspond to a set of emotions. SER is usually tackled as a problem of supervised learning. Figure 12-1 depicts all the stages and possible loops of this process. The explanation follows below.

Let there be c possible classes in the problem, with labels from:

$$W = \{w_1, w_2, \ldots w_c\}. \tag{1}$$

Table 12–1. Comparison of classifiers in speaker-dependent and -independent conditions

Classifier	S IND Error %	S DEP Error %
kMeans	57.05	27.38
kNN	30.41	17.39
GMM	25.17	10.88
MLP	26.85	9.36
SVM	23.88	7.05
ML-SVM	18.71	9.05

Note. This table shows predominance of Support Vector Machines. The classifier is increasingly popular for different tasks (see Abe & Inoue, 2005; Kecman, 2005). For experiments of SER done with SVM as a classifier, see McGilloway et al., 2000. Data are from *Report on Implementation of Audio, Video, and Multimodal Algorithms*, by Augmented Multiparty Interaction, Integrated Project, 2004 [AMI] D 4.1. Retrieved October 22, 2005, from http://www.ami project.org/annual_report_04.php

Feature values for a given object form an n-dimensional vector:

$$x = [x_1 \ldots x_n]^T \in {}^n. \tag{2}$$

The real space $\in^n$ is called the feature space, with every axis corresponding

Table 12–2. Comparison of classifiers in speaker-dependent conditions (two speakers)

Classifier	Speaker 1 (error) %	Speaker 2 (error) %
1-NN	13	8
5-NN	10	8
10-NN	13	9
Decision trees/ C4.5	15	8
Decision rules/ PART	14	7
Kernel density	13	9
Kstar	14	10
Linear regression	17	11
LWR	13	11
Voted perceptrons	35	22
SVM degree 1	13	9
SVM degree 2	10	4
SVM degree 3	11	6
VFI	17	8
M5Prime	12	5
Naïve Bayes	11	7
AdaBoost M1/ C4.5	10	4
AdaBoost M1/ PART	10	4

Note. Data are from "Novel Useful Features and Algorithms for the Recognition of Emotions in Human Speech," by P.-Y. Oudeyer, 2002, *Speech Prosody*, p. 39.

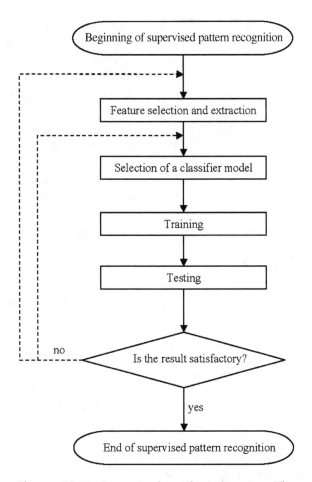

Figure 12–1. Supervised machine learning. The dashed lines show that loops of model tuning can be closed at different places: to use the same classifier model, but redo the training with different parameters, or to change the classifier model.

to a particular feature. The data set is denoted as,

$$Z = \{z_1, \ldots, z_N\}, z_j \in {}^n; \tag{3}$$

Let $l(z_j)$ denote the class label of z_j, and $l(z_j) \in$, where $j = 1, \ldots, N$. A classifier D is a function:

$$D: {}^n \rightarrow |. \tag{4}$$

In the canonical model of classifier (Figure 12–2) a set of c discriminant functions is considered:

$$G = \{g_1(x), \ldots, g_c(x)\}, \text{where} \tag{5}$$

$$g_i: \Re^n \Re, \text{for all } i = 1, \ldots, c. \tag{6}$$

Every function yields a score for the representative class, and x is assigned the

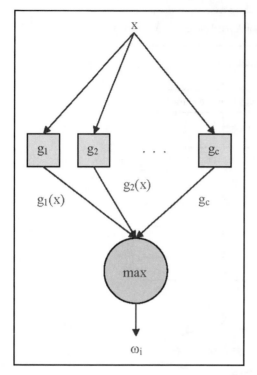

Figure 12–2. Canonical model of a classifier.

label of the highest scoring class. The maximum membership rule can be stated as

$$D(x) = w_j \in \Omega \Leftrightarrow j = \arg\max_i\{g_i(x)\}. \quad (7)$$

Ties are resolved randomly, i.e., x is assigned randomly to one of the tied classes. The discriminant functions divide the feature space $\Re^n$ into c, not necessarily compact, classification regions, R_1, ..., R_c:

$$R_c = \{\mathbf{x}\ \mathbf{x} \in \Re^n, g_c(\mathbf{x}) = \max g_k(\mathbf{x}),$$
$$k = 1, \ldots, c\}, i = 1, \ldots, c. \quad (8)$$

The points for which the ith discriminant function has the highest score constitute the decision region for class w_i. By (7), all points in decision region R_i are

assigned in class w_i. The decision regions are defined by classifier D, or, equivalently, by discriminant functions G. The *classification boundaries* of the decision regions contain the points for which two or more discriminant functions return the same value. A point on the boundary can be assigned to any of the adjacent classes. The classes w_i and w_j are said to be overlapping if a decision region R_i contains data points from the labeled set $\mathbf{Z}$ with true class label w_j, with $j \neq i$. If classes overlap given a particular partition of the feature space, they also can be non-overlapping, if the feature space were to be partitioned differently.

To know exactly how accurate D is, it must be run on all possible input objects. Since this is not possible, the counting estimator Error (D) is used to characterize accuracy. Assume a labeled data set Z_{test} with N_{test} objects in it is available for testing the accuracy of a classifier D. After running D on Z_{test}, calculate Error(D):

$$\text{Error}(D) = \frac{N_{error}}{N_{test}}, \quad (9)$$

where N_{error} is the number of misclassifications made by D, and N_{test} is the total number of objects in the test data set.

Another question is which subsets of $\mathbf{Z}$ it takes for training and testing purposes. The main choices are:

- Resubstitution (R-method): In this method classifier D is trained on $\mathbf{Z}$ and is tested on it as well. *Overfitting,* whereby a classifier learns the training data perfectly but fails on unseen data, is a distinct possibility in such a scenario.
- Bootstrapping: This method is an extension of R-method. It corrects the optimistic bias of the R-method by

randomly generating L sets of cardinality N from the original set Z, with replacement. Then the average error is assessed.

- Hold-out (H-method): Z is split into halves, one for training and the other for testing. Splits can be performed in other proportions too. Data shuffle is a variant of this method wherein Z is randomly split L times into training and testing parts and average Error(D) of all L is estimated.
- Cross-validation (π - or rotation method): The data set Z is randomly divided into K subsets of size N/K, where the integer K is preferably a factor of N. Then one subset is used to test the performance of D trained on the union of the remaining K-1 subsets. This procedure is repeated K times and the average error over all K trials is taken as Error(D).

To know how the misclassifications are distributed across the classes, confusion matrices are built for Z_{test}. The entry a_{ij} of a confusion matrix denotes the number of elements from Z_{test} whose true class is w_i, and which are classified by D as belonging to the class w_j.

A rapidly evolving area in pattern recognition research is the combination of classifiers to form so-called classifier ensembles. For a number of reasons, ranging from statistical to computational and representational aspects, ensembles of classifiers tend to outperform single classifiers. In the field of speech processing classifier ensembles have also proven to be adequate for the SER task (Dellaert, Polzin, & Waibel, 1996; Petrushin, 2000).

k-Nearest Neighbor (k-NN)

The k-NN is a classical prototype classifier where a comparison is made between the prototypes from a training set and the vector x to be classified (Duda, Hart, & Stork, Section 4.4, 2001). It has quite often been used in SER.

Let V denote a labeled reference set containing v points in $\Re^n$, referred to as the prototypes:

$$V = \{v_1, \ldots, v_v\} \tag{10}$$

The prototypes in V are labeled; i.e., for any $v_i \in V$, its class label $l(v_i) \in \Omega$ is known. In the k-NN design, V is the whole of Z. In order to classify an input x, the k-NN prototypes are retrieved from V together with their class labels. The input x is assigned the label of the nearest prototype in a Euclidean sense. In Figure 12–3a, 1-nn (k = 1) and 3-nn (k = 3) rule on a randomly generated data set with two classes. The star represents the vector to be classified and the arrows join this vector to its three nearest neighbors. The new object is assigned to the class *diamonds* by the 1-NN rule because such is the label of the closest neighbor. The 3-NN rule labels the object as a *cross* because such were the labels of the second and third neighbors (by majority vote: 2 out of 3). The classification regions obtained by the 1-nn rule are depicted using Voronoi diagrams,[6] as shown in Figure 12–3. The Voronoi bin V for $z_{j \in} Z$ is the set of points in $\Re^n$, whose nearest neighbor from Z is z_j, that is,

$$V(z_j) = \{x \mid x \in \Re^n, d(z_j, x) = \min_k d(z_k, x) \text{ for all } z_k \in Z \}, \tag{11}$$

---

[6]Voronoi diagrams are decompositions of the metric space calculated from the distances between a discrete set of points in the space.

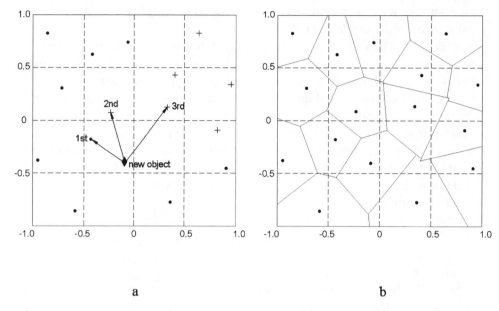

Figure 12–3. Illustration of the 1-nn and 3-nn classification rules (**a**) and Voronoi diagrams (**b**).

where $d(z,x)$ is the Euclidean distance between z and x in $\mathfrak{R}^n$.

The k-NN classifier design can differ in three respects: there can be different values of k; there can be different distance metrics in $\mathfrak{R}^n$; and there can be different reduced versions of Z as prototype sets V.

There are two major ways for finding k-NN prototypes: prototype selection (Hart's method, Wilson's method, random editing, etc.) and prototype extraction (competitive learning, using gradient descent, Chang, modified Chang etc.).[7] Naturally, while contracting the cardinality of Z, for SER one usually would want to have every emotion represented in V.

The main advantage of the k-NN classifier is its simplicity. The drawbacks of classical k-NN are a long list: are compu-tationally expensive; intolerant to noise in features; they treat all vector components as if they were of equal importance; they are intolerant to redundant features; they often perform poorly when confronted with high dimensional features; they are sensitive to the choice of the similarity function; they have no natural similarity measure for nominal-valued features; they have no natural capacity for handling missing values; and they provide little information regarding the structure of the data. Moreover, the number of classes k distinguished between, must be kept small, especially if the distance between the classes is small.

These drawbacks motivated the investigation of many k-NN variants (Wettschereck, Aha, & Mohri, 1995). These k-NN variants have frequently been shown to

---

[7]For a presentation of many of these methods of acquiring the prototypes, see Bezdek and Kuncheva (2000) and the literature cited therein.

provide superior classification performance as compared to the conventional k-NN algorithm. Unfortunately, such sophisticated variants have been largely ignored in the SER literature.

Dellaert, Polzin, & Waibel (1996) was among the first to consider the problem of classifying utterances of human speech according to their emotional content. They considered two sets of features: The first feature set of features was global statistics about the behavior of F0, the fundamental frequency, during voiced regions of the speech. These statistics included mean, standard deviation, minimum, maximum, and range, which was defined as the minimum F0 subtracted from the maximum. Slope was defined through a linear regression on F0 during voiced speech segments, and speaking rate was defined as the inverse of the average length of voiced segments. The second feature set included 17 features total, all of which were based on estimating cubic splines for the F0 contour during voiced segments. Among these were statistics related to rhythm, to global characteristics, such as minimum, maximum, median and standard deviation, the individual voiced segments and the slopes thereof. In Dellaert Polzin, & Waibel (1996), the performance of a k-NN classifier was compared to both a maximum likelihood Bayes (MLB) classifier as well as a kernel regression (KR) classifier. They conducted experiments on a corpus of over 1,000 utterances from several different speakers, which were to be classified according to four emotions, namely, happiness, sadness, anger, and fear. Their results indicated that the k-NN classifier was significantly better than either the MLB or KR classifiers for both feature sets. They also found that the performance of the k-NN classifier could be sig-

nificantly improved by adjusting the importance assigned to each feature in a weighted Euclidean distance metric. Moreover, they obtained further reductions in classification error when multiple classifiers based on different feature sets were combined.

Oudeyer (2002) was the first researcher to apply a truly large number of classification algorithms developed by the machine learning community to the SER problem. He also considered a large feature set, including mel-frequency cepstral coefficients, pitch, and intensity. The findings reported in that work demonstrated that several classifiers performed better than k-NN when all features were used for classification, most notably decision trees trained with adaboost. The performance differences among the classifiers were greatly reduced, however, when the features were selected according to a number of different schemes. Interestingly, the most effective parameters were related to the intensity of the speech after low pass filtering. Indeed, four rules in a decision tree, all of which were related to low pass-filtered intensity, enabled the correct recognition of three emotions, anger, happiness, and sadness, as well as a single neutral state with an error rate of only 6%. Surprisingly, many of the features proposed in the psychoacoustic literature turned out to be not particularly effective for this machine-learning task.

Toivanen, Seppänen, & Väyrynen, (2004) used a k-NN classifier exclusively to test emotion recognition accuracy in spoken Finnish. They considered three sets of features. The first set was based on F0 and included of mean, median, maximum, minimum, range, and variance. The second set consisted of the same statistics, but as applied to intensity, and the third as applied to duration. Out of three emotions, anger, happiness, and sadness, as well as a neutral state, they found that sadness was consistently the easiest to classify. Moreover, their results indicated that performance degraded significantly when performing speaker independent, as opposed to speaker dependent, classification.

In Toivanen, Seppänen, & Väyrynen, (2004), the selection of training and testing materials was performed according to the leave-one-out principle, a variant of the cross-validation technique. Choosing $k = 1$ and prior speaker identification led to 80.7% of correct emotion recognition. Choosing $k = 3$ with no prior speaker identification led to 75.4%; with $k = 5$, 60% of speaker-independent recognition was reached.

The effective application of the k-NN classifier to a problem such as SER requires a significant amount of parameter tuning. It is always advisable to try different values of k, as well as different distance metrics, such as the Mahalanobis and Minkowski metrics, and the tangent distance; see (Duda, Hart, & Stork, Section 4.6, 2001) for a discussion of metrics for use with k-NN classifiers.

Neural Networks

Artificial neural networks (NNs) are designed with the idea to model mathematically human intellectual abilities by biologically plausible engineering design and to benefit from parallel computation. The multilayer perceptron (MLP) is the most widely used NN variant. For quite a long time NNs have been a popular classifier choice in SER experiments (AMI, 2004; Hozjan & Kacic, 2003a; 2003b; Petrushin, 2000; Tosa & Nakatsu, 1996).

For an n-dimensional pattern recognition problem with c classes, a neural network obtains a feature vector $\boldsymbol{x} = [\mathrm{x}_1 \ldots \mathrm{x}_n]^T \in \mathfrak{R}^n$ as its input, and produces values for the c discriminant functions $g_1(\boldsymbol{x})$, $\ldots$, $g_c(\boldsymbol{x})$ as its output. A NN is usually trained to minimize the squared error E on a labeled training set $\boldsymbol{Z} = \{z_1, \ldots, z_n\}$, $z_i \in \mathfrak{R}^n$, and $\mathrm{l}(z_i) \in \Omega$:

$$E = \frac{1}{2} \sum_{j=1}^{N} \sum_{i=1}^{c} \{g_i(\mathbf{z}_j) - I(\mathbf{w}_i, \mathrm{l}(z_j))\}^2, \quad (12)$$

where I is an indicator function.

Neurons are processing units of the human brain. The computational model of neuron is presented in Figure 12–4. Let $\boldsymbol{u}$ be the input vector to the node:

$$\mathrm{u} = [\mathrm{u}_0 \cdots \mathrm{u}_q]^T \in \mathfrak{R}^{q+1} \quad (13)$$

and $v \in \mathfrak{R}$ be the output. Let $\boldsymbol{w}$ be a vector of synaptic weights:

$$\mathrm{w} = [\mathrm{w}_0, \ldots, \mathrm{w}_q] \in \mathfrak{R}^{q+1} \quad (14)$$

The processing element implements the function:

$$v = \phi(\xi), \text{ where } \xi = \sum_{i=0}^{q} \mathrm{w}_i \mathrm{u}_i \quad (15)$$

where $\phi: \mathfrak{R} \to \mathfrak{R}$ is the activation function and ξ is the net sum. Typical choices for ϕ are:

■ The threshold function:

$$\phi(\xi) = \begin{cases} 1, \text{if } \xi \geq 0, \\ \\ 0, \text{otherwise} \end{cases} \quad (16)$$

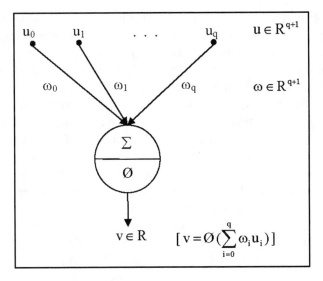

Figure 12–4. The computational model of neuron.

■ The sigmoid function:

$$\phi(\xi) = \frac{1}{1 + \exp(-\xi)} \tag{17}$$

■ The identity function:

$$\phi(\xi) = \xi. \tag{18}$$

■ The hyperbolic tangent function:

$$\phi(\xi) = \text{than}(\xi) \tag{19}$$

The weight $-w_0$ is used as a bias, and the corresponding input value u_0 is set to 1. Expression (15) can be rewritten as:

$$v = \phi[\zeta - (-w_0)] = \phi[\sum_{i=1}^{q} w_i u_i - (-w_0)], \tag{20}$$

where ζ is now the weighted sum of the weighted inputs from 1 to q. Equation (21) defines a hyperplane in $\Re^q$:

$$\sum_{i=1}^{q} w_i u_i - (-w_0) = 0 \tag{21}$$

In the late 1950s Rosenblatt (1957) defined the famous perceptron with its training algorithm. The perceptron was implemented as defined in (15); its threshold activation function:

$$\phi(\xi) = \begin{cases} 1, & \text{if } \xi \geq 0, \\ \\ -1, & \text{otherwise} \end{cases} \tag{22}$$

This single-neuron classifier separates two classes in $\Re^n$ with $\xi = 0$. The learning algorithm starts with random initial weights w and modifies them, while each subsequent sample from Z is "fed" to the perceptron. The change is made only in case of misclassification of the current vector z_j, i.e., point representing z_j appears on the wrong side of the hyperplane. The weights are corrected by

$$w \leftarrow w - v\eta\, z_j, \tag{23}$$

where v is the output of the perceptron for z_j and η is the learning rate.

Multilayer perceptron (MLP) is an NN structure comprised by perceptrons. MLP has an input layer, a hidden layer, and an output layer connected in a feed-forward manner; that is, each neuron receives signals from the previous layer as well as sends connections to the next layer (Figure 12–5), and there are no connections between the nodes of the same level. Weights are associated to each input and every connection. MLP receives an input pattern (x) and maps this into c discriminant functions $g_1(x), \ldots, g_c(x)$ at the output layer. The default perceptron properties are:

- For input layers, the activation function is the identity function (18).
- Feed-forward structure.
- Non-adjacent layers are not directly connected.
- All nodes at all hidden layers have the same activation function.

This model is no constraint model: MLP with a single hidden layer and threshold nodes can approximate any function with a specified precision. Figure 12–6 shows classification regions that could be formed by an MLP with one, two, and three layers of threshold nodes.

After the MLP structure (number of hidden layers, number of nodes at each layer, activation functions) is defined, the learning problem determines weights for all nodes.

Let θ be a parameter of the NN and $J(\theta)$ be some error function to be minimized. The gradient descent method updates by

$$\theta \leftarrow \theta - \eta \frac{\partial J}{\partial \theta}, \tag{24}$$

where $\eta > 0$ is the learning rate.

Backpropagation training algorithm:

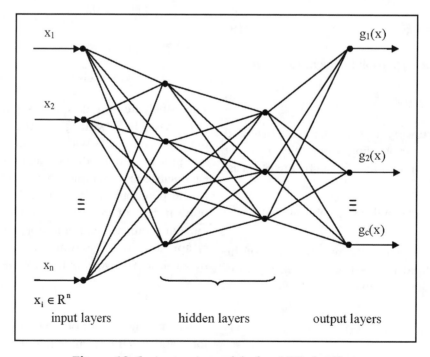

Figure 12–5. A generic model of an MLP classifier.

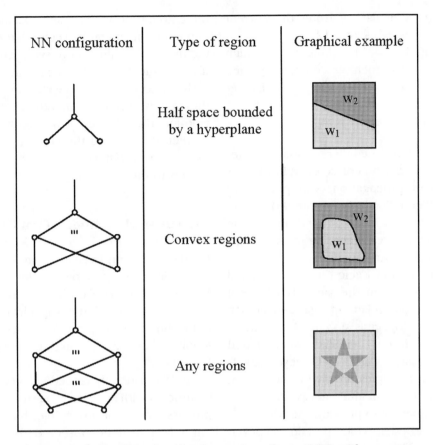

NN configuration	Type of region	Graphical example

Half space bounded by a hyperplane — w_2, w_1

Convex regions — w_2, w_1

Any regions

Figure 12–6. Possible classification regions for an MLP with one, two, and three layers of threshold nodes (in this example, the number of layers is important, not the number of neurons in every layer).

1. Initialize the training procedure: assign small random values to all weights (including biases) of the MLP. Specify the learning rate $\eta > 0$, the max number of epochs T,[8] and the error goal $\varepsilon > 0$.
2. Set $E = \bullet$, the epoch counter $t = 1$ and the object counter $j = 1$.
3. While ($E > \varepsilon$ and $t \leq T$) do
    (a) Submit z_j as the next training example.
    (b) Calculate the output of every node of the NN with the current weights (forward propagation).
    (c) Calculate the error term at each node at the output layer by $\delta = \delta^0_i$.
    (d) Calculate recursively all error terms at the nodes of the hidden layers using (back-propagation).

    $$\delta^b_k = (\sum_{i=1}^{c} \delta^0_i w^0_{ik}) \frac{\partial \phi(\xi^b_k)}{\partial \xi^b_k} \quad (25)$$

    (e) For each hidden and each output node update the weights by

    $$w_{new} = w_{old} - \eta \, \delta \, u, \quad (26)$$

---

[8]A pass through the whole $\mathbf{Z}$ is called an epoch.

(f) Calculate E using the current weights and (12).

(g) If $j = N$ [a whole pass through **Z** (epoch) is completed], then set $t = t + 1$ and $j = 0$. Else, set $j = j + 1$.

4. End while.

To overcome the inherent disadvantages of the pure gradient descent, RProp (for resilient propagation) was proposed;[9] see Riedmiller & Braun, (1993). RProp performs a local adaptation of the weight-updates according to the behavior of the error function.

Hozjan and Kacic (2003) conducted experiments on the same data base of English, Slovenian, Spanish and French used by Nogueiras Moreno, Bonafonte, & Marino (2001). Their SER system is based on all features used by Oudeyer (2002) with duration features, with the sum of absolute pitch and energy difference which pertain to prosody, and with shimmer and jitter, which pertain to speech quality. Their classification system was based on a MLP with 144 input neurons, 7 output neurons, one for each of six emotional states in addition to the neutral condition, and 49 neurons in the hidden layer. The MLP was trained with the R-prop algorithm using Stuttgart Neural Network Simulator version 4.2. Readers should note that most of these capabilities are also available in Weka (Witten and Frank, 2005). Eighty percent of all sentences from the database were randomly selected for the training of the neural network, and the remaining 20% were used for testing. The max-correct method (Noam, Kerret, and Karlinski, 2001) was used to evaluate the correctness of the entire vector. One output vector denoted the emotion of one utterance. Elements in the output and target vector that have the maximum values were searched for. If the element with the maximum value in the target vector and the element with the highest vector denoted the same emotion, then the vector was defined as correct. It evaluated the correctness of the entire output vector, which corresponds to the emotion.

Hidden Markov Models (HMM)

HMMs have long been used in several human language technologies, including SER (e.g., De Silva & Chi Ng, 2000; Kwon, Chan, Hao, & Lee, 2003; Nogueiras, Moreno, Bonafonte, & Marino 2001; Schulle, Rigoll, & Lang, 2003; Song Bu, Chen, & Li, 2004).

HMM is a doubly embedded stochastic process with an underlying stochastic process that is not observable (hidden), but which can be observed through another set of stochastic processes that produce the sequence of observations. HMMs are the probabilistic counterpart of finite automata.

HMM is a 5-tuple A = (N, M, A, B, π), where variables denote the following. N is the number of states in the model. Let the set of states S,

$$S = \{S_1, S_2, \ldots, S_N\}, \tag{27}$$

and the set at time t is q_t. Let O = O_1 $O_2 \ldots O_T$ denote a vector sequence of continuous-valued observations where T is the total number of observations in the sequence. The specific features comprising the observation vector vary from author to author, as discussed below.

---

[9]Also read about RProp at http://openai.sourceforge.net/docs/nn_algorithms/networksarticle/rules.html

A is the state transition probability distribution, $A=\{a_{ij}\}$, where

$$a_{ij} = P[q_{t+1} = S_j | q_t = S_i], \ 1 \leq i, j \leq N. \quad (28)$$

Let B denote the set of Gaussian mixture models used to calculate the state-dependent likelihood of observation. For state j, this conditional likelihood can be expressed as

$$b_j(O_t) = \sum_{k=1}^{K} w_k N(O_{t;}, \mu_{jk}, \Sigma_{jk}), \quad (29)$$

where, w_{jk}, μ_{jk} and Σ_{jk} are the mixture weight, mean vector and covariance matrix, respectively, for the kth Gaussian component of the jth state, and $N (O, \mu, \Sigma)$ denotes a multidimensional Gaussian probability density function (pdf) with mean vector and covariance matrix Σ. In order to ensure a valid pdf, we require that $w_k \geq 0 \ \forall \, k$ and $\sum_{k=1}^{K} = 1$.

Let π_i denote the initial state distribution $\pi = \{\pi_i\}$, where

$$\pi_i = P[q_1 = S_i], \ 1 \leq i \leq N \quad (30)$$

An HMM is a left to right model, if the state transition coefficients have the property:

$$a_{ij} = 0, j < i \quad (31)$$

In other words, the state sequence associated with the model has the property that as time increases the state index increases or stays the same. In the ergodic model all the states are reachable from a given state after a finite number of transitions. See Figure 12-7.

Let $\lambda = (A, B, \pi)$ denote the current parameter set specifying a HMM. Suppose we wish to evaluate the likelihood $P(O|\lambda)$ of a sequence of observations

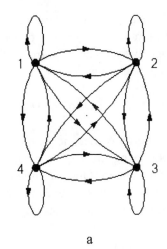

a

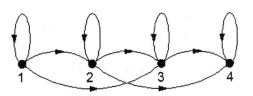

b

Figure 12–7. (a) A four-state ergodic model. **(b)** A four-state left-to-right model. *Note.* From "A Tutorial on Hidden Markov Models and Selected Applications in Speech Recognition," by L. R. Rabiner, 1989, *Proceedings of the IEEE*, 77(2), p. 266. Copyright 1989 IEEE.

$$O = O_1 O_2 \ldots O_T, \quad (32)$$

based on λ. A naïve solution to this problem would be to enumerate every possible state sequence of length T, then to sum up the observation likelihoods conditioned on all such sequences. But this would be computationally prohibitive for sequences of even modest length, in that it would require approximately

$2T \times N^T$ floating point operations. A better solution is the forward procedure, explained below. The forward probability $\alpha_t(i)$ is defined as

$$\alpha_t(i) = P(O_1 \, O_2 \ldots O_t, q_t = S_i | \lambda). \qquad (33)$$

In other words, $\alpha_t(i)$ is the joint probability of observing the sequence $O_1 \, O_2 \ldots O_t$ and finishing in state S_i at time t, given the parameter set λ. We can solve for $\alpha_t(i)$ inductively as follows:

1. Initialization:

$$\alpha_1(i) = \pi_i b_i(O_1), \; 1 \leq i \leq N. \qquad (34)$$

2. Induction:

$$\alpha_{t+1}(j) = \sum_{i=1}^{N} \alpha_t(i) \, a_{ij} \, b_j(O_{t+1}),$$
$$1 \leq t \leq T\text{-}1, \; 1 \leq j \leq N. \qquad (35)$$

3. Termination:

$$P(O|\lambda) = \sum_{i=1}^{N} \alpha_T(i). \qquad (36)$$

The induction step is illustrated in Figure 12–8.

Suppose that we wish to find the optimal sequence of states $q_1 q_2 \ldots q_t$ conditioned on the observation sequence $O = O_1 \, O_2 \ldots O_T$ under the current parameter set λ. A polynomial-time solution to this problem is the *Viterbi* algorithm, which we now explain. Let

$$\delta_t(i) = \max_{q_1, q_2 \ldots q_{t-1}} P[q_1 q_2 \ldots q_t =$$
$$S_i, O_1 O_2 \ldots O_t | \lambda] \qquad (37)$$

denote the likelihood of the most probable path which accounts for the first t observations and ends in state S_i. The Viterbi algorithm is based on the recursion

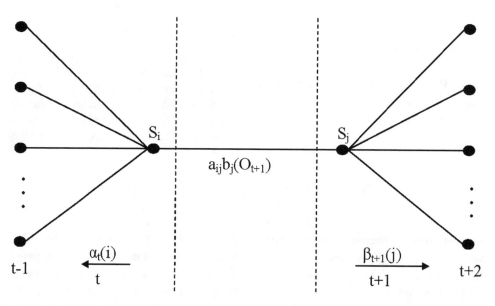

Figure 12–8. State Sj can be reached at time t + 1 from the N possible states, Si, $1 \leq I \leq N$, at time t. From "A Tutorial on Hidden Markov Models and Selected Applications in Speech Recognition," by L. R. Rabiner, 1989, *Proceedings of the IEEE*, 77(2), p. 264. Copyright 1989 IEEE.

$\delta_{t+1}(j) = [\max_i \delta_t(i)a_{ij}] \times b_j(O_{t+1}).$ (38)

Let $\psi_t(j)$ denote the index of the previous state along the most likely path ending in state S_j at time t. The complete Viterbi algorithm can then be stated as:

1. Initialization:

$$\delta_1(i) = \pi_i b_i(O_1), \ 1 \le i \le N \qquad (39)$$

$$\psi_1(i) = 0 \qquad (40)$$

2. Recursion:

$$\delta_t(j) = \max_{1 \le i \le N} [\delta_{t-1}(i)a_{ij}]b_j(O_t),$$
$$2 \le t \le T, \ 1 \le j \le N. \qquad (41)$$

$$\psi_t(j) = \arg\max_{1 \le i \le N} [\delta_{t-1}(i)a_{ij}],$$
$$2 \le t \le T, \ 1 \le j \le N. \qquad (42)$$

3. Termination:

$$p^* = \arg \max_{1 \le i \le N} [\delta_T(i)]$$

$$q_T^* = \arg\max_{1 \le i \le N} [\psi_T(i)]. \qquad (43)$$

4. Path (state sequence) back tracing:

$$q_t^* = \psi_{t+1}(q_{t+1}^*),$$
$$t = T\text{-}1, T\text{-}2, \ldots, 1. \qquad (44)$$

The final issue to be resolved before a HMM can be applied to a pattern classification problem is the optimization of the model parameters (A, B, π) in order to maximize the probability of an observation sequence given the model. As there is no known way to solve the maximum likelihood model analytically, an iterative procedure, such as the Baum-Welch method discussed here, or gradient techniques must be used for optimization.

To describe how to (re)estimate HMM parameters, let us define $\xi_t(i, j)$ as

$$\xi_t(i, j) = P(i_t = S_i, i_{t+1} = S_j | O, \lambda); \qquad (45)$$

i.e., the probability of a path being in state S_i at time t and making a transition to state S_j at time $t + 1$, given the observation sequence and the model; $\xi_t(i, j)$ can be rewritten as

$$\xi_t(i, j) = \frac{\alpha_t(i)a_{ij}b_j(O_{t+1})\beta_{t+1}(j)}{P(O|\lambda)}, \qquad (46)$$

where $\alpha_t(i)$ accounts for the first t observations ending in state S_i at time t; the term a_{ij} accounts for the transition to state S_j at time $t + 1$, the term $b_j(O_{t+1})$ is the likelihood of the observation O_{t+1} conditioned on state S_j; and the term) $\beta_{t+1}(j)$ accounts for the reminder of the observation sequence, such that,

$$\beta_{t+1}(j) = \sum_i \beta_{t+2}(i) p_{i|j} b_i(O_{t+2}).$$

The normalization factor $P(O|\lambda)$ in the denominator of (46) ensures that the sum of $\xi_t(i, j)$ over all i and j is unity.

Let $\gamma_t(i)$ be the probability of being in state q_i at time t, given the observation sequence and the model, which can be calculated according to

$$\gamma_t(i) = \sum_{j=1}^{N} \xi_t(i, j). \qquad (47)$$

Summing $\gamma_t(i)$ over the time index t, we get a quantity that can be interpreted as the expected (over time) number of times that state S_i is visited, or equivalently, the expected number of transitions made from state S_i, if we exclude the last moment, T, in the summation. Similarly, summation of $\xi_t(i, j)$ over t

from $t = 1$ to $t = T$ can be regarded as the expected number of transitions from state S_i to state S_j.

Using the above formulae, one can use the Baum-Welch method to re-estimate values of the HMM parameters. The re-estimation formulae for π, A, and B are:

1. $\bar{\pi}_i = \gamma_1(i)$ $1 \leq i \leq N$;

2. $\bar{a}_{ij} = \sum_{t=1}^{T} \xi_t(i,j) / \sum_{t=1}^{T} \gamma_t(i)$;

3. $\bar{\mu}_{jk} = \sum_{t=1} \gamma_t(j) \dfrac{O_t w_{jk} N(O_t; \mu_{jk}, \Sigma_{jk})}{\sum_{l=1}^{K} w_{jl} N(O_t; \mu_{jl}, \Sigma_{jl})}$,

$$\bar{\Sigma}_{jk} = \sum_t \gamma_t(j) \dfrac{O_t O_t^T w_{jk} N(O_t; \mu_{jk}, \Sigma_{jk})}{\sum_{l=1}^{K} w_{jl} N(O_t; \mu_{jl}, \Sigma_{jl})}$$
$$- \bar{\mu}_{jk} \bar{\mu}_{jk}^T$$

$$\bar{w}_{jk} = \sum_t \gamma_t(j) \dfrac{w_{jk} N(O_t; \mu_{jk}, \Sigma_{jk})}{\sum_{l=1}^{K} w_{jl} N(O_t; \mu_{jl}, \Sigma_{jl})}$$

The re-estimation formula for π_i is the probability of being in the state S_i at $t = 1$. The re-estimation formula for a_{ij} is the ratio of the expected number of transitions from state S_i S_j divided by the expected number of transitions out of the state S_i. If we define the initial model as λ and the re-estimation model as $\bar{\lambda}$, consisting of the above $\bar{\pi}_i$, $\bar{a}_{ij}$, $\bar{\mu}_{jk}$, $\bar{\Sigma}_{jk}$, and $\bar{w}_{jk}$ then it can be proven that either:

1. The initial model defines a critical point of the likelihood function, in which case $\bar{\lambda} = \lambda$; or
2. Model $\bar{\lambda}$ is more likely in the sense that $P(O|\bar{\lambda}) > P(O|\lambda)$.

Therefore if $\bar{\lambda}$ is iteratively used in place of λ, then the probability of O being observed from the model will be improved until some limiting point is reached. The result is the estimated model.

Semicontinuous models are HHMs, where the score of a frame being at a certain state is given by a probability distribution function (pdf) that takes the form of a Gaussian mixture, i.e., a weighted sum of Gaussian contributors. In the case of continuous models, each state has its own Gaussians. In the case of semicontinuous models all the states share all the Gaussians that form a codebook that quantifies the feature space.

Nogueiras, Moreno, Bonafonte, & Marino (2001) investigated the classification of emotions in speech with a HMM. They tested different HMM configurations and found that increasing the number of states from one to 64 monotonically improved the recognition accuracy. The best reported recognition accuracy was 82.5%, which was obtained using HMMs with 64 states and all 11 features based on energy and pitch. The features used for these investigations were derived entirely from energy and pitch, their absolute values as well as their first and second derivatives, they found that using all 11 features based on energy and pitch yielded the best classification accuracy. The SER experiments were conducted on a corpus of speech in French, English, Slovenian, and Spanish that had been recorded by two professional actors, one male and one female, per language. The classification task was to distinguish between the six emotional styles defined in the MPEG-4 standard, namely, anger, disgust, fear, joy, sadness, and surprise, in addition to one neutral style. For these experiments, one semicontinuous HMM was trained for each of the seven emotional styles above. The chosen model implies that low level features used must model the short-time behavior of voice. At recognition time, the likelihood that the utterance was produced by each of the HMMs was computed, and the emotion with highest score was chosen as the recognition result. Classification could thus be performed with the Viterbi algorithm discussed above. Testing and training sets were chosen to be disjoint. Another interesting aspect of that work was the comparison of automatic and human recognition accuracy. In order to assess human recognition performance for this task, 16 non-professional listeners were asked to assign 56 utterances to one of the seven emotional styles, and were allowed to specify a second choice in cases where they were not confident about their first choice. These experiments revealed that human SER accuracy was approximately 80% when only the first choice was considered, and nearly 90% when both first and second choices were considered. If only the first choice is considered, the performance of the automatic HMM-based system is very comparable to human performance on this task.

Kwon, Chan, Hao, Lee, (2003) compared the performance of a HMM-based SER system with that of a system based on Gaussian kernel support vector machine (GSVM). The feature set used in that study for the HMM-based system consisted of pitch, log energy, formant frequencies, band energies, and mel-frequency cepstral coefficients (MFCCs), which were calculated every 10 ms. In addition to the static features, the feature set also included first and second derivatives of the pitch and the MFCCs. For the GSVM, the feature streams were converted to a single fixed length vector per utterance by computing a set of global statistics over the entire utterance.

The experimental results reported in Kwon, Chan, Hao, & Lee, (2003) were obtained on a data set recorded in German with the Sony entertainment robot. The utterances in this corpus consisted of short commands or greetings of several words. In this case, the recognition task was to distinguish between the emotional states angry, bored, happy, neutral, and sad. Kwon, Chan, Hao, & Lee, (2003) found that the HMM-based system achieved a classification accuracy of 40.8%. This was somewhat inferior to the accuracy of 42.8% obtained with the system based on a GSVM.

Tree Grammar Inference and Decision Trees

This section presents one more "combined" classifier, specially tailored for SER. The combination is more complex than an ensemble; the structure of the syntactic classifier is used within the statistical classifier (the basic difference between the two approaches is explained in Figure 12–9). It seems that such combinations are quite heuristic in nature, and every classification problem would have a specifically tailored combination method. The philosophy of the method was presented in Sempere and Lopez (2003) for the task of optical character recognition, and then adapted for SER (Sidorova, 2005).

Step 1: Convert sentences to tree structures

Utterances are converted into tree structures with the same skeleton representing

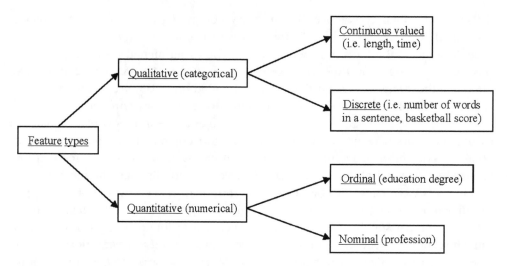

Figure 12–9. Feature types. Syntactic pattern recognition deals with qualitative features exclusively and is opposed to statistical pattern recognition.

the structure of the utterance from the linguistic point of view, the *skeleton* of which is defined by the grammar (Figure 12–10):

Acoustics_of_the_utterance → Prosody Segmental_information;

Prosody → Pitch Intensity Temporal_information;

Segmental_information → Energy Formants;

Pitch → Mean_F0 Median_F0 max_F0 min_F0 F0_range F0_variance average_F0_rise Min_F0_rise max_F0_rise Average_F0_fall Min_F0_fall Max_F0_fall Average_steepness_of_F0_rise average_steepness_of_F0_fall;

Intensity → Mean_RMS_intensity Median_RMS_intensity Max_RMS_intensity Min_RMS_intensity Intensity_range Intensity_variance;

Temporal_information → Average_duration_of_vowels Average_duration_of_consonants Speech_rate Silence-to-speech_ratio;

Energy → Proportion_of_energy_below_500_Hz Proportion_of_energy_below_100_Hz;

Formants → Mean_of_F1 Mean_of_F2 Mean_of_F3 Mean_of_F4 Mean_of_F1_bandwidth Mean_of_F2_bandwidth Mean_of_F3_bandwidth Mean_of_F4_bandwidth.

Leaves are numerical values of low level speech parameters (of variables that do not occur on the left side of the productions above) extracted from every utterance. Eight sets of trees were ob-

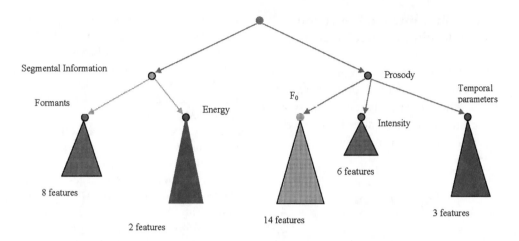

Figure 12–10. Skeleton of the tree expression.

tained: in each set trees are of emotional utterances of one type—anger, irony, surprise, fear, annoyance, joy, shame, and neutral utterances.

España (2002) was applied. The result of this step was eight different automata, each for one of the eight emotions to be recognized.

Step 2: Tree grammar inference to learn eight automata accepting a different type of emotional utterances each

Grammar inference is a method to learn grammar from examples (Sakakibara, 1997). In our case it is tree grammar inference, because we deal with trees representing utterances. More precisely, grammar inference learns the possible intervals for low level parameters of a given type of emotional utterances. The general idea is that at first the grammar is empty, then with each example it augments itself to be able to accept the example being processed or it stays the same, if the example can already be accepted. Several algorithms have been proposed to infer tree languages from examples; here the one proposed in Lopez and

Step 3: Calculate edit distances between obtained tree automata and trees in the training set, put the result into matrix

Edit distances are then calculated between every tree automaton obtained at step two and at every tree representing utterances from the training set. The notion of edit distance for tree languages is a measure of how different the trees really are: first the mapping of one tree to another needs to be done, and then the minimum number of substitution, deletion, and insertion operations is taken into account to make the tree structures isomorphic. Different weights can be assigned to different types of operation if needed. The calculated edit distances are put into a matrix of size 162 (cardinality of the training set) by 8 (cardinality of tree automata learned).

Step 4: Running C4.5 over the matrix to obtain a decision tree

C4.5 (Quinlan, 1993) is run on this matrix in order to obtain a decision tree, classifying each utterance as eight emotion types, according to edit distances between this utterance and eight tree automata.

Conclusions

SER is a dynamically evolving research field. In this paper we presented a general overview of the task with the emphasis put on classifier models. A rather detailed explanation of the three most popular (and taxonomically different) classifiers was presented and the discussion was followed by a new experimental classifier method of a combined nature referred to as Tree Inference and Decision Tree. We also summarized recent publications in which one or more of these classifiers were applied to the SER task.

Acknowledgments. The authors are very grateful to Dr. Artem Kozmin, Prof. Ludmila Kuncheva, Prof. Albino Nogueiras, and Prof. Enric Monte for some of their valuable suggestions and explanations.

References

Abe, S., & Inoue, T. (2002). Fuzzy support vector machines for multiclass problems. In *Proceedings of the European Symposium on Artificial Neural Networks* (pp. 113–118). Berlin, Germany: Springer-Verlag.

Aina, O. O., Hartmann, K., & Strothotte, T. (2003). Extracting emotion from speech: Towards emotional speech-driven facial animations. In A. Butz, A. Krüger, & P. Olivier (Eds.), *Smart graphics 2003* (pp. 162–171). Berlin, Germany: Springer-Verlag.

Augmented Multiparty Interaction, Integrated Project. (2004). [AMI] D 4.1. Report on Implementation of Audio, Video, and Multimodal Algorithms.

Bezdek, J. C., & Kuncheva, L. (2000). Some notes on twenty one (20) nearest prototypes classifiers. In C. Baukhage, S. Kronenberg, F. Kummert, & G. Sagerer (Eds.), *Proceedings of the Joint IAPR International Workshops on Advances in Pattern Recognition: Vol. 1876: Lecture notes in computer science* (pp. 1–16). London: Springer-Verlag.

Dellaert, F., Polzin, T., & Waibel, A. (1996). Recognizing emotions in speech. *Proceedings of the Fourth International Conference on Spoken Language Processing.* Philadelphia.

Deller L., Proakis, J. G., & Hansen, J. H. L (1993). *Discrete-time processing of speech signals.* Macmillan.

De Silva, L. C., & Chi Ng, P. (2000). Bimodal emotion recognition. *Proceedings of the IEEE International Conference on Automatic Face and Gesture Recognition* (p. 332). Grenoble, France.

Devillers, L., Vidrascu, L., & Lamel, L. (2005). Annotation and detection of blended emotions in real human-human dialogs recorded in a call centre. *Proceedings of IEEE ICME.* July. Amsterdam, Netherlands.

Duda, R. O., Hart, P. E., & Stork, D. G. (2001), *Pattern Classification* (2nd ed.). Wiley.

Hozjan, V., &, Kaãiã, Z. (2003). Context-independent multilingual emotion recognition from speech signals. *International Journal of Speech Technology, 6,* 311–320.

Hozjan, V., & Kacic, Z. (2003). Improved emotion recognition with large set of statistical features. *Proceedings of Eurospeech* (pp. 133–136).

Karpouzis, K., & Kollias, S. (2005, July). Multimodal emotion recognition and expressivity analysis. *Proceedings of the IEEE International Conference on Multimedia and Expo* (pp. 779–783). Amsterdam, Netherlands.

Kim, J., Andre, E., Rehm, M., Vogt, T., & Wagner, J. (2005). Integrating information from speech and physiological signals to achieve emotional sensitivity. In *Proceedings of the 9th European Conference on Speech Communication and Technology, 2005* (pp. 354–363).

Kuncheva, L. I. (2004). *Combining pattern classifiers: Methods and algorithms.* Wiley-Interscience.

Kwon, O.-W., Chan, K., Hao, J., & Lee, T.-W. (2003). Emotion recognition by speech signal. *Proceedings of Eurospeech 2003* (pp.125–128). Geneva, Switzerland

Li, Y., & Zhao, Y. (1998). Recognizing emotions in speech using short-term and long-term features. In *Proceedings of the International Conference on Speech and Language Processing* (pp. 2255–2258). Sydney Australia.

Lopez, D., Espana, S. (2002) Error correcting tree-language inference. *Pattern Recognition Letters 23*, 1–12.

McGilloway, S., Cowie, R., Douglas-Cowie, E., Gielen, S., Westerdijk, M., Stroeve, S. (2000). Approaching automatic recognition of emotion from voice: A rough benchmark. In *Proceedings of the ISCA Workshop on Speech and Emotion* (pp. 207-212). Northern Ireland, Belfast.

Montero, J. M., Gutierrez-Arriola, J., Cordoba, R., Enriquez, E., & Pardo, J. M. (1998). Spanish emotional speech: Towards concatenative synthesis. In E. Keller, G. Bailly, A. Monaghan, J. Terken, & M. Huckvale (Eds.), *Improvements in Speech Synthesis. Cost 258: The Naturalness of Synthetic Speech* (pp. 246–251). Chichester, UK: John Wiley & Sons.

Moriyama, T., & Ozawa, O. (1999, October). Emotion recognition and synthesis system on speech. In *Proceedings of the IEEE Int. Conf. Multimedia Computing and Systems* (Vol. 1, pp. 840–844). Florence, Italy.

Müller, R., Schuller, B., Rigoll, G. (2004, September). Enhanced robustness in speech emotion recognition combining acoustic and semantic analyses from signals to signs of emotion and vice versa. *Proceedings of the EU-IST FP6 Network of Excellence HUMAINE Workshop*, Santorini, Greece.

Noam, A., Kerret, O. & Karlinski, D. (2001). Classifying emotions in speech: A comparison of methods. In *Proceedings of Eurospeech 2001* (pp. 127–130). Scandinavia.

Nogueiras, A., Moreno, A., Bonafonte, A., & Marino, B. (2001). Speech emotion recognition using Hidden Markov models. In *Proceedings of Eurospeech 2001* (pp. 2679–2682). Scandinavia.

Oudeyer, P.-Y. (2002, April). Novel useful features and algorithms for the recognition of emotions in human speech. In *Proceedings of the 1st Int. Conf. on Speech Prosody.* Aix-en-Provence, France.

Petrushin, V. A. (2000). Emotion recognition in speech signal: Experimental study, development, and application. *Proceedings of the 6th International Conference on Spoken Language Processing* (Vol.2, pp. 222–225).

Quinlan, J.R. (1993) *C4.5: Programms for Machine Learning.* San Mateo, CA: Morgan Kaufman.

Riedmiller, M., & Braun, H. (1993). A direct adaptive method for faster Backpropagation learning: The RPROP algorithm. In *Proceedings of the IEEE International Conference on Neural Networks 1993* (pp. 586–591).

Rosenblatt, F. (1957). The perceptron: A probabilistic model for information storage and organization in the brain. *Psychological Review, 65*(6), (pp. 386-408).

Sakakibara, Y. (1997) Recent advances of grammatical inference. *Theoretical Computer Science 185* (pp. 15–45). Elsevier.

Scherer, K. (2000). A cross-cultural investigation of emotion inferences from voice and speech: Implications for speech technology. In *Proceedings of the Sixth International Conference on Spoken Language Processing* (Vol. 2, pp. 379–382).

Schuller, B., Rigoll, G., & Lang, M. (2003). Hidden Markov Model-based speech emotion recognition. In *Proceedings of ICME 2003, 4th International Conference on Multimedia and Expo, IEEE: Speech Coding, Analysis and Synthesis* (Vol. I, pp. 401–404).

Sempere, J. M., & Lopez, D. (2003). Learning decision trees and tree automata for a syntactic pattern recognition task. In *Proceedings of the 1st Iberian Conference on Pattern Recognition and Image Analysis* (pp. 943–950). Puerto de Andratx, Mallorca, Spain.

Sidorova, J. A. (2005, September). *Building an agent, sensible to speech emotion of the user.* Paper presented at the 5th Conference on Language Engineering, Cairo, Egypt.

Song, M., Bu, J., Chen, C., & Li, N. (2004). Audio-visual based emotion recognition—A new approach. In *Proceedings of the 2004 IEEE Computer Society Conference on Computer Vision and Pattern Recognition* (Vol. 2, pp. II-1020–II-1025).

Toivanen, J., Seppänen, T., & Väyrynen, E. (2004). Automatic recognition of emotion in spoken Finnish: A preliminary study. *Language and Speech, 47*(4), 383–412.

Tosa, N., & Nakatsu, R. (1996). Life-like communication agent. *Proceedings of the IEEE International Conference on Multimedia Computing and Systems* (pp. 12–19).

Vogt, T., & André, E. (2005). Comparing feature sets for acted and spontaneous speech in view of automatic emotion recognition. *Proceedings of the IEEE International Conference on Multimedia and Expo,* (pp. 474-477).

Wettschereck, D., Aha, D. W., & Mohri, T. A. (1995). Review and empirical evaluation of feature weighting methods for a class of lazy learning algorithms. In *Proceedings of the 1st International Conference on Case-Based Reasoning* (pp. 273–314). Springer, Netherlands.

Williams, C. E., & Stevens, K. N. (1972). Emotions and speech: Some acoustical correlates. *Journal of the Acoustical Society of America, 52,* 1238–1250.

Wilson, D. L. (1972). Asymptotic properties of nearest neighbor rules using edited data. *IEEE Transactions on Systems, Man, and Cybernetics, 2,* 408–421.

Witten I., Frank E. (2005) *Data Mining: Practical machine learning tools and techniques* (2nd ed.). San Francisco: Morgan Kaufmann.

CHAPTER 13

The Context of Voice and Emotion: A Voice-Over Artist's Perspective

Kathleen Antonia Tarr

Abstract

This chapter reflects the perspective of an actor on the creation and understanding of believable vocalized emotions.

Introduction

Radio ads and commentary. Audio books. Phone calls and voice mail. There are very few other venues that are home to voice and emotion without visual context. However, whether the audience sees the speaker or other visual cue, the body is key to emotional expression. As a voice-over artist, I cannot act the part vocally if physically I am disconnected from the emotion. If I am disconnected, the audience will be disconnected, too. If I am on stage, any personal disconnection from the emotion I intend to portray also disconnects the audience. The same is true of film, and the same is true whether one can see me or only hear my voice.

The Sense, the Context, and the Know-How

In addition to my emotional intention, the effort to produce emotions in voice requires a physical *context*. It is not enough to be a snapshot: lips upturned, a furrowed brow, a feeling of disgust. Context requires incorporation of the moments before and after, the bookends. Context in written form is how one knows the difference between *tear*—to rip—and *tear*—to cry. In visual form, an onlooker can look at a smile and try to decipher the supporting emotion of the smiler, but can fail to detect whether this person is truly happy—or perhaps instead complicit—if she doesn't know the situation that inspired the moment. Hence, one crucial key to understanding emotion in voice is understanding the context.

Take, for example, the quick image of me in a Sunsweet prunes (rather, "dried plums") commercial (still airing as of this printing: Editor). I look down at a dried plum held between my fingers and say, "*Wow*." That's it.

After this commercial aired during the 2006 *Golden Globe Awards*, I received several phone calls asking about the ad, always with the tag, "You sure were enjoying that prune!"

Was I? The context suggests so. Images of others bookended mine, all with more dialog, all truly enjoying Sunsweet dried plums. Although I am not shown biting into the prune, there seems to be something in my mouth, and with prune in hand, the "wow" is correctly interpreted as referring to that item. My nose isn't scrunched up, my eyes and brow are raised, and I am looking at the prune. Context. I could have meant, "*Wow*! This is the most distasteful thing I've eaten all day!" but in addition to the context of my own expression and others' in the commercial, audiences prejudge correctly that a company is not going to include the image of someone who hates its product in a promotional ad and thus correctly conclude that I like the taste. It is interesting that of those who watched the *Golden Globes*—wherein there was an overflow of enjoyment and "Wow!"—many made the observation, "You sure were enjoying that prune!" During previous airings, say, during *The Amazing Race*—a show with, yes, enjoyment, but also quite a bit of "ugh"—I did not receive characterizations of my dried plums performance that stressed the depth of my delight.

Contrast two other wows. A friend of mine who once at dinner accidentally put an entire chili pepper in her mouth, thinking it was a sweet green pepper, kept repeating "Wow" as she brushed her tongue with her napkin and followed up with a gallon of water. My sister—whom I had forewarned about the foulness of fermenting yeast—put Vegemite on toast and took a bite. Her wows were interspersed with chugs of guava juice. In fact, both my friend and my sister were smiling during their ordeals. One snapshot of the action, and they could easily have taken my spot in the Sunsweet dried plums commercial and fooled an audience into thinking they were enjoying their moments. But they weren't. Quite the opposite. Why would the snapshot work?

Well, all three of us were sharing the feeling of "That's incredible." I was actually enjoying the flavor of my item, but my sense at that moment regarded the infusion of orange into the prune. Surprising! Delicious! My friend was also surprised but taken aback by "Pain! Help!" My sister predominated by "Yuck! My God, this is the most disgusting thing I have ever tasted!" And because they both have excellent senses of humor, smiles, raised eyes, and raised brows.

More of Context

Because I know my friend and sister, and because I was there for their entire taste disaster experiences, I knew that the smiles under the wows were not expressing happiness or enjoyment about the flavors consuming their consumption. Someone on the scene with less experience or detail about the players and the stories might not have figured it out as quickly. They might have wondered about why these two women were having so much dramatic fun. As they watched, they might have figured out that the moments actually involved quite a bit of

displeasure, but only in the context of the players, two people who see comedy in almost everything.

It is easy to conclude, then, that understanding the emotion of a particular vocal moment is not only about external context but also about understanding one's own biases, expectations, and interpretive patterns. Biases can be benign or even insightful, as above. But here is also where interpretations of emotions and voice can take sickening turns.

Racism, sexism, homophobia, and other mental delusions all carry with them fallacies of interpretation of emotions and of the voice. The same phrase uttered by a white person may be interpreted by a racist with black bias as a casual statement in the former demographic scenario, but if uttered by an African American, as asserting superiority: "I disagree. I think all people are equal." Someone without racist delusions can hear that statement from someone of another race and not usually be threatened.

Someone with racist delusions most often cannot. It depends upon the context one projects. If it is simply an intellectual discussion, and *both parties have similar understanding*, disagreements are not typically threatening. If one party thinks that disagreement means the other doesn't know her "place" or thinks he is smarter—emotionally that the other feels confident when she should feel subservient or when he should feel deferential—then problems arise.

I used to play tackle football with men who were high school and college team standouts. Notoriously, a couple of them who had never played with or against me taunted me in the days before a game. "You're not even going to show up. Women can't play football. What are you? The cheerleader?" "I'll see you on

Sunday," was my common reply. "I'll see you on Sunday," infuriated many of them. They believed I was saying that they were weak, that they weren't really men, that *they* might as well play the cheerleader. What did I mean? That none of their posturing meant anything to me. Skill would be decided on the field, not by argument. Did I think I was the better player? Hell yes! But did I think they were weak, unmanly, cheerleader types? No. I wasn't thinking of them at all. I had no *feeling* for them at all. But for what they believed I thought and felt, I was threatened on several occasions with violence.

One's own bias and prejudgment are the great interpreters of voice and emotions. They are as, if not more, important than any other measurement. Compare the "problem" with people affected by physical disorders that impact vocal tone or physicality, including facial expression. The difficulties they face with connecting the emotion to the voice are in the *interpretation*, not in the manifestation. (More on this subject is provided in Chapter 8, 16, and 17 in Volume 2 of these series: Editor.)

The speaker has all of the emotions, *speaks* with all of the emotions supporting the speech. The failure in understanding the emotion is in the interpretation of the voice. Someone more familiar with the speaker will do a better job of understanding. It is like any language. Someone without fluency will not as easily get it.

The search for the perfect robotic display of vocal emotion is the search for the language of the masses. Attempts to create authentic computerized voices are not in fact efforts to make the speech more decipherable but instead more comfortable for the listener, somehow more sincere, warmer. If people took a moment, they would realize that the computerized voice pleasantly speaking to them has no feeling for them whatsoever, and in the end, it doesn't really matter whether it is monotonous or "kind." In fact, much of the fury over the delighted voices of multi-prompters seems to be the result of frustration over *not* being acknowledged by the voice on the other end of the phone, a voice that *sounds* warm, more human, less monotone, and computerized.

I'm on the phone having a fit because I'm on my 10th prompt transfer and "someone" is having a lovely day, telling me, "I'm sorry" yet again, and *with an audible smile*! I've been less put out by monotones prompting me to enter my account number over and over again. I can *hear* that they don't care. Hey, I admit it. I'm human, biased and deceived and led places by voices without real feeling like a lamb to the slaughter—which brings me back to my job.

Tricks

There are certain tricks I use to help audiences correctly interpret the emotions I intend to project. When I play restrained anger, I might smile with my mouth, but I am predatory with my eyes, scrunched, pinpointing attack.

When I play restrained derangement, I smile with my mouth, and my eyes remain neutral. The words then flow from these places. Anger, they do not leave the throat easily. Derangement, they flow smoothly. My face might transform a thousand compositions, but because the voice and eyes are specific, the emotion is fairly transparent. In fact, acting any part, voice only or not, I rely primarily upon my throat and eyes. My face follows, but its expressions are only important in as much as they reflect the secondary emotion, i.e., the one my *character* is hoping to project in the scene. What the character is actually feeling, the emotion *I* primarily want understood, is not found there.

There is a scene in *Kill Bill, Vol. 2* in which Uma Thurman's character is going to be buried alive. The camera gives the audience a shot of her face as the grave-digger exclaims, "Look at those eyes. This bitch is furious!" She is still above ground during this scene, not yet confined to her casket six feet under. The shot is only of her eyes, partial forehead, bridge of nose. She doesn't look furious to me. She looks frightened. When her casket is being closed, the camera reveals a cut of the same sequence. The lighting is the same. The point of view the same. She looks frightened. It makes sense. The earlier usage is obviously the same take, nonsensical, above ground, only by virtue of the editor's effort to substitute for an otherwise unavailable shot. Had she spoken and sounded furious in the earlier shot, I might have then thought the character was deranged. When the eyes and voice don't match, insanity. Open the eyes wide in utter surprise and smile. No, I mean it. Go look at yourself in the mirror. Say "Hi there" or something. Next Bride of Chucky, huh?

But here again, it is my projection, my bias that does most of the emotional interpretation. A wide-eyed smile may just mean someone had really bad plastic surgery. I'm fairly astute, so usually I can detect bad surgery, and usually I simply know what someone is feeling, even if the emotion is only found in the voice and eyes. It's why people think I listen well. I hear more than what is being said.

I can *reflect* more than what is said. But like I wrote, it is like any language, and I just happen to be very good at language.

Ability, Bias, and Observations

If one is unable to learn a new language, unable to precisely imitate tones and inflections and body movements, one undoubtedly has limitations in the ability to interpret emotions. If one has no baseline understanding of how an individual or group expresses itself, then the context is askew.

In language, I best learn new words by closely watching how sounds are used. *Watching* how they are used. My bias: someone walks into a room, if she speaks, she is probably going to say "Hello" or some similar greeting. Next, she will probably be asked how she is, and she will answer.

Observation: if she answers the equivalent to "I'm well," her voice will rise, she will smile. If she is not so well, she will support the words with emotional consistency, maybe heavy, slumping shoulders, down turned eyes, and a cringe for "awful." One can interpret more complicated responses accordingly. When I learn language, I come to understand not only the tone and thus vocabulary and grammar but also the presentation. More importantly, to *mimic* the presentation. The context. I very rarely do a word-for-word translation, even in my native American English, and likely few of us did when we were first learning to speak. It is the sound of the whole thought or phrase and the trumpeter's performance that teaches the voice associated with the feeling, and *that* becomes the music to play.

Job

What am I, a poet? Back to my job as a voice-over artist. I passed over it fairly quickly, but did you know that you can hear a smile? "Smile" is a frequent instruction in the recording studio, particularly for commercials, jingles, or spoken word. Is it actually the case that the smile itself changes the voice? Very little. It is the emotion behind smile that does most of the work. It is what causes you to smile that changes the tone of voice. I can smile and sound like I am about to enter a boxing ring. But if I think of something that makes me happy ("be happy" probably being the more precise direction than "smile"), I can then sing or talk and sell to an unsuspecting audience the notion that the product I'm singing or talking about is making me happy.

I must say that the best voice-over audition I ever had, one for which I did *not* book the job, was for one of George Lucas's animated projects. I auditioned for the role of an intelligent, older, woman whose temper was frightening and mystical. Let's suppose the dialog was:

> That's fine, but if you ever again persist in disregarding my direct order, I shall see to it that you fall into the deepest trenches of Hell and burn for an eternity without one hope of escape that is not suffocated by the stench of your damnation.

Wow. That's pretty wicked. I'm sure George Lucas wrote a kinder, gentler, script . . . but let's get on with it.

A good performance has contrasts, conflict, and intrigue. "That's fine." Spoken with a gentle, flowing vocal projection, intended to give the audience a (false) sense of safety, ease, and relaxation. Eyes soft. "But if you ever again persist" begins with a steadily widening eye squint and a steady increase in vocal volume and tempo—interlaced with normal spoken variants—that peaks at *stench* and rumbles to a stop at *damnation*.

For age effect, the baseline voice grumbled deeply in my throat. The result is a line that reads as a growl with small barks interlaced, building until one major threatening bark that then falls to a growl to conclude the thought. Maintaining some restraint in vocal projection, even at the peak, builds the threat by making the speaker seem on the verge of full out attack at any moment. This means for the audience that as scary as the character may sound, the situation can get scarier. Deepening the tone without altering the pitch builds the threat similarly. The audience begins relieved, then becomes tense, then ends assured that the immediate threat has passed but remains on edge that danger still lingers. Mission accomplished! . . . except for the booking, but honestly, just because a performer doesn't book a job, it doesn't mean the audition wasn't stupendous. Isn't that right, George?

Even without hearing my voice, you have an imagining about what I would sound like asking, "Isn't that right, George?," what I would look like while I speak. Perhaps you envision me laughing or smiling, at least in the eyes. You have given me a voice without hearing me or seeing me, and the emotion you attribute is the real measure. Perhaps even more interesting is the emotion with which you respond to the projection.

It's the feeling that counts.

Author's Publications

Tarr,K. T. (2002) Preaching to the convicted. In R. Solomon (Ed.), *That Takes Ovaries!* (pp. 22–24). New York, NY: Three Rivers Press.

CHAPTER 14

Tokin Tuf: True Grit in the Voice of Virility

Claude Steinberg

In speech science, as well as in economics, sociology, medicine, and the physical sciences, new theories tend to evolve from difficulties accounting for recalcitrant experimental data. On occasion, however, researchers in these fields will take an inventory of naturally occurring rather than experimentally induced physical and behavioral phenomena and develop new theories to account for them. The latter approach has justifiably been eschewed in the cognitive, emotional, and social psychology of individuals (as opposed to behavioral studies of groups) because, although physical and behavioral phenomena abound for human individuals to react to, there are no human cognitive, social, or emotional reactions lying around for researchers to gather, classify, and theorize about.

Of necessity, these artifacts of subjective human experience must be gathered through research, if not in laboratory settings then through informal interviews, and are rarely presented to other researchers in the form in which they were collected. When subjective responses are involved, even raw data presented in appendices of published papers will have been selectively edited and formatted by the researcher. Aspects of a human response not relevant to the research topic may never appear in print and may remain forever inaccessible to other researchers. As a result, psychological phenomena not significant for a particular current theory may never be discovered.

In my experience, this problem is only compounded in industrial applications such as market research and human factors research, where data on individual respondents may be subject to privacy restrictions, and where even aggregate data on subjective response may be subject to corporate nondisclosure agreements. When companies cannot see the results of studies their competitors have commissioned, they are often forced to repeat a research program from scratch, requesting replications of established findings. The expense involved, which includes incentive payments to human subjects who must represent a target demographic, not necessarily undergraduate students, often means that not enough subjects can be recruited to obtain statistical significance. In these situations, an organization may find it more cost effective to commission an expert review from a researcher who is experienced in eliciting human responses in a particular domain.

Rather than testing the product on other people, the expert will audition the product herself and attempt to think and behave in a manner characteristic of users she has studied reacting to similar products. The expert cannot guarantee that the majority of consumers will respond as she has; all she can do is provide an informed critique from a consumer's perspective that will help the organization refine its product. In attempting to understand emotional response to the voice, similar pragmatic considerations make this the approach taken here. In this paper, I intend to prove nothing, nor provide what I would consider scientifically legitimate support for anything. In gathering, reviewing, and presenting my emotional experiences of speech patterns as a representative listener, I cannot know whether I speak for the norm or the outlier in a population of responsive listeners. All I can do is present subjective responses that may have been overlooked in other studies, and develop a theory to account for heretofore unexplained emotional response to auditory phenomena.

Research in speech perception often involves the listener hearing diverse experimentally manipulated context-independent stimuli and selecting from among several response options for each stimulus. As the goal here is to obtain open-ended or free emotional response

during the experience of listening to a naturally occurring speech artifact, namely radio plays, the method employed is instead to have the listener meta-cognize about his experience of listening, an approach once again more characteristic of user experience testing in applied human factors research than of academic experimental psychology. Furthermore, as the analysis is not of the human voice per se but of emotional response to it, the method is not acoustic analysis but auditory analysis, though spectrographic analysis is occasionally used to verify or illustrate perceptions. That these two methods of analysis do not always correspond I discovered accidentally while pursuing my thesis research on an entirely unrelated topic. It turns out listeners often do not hear F0 drops resulting from glottalization as constituting either a categorical drop to low tone or a gradient pitch variation; instead, they hear the previous pitch level as continuing into the glottalized portion of the waveform despite clear evidence to the contrary from pitch tracking software. That is, they hear timbral differentiation, but no variation in pitch. Apparently, the ear compensates for the glottalization and produces the auditory illusion of a fundamental frequency an octave higher than it actually is. While it can be observed that the period of the original waveform is an exact multiple of the period of the glottalized waveform, researchers wedded to an acoustic approach would never know to magnify the waveform to check for this and would simply assume the speaker's voice has been heard to have dropped. Similar auditory-acoustic mismatches have been identified in studies of musical information processing, for instance, in similarity judgment tasks in which tones farther apart from each other in frequency are heard as more similar to each other than tones closer together in frequency despite evidence for a natural correspondence between acoustic frequency and wavelength perceptors along the basilar membrane (Krumhansl & Shepard, 1979, as cited in Hubbard & Stoeckig, 1992, p. 202), as well as in dichotic listening tasks in which scale tones randomly assigned to each ear are mentally reassigned by the listener so that an ascending scale is heard in one ear and a descending scale in the other (Deutsch, 1975, as cited in Deutsch & Pierce, 1992, p. 257). Acoustics is not psychology, and spectrographic analysis should never be interpreted as a visual representation of auditory perception.

Having justified the use of both auditory analysis and naturalistic data, I turn to the question of the naturalness of the data. Sacrificing experimental control for the sake of studying response to purported naturally occurring phenomena may be defended only if there is reason to believe the phenomena are truly more natural than laboratory stimuli. An objection that can be made to treating actors' voices as natural speech is that, much like experimental speech stimuli, these voices may be developed to elicit more specific emotional responses and command more attention than the voices of the majority of the population. However, the actors whose classic voices are examined herein are not simply playing roles but embodying classic character types subsequently imitated on stage and screen. Their voices may have evolved as a synthesis of prior individual variants or as a reaction against contrasting vocal styles, and the 50-year-old characters may have been somewhat more unique when they were first heard, but as popular personalities they came to represent stereotypes of law enforcer and criminal investigator, setting a public standard for naturalness against which real-life sheriffs and detectives could be judged.[1] Furthermore, through their interactions with other characters with less stylized, less recognizable voices, the voices of classic character types can be understood as a type of commentary on or reaction to vocal styles of the public at large. So if the voices are not necessarily representative of how the general public expresses or elicits emotion, they are natural to the extent that they represent cultural archetypes of emotion expression.

Through describing my experiences listening to several episodes of two radio plays featuring manly-sounding heroes, the goal here is to demonstrate that a feeling of trust, perhaps inspiring concomitant emotions of attachment and loyalty, can be elicited in a listener through vocal behaviors that iconically, symbolically, or metaphorically connote fitness for duty through demonstrable action. These vocal behaviors exhibit auditory patterns analogous to aspects of mental or physical labor, including specifically preparation, prioritization, and simplification of complex processes, all skills

---

[1]This is particularly true of the voice of the U.S. marshal in *Gunsmoke*, since the radio play was succeeded by a 20-year run on television, from 1955 through 1975, where, according to Horace Newcomb of the Museum of Broadcast Communications in Chicago, Illinois, it was consistently one of the 20 most popular television programs and the single most popular for several years running. Yet it is also true of Sam Spade, echoes of whose voice can be heard in the detective Stone in the contemporary musical *City of Angels*. It is not unreasonable to suppose that when real-life mobsters adopt the term *godfather* only after seeing the eponymous movie (as indicated on the Web site http://www.moviemistakes.com/film544/trivia), and when "FBI wiretaps have recorded New York gangsters talking about plot lines from the 'Sopranos'" (Fields, 2001, p. 3), life would imitate art to the extent that real people on the other side of the law would model themselves on fictional characters.

one would expect from an accomplished tradesperson or professional. The vocal behaviors connote competence but not necessarily impeccable craftsmanship, which I will suggest listeners may associate with craftiness and duplicity if not downright diabolical intent, for example, the sort of craftsmanship that might characterize a plan to launch two September 11 attacks on the World Trade Center almost exactly at 9:11 AM. It is vocal connotations of reliability, of knowledge and experience, I will suggest, that distinguish classic American radio heroes, not vocal connotations of friendliness (which may actually be more characteristic of villains), and it is these same vocal indicators of worldly competence, not vocal analogs of bravery or strength, I will argue, that identify these characters as manly men (connotations of naïve honesty being associated more with boyishness).

Although the "fitness for duty" portion of the theory may seem commonsensical, predicting just the trusting emotional response one might expect in a listener hearing well-crafted, workmanlike speech, it offers an explanatory psychological framework for previous findings associating physical qualities of the voice with attributions of personality characteristics to speakers. For instance, it may be fitness for a given task—more than fastness or absolute physical fitness—that people trust. That is, a correlation previously noted between greater fluency (faster speech rate) and greater credibility (Miller, Maruyama, Beaber, & Valone, 1976) may be more contingent than previously imagined.[2] The trustworthy sounding speakers I present herein, one in particular, sometimes talk fast, but not consistently fast. By assigning equal duration to a series of unstressed syllables as to a single stressed syllable, they assign a measured consideration to their words that enhances their credibility more than one might expect from the more consistently fast speech of an inconsiderate fast-talking salesman, insensitive to his audience and his own words.

Besides helping to explain response to physical qualities of the voice in terms of interpersonal psychology, the theory also suggests certain aversive emotional responses to message delivery that were previously viewed as being entirely the result of limitations on cognitive processing may actually result from social attributions. For instance, because the trust response described herein is shown not to be elicited through vocal behaviors connoting self-promotion, virtuosity, or ease and comfort with complexity, the theory is consistent with past research by Smith and Shaffer (2000) and Frey and Eagly (1993) somewhat incongruously suggesting that intense, vivid language may undermine persuasiveness if vivid descriptions are gratuitous. Yet whereas these researchers conclude that displays of irrelevant virtuosity merely distract the listener from the message, thereby interfering with information processing, I claim that because such displays appear motivated by the desire to impress rather than the imperative of attending carefully to one's work, vocal virtuosity, like linguistic virtuosity, may actually arouse suspicion and encourage distrust.

In addition to offering an explanatory social psychological framework to better account for previously identified relations both between speech rate and credibility

---

[2]This is indeed implied in a study by Woodall and Burgoon (1984), cited in Pittam (1994, p. 107), which contrary to Miller et al. (1976), obtained lower ratings for trustworthiness and honesty in response to fast speech.

and between virtuosity and failure to persuade, the examples I will present provide more detail about emotion-eliciting vocal behaviors than typically appear in articles describing social psychological experimental studies on the voice, articles which arguably appear rhetorically constructed to encourage overgeneralization about rather subtle vocal qualities. For example, the theory developed herein is quite consistent with the findings of a study by Pearce and Brommel (1972) demonstrating that a speaker using a conversational style of delivery was perceived as more trustworthy than—while just as competent as—the same speaker using a dynamic style (presented to a different set of listeners). Yet as is typical of social psychological research on speech styles, Pearce and Brommel provide only vague and incomplete accounts of the acoustic and perceptual features that distinguish the two styles. The dynamic style is said to be "more orotund" and contain more dramatic "pauses" and "loudness for emphasis," but this is the extent of the assistance the researchers provide to anyone attempting to replicate the more and less trustworthy styles they have identified. The researchers characterize the styles as whatever the expert speaker who recorded the samples did with his voice that could have caused an additional set of human subjects hearing the samples in pre-experimental manipulation check to rate them as either "dynamic" or "conversational," without specifying what distinguishes them either acoustically, in articulatory terms, or in terms of epiphenomenal auditory events consistently evoked for listeners in certain acoustic contexts. Because the authors don't really define the qualities of the speech they study, a credulous reader might

infer from Pearce and Brommel (1972) that all exaggerated-sounding speech is necessarily as uncredible sounding as incredible sounding. On the contrary, through analysis of the actual auditory characteristics of tough talking classic radio play personalities, I will suggest that a stylized, paradoxically exaggerated simplicity in their voices can, at least in the appropriate social contexts examined, produce an emotional response of devotion to and reliance on the speaker, a response presumably more emotionally intense than the cognitive attribution of credibility in response to unexaggerated conversational speech which Pearce and Brommel identified.

Howdy Stranger

Some visitors to the United States claim that honest, good-hearted Americans are more superficially courteous to strangers (at least those they meet on public property) than are people of certain other nationalities, but this generalization fails to characterize a number of situations. Scotton and Bernsten (1988) suggest that the amiable formulaic English conversation patterns taught to nonnative English speakers in American ESOL classes are poor preparation for the way friendly strangers actually speak to each other. According to Scotton and Bernsten, the more common sort of response to a foreigner's request like, "Can you tell me how to get to the animals in the park?" is unlikely to involve conventions for polite social interaction, as in "Sure, I'd be happy to; to get to the zoo, you turn left, then make a right . . . " or "I'm very sorry, I don't know." The responder is far more likely to be concerned about providing an accurate response, as in "Tsk, tsk . . . that's a tough one; you're going the wrong way!" or "Aw jeez . . . do you know where the fountain is?" or even "Did you say 'enemies' or 'enemas'?" If foreign speakers are to become comfortable with genuine American speech patterns, it appears they must learn to expect uncouth expressions of concern, not necessarily expressions of courtesy.

To win friends and influence people at a cocktail party, it may help to sound charming, but if one is being cross-examined in a courtroom, straightforward testimony would likely be more appreciated by a judge or jury than would sparkling repartee. As clinical pathologists and speech trainers, do we always want to help our clients to sound friendly and competent at the expense of their possibly sounding unnatural and false? Fluent speech may help speakers sound competent, credible, and persuasive, but this may not be an advantage in all situations. On the contrary, Street, Brady, and Putman (1983) found that fast speech is more noticeable, and slow speech less noticeable, in job interviews than in casual conversation, perhaps because in a job interview setting, fast speech is indicative of scripted preparation, nervousness, and evasion, while slow speech, though initially less impressive, is indicative of careful appraisal and attentiveness. By training dysfluent job candidates to become more fluent, we are not necessarily helping them obtain jobs.

Euchred by Hornswogglers

All the effort a speaker invests in polishing his or her speech may be for naught if the effort at improving style is per-ceived as an attempt to mask or distract attention from deficiencies in substance or character. In the context of a talk on the voices of cartoon villains at the Pacific Voice and Speech Foundation 2005 Conference on Voice Quality and Emotions, I presented two examples of the same expression of sympathy, "Aww, that's so sweet," spoken by the same speaker with the same intonation pattern but in one case sincerely and ingenuously, in the other patronizingly and with deceitful malice. The spectrograms of the genuine version (Figure 14–1a) and the snide version (Figure 14–1b) exhibit numerous subtle differences, including the snide version's narrower, stronger, more consistent bands of nasal resonance in the 6000- and 8000-Hz range (connoting haughtiness or condescension), the smaller range but steeper, more parabolic pitch falls in the snide version's fundamental frequency (connoting faster movement to a place of rest), the glottal fry perturbations at the bottom of the snide version's pitch declination (between 60 and 80 Hz, reminiscent of feline purring, connoting the ease and comfort of a vibration so slow that individual periods can be heard as separate from each other), as well as the addition in the snide version of microtonal rises from an already high pitch before the high pitch falls on "Aww" and "sweet" (0.10 second in length and one fifth of the frequency range of the fall itself), connoting underhanded dexterity (the apparent rise and fall from a completely vertical F0 in the genuine version being merely artifacts of transition from a stop or fricative). More generally, the genuine version differs from the snide version mostly in what it does not contain. Looked at as gestalts, the two versions differ in that the snide version exhibits more effortful complexity.

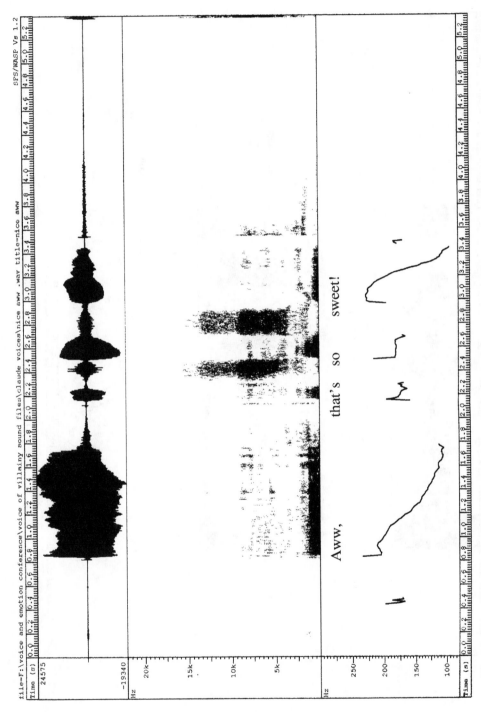

Figure 14–1a. Amplitude waveform, spectra, and F0 contour for genuine expression of sympathy: "Aww, that's so sweet!"

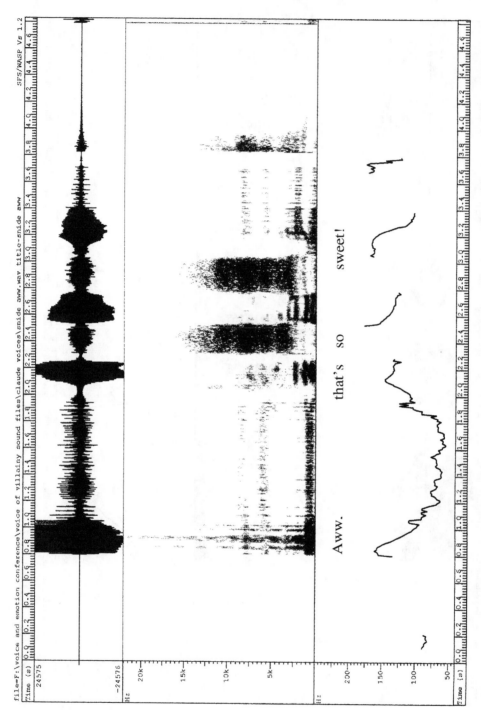

Figure 14–1b. Amplitude waveform, spectra, and F0 contour for "Aww, that's so sweet!" articulated by disdainful individual pretending to be sympathetic.

The pattern of high frequencies in the genuine version may appear to the eye more complex than that of the snide version, but the former is only complex in the sense that more random noise, less channeled energy is being produced. Consciously or unconsciously, the duplicitous speaker is trying harder and doing more with the voice than is the honest speaker with more generous but nearly linear pitch falls, and though the duplicitous speaker may sound friendlier or more superficially attractive as a result, such speech is not necessarily something we should be encouraging honest people aspiring to speak more successfully to imitate.

Politicians like John Kerry and Al Gore have been cursed in many ways, one of which is being thought not to sound like "real Americans." It is ironic that decent orators like these, people who work on their speeches and presumably think of themselves as good speakers, should be perceived as unconvincing. Sounding convincing when speaking in the American heartland is a particular challenge for intelligent, articulate men, because, after all, the conventional wisdom goes, real American men don't say much, and if they say anything, they mumble it. If the speech of archetypal American heroes exhibits qualities beyond these, it would surely behoove accomplished orators to know of them. Just what do they have to do, and how much do they have to simplify to get their points across credibly? Would it help them to tackle the tough issues Howard Dean addressed in the 2004 U.S. presidential campaign, or would it help more to sound like him, apart from his notorious holler? For guidance on this issue, it would seem appropriate to examine the speech of what more astute and successful if less accomplished politicians seem to have identified as an archetypal honest sounding American male, the cowboy.

Mudsill, Tenderfoot, or Ace-High Thoroughbred?

For urban cosmopolitans, the idea of cowboy speech may conjure up notions of Southern drawls, Western twangs, and Howard Dean's notorious hoot, yip, or rebel yell. It may thus come as a bit of a surprise to learn that the cowboy caricature in accomplished mimic Robin Williams' radio rendition of the story of Pecos Bill sports a more Northern and Eastern sounding accent than either the narrator or Pecos Bill himself (who, allegedly raised by coyotes, initially considers himself a coyote, not a cowboy). It appears the Northern accent may connote some degree of respectability in the despicable world of the lawless West.[3] Williams' caricatures of the narrator and Pecos Bill do suggest ignorant "low-life" or "backwoods" characters unconcerned with the finer points of decorum as long as they can be understood. They exhibit neutralization of vowels to schwa, their replacement of "cowbo-ee" with "cowbo-ah" suggesting that for them, the thought of moving the mouth all the way from one vowel extreme to another has connotations of fastidious delicacy. And when they do insert a second vowel sound into a syllable that in standard speech contains but one vowel, it's always a neutral schwa, as in the diphthongized "Bee-uhll" for Bill, "fluh-eez" for "fleas," and "muh-oon" for "moon."

---

[3] Indeed on my first trip to the Northwestern state of Wyoming, though I found myself trying to ingratiate myself with gentlemen sporting cowboy hats by adoping a bit of a Southwest Texas drawl, they responded with no trace of one.

But the cowboy himself doesn't speak this way. Williams' cowboy caricature, far less typified by vowel neutralization and schwa insertion, suggests manliness through articulation farther back in the throat than is presumably natural for Williams, lengthening the resonating chamber and reducing resonance in the nasal cavity, and as we will see with other manly speakers, the amount of time devoted to syllable-final or syllable-initial stop gap silence is greater than in standard speech, creating an impression of tougher than normal articulation.

Though manly and more intelligent sounding than the voices of the narrator and Pecos Bill, the voice of this cowboy is nevertheless not particularly heroic. The most noticeable characteristic of this voice, which seems to parody the speech of actor John Wayne in less responsible roles, is that each syllable nucleus is produced so as to be perceived as of the same duration as every other syllable nucleus, until the last syllable of an intonation phrase, where the final syllable's nucleus is prolonged if the syllable is stressed. Points of sentential stress virtually disappear (or recur on every syllable), as if the cowboy were speaking with French prosody or a slowed down, spoken version of opera recitative, a style more appropriate to Italian than English prosody. This is the voice of the naïve, good-natured though manly cowboy, who works hard to give equal weight to everything he encounters, unaware that certain unworthy elements do not merit his undivided attention. He is the sort who will be cheated by the villain before he learns his lesson and gets his revenge, and he is unlikely to earn any more respect from the public than

would an automated telephone voice based on a rudimentary speech synthesis algorithm that had not learned to prioritize stresses. Curiously, in a 1951 Lux Radio Theater adaptation of John Ford's film "She Wore a Yellow Ribbon" starring John Wayne as a responsible senior military officer, Captain Nathan Brittles, Wayne only resorts to producing perceptually equally timed syllable nuclei throughout an utterance in moments of emotional trauma.

To identify a more appropriate honest sounding model than the cowboy for the accomplished and socially responsible but politically inept aspiring political candidate in America requires examining the speech of an American archetype who is perceived as not simply honest, but also responsible, experienced, and knowledgeable. For American law enforcement officers and criminal investigators, rural and urban alike, the dangers of criminal elements make knowledge and experience a matter of life and death, while the responsibilities of the position make integrity equally paramount. Where the cowboy may sound tough, simple, and honest, but also naïve, the heroic enforcer or investigator sounds much savvier, as savvy as a villain even, while paradoxically managing to sound equally simple and honest. How is this possible? How is this feat accomplished?

Walkin' Quicksand over Hell[4]

At first hearing, Matt Dillon, hero of the classic American radio drama *Gunsmoke*, sounds a slight bit like Williams' caricatures of the narrator and Pecos Bill.

---

[4]This is a cowboy characterization of being in a dangerous situation (Adams, 2000, p. 233). Significantly, the trope characterizes situational awareness rather than feelings experienced.

Officially, he may be a United ("Ee-oo-nah-ee-tud") States marshal, but he introduces himself during the opening of each program as a "Yuh-nah-dud" States marshal. Yet almost immediately we learn that he's not as dumb as he might sound, his vowel neutralization being as consistent with a personality that doesn't see any personal advantage in pretense as with an ignoramus who doesn't know how to tackle the intricacies of diphthongs and articulatory extremes. Immediately Dillon tells us he's the "first man [people out West] look for and theIll-ast they wannammm-eet." This vocal anomaly recurs in his dialog in various episodes of the program, for example, "Yeah, maybe I oughta take alll-otta time off" and "there's always ann-othermmm-an to kill." That is, his word-initial sonorants are anticipated as the previous word is still being completed and held longer than would be typical when articulating the syllable they initiate, while the nucleus and coda of the syllable they initiate are perceptually correspondingly shortened. The prolonged syllable-initial sonorant serves as an admonition, the perceived rush to the following coda consonant as an explosive attack, much like the "grrrrruff" sound a dog makes when first growling and then barking. If it seems odd that anyone who might expect to be perceived as a respectable hero would adopt vocal mannerisms connoting bestial hostility, consider that while Dillon may be rough, like a dog, he's also instinctually wary, alert to, and suspicious of superficially appealing baits. Like a watchdog, this man is to be

trusted as an able protector. He may be tough as an animal, but he also shows foresight in guarding his throat. Relative to other speakers, he shortens the time he leaves his vocal tract open and exposed when producing a vowel, and when he does sustain higher frequency resonances characteristic of open-mouthed vowels, he does so through the more protective constriction of sonorant articulation.[5]

Elsewhere, Dillon anticipates and prolongs not only sonorants but fricatives as well as stop gaps, yielding a harder, less breathy attack (a series of identical stops in the transliterations that follow indicating prolonged constricted silence and absence of predicted aspiration, not repeated consonant articulation): "as fast as theykkk-ome," "and he's wrong about mylll-ikin' takkk-ill men," "I haven'tsss-lept since I rode outa here 2 days ago," "got some o' thesss-leep," I'mtt-oott-ired to walk to my room," "outtajjj-ail yet," "you've seen hisppp-icture, Chester." In contrast to the friendly cartoon villain, who prolongs vowels, leaving his mouth open longer than expected to lure victims into a false sense of security via gradual F0 declination, the wary Western hero shortens his vowels and prolongs his consonants. He demonstrates the latent ability to release a lot of energy through patterns of prolonged consonants and quickly released vowels, suggesting he is a repository of raw strength, but not of dexterity or finesse. Powerful and prepared, this hero is not prone to self-promotion. He is obviously able but not obviously adept. Yet like the film character Indiana Jones, who in *Raiders of the*

---

[5]In the episode variously titled "Sweet and Sour" or "Pretty Rena's Deadly Ways" from August 5, 1956, it should be noted, a villain speaks this way as well, but only when trying to appear tough, when bluffing the hero and when first introducing himself to a lady, not when attempting to seduce her. When attempting to seduce the lady, the villain begins with even, smooth syllables, and when things aren't working, he reverts to the overly solicitous snide slides of a villain, devilishly versatile falls from high tone within a single syllable and controlled, evenly timed, forced false laughter.

Lost Ark pulls the trigger of his gun when confronted with a man swinging a sword, it is more important that Dillon be able to quickly dispatch villains than engage in exciting swordplay, wordplay, or heard play.

The impression of vigilant wariness conveyed through Dillon's anticipation and prolongation of syllable-initial consonants is reinforced through his pitch range. When he asks "Oh? Why?" he rises on "Oh?" but starts the word "Why?" with a restrained downstep rather than a complete rise-fall more typical of stylized overt curiosity. His attention to pitch range is most apparent in Dillon's expressions of assurance. Reassuring expressions of sympathy, whether genuinely solicitous or duplicitous, are usually articulated at the bottom of a speaker's natural range and/or involve a fall to that range. The use of the low range may elicit emotional associations not only with calmness (relaxed, slower vibrations), but also with empathy, coming down to the listener's level. Such reassurances, at least as they are portrayed in children's cartoons like Spiderman and Disney's Snow White and The Lion King, are also articulated with extra long vowels on stressed syllables. Dillon, however, though he reassures a seemingly frightened woman several times in the course of a single program episode, speaks quickly, never lengthening his vowels, and fails to drop to the bottom of his range during

the actual reassurance ("Now don't you worry, miss"), conceding no more than a downstepped high tone. While this may not be immediately apparent from a spectrogram of the isolated utterance, since the downstepped high tone is near the bottom of some men's range (70 Hz), Dillon is intriguingly capable of producing an unnaturally low bottom register, and of doing so more or less naturally, without glottal fry (50–60 Hz). The downstep on the reassurances proper becomes apparent by contrast with what follows, namely, more precipitous falls to the speaker's lower range accompanying the verbal exergasias "He won't bother ya" in one case, and "Nothin'll happen to ya" in another. Yet even in these contrasting amplifications, the speaker's lowest tones do not correspond to stressed syllables; the stressed syllables in the exergasias are low pitched in absolute terms, but still categorically high relative to the unstressed ones. Because the lowest 50–60 Hz sounds in the amplifications are aligned only with syllables of shortest relative duration, hence not emphasized, they lead Dillon to sound more dismissive than concerned, merely acknowledging the lady and throwing her some vocal crumbs for decency's sake. In a safer setting, his voice might be perceived as insensitive.[6] Yet in the social context of the Wild West, a lady's still going to trust a guy who's ever watchful and doesn't let down his

---

[6]How dependent interpretation of this vocal behavior is on cultural context becomes still more apparent if one attempts to analyze it from a culture-independent perspective like Gricean linguistic pragmatics. This tradition often treats form-function relationships as invariant if not arbitrary. A Gricean view would recognize incomplete falls in the downstepped initial reassurances (not the amplifications) as using inappropriate intonation, hence possibly what Griceans call violations of the conversational maxim of relevance, but because the approach stops short of exploring what makes a behavior relevant, it would seek a more satisfying explanation in other conversational maxims. By treating Dillon's speech as,,to use Gricean terminology, flouting (intentional violation) of the conversational maxim of manner (avoid obscurity and ambiguity) or maxim of quantity (say as much as necessary but no more than necessary), the incompleteness might be viewed as

guard. When she's surrounded by vicious outlaws, a woman doesn't need a speaker who can come off his high horse and feel her pain. She needs a man who's reliable, who is not overwhelmed by feminine charms, and who can be counted on when confronted with unanticipated challenges. Reliability inspires trust, and trust presupposes integrity on the part of whoever is trusted. Dillon is likeable because he sounds trustworthy, though he may not sound very nice.

Sand in His Craw; Gravel in His Gizzard[7]

There are certain points, including in the 50 to 60 Hz reassurance amplifications just discussed, where Dillon deals with a rense interpersonal situation by sounding tense himself, but at the same time, unusually deep and powerful. Inspection of waveforms of these isolated portions of Dillon's speech, magnified to display repeating periods of amplitude modulation, reveals a repeated series of successively lower but smoothly parabolic amplitude peaks mirroring the amplitude modulation of what Sakakibara et al. (2001) refer to as *kargyraa voice*, an extra-low pitched voice characteristic of Asian "throat singing" that involves vibration of false vocal folds at half the period of the acoustic waveform. According to Agarwal, Scherer, and De Witt (2004), partial adduction of the false vocal folds

generally dissipates energy and reduces translaryngeal airflow, though when the false vocal fold gap gets small enough, equal to or smaller than the glottal diameter, airflow again increases. This suggests that in order to produce a powerful sounding but exceedinglylow-pitched voice, a speaker may need to occlude the vocal tract at some point between the glottis and the false vocal folds to maintain intensity.

Because most American and European listeners are unaccustomed to using the ventricular folds to produce speech sounds, they are unlikely to have developed a kinesthetic association between the sound produced by the ventricular folds and physical motions iconic of particular emotions. It is therefore more difficult to characterize the emotional qualities English speakers are likely associate with pharyngeal tension used to force a louder ventricular vibration than to develop hypotheses about the emotional qualities of more familiar speech sounds. Yet while pharyngeal sounds are not phonemically distinctive in English words, the meanings English speakers associate with them can be inferred from examining how English speakers refer to these sounds when they appear in other languages. A cursory examination of this issue might suggest that English speakers perceive pharyngeal sounds as having unsavory connotations, as being more appropriate to villains than heroes, but such a conclusion would be compromised by an imprecise use of the term "pharyngeal." A class of throat-articulated sounds

---

implicating speaker uncertainty and leading the listener to doubt the speaker for seeming to doubt himself, an interpretation which does not seem at all tenable in this situation.

[7]Typical cowboy characterizations of a brave colleague (Adams, 2000, p. 209), as in "He had more sand in his craw than the Mohave Desert."

foreign to many European ears, the uvular, pharyngeal, and laryngeal sounds of Arabic (including a kind of glottal fry frication) are often referred to as "guttural" (Zawaydeh, 1997), a term which the American Heritage College Dictionary of 1997 defines as "having a harsh or grating quality." Because this nontechnical meaning is not attested in an earlier edition of the American College Dictionary from the 1960s, it may have acquired new connotations, perhaps from the similar sounding word *gutter*, but perhaps also through English speakers' perception of these sounds. Academic literature refers to optional pharyngealization of Arabic consonants primarily produced with articulators higher in the vocal tract as "emphatic" (Amayreh, 2003), a choice that suggests the sound is heard as at least more assertive if not more aggressive than other sounds. However, among Arabic grammarians, what English linguists call pharyngeal "emphasis" is referred to as *ʔitbaq*, literally "covering" (Al-Masri & Jongman, 2003). To Arabic ears, the sound may be more defensive than assertive, more shielding than hostile. Partial justification for this impression can be found through comparing the acoustic patterning of so-called emphatic and nonemphatic sounds. Just as vowels with less clearly separated formant regions may be heard as "darker" (Tsur, 1992, pp. 8–29), Al-Masri and Jongman find that the characteristic lowering of the F2 formant in pharyngealized "emphatics" produces a tighter, "more compact spectrogram" presumably indicative of articulatory containment rather than egression. To Arabic speakers, pharyngealization of consonants normally articulated primarily in the mouth area may also have connotations of preparedness, of the careful planning characteristic of responsible heroes rather than of the impetuous display of emphatic speech. According to Watson (1999), emphatic pharyngealization in Arabic consistently spreads "leftward" (though presumably rightward from the standpoint of Arabic writing) to phonemes articulated earlier in a word or syllable because the pharynx must narrow early in the process, producing an anticipatory effect. While pharyngealization may sometimes spread "rightward" as well (to subsequent phonemes), it is often blocked from rightward spread by high vowels that cannot be easily articulated with the retracted tongue root characteristic of emphatics. That pharyngealization may be a powerful but not necessarily aggressive style of speaking is also suggested by the fact that although it appears to be more accentuated among male than female Arabic speakers in Cairo (Kahn, 1975, as cited in Al-Masri & Jongman, 2003), the opposite trend is evident among female and male Arabic speakers in Jordan (Al-Masri & Jongman, 2003). Thus, for Arabic speakers at least, there is reason to believe pharyngealization may indeed connote the guarded gentlemanly vigilance one might expect of a professional guardian of justice or of an American aspiring to be elected the world's policeman.

However, this all argues for differences between Arabic and English perceptions of pharyngealization. None of this suggests pharyngealization sounds any less harsh or assertive to English speakers, particularly in the context of Arabic given the current political climate in America. Yet, what is often loosely referred to as "pharyngealization" is quite often actually sub-uvular frication. According to Ghazeli (1977), emphatic pharyngealization of nonpharyngeal consonants in Arabic is produced with the upper pharynx.

The actual pharyngeal phonemes of Arabic are very different sounds produced below the epiglottis. The significance of this distinction becomes more apparent in the artificial language Klingon created by an English-speaking linguist, Marc Okrand, for a race of arch-villains in a series of popular science fiction films. The Web site of a society devoted to preserving this language (http://www.kli.org) characterizes both its uvular sound as "a little like choking" and its pharyngeal sound as "a lot like choking." Indeed, the Klingon word for *choke*, *voQ*, contains a pharyngeal. The Klingon word *Qaq*, meaning "to behave falsely honorably," a particular type of cowardly deception characteristic of villains, begins with a pharyngeal fricative. However, it is important to note that the word also ends with a uvular fricative. According to the Klingon Pocket Dictionary (http://www.klingonska.org/dict), other more overtly antagonistic Klingon words like *ghob* for *fight* and *Hegh* for *die* are characterized by velar fricatives, throaty sounds produced even higher in the throat. Indeed, one of the nicest words in the Klingon lexicon[8] is the Klingon word for *good*. Pronounced *QaQ*, it both begins and ends with a pharyngeal fricative. This pattern, in a language created to titillate native speakers of American English with sonic caricatures of foreignness and barbarity, again suggests that pharyngeal articulation per se, at least when produced very low in the vocal tract, is not necessarily associated with hostility or duplicity.

What English speakers do hear in lower pharyngeals may be some of the same qualities that those for whom the articulation is phonemically distinctive hear. Dr. Johanna Nichols, author of Ingush-English/English-Ingush and Chechen-English/English-Chechen dictionaries and a coeditor of a book entitled *Sound Symbolism*, noted (J. Nichols, personal communication, November 14, 2005) that in these languages of the Caucasus Mountains, pharyngeal consonants are statistically more prevalent in one of four noun classes, a neutral gender class that includes the sun, moon, some body parts, some fruits, and some large animals. This finding would be consistent with a universal tendency to hear low pharyngealization as being superficially as rough and irregular as an orange's skin, a rhino's plates, or a celestial body's halo, yet as fundamentally rotund, full, and dense as the contents these surfaces circumscribe.[9]

Thus, when Western listeners hear someone like Dillon using false vocal fold articulation, they are likely to be impressed by a magically resonant, immensely strong masculine voice emerging from what seems to be the vocal equivalent of shackles. In contrast to the slow, relaxed beats of a cartoon villain's glottal fry, the

---

[8]There seems to be no word in the on-line pocket dictionary for *nice*, and the word for *fine* means "tax or fee."

[9]Some confusion may still arise from the fact that in some languages like Rengao, a language of Vietnam (Gregerson, 1984), both vowels and consonants involving a smaller pharyngeal cavity may be statistically more common in words for smaller objects, since the smaller cavity is created by motion backward down the throat, retracted tongue root. However, it is important to bear in mind that the tongue root, while shaping and filtering the sound, is not a vibrating articulator across which air travels to make these sounds; they are not pharyngeal fricatives. Also, movement of the tongue root toward the soft palate, creating constriction and the smaller space presumably iconic of smaller objects, occurs not within the pharyngeal cavity but above it. Thus, Gregerson's findings should in no way be interpreted as suggesting that pharyngeal frication itself should be associated with smallness rather than fullness.

hero's rigid pharyngeal shield presents the physiologic equivalent of a blockade against unexpected assault, but amazingly, without restricting the speaker's freedom of motion. Dillon does not appear to be using pharyngeal frication as a way to add noise to or filter laryngeal production, in the manner of the growling jazz singer Louis Armstrong, whose glottalized amplitude modulation, shown in Figure 14–2a (Armstrong growling "uh" in the word "brothers" in a spoken introduction to the song "When the Saints Go Marching In"), is visibly far more irregular and less periodic than that of Dillon shown in Figure 14–2b (uttering the same phoneme "uh," in "Shut up" with an open throated buzz rather than a glottalized growl). Instead, Dillon appears to be using audible pharyngeal tightness to force more air past a supplemental set of vibrating vocal folds to produce a loud, resonant, extremely low-pitched sound that involves no strain. Furthermore, unlike a cartoon villain who typically likes to exhibit his vocal virtuosity through such feats as articulating a single syllable by sliding among three pitch centers, the responsible gunslinger's unheard of vocal capabilities are modestly hidden amidst unfamiliar articulatory gestures known only to the expert speaker himself, not presented for public display.

Moseyin' ta Town

Lest this characterization of the voice of virility be equated with the voice of the Western lawman only, Fuks (1999) has identified acoustic correlates of these same superficially constricted but imperceptibly deft articulatory characteristics

in the strong but gravelly voice (averaging 50 Hz below the natural male range) of a powerful and heroic but not particularly suave classic American cartoon character, Popeye the Sailor, who despite his powerful voice, self-effacingly mumbles his words. I myself noticed the same low-pitched but high-intensity buzz above a tight throat in a caricature of the voice of the somewhat less self-effacing governor Arnold Schwarzenegger on the NPR comedy quiz show *Wait Wait, Don't Tell Me* aired August 20, 2005. Although the governor's radio address of the same date (available at http://gov.ca.gov), suggests that the real Schwarzenegger may not actually use his ventricular folds outside the movies, the movie voice may be more familiar to the public. A poll conducted by *USA Today*, CNN, and Gallup in November 2004 found that Americans' opposition to allowing a foreign-born citizen to become president dropped from 67% to 58% when Schwarzenegger's name was included in the question (Kasindorf, 2004), suggesting that a significant proportion of Americans may consider this Austrian-born actor turned U.S. governor to be a public voice at least as representative of "real America" as the born and bred but politically challenged Americans Kerry and Gore.

Giddiyup 'n' Whoa Pardner

The formal characteristics of Matt Dillon's speech are less evident in the speech of a more urbane contemporary, the "hard boiled" San Francisco radio detective Sam Spade in *The Adventures of Sam Spade, P.I.* yet Spade's speech produces the same emotional impact as

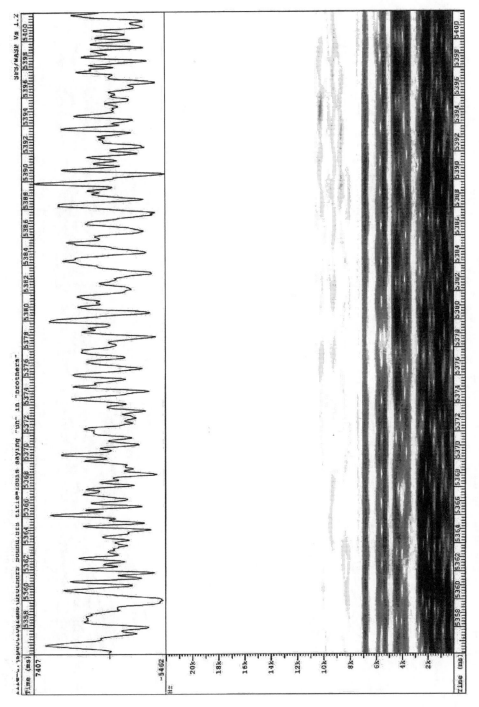

Figure 14-2a. Amplitude waveform and spectra for Louis Armstrong growling "uh" in "brothers."

255

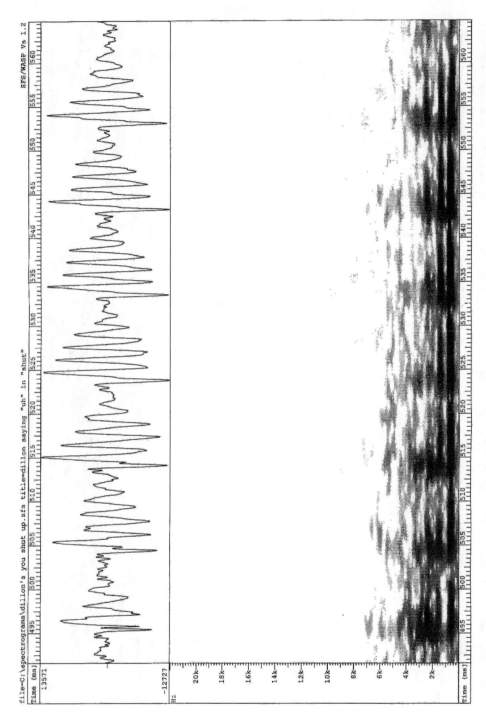

Figure 14–2b. Amplitude waveform and spectra for Matt Dillon saying "uh" in "shut" with deep resonance, seemingly lengthened vocal tract, and pharyngeal constriction.

Dillon's through different formal means. While Spade occasionally expresses toughness at the phoneme-in-word level, anticipating syllable initial consonants as in "whether youss-ee it orsss-ell it," and "match up with this piece of thesshh-irt with his initials on it," Spade generally produces a more refined but analogous warning-attack pattern at the less primal syllable-in-phrase level. Rather than tending to alternate strong and weak syllables, as in more standard speech, Spade articulates strings of three to five weak syllables run together in the temporal space another speaker might allot to a single weak syllable, followed by a single strong one, as in such phrases as "thefronovhuh NEGligée," "Ilookedfuhthu WOUND," "SIttinginfron'ov'a DRESSing table," and "broken GLASS allovathu FLOOR." The speaker's periodic alternation between a fast unstressed and slow stressed speech rate creates an emotional impression of animated power and control that contrasts as strongly with a runaway, invariably fast speech rate as with the ponderous, obtuse quality of slower alternating strong and weak syllables. Simultaneously assertive and exuberant, this syllable-compressing style is refined and professional, not at all the speech of an inexpressive ruffian. Far from being a "macho" style, it was actually a women's speaking style as well, typical of the "tough broads" and professional women portrayed in movies of the 1930s and 1940s, hardened by the Great Depression or by the Great War

that took men out of the civilian workforce. But by the radio drama heyday of the 1950s, in an age when the sport of boxing was surpassed in popularity only by that of baseball, Spade's strong syllables may have been heard as analogous to the quick jabs of a prize fighter, the intervening strings of weak syllables as the fighter's recoiling from his opponent while keeping his arms engaged.[10]

However, the retracted arms would not have been engaged in any elaborate feints; they would simply have prepared for the next punch. That is to say, little in Spade's speech other than the volley of unstressed syllables itself testifies to vocal agility. Many of Spade's consonants, far from being emphasized, are, when they appear in weak syllables, actually dropped or replaced with less effortful substitutions, as in when a dental stop is replaced with a dental sonorant, not just in word-final position, but consistently: "You say this girl came na [sic] yer aparnmen [sic] in a jealous rage." That is, Spade compromises articulation for the sake of speed. Sentences describing elements of the scene of a crime are articulated with an invariant, parallel series of rising "list" intonation patterns, suggesting a jaded emotional detachment from the horrors the speaker is describing. Even Spade's rapid-fire articulations, though more refined than Dillon's consonant prolongations, connote a kind of callousness by ignoring the stress possibilities of intervening syllables.[11]

---

[10]The style can be heard in other detective dramas of the same period, as in *Dragnet*, "A man was TALKintaoneo'the OFFicers," and even occasionally in the speech of *Gunsmoke*'s Matt Dillon himself, as in "MAYbehewantstafind OUT if," "As much TROUbleasyoucan HANDle," and "NAIL'emoverthe WINdow."

[11]This is not to say Spade isn't highly intelligent. He reasons deductively to solve crimes and on occasion may sound somewhat more sophisticated. The few stylistic exceptions in his vocal expression involve vowel and sonorant prolongation while he is reasoning or planning aloud, devising an ingenious solution, as in "A little AIRRR won't do this DInnerrrr any HARRRM," or when he is stumped, notices something odd or suspicious, or tentatively auditions a new idea, as in "CHANGED MY MIND," or certain points such as "TWO TYPEwritten

The quick jabs of Spade's stressed syllables may sound manly in the context of accelerated surrounding syllables, but given then that Spade slurs his words together, drops his *T*'s and doesn't seem to feel enough emotionally to vary his pitch unpredictably, what could possibly be considered heroic, as opposed to simply manly, in his vocal expression? Well, as with Dillon's downstepped reassurances, Spade's rushed unstressed syllables suggest he isn't distracted by unimportant details. Mature and responsible, he only concentrates on the most important words, not other interesting words, attention to which might put him at a disadvantage. Spade's predictable intonation patterns suggest he won't get emotionally involved in matters that might compromise his ability to do his job, in short, that he is dependable and trustworthy. His apparent disregard for accuracy in vocal presentation also suggests he is honest, that he does not seek to create a falsely favorable impression through impeccable vocal style.

The Roundup

The speech of Dillon and Spade is fluent, but in Dillon's case not effortless, and in Spade's, not flawless in the sense of the accomplished performance of a practiced athlete. Their superficial coarseness and apparent disdain for and inattentiveness to vocal niceties in intonation and articulation suggest they are not interested in impressing others. A listener naturally concludes that they are not trying to

deceive others either. Though they may not be Princes Charming, what makes them heroes, or at least anti-villains, is simply their honesty. Their voices may lack enthusiasm yet retain the ring of truth. They help protect people from villains because it's their job and because it's right, but not because it's fun. In one of Gunsmoke episodes, a trigger-happy cowboy and a woman who encourages cowboys to pick fights over her and kill each other for her own amusement sound far happier than the emotionally restrained U.S. marshal who chases them down. The American popular culture view of good and evil presented in the voices of classic American radio drama is far from the revisionist Miltonic vision of jubilant, well-adjusted angels singing hallelujahs until besieged and existentially challenged by devils incessantly driven to speak unwelcome truths to God and man. It is a more authentically puritanical one, in which virtue is a duty, not a joy, and in which people who are heard as exulting, laughing ecstatically, and expressing themselves without reservation can't help but disguise some ill intent through their superficial vocal ornamentation and must eventually be unmasked for their moral turpitude. A sobering thought for communication consultants tasked with training leaders accused of sounding stiff and formal to sound "more expressive."

We have seen that in contrast to the exaggerated pitch slides and extreme (extra high and glottalized) registers that characterize baby talk or motherese and expressions of sympathy, as well as the speech of cartoon villains, the simple,

---

LINES in it," and "FAINT GHOSTly GLIMMmer of LIGHT, OverHEAD." In these instances, the relative proportion of stressed to unstressed syllables shifts in the direction opposite that of rapid-fire speech, with some stressed syllables even appearing adjacent to each other.

conversational speech of trusted American heroes contains less variety, but offers correspondingly less reason for listeners to suspect the speaker of disguising his voice or speaking falsely. Furthermore, what little divergence from standard speech the hero exhibits signals the reliability and competence a listener would expect from someone he would trust to keep him safe. Ironically, it is not vocal expressions of courage or strength but these attributions of honesty, reliability, and competence, qualities that one might just as easily associate with mothers, grandmothers, and big sisters, that make these heroes sound manly. When greater than expected emphasis on articulatory constriction through consonant prolongation occurs word-initially, significantly not word-finally, it can sound to the listener as if it signals a state of preparedness for aggressive action rather than aggression itself, while corresponding reduction of the duration of sounds produced with more open articulation, word-medial vowels, can signal guardedness or protectiveness. In the social context of an unsafe environment, refusal to conform to societal standards for vocal expression of sympathy can be heard as a socially appropriate vocal expression of wariness, of attentiveness more to the potential for future victimization of a likely victim than of immediate concern for the potential victim's feelings. An extremely low-pitched sound produced through articulatory constriction low in the throat, yet crucially, without the irregular, aperiodic amplitude variation characterizing glottal fry, can simultaneously convey a sense of strength and protectiveness, yet without the self-promoting qualities one might associate with more forward sounding articulation. Assigning the same amount of time to one impor-

tant syllable as to a whole slew of unimportant syllables conveys the skill at prioritization and ability to work efficiently one would expect of a trustworthy private investigator.

Up Yonder

These findings on the vocal qualities responsible for speech sounding honest and trustworthy to American ears suggest opportunities for future research in both applied and theoretical settings. The findings can be applied to speech coaching in the political arena and can inform cross-cultural research on speaking styles and audience response.

That two such distinct speaking styles, that of an urban detective and that of a Western lawman, should be capable of eliciting such similar emotional reactions argues for an evolutionary perspective on vocal expression of emotion grounded in speakers' and listeners' behavioral adaptation to cultural constraints, as opposed to a strict one-to-one semiology pairing acoustic and articulatory forms with the emotions they elicit. It follows that a speaker may be able to sound more honest and believable by working backward from a desired result to emphasize existing properties of his own cultural dialect. By simply analyzing—rather than imitating—the speech of classic American heroes, American political candidates male and female alike may gain a greater awareness of elements in their own speech that may be perceived by the American public as insincere and learn to cultivate aspects of their speech that can suggest the sense of integrity, awareness, and vigilance that some listeners, particularly those in rural areas, high crime urban settings, and disaster-prone regions, may feel is missing in these speakers' voices and political outlook. While avoiding the embarrassingly incongruous mimicry that characterized Al Gore's attempt to growl like a black preacher when visiting an African American church, politicians can thereby speak naturally to their skeptics' sensitivities.

The lessons that examining the voice of virility offers for cultures outside the United States are less clear. Several papers presented at the Pacific Voice and Speech Foundation 2005 conference suggested that the acoustic and articulatory characteristics of a caricatured voice of villainy may be cultural universals, but an insincere sounding voice may be less sensitive to context and culture than an honest sounding one. This may sound paradoxical until one considers that the insincere voice of the dissembling villain may be a stereotype of awkward politeness, which presumably sounds wrong to many ears, whereas the truly sincere voice must adjust to situational and cultural circumstances to show empathy with the interlocutor. Certain other cultures may value "straight talk" over affected talk as much as the findings herein suggest American listeners do. This is probably the case among Israeli Jews, among whom *dugri* speech, a simple and straightforward style, has evolved as a reaction to the deferential circumlocutions of international diplomacy, which have been viewed by Jews as symbolic of weakness and capitulation to Arab and Christian interests (Katriel, 1986). As a symbol of honesty, according to Katriel, it has even been used by duplicitous politicians to dispel suspicion. Nevertheless, the association of straight talk with honesty may be weaker in other cultures, or may apply only in certain situations, with the result that what sounds honest in one context sounds untrustworthy in another. This appears to be the case in Portugal since its 1974 revolution. According to Reed (1990, p. 139), formerly oppressed commoners have adopted the subtler, cultivated speech of the former ruling elite, at least in formal settings or when speaking in the presence of members of the former elite, to symbolically demonstrate that they are equal to them. Users of the cultivated style in formal settings are not considered pretentious; nor are they suspected of duplicity, of representing adversarial upper class interests; instead, they are viewed as worthy competitors. Thus, in formal settings, appeals to Portuguese listeners that invoke a simple, straightforward style may not convey the sense of practical skill and competence necessary to inspire a feeling of trust, though the style may be quite proper in informal settings, where the speaker would wish to avoid the appearance of showing off. People in still another set of cultures may, like the American listener, associate straight talk with honesty and yet refuse to judge the speaker solely on the style of his speech. On Tanna, an island in Melanesia, according to Lindstrom (1990), straightforward speech is valued in theory, but everyone recognizes that one cannot expect speakers to be as honest as they sound. Thus, owing to listeners' justifiable mistrust, straightforward sounding speech on Tanna may elicit emotions of amusement or disgust rather than confidence in the speaker. Without further research, it is not a simple matter to predict how listeners from other cultures might respond to the serious and unpretentious but perhaps not universally trustworthy voices of Dillon and Spade. To characterize acoustic and articulatory properties of virile American voices and relate them to analogs in the physical motion of larger bodies potentially responsible for our emotional response is one thing, but to characterize vocal naturalness and sincerity in general is a far more complex, culturally contingent task, one which will require a lot tougher analyses to tackle.

References

Adams, R. F. (2000). *Cowboy lingo: A dictionary of the slack-jaw words and whangdoodle ways of the American West*. New York: Houghton Mifflin.

Agarwal, M., Scherer, R. C., & De Witt, K. J. (2004). *The effects of the false vocal folds on translaryngeal airflow resistance.* Paper presented at 2004 International Conference on Voice Physiology and Biomechanics, Marseille. Retrieved from http://icv2004.free.fr/download%20bis/meena.pdf

Al-Masri, M., & Jongman, A. (2004). Acoustic correlates of emphasis in Jordanian Arabic: Preliminary results. In A. Agwuele, W. Warren, & S. Park (Eds.), *Proceedings of the 2003 Texas Linguistics Society* (pp. 96–106). Somerville, MA: Cascadilla Proceedings Project. Retrieved November 4, 2007 from http://www.lingref.com/cpp/tls/2003/paper1071.pdf

Amayreh, M. (2003). Completion of the consonant inventory of Arabic. *Journal of Speech, Language, and Hearing Research*, 46(June), 517–529.

Deutsch, D. (1975). Two-channel listening to musical scales. *Journal of the Acoustical Society of America*, 57, 1156–1160.

Deutsch, D., & Pierce, J. R. (1992). The climate of auditory imagery and music. In D. Reisberg (Ed.), *Auditory imagery* (pp. 237–260). Hillsdale, NJ: Lawrence Erlbaum Associates.

Fields, S. (2001, March 27). Crime and punishment on the small screen. *Jewish World Review*, retrieved November 4, 2007 from http://www.jewishworldreview.com/cols/fields032701.asp

Frey, K. P., & Eagly, A. H. (1993). Vividness can undermine the persuasiveness of messages. *Journal of Personality and Social Psychology*, 65(1), 32–44.

Fuks, L. (1999). *Computer-aided musical analysis of extended vocal techniques for compositional applications*. Paper presented at VI Simpósio Brasileiro de Computação Música, Rio de Janeiro. Retrieved November 4, 2007 from http://gsd.ime.usp.br/sbcm/1999/papers/Leonardo_Fuks.pdf

Ghazeli, S. (1977). *Back consonants and backing coarticulation in Arabic*. Unpublished doctoral dissertation, University of Texas at Austin.

Gregerson, K. (1984). Pharynx symbolism and Rengao phonology. *Lingua*, 62, 209–238.

Hubbard, T. L., & Stoeckig, K. (1992). The representation of pitch in musical images. In D. Reisberg (Ed.), *Auditory imagery* (pp. 199–235). Hillsdale, NJ: Lawrence Erlbaum Associates.

Kahn, M. (1975). Arabic emphasis: The evidence for cultural determinants of phonetic sex-typing. *Phonetica*, *31*, 38–50.

Kasindorf, M. (2004, December 2). Should the constitution be amended for Arnold? *USA Today*. Retrieved November 4, 2007 from http://www.usatoday.com/news/politicselections/2004-12-02-schwarzenegger-amendment_x.htm

Katriel, T. (1986). *Talking straight: Dugri speech in Israeli Sabra culture*. Cambridge, UK: Cambridge University Press.

Krumhansl, C. L., & Shepard, R. N. (1979). Quantification of the hierarchy of tonal functions within a diatonic context. *Journal of Experimental Psychology: Human Perception and Performance*, *5*, 579–594.

Lindstrom, L. (1990). Straight talk on Tanna. In K. A. Watson-Gegeo & G. M. White (Eds.), *Disentangling: Conflict discourse in Pacific societies* (pp. 373-411). Stanford, CA: Stanford University Press.

Miller, M., Maruyama, G., Beaber, R. J., & Valone, K. (1976). Speed of speech and persuasion. *Journal of Personality and Social Psychology, 34*(4), 615-624.

Pearce, W. B., & Brommel, B. J. (1972). Vocalic communication in persuasion. *Quarterly Journal of Speech, 58*, 298-306.

Pittam, J. (1994). *Language and language behaviors: Volume 5. Voice in social interaction: An interdisciplinary approach.* Thousand Oaks, CA: Sage.

Reed, R. R. (1990). Are Robert's Rules of Order counterrevolutionary? Rhetoric and the reconstruction of Portuguese politics. *Anthropological Quarterly, 63*, 134-144.

Sakakibara, K. I., Imagawa, H., Konishi, T., Kondo, K., Murano, E. Z., Kumada, M., et al. (2001). Vocal fold and false vocal fold vibrations and synthesis of khöömoi. In *Proceedings of the International Computer Music Conference 2001* (pp. 135-138). Retrieved November 4, 2007 from http://www.brl.ntt.co.jp/people/kis/paper/icmc2001.pdf

Scotton, C. M., & Bernsten, J. (1988). Natural conversations as a model for textbook dialogue. *Applied Linguistics, 9*(4), 372-384.

Smith, S. M., & Shaffer, D. R. (2000). Vividness can undermine or enhance message processing: The moderating role of vividness congruency. *Personality and Social Psychology Bulletin, 26*, 759-779.

Street, R. L., Jr., Brady, R. M., & Putman, W. B. (1983). The influence of speech rate stereotypes and rate similarity or [sic] listeners' evaluations of speakers. *Journal of Language and Social Psychology, 2*(1), 37-56.

Tsur, R. (1992). *What makes sound patterns expressive? The poetic mode of speech perception.* Durham, NC: Duke University.

Watson, J. (1999). Remarks and replies: The directionality of emphasis spread in Arabic. *Linguistic Inquiry, 30*(2), 289-300.

Woodall, W. G., & Burgoon, J. K. (1984). Talking fast and changing attitudes: A critique and clarification. *Journal of Nonverbal Behavior, 8*, 126-142.

Zawaydeh, B. (1997). Endoscopic and acoustic evidence of the gutteral natural class. *Journal of the Acoustical Society of America, 102*(5), 3093.

CHAPTER 15

Vocal Expressions of Emotions and Personalities in Japanese *Anime*

Mihoko Teshigawara

Introduction

Vocal stereotyping plays an important role in our daily lives. For instance, upon hearing a voice on the telephone, we can attribute certain age, gender, personality, and physical characteristics to a speaker we have never met. While such judgments do not necessarily coincide with the true attributes of the speaker, they are nonetheless surprisingly consistent among listeners from the same culture because they share the same vocal stereotypes. Previous studies on vocal stereotypes (Hecht & LaFrance, 1996; Yarmey, 1993; Zuckerman & Miyake, 1993), in which listeners listen to voices and rate personality and vocal characteristics, reveal that people infer similar personality traits from voices, as is the case in everyday life. The results of Erickson et al.'s (2006) study suggest

the importance of vocal stereotypes in the perception of emotional speech as well. In their perception test, sad speech that was produced in imitation of genuinely sad utterances was perceived as sadder than the original sad speech, which was recorded while the speakers were talking about a sad event (e.g., the speakers' mothers had recently died or were gravely ill).

Turning to the world of animated cartoons, voices need to reflect the attributes of the characters in terms of age, gender, appearance, and personality and portray emotions appropriate to the scenes. In other words, the voices need to reflect the vocal stereotypes that consumers, filmmakers, and voice actors share. This medium, therefore, is a rich source for research on vocal stereotypes. A phonetic analysis of voices in animated cartoons is a good starting point for the

263

investigation of the phonetic correlates of vocal stereotypes in particular cultures.

In this article, I provide an overview of a series of studies that focus on the *voice qualitie*s of heroes and villains in Japanese animated cartoons (*anime*) (Teshigawara, 2003; 2004). Most previous studies of vocal stereotypes have used computer programs or systematic control by speakers to investigate the effects of prosody (i.e., pitch, loudness, and speech rate) on impression formation (Nass & Lee, 2001; Ray, 1986). However, to my knowledge, only one study has systematically examined the effects of voice quality on impression formation (Addington, 1968). In a similar vein, while there is a growing interest in research on vocal cues to emotion and other paralinguistic information, most of the studies focus on the acoustic correlates of prosody; and only a few have considered voice quality (Campbell & Mokhtari, 2003; Fujimoto & Maekawa, 2003; Gobl & Ní Chasaide, 2003). (See Teshigawara, 2003, for a detailed review of studies in this vein.)

In line with the work of Laver (1980; 1994) and Esling (1978; 1994), in this study, the term *voice quality* refers to "those characteristics which are present more or less all the time that a person is talking: it is a quasi-permanent quality running through all the sound that issues from his [sic] mouth" (Abercrombie, 1967, p.91). In other words, upon hearing a stretch of speech exhibiting a certain voice quality, we are able to extract certain consistent characteristics from the voice. The source of this consistency is long-term laryngeal postures (i.e., phonation types) and/or supralaryngeal postures. For example, if a speaker smiles throughout an utterance—a habit prevalent among Japanese female TV reporters

—we are able to extract the auditory cues associated with constant lip spreading. It seems reasonable to assume that such long-term laryngeal and supralaryngeal postures contribute to listeners' shared impressions of long-term speaker attributes, as well as their impressions of short-term features such as the expression of emotion. By examining the voice qualities of *anime* characters, I hope to shed light on phonetic aspects of speech communication that have not yet been fully investigated.

In the next section of this article, I will describe the data analyzed in this study, along with my modified version of Laver's (1994; 2000) framework for the auditory analysis of voice quality. In the following section, I will describe my perceptual experiment and discuss my results in relation to phonetic correlates. In the last section, I will discuss the implications of my findings for future research.

Materials

I chose the materials for this study from 20 Japanese animated cartoons in which there was an obvious contrast between heroes and villains. The materials were selected from TV series and movies produced from the 1960s through to the 1990s (see Teshigawara, 2003 and 2004, for a complete list of titles selected for the study). From these sources, I compiled noise-free speech samples longer than 5 seconds for the selected characters. The speech samples were digitized onto a personal computer at 22,050 samples per second, 16-bit for acoustic analysis. In total, I analyzed the voices of 88 heroes, villains, and supporting roles, distributed as follows: 44 heroes (25 males, 19 females); 42 villains (30 males, 12 females); and 2 villainous-sounding supporting characters.

Auditory Analysis

Hypotheses

Prior to the auditory analysis, I reviewed psychological studies on vocal stereotypes and vocal cues to personality and emotion to help formulate hypotheses about the auditory and acoustic characteristics of the voices of heroes and villains. Two of the hypotheses formulated in Teshigawara (2003) are discussed below.

Following an initial auditory review of the voices of heroes and villains in the materials in this study, I noted that, while heroes expressed a wide variety of positive and negative emotions, villains expressed primarily negative emotions such as anger, disgust, frustration, etc. Therefore, it is reasonable to expect that vocal cues associated with these negative emotions would be consistently found in villains' voices. Based on Scherer's (1986) predictions for the four relevant emotions of displeasure/disgust, contempt/scorn, irritation/cold anger, and rage/hot anger, I hypothesized that the articulatory correlates of villains' voices would be: pharyngeal constriction, overall tensing of the vocal tract, and raised larynx (Hypothesis 1).

Drawing on Yarmey (1993), who suggests that the schemata for good characters are more typical and likeable, while those for bad characters are more distinctive and less enjoyable, I hypothesized that the auditory and acoustic character-

istics of heroes' voices would be more salient and easier to generalize than those of villains, which I presumed would deviate within a wider range and would exhibit greater variety (Hypothesis 2).

Method

In Laver's (1994; 2000) framework for voice quality description, after listening to a stretch of speech, the phonetician introspectively deduces the quasi-permanent articulatory characteristics of the speaker. Laver, Wirz, Mackenzie, and Hiller (1981/ 1991) report generally high agreement among phoneticians trained in this method. No direct articulatory (physiological) experiments and measurements were used in the present study; however, in combination with techniques such as magnetic resonance imaging (MRI), the auditorily identified characteristics were confirmed physiologically (Teshigawara & Murano, 2004).

The phonetic quality of a voice is created by a combination of *settings.* Laver defines a phonetic setting as "any co-ordinatory tendency underlying the production of the chain of segments in speech towards maintaining a particular configuration or state of the vocal apparatus" (Laver, 1994, p. 396). Of the four groups of settings that are distinguished in Laver (1994; 2000), two were considered in this analysis: articulatory settings (supralaryngeal settings) and phonatory settings (laryngeal settings). These two settings are subdivided into smaller groups, which also consist of multiple settings, most of which represent the activity of individual articulators, such as the jaw or tongue body (see Laver, 1994, p. 154, for a vocal profile protocol).

Based on the results of the preliminary auditory analysis, I made the following modifications to Laver's (1994; 2000) descriptive framework for voice quality (see Teshigawara, 2004, pp. 64–65; Teshigawara, 2003, pp. 40–46, for more details). Of the modifications made, I would like to highlight the addition of *laryngeal constriction* (corresponding to *laryngeal sphinctering* in Teshigawara, 2003 and 2004) and *larynx lowering* (combining *pharyngeal expansion* and *lowered larynx* in Teshigawara, 2003 and 2004), since these articulatory features played a principal role in distinguishing the voices of heroes and villains. The laryngeal constriction mechanism has been extensively investigated by Esling and his colleagues (e.g., Edmondson & Esling, 2005; Esling, 1999; Esling & Harris, 2005). I follow their use of the term *laryngeal constriction* to refer to the three components of this mechanism, that is, aryepiglottic constriction, tongue retraction, and larynx raising, which are hierarchically ordered. Aryepiglottic constriction occurs first, followed by tongue retraction and larynx raising. (For the articulatory basis of this activity, see the studies cited above and other work by Esling and his colleagues.) An auditory comparison of voice qualities in the present corpus and in the work of Esling and his colleagues revealed that even a slight degree of laryngeal constriction is likely to involve aryepiglottic constriction. On the other hand, pharyngeal expansion is achieved by lowering the larynx and/or advancing the tongue root.

Within my modified version of Laver's (1994; 2000) descriptive framework for voice quality, each voice quality description essentially represents the listener's estimation of a particular degree of deviation from a neutral setting. The neutral

reference setting is the neutral disposition of the vocal tract: for articulatory settings, the neutral reference setting refers to the setting that would result in the production of the central unrounded vowel [ə]; for phonatory settings, the neutral reference setting is that which would result in modal phonation (see Laver 1994, pp. 402–404, for more detail). Deviations from the neutral reference setting are accorded a value in terms of three scalar degrees: 1 represents a slight degree of deviation from neutral; 2 a moderate degree; and 3 an extreme degree.

After listening repeatedly to the speech samples for each character, I deduced the movement of each articulator. In this way, I developed a vocal profile for each character, using Laver's protocol. In Teshigawara (2003), the auditory characteristics of the voices of heroes and villains are discussed separately according to gender and age; however, in the next subsection, I highlight only general tendencies.

Results and Discussion

With regard to the overall distribution of articulatory and phonatory settings, heroes appeared to converge on selected settings and the incidence of neutral settings was high. In contrast, the settings of the villains were more widely distributed over the entire range of settings and the incidence of neutral settings was low. Below, I identify the combinations of settings that distinguished different character and subcharacter types. Supraglottic states (i.e., laryngeal constriction and larynx lowering) were key features in distinguishing the various character types.

There are two combinations of settings judged to occur in heroes:

1. Hero Type I: no laryngeal constriction with/without breathy voice
2. Hero Type II: slight or intermittent laryngeal constriction

Among the Hero Type I voices, 79% were judged to exhibit breathiness to some degree. In addition, the voices produced by the male voice actors were noted to exhibit intermittent, slight, or moderate larynx lowering. The voices produced by female voice actors tended to show fronted tongue body and an open jaw; about half of the voices exhibited lip spreading. All but two heroes played by female voice actors were identified as Hero Type I voices.

Hero Type II voices were not notable for their breathiness. Rather, these voices gave an auditory impression of somewhat greater loudness and of a greater degree of ringing quality.

By contrast, the combinations of settings judged to be common in villains exhibited much greater deviation from the neutral setting than those found in the heroic voices:

1. Villain Type I: moderate or extreme laryngeal constriction accompanied by raised larynx, jaw protrusion, labial constriction, close jaw, and harsh voice
2. Villain Type II: lowered larynx, with/without slight jaw protrusion, and slight labial constriction

The jaw protrusion and labial constriction noted in Villain Types I and II were reflected in an auditory impression of tightness in the lips and jaw, limiting the capacity of the jaw to open more than slightly. The restricted articulatory movements caused by these features can be associated with overall tensing of the vocal tract. Therefore, the Villain Type I voices exhibited the articulatory characteristics predicted for villains' voices in Hypothesis 1: pharyngeal constriction, overall tensing of the vocal tract, and raised larynx. In addition, 63% of the Villain Type I voices were deemed to have intermittent aryepiglottic/ventricular fold vibration concomitant with vocal fold vibration, which enhanced the auditory impression of a low-pitched voice. On the other hand, the articulatory characteristics of the Villain Type II voices were not predicted by Hypothesis 1, with the exception of the tenseness in the lips and jaw mentioned above.

The combination patterns observed in heroes (Hero Types I and II) were also noted in villains, although breathy voice was not noted among the villains, except for three out of eight Villain Type I speakers. As illustrated in the foregoing discussion, villains' voices seem to exhibit a wider range of deviation and greater variety than those of heroes—an observation that is consistent with Hypothesis 2.

It is also notable that the overall distribution patterns of the heroic and villainous voice types differed depending on the sex of the voice actors. As already noted, the heroes played by female voice actors were almost exclusively identified as Hero Type I voices (absence of supraglottic constriction). As for the villainous voices, while the majority of male voice actors in these roles had Villain Type I voices (with laryngeal constriction), the majority of female voice actors playing villainous roles had Villain Type II voices (with larynx lowering; see Chapter 3 of Teshigawara, 2003, for more details). Future studies should take into account the relationship between voice quality settings and the sex of the speaker.

To summarize, in this study I auditorily identified four voice types for heroes and villains (and supporting roles); supra-glottic states played an important role in differentiating these four voice types. Among the four voice types, the articulatory characteristics of Villain Type I were consistent with those predicted by Hypothesis 1. Hypothesis 2 was confirmed in the finding that villains' voices seem to exhibit a wider range of deviation and greater variety than those of heroes.

The articulatory characteristics of Villain Type II voices do not have any counterpart in Scherer's (1986) predictions about vocal cues to emotion. However, the following facts seem to suggest a connection between Villain Type II voices and negative emotions. First, the perceptual experiment (see next section below), in which a selected set of voices from the present corpus was used as stimuli, showed that Villain Type II voices were rated as having more negative emotional states than the other voice types (Teshigawara, 2003, Section 5.2.8, pp. 156–159; 2004, p. 70–71). In addition, in a free-answer portion of the perceptual experiment, listeners almost invariably provided the label "anger" (a negative emotion) in response to the two Villain Type II voices they heard (Teshigawara, 2003, p. 159; 2004, p. 72). Second, according to the observations of Poedjosoedarmo (1986) for Javanese speech, pharyngeal configuration plays not only a linguistic role in distinguishing the light and heavy stops, but also a paralinguistic and extralinguistic role. Vocal stereotypes exploited in *wayang* (shadow puppet) involve pharyngeal configuration and intonation. Whereas pharyngeal constriction tends to be associated with particular social groups, "[p]haryngeal expansion combined with rounded and protruding lips may be adopted on occasion to express anger, irritation, or other negative emo-

tions" (Poedjosoedarmo, 1986, p. 34). Therefore, we may say that the articulatory characteristics of both Villain Types I and II are associated with vocal cues to negative emotions.

Perceptual Experiment

In order to investigate whether the identified auditory characteristics contribute to people's perceptions of the characters as good or bad, I examined Japanese lay-persons' perceptions of selected speech samples in an experimental setting. I hypothesized that participants would attribute less favorable physical traits, personality traits, emotional states, and vocal characteristics to speakers who exhibited non-neutral supraglottic states (laryngeal constriction or lowered larynx) regardless of the roles they played in the original cartoons. Pearson's correlations were calculated between the trait ratings and selected phonetic measures, in order to examine the relationship between the results of the perceptual experiment and the identified phonetic correlates.

Method

Stimuli

Twenty-seven of the 88 character voices were selected for the perceptual experiment; the selected characters differed in degrees of laryngeal constriction/larynx lowering. In order to elicit listeners' responses to the voices independent of verbal content, I masked the contents of the speech samples. Of the five content-masking techniques investigated by Scherer, Feldstein, Bond, and Rosenthal

(1985), I chose the random splicing technique because this method alone retains voice quality information, which is the focus of this study.

First, in order to create stimuli representative of each speaker, speech portions produced with a voice quality setting deviating from the speaker's normal setting were removed, with the exception of characters who were consistently angry or shouting. In line with previous research using the random-splicing technique (Friend & Farrar, 1994; Scherer, Feldstein, Bond, & Rosenthal, 1985; van Bezooijen & Boves, 1986), following the removal of pauses, the digitized speech samples were divided into 250-ms segments. The first and last 3 ms of each segment were linearly attenuated to zero amplitude in order to avoid the introduction of transients (Friend & Farrar, 1994). In order to create a 5-s stimulus for each speaker, 20 250-ms segments were prepared and rearranged so that segments could not occur in the same relative order in the spliced stimulus as in the original.

Questionnaire, Participants, and Procedures

Twenty-one trait items were used in the questionnaire for the rating session, of which 19 are discussed here. The listeners were given adjectival labels and were asked to rate the characters on 7-point scales, from 1 (*not at all true*) to 7 (*extremely true*). English translations are given for the items as follows: two physical characteristics (*big, good-looking*); one emotional state (*positive emotion*); five vocal characteristics (*high-pitched, loud, relaxed, pleasant, attractive*); and 11 personality traits, of which 3 were chosen for their pertinence to heroes of Japanese *anime* in particular (*selfless,*

loyal, perseverant) (Levi, 1998), 3 were thought to be universal characteristics of heroes (*brave, intelligent, strong*), and 5 represented each of the five factors in the NEO Personality Inventory (*sociable, calm, curious, conscientious, sympathetic*) (see McCrae & Costa, 1987).

Thirty-two participants (15 males, 17 females; average age 22.8 years old) were recruited from Nagoya University, Japan, and the vicinity. Experimental sessions were run in groups of up to 7 in a sound-attenuated room. For each speaker, the participants twice heard a 5-s content-masked cartoon speech excerpt, and rated their impressions of the speakers' traits during the 70 s of silence that occurred between speakers. Each session lasted less than 1 hour.

Phonetic Measures

The following three articulatory and phonatory settings, which were previously found to correlate well with perceptions of trait items (Teshigawara, 2003), were included for the correlation analysis with trait ratings: laryngeal constriction, larynx lowering, and breathiness.

The acoustic parameters investigated in this study were related to pitch (F0) and vowel quality (F2 for a Japanese vowel /a/). The mean (and the standard deviation, SD, for F0) of each parameter was estimated over the voiced frames of the vowel portions for each utterance. The mean F0 and F0 SD are used as indices of pitch height and pitch range, respectively. In addition, since it was found that the second formants of vowels were negatively correlated with trait items *big, brave,* and *strong* in Teshigawara (2003), the F2 was measured for each /a/, which was the most consistently occurring vowel across the stimulus phrases, and the mean value was calculated for each stimulus.

Results

In order to examine the consistency of participants' trait ratings, Pearson's correlations were calculated for each participant relative to the average ratings of all participants, separately for each item. Because one participant's responses correlated significantly with the average ratings for only 6 out of 21 items ($p < .05$), results for this participant were removed from the rest of the analysis, resulting in a total of 31 participants.

Because the main concern of this study was to identify the overall trends in participant ratings, rather than in individual ratings, ratings were averaged across participants. In order to standardize the ranges of scalar degrees used by participants, for each trait item, z-scores were calculated for each participant across stimuli. Then, averaging the resulting z-scores across participants for each speaker, Pearson's correlations were calculated for the 19 adjective trait items for all 27 speakers used in the experiment, separately for male ($n = 9$) and female ($n = 18$) voice actors. (See Teshigawara, 2003 and 2004, for an analysis where correlations were calculated combining the two sexes.) Although this measure reduced the sample sizes, I considered it better to calculate the correlations separately, given that trends in articulatory behaviors differed between the two sexes (see Results and Discussion above). The overall correlation patterns among trait items were more or less similar between the two sexes; the same items showed significant correlations with one another,

except for the following items that showed more pronounced differences in male and female ratings: *brave, perseverant, conscientious, positive emotion, high-pitched, loud,* and (vocally) *relaxed*. (For the constituents of the two groups, see the discussion below about correlations between trait items and phonetic measures.) I found that in general, positive trait items such as *good-looking, loyal,* and *intelligent* were correlated with one another in the ratings of both sexes.

In order to examine the relationship between the results of the perceptual experiment and the phonetic correlates, Pearson's correlations were calculated between trait ratings and the selected phonetic measures, separately for the two sexes (see Table 15–1). Generally speaking, the correlational patterns between trait items and phonetic measures were the same for the two sexes: degrees of laryngeal constriction were correlated with quite a few positive trait items (e.g., *good-looking, loyal, intelligent*), whereas degrees of larynx lowering were correlated with only a few items. In addition, the direction of the correlations was also shared between the two sexes. Below I examine the correlational patterns more closely in terms of the phonetic measures.

The degree of laryngeal constriction had the largest number of significant correlations with trait items: 10 items for male voice actors and 12 for female voice actors. The direction of the correlations was negative, suggesting that an increased degree of laryngeal constriction elicited lower ratings for favorable traits, which conforms to the prediction that participants would attribute less favorable traits and characteristics to voices exhibiting non-neutral supraglottic states. We can also say that one supraglottic state,

Table 15–1. Correlations between perceptual experiment items and phonetic measures

	Auditory measures						Acoustic measures					
	Laryngeal const.		Larynx lower.		Breathy		Mean F0		F0 SD		F2 for /a/	
Trait items	M	F	M	F	M	F	M	F	M	F	M	F
Physical char.												
Big	-.37	-.18	.69*	.58*	-.02*	-.04	-.31	-.17	-.58	-.14	-.93**	-.35
Good–looking	-.93**	-.76**	.25	-.05	.50	.39	-.87**	.69**	-.58	-.19	-.21	.37
Personality												
Brave	-.67	-.60**	.68*	.26	.24	.29	-.56	.18	-.66	-.01	-.75*	-.36
Selfless	-.59	-.76**	.07	.01	.43	.60**	-.09	.64**	-.57	-.25	-.35	.29
Loyal	-.82**	-.84**	.22	.02	.40	.60**	-.33	.56*	-.68*	-.26	-.38	.21
Perseverant	.19	-.74**	.02	-.06	.23	.37	.50	.64**	.02	-.21	.00	.27
Intelligent	-.90**	-.64**	.46	.19	.15	.50*	-.82**	.38	-.71*	-.25	-.44	.20
Strong	-.53	.02	.78*	.63**	.16	-.21	-.59	-.46	-.53	.12	-.77*	-.54*
Sociable	-.23	-.56*	-.57	-.18	.70*	.16	.14	.62**	.06	-.13	.32	.30
Calm	-.89**	-.66**	.11	-.18	.37	.77**	-.76*	.38	-.65	-.19	-.27	.18
Curious	.34	.00	-.58	-.35	.35	-.13	.24	.12	.80**	.15	.88**	.04
Conscientious	-.69*	-.81**	.38	.06	.13	.56*	-.21	.63**	-.78*	-.29	-.59	.29
Sympathetic	-.80**	-.82**	.07	-.06	.65	.60**	-.56	.58*	-.45	-.22	-.13	.24
Emotion												
Positive	-.30	-.17	-.56	-.53*	.35	.36	-.16	.12	.12	-.01	.38	.20
Vocal char.												
High–pitched	.12	-.37	-.82**	-.33	.22	.11	.28	.76**	.27	-.09	.75*	.58*
Loud	.85**	.37	.08	.26	-.53	-.70**	.72*	-.06	.56	-.02	-.02	-.04
Relaxed	-.67*	-.03	-.07	-.47*	.42	.36	-.74*	-.16	-.28	.00	.03	.03
Pleasant	-.86**	-.76**	.21	-.22	.54	.60**	-.86**	.47*	-.45	-.07	-.18	.23
Attractive	-.82**	-.82**	.31	-.11	.45	.56*	-.88**	.57*	-.41	-.13	-.15	.32

Note. M (males): *n* = 9, except mean F0 and F0 SD, where *n* = 8. F (females): *n* = 18. * *p* < .05. ** *p* < .01.

laryngeal constriction, played an important role in laypersons' perceptions of heroic and villainous voices in the present experiment.

There were other phonetic measures that showed similar correlation patterns with trait items for degrees of laryngeal constriction, namely degrees of breathiness and mean F0 for female voice actors and, to a lesser extent, mean F0 and SD of F0 for male voice actors. The direction of correlations for breathiness and mean F0 for females is opposite to that for laryngeal constriction; the breathier or higher-pitched the voices were, the higher the ratings they received for favorable traits such as *selfless*, although the correlations were generally slightly weaker compared to those for laryngeal constriction. As for the two F0-related measures for males, a smaller number of significant but slightly weaker correlations with trait items emerged. The direction of correlations was negative, suggesting that a higher mean F0 and a wider F0 range led to negative ratings for items such as *intelligent*.

With respect to the other supraglottic state, larynx lowering, a smaller number of significant correlations with trait items were found. The items with significant correlations for both sexes were the physical characteristic *big* and the personality trait *strong*. The direction of correlations was positive, meaning that an increased degree of larynx lowering elicited the impression of greater size and strength from listeners. Therefore, we can say that while the number of significant correlations with trait items was not high, larynx lowering also played a role in laypersons' perceptions.

Another phonetic measure that showed similar, although weaker, correlation patterns with trait items for degrees of larynx lowering for both sexes was mean F2 for /a/. The direction of correlation for this measure was the opposite of that for larynx lowering; that is, a higher mean F0 for /a/ elicited lower ratings for *big* and *strong* (and higher ratings for *high-pitched*).

As has been partially noted in the foregoing discussion, mean F0 seems to elicit different correlation patterns between the two sexes; for males, a lower F0 elicited positive impressions for such items as *good-looking, intelligent,* and (vocally) *attractive*; whereas for females, a higher F0 was associated with more positive ratings for such items as *good-looking, selfless,* and *conscientious*, as well as *high-pitched*. This difference is consistent with van Bezooijen's (1995) questionnaire survey about ideal pitches in Japanese and Dutch cultures, which suggested that there was a strong differentiation between the ideal man and woman in Japanese culture.

Lastly, no phonetic measure used in the present analysis was strongly correlated with the item *positive emotion*. It seems necessary to consider other phonetic measures in order to be able to quantify emotional speech phonetically. However, it is also possible that ratings for this item are not linearly correlated with phonetic properties (see Section 5.2.8 of Teshigawara, 2003, and 2004, for the possibility of combining voice types with F0-related measures).

In summary, the goal of my perceptual experiment was to investigate whether auditorily identified characteristics (laryngeal constriction and larynx lowering, along with other articulatory characteristics) contribute to listeners' perceptions of good and bad characters. The hypothesis that participants would attribute less favorable physical traits, personality traits, emotional states, and vocal characteristics to speakers who exhibited non-neutral supraglottic states was partially confirmed, in that the degree of laryngeal constriction was negatively correlated with ratings of favorable traits. The study also confirmed that supraglottic states (especially degrees of laryngeal constriction), which played an important role in differentiating heroic and villainous voices in the auditory analysis, played an important role in participants' perceptions of characters as well.

Conclusions and Future Studies

In this study, I investigated phonetic properties of Japanese *anime* voices through (a) auditory analysis, using a modified version of Laver's (1994; 2000) framework for voice quality description (Teshigawara, 2003; 2004); and (b) a perceptual experiment with lay Japanese listeners, using a selection of content-masked *anime* voices. In the auditory analysis, I found that supraglottic states, namely laryngeal constriction and larynx lowering, played an important role in differentiating the articulatory characteristics of heroic and villainous voices. There also appeared to be a relationship between the articulatory profile of negative emotions and that of villainous voices. The perceptual experiment revealed that supraglottic states, especially laryngeal constriction, correlated well with participants' ratings of favorable trait items, which suggests the importance of these articulatory characteristics in listeners' perception of voices.

The results of the present study can be extended in a variety of directions in future research, a few of which I suggest below. First, the present results are based on a small number of samples. Therefore, it is necessary to confirm whether these results can be generalized to a larger sample. Second, beyond a few simple measurements, this study did not involve acoustic analysis. The nature of the data provides numerous challenges to acoustic analysis: the voices are produced by speakers with different vocal tract lengths, portraying characters with physical traits, ages, and genders that often differ from their own, under unknown recording conditions. In order to eliminate such confounding factors and capture the acoustic characteristics of the articulatory behaviors of interest, it would be necessary to record speakers who can control the supraglottic states and other articulatory behaviors of interest under consistent recording conditions. Third, the auditory descriptions in the present study should be compared with physiological observations of the pharyngeal and laryngeal areas in order to confirm their validity. Teshigawara and Murano (2004) is one example of an attempt to provide measurements of supraglottic states using MRI. Finally, considering that there appears to be some universality with respect to emotional speech (Scherer, Banse, & Wallbott, 2001), and that universal characteristics of emotional speech have some relevance to vocal stereotypes of good and bad characters, it would be interesting to see whether the present findings can be extended to other cultures. Preliminary results of an ongoing study in an Israeli setting is discussed in Chapter 10.

References

Abercrombie, D. (1967). *Elements of general phonetics*. Edinburgh, UK: Edinburgh University Press.

Addington, D. W. (1968). The relationship of selected vocal characteristics to personality perception. *Speech Monographs, 35,* 492-503.

Campbell, N., & Mokhtari, P. (2003). Voice quality: The 4th prosodic dimension. In M. J. Sole, D. Recasens & J. Romero (Eds.), *Proceedings of the 15th International Congress of Phonetic Sciences, Barcelona, Spain* (pp. 2417-2420). Adelaide, Australia: Casual Productions.

Edmondson, J. A., & Esling, J. H. (2005). *The valves of the throat and their functioning in tone, vocal register, and stress: Laryngoscopic case studies*. Manuscript submitted for publication.

Erickson, D., Yoshida, K., Menezes, C., Fujino, A., Mochida, T., & Shibuya, Y. (2006). An exploratory study of some acoustic and articulatory characteristics of *sad* speech. *Phonetica, 63,* 1-25.

Esling, J. H. (1978). *Voice quality in Edinburgh: A sociolinguistic and phonetic study*. Unpublished doctoral dissertation, University of Edinburgh, UK.

Esling, J. H. (1994). Voice quality. In *The encyclopedia of language and linguistics* (Vol. 9, pp. 4950-4953). Oxford, UK: Pergamon Press.

Esling, J. H. (1999). The IPA categories "pharyngeal" and "epiglottal": Laryngoscopic observations of pharyngeal articulations and larynx height. *Language and Speech, 42,* 349-372.

Esling, J. H., & Harris, J. G. (2005). States of the glottis: An articulatory phonetic model based on laryngoscopic observations. In W. J. Hardcastle & J. M. Beck (Eds.), *A figure of speech: A festschrift for John Laver* (pp. 347-383). Mahwah, NJ: Lawrence Erlbaum Associates.

Friend, M., & Farrar, M. J. (1994). A comparison of content-masking procedures for obtaining judgments of discrete affective states. *Journal of the Acoustical Society of America, 96,* 1283-1290.

Fujimoto, M., & Maekawa, K. (2003). Variation in phonation types due to paralinguistic information: An analysis of high-speed video images. In M. J. Sole, D. Recasens & J. Romero (Eds.), *Proceedings of the 15th International Congress of Phonetic Sciences, Barcelona, Spain* (pp. 2401-2404). Adelaide, Australia: Casual Productions.

Gobl, C., & Ní Chasaide, A. (2003). The role of voice quality in communicating emotion, mood and attitude. *Speech Communication, 40,* 189-212.

Hecht, M. A., & LaFrance, M. (1995). How (fast) can I help you? Tone of voice and telephone operator efficiency in interactions. *Journal of Applied Social Psychology, 25,* 2086-2098.

Laver, J. (1980). *The phonetic description of voice quality*. Cambridge, UK: Cambridge University Press.

Laver, J. (1994). *Principles of phonetics*. Cambridge, UK: Cambridge University Press.

Laver, J. (2000). Phonetic evaluation of voice quality. In R. D. Kent & M. J. Ball (Eds.), *Voice quality measurement* (pp. 37-48). San Diego, CA: Singular.

Laver, J., Wirz, S., Mackenzie, J., & Hiller, S. M. (1991). A perceptual protocol for the analysis of vocal profiles. In J. Laver (Ed.), *Gift of speech: Papers in the analysis of speech and voice* (pp. 264-280). Edinburgh, UK: Edinburgh University Press. (Original work published 1981).

Levi, A. (1998). The new American hero: Made in Japan. In M. L. Kittelson (Ed.), *The soul of popular culture: Looking at contemporary heroes, myths, and monsters* (pp. 68-83). Chicago: Open Court.

McCrae, R. R., & Costa, P. T., Jr. (1987). Validation of the five-factor model of personality across instruments and observers. *Journal of Personality and Social Psychology, 52,* 81-90.

Nass, C., & Lee, K. M. (2001). Does computer-synthesized speech manifest personality? Experimental tests of recognition, similarity-attraction, and consistency-attraction. *Journal of Experimental Psychology: Applied, 7*, 171–181.

Poedjosoedarmo, G. (1986). The symbolic significance of pharyngeal configuration in Javanese speech: Some preliminary notes. *NUSA, Linguistic Studies in Indonesian and Languages in Indonesia, 25*, 31–37.

Ray, G. B. (1986). Vocally cued personality prototypes: An implicit personality theory approach. *Communication Monographs, 53*, 266–276.

Scherer, K. R. (1986). Vocal affect expression: A review and a model for future research. *Psychological Bulletin, 99*, 143–165.

Scherer, K. R., Banse, R., & Wallbott, H. G. (2001). Emotion inferences from vocal expression correlate across languages and cultures. *Journal of Cross-Cultural Psychology, 32*, 76–92.

Scherer, K. R., Feldstein, S., Bond, R. N., & Rosenthal, R. (1985). Vocal cues to deception: A comparative channel approach. *Journal of Psycholinguistic Research, 14*, 409–425.

Teshigawara, M. (2003). Voices in Japanese animation: A phonetic study of vocal stereotypes of heroes and villains in Japanese culture. Unpublished doctoral dissertation, University of Victoria, Canada. [Retrievable from http://web.uvic.ca/ling/students/graduate/Dissertation_Teshigawara.pdf]

Teshigawara, M. (2004). Vocally expressed emotions and stereotypes in Japanese animation: Voice qualities of the bad guys compared to those of the good guys. *Journal of the Phonetic Society of Japan, 8*(1), 60–76.

Teshigawara, M., & Murano, E. Z. (2004). Articulatory correlates of voice qualities of good guys and bad guys in Japanese *anime*: An MRI study. In S. H. Kim & D. H. Youn (Eds.), *Proceedings of INTERSPEECH 2004—8th ICSLP* (vol. 2, pp. 1249–1252). Jeju Island, Korea: Sujin Printing.

van Bezooijen, R. (1995). Sociocultural aspects of pitch differences between Japanese and Dutch women. *Language and Speech, 38*, 253–265.

van Bezooijen, R., & Boves, L. (1986). The effects of low-pass filtering and random splicing on the perception of speech. *Journal of Psycholinguistic Research, 15*, 403–417.

Yarmey, A. D. (1993). Stereotypes and recognition memory for faces and voices of good guys and bad guys. *Applied Cognitive Psychology, 7*, 419–431.

Zuckerman, M., & Miyake, K. (1993). The attractive voice: What makes it so? *Journal of Nonverbal Behavior, 17*, 119–135.

CHAPTER 16

Preserving Vocal Emotions while Dubbing into Brazilian Portuguese

An Analysis of Characters' Voices in Children's Movies

Mara Behlau and Gisele Gasparini

Abstract

The goal of this chapter is to demonstrate the process of dubbing children's movies into Brazilian Portuguese. We show how vocal emotions are preserved and how the originally intended voice quality is retained in the dubbing and localization processes of foreign movies into Brazilian Portuguese language and to explore some other challenges of dubbing English material—for the Brazilian audiences. The advisory role of the voice pathologist in this process and the dubbing industry is demonstrated.

Introduction

The history of dubbing in Brazil dates from 1950 when the first Brazilian movies were dubbed into Brazilian Portuguese at the Estúdios Vera Cruz (Vera Cruz Studios). At that time, the Brazilian actors had to dub their voices twice because of the poor quality of direct sound capture. After completion of the initial dubbing, the movie was reproduced again, but this time on a large screen at the studios' theater, with all of the actors involved in the same scene replacing the originally recorded voices by following the scenes, take by take.

Dubbing was performed for two main reasons: (a) to value the national language, according to the "nationalism philosophy" dominant in the 1950s, and (b) to attract more customers to the theaters due to audience reading limitations. By 1964, Brazil introduced a federal law (Leonardo, 2004) requiring the dubbing of all films and cartoons for TV showing. This law is no longer enforced, and TV films can be seen both in the original language and Brazilian Portuguese, using a SAP key. Some TV stations still show dubbed features, because of a variety of reasons, such as social-economic preferences, prevalence of slow readers, and the notion that a busy audience will prefer to listen to the dubbed version (while watching TV at home) and not be stuck in front of a TV monitor. In movie theaters however films, cartoons, and *anime* directed to children and adolescents are shown in both versions, original and dubbed.

The Dubbing Process

In Brazil, all dubbing actors need to be licensed by a governmental institution that legalizes this activity, getting the des-ignation DRT register. Because Brazilian law prohibits employment of adolescents under 16 years of age, with exceptions for special conditions, children cannot usually work as dubbers. This means that children's voices are replaced by adult females mimicking infantile vocal production. Besides legal limitations, there is also an economical reason for not hiring children for dubbing purposes, namely speed—as adults dub faster—and economy because all dubbing is paid on an hourly basis. Dubbing studios are centrally located around the cities Sao Paulo and Rio de Janeiro, and now employ close to 400 actors, because TV cable introduction required a great amount of specialized professional voices for documentaries, soap operas, sitcoms, films, and the traditionally dubbed material, such as films and cartoons. This workforce is very busy and often requires help from a voice pathologist to maintain vocal health and employment.

A good dubbing is essential to the success and economical survival of the film, series, or animation. The classic example of this situation in Brazil is the huge success of the Japanese series, *National Kid,* which had two superb dubbing versions, one in 1960 and another in 1990. It is interesting to comment that the character of Prof. Masao Hato (the central hero of the series) was dubbed both times 30 years apart by the same actor, Emerson Camargo, to preserve the vocal identity of the character, as Mr. Camargo's vocal quality was essential to the sustaining success of the Brazilian version.

There is no formal dubbing course or education in Brazil; however, occasionally studios organize short courses to either identify new dubbers or to develop dubbers' abilities. Besides being a professional registered actor, the prerequisites to work as a dubber require special skills such as fast auditory processing, vocal flexibility for producing several different voices, accurate "vocal trigger" or an ability to interpret correctly moods and feelings, ability to play different parts within the same feature, excellent reading skills, fast word replacement strategy to improve last moment changes, precise speech articulation rate and rhythm, as well as superb visual-vocal synchronization (Behlau et al., 2005).

Contrary to famous screen actors, dubbers cannot have an idiosyncratic vocal quality that can be easily identified by the listener. This is based on the idea that it would be weird to listen to Lucile Ball's Brazilian voice and then recognize the same voice quality in the Brazilian character of Virginia Woolf played by Nicole Kidman (*The Hours*) or Meryl Streep's character in *Sophie's Choice*. Therefore, the preferred voice of a dubber is the voice of the actor with a wide vocal plasticity, and with the ability of producing fast changes in all vocal and speech settings (Behlau, 2001).

Dubbers not only have to master the dubbing techniques but also to conquer the public by an immediate interpretation of characters' psychological traits, context and circumstances, facial expression of the original actor, and countless details included in the original version, using only his or her voice. Since there is no straight synchronization between articulatory movements and speech output of the original and dubbed versions, the sound of the voice acquires a unique importance for blending the image to the ongoing message. The public needs to have the illusion that the movie was originally recorded in the dubbed language.

The perceived importance of the dubbing industry is enormous on the Brazilian public, to the point that in 2003, the first Dubbing Oscar was established (Yamato Award, 2005). While five thousand people attended the first award ceremony, the second award ceremony held only a year later had a total of 11,000 people who voted on the nominees using Internet. So far, a total of 13 awards were given to recognize the excellence of the dubbing actors, with four awards going to *Finding Nemo* (best dubbing, best translation, best actress in a supporting role, and best sound technician). In 2005, at the third ceremony, *The Incredibles* won best dubbing and best actress.

Typically, the dubbing process comprises of the following five-step sequence: Step 1, specialized translation of the original movie; Step 2, selection of the actors; Step 3, the actual dubbing process; Step 4, the monitoring of oral precision and interpretation, and finally Step 5, technical equalization.

Step 1. Specialized Translation of the Original Movie

The translation process starts with transferring the written script into the target language. This involves understanding of all dubbing constraints, such as speech duration, speech rate, and the range and character of labial movements to avoid creating artificial or even ridiculous situations in the dubbed version. To help to achieve expected results, a translator team specialized in localizing the original text is employed. Because the use of proper vocabulary is one of the most essential aspects for dubbing success, some of the text must be entirely changed (localized, not translated verbatim) and the original films in the English, Japanese, and Italian languages are treated accordingly to correspond to the target Brazilian Portuguese.

For example, localization-translation problems are often paramount, when dubbing from a concise type language (e.g., English) into Brazilian Portuguese, which requires on the average 40% more words per equal expression. Thus, to translate a short sentence from English to a short sentence in Brazilian Portuguese and match the lip motions and still retain the message may be very challenging. This is the reason why in some English films dubbed to Portuguese the dubbing actor needs to speak much faster as not to overrun the frame numbers on the screen.

An even more difficult task is to dub from a Japanese feature because Portuguese is a more descriptive language and a larger number of words are used to say the same sentence.

On the other hand, Italian movies are easier to handle because of the similarity of sounds and length of sentences between these two Latin languages, which allows a closer version to the original. Because the national and cultural specificity of Brazil has to be taken into account when preparing films for dubbing, Portuguese language from Portugal is not accepted for Brazilian audiences. The same applies to the Spanish language. Jokes, proverbs, slang, and idiomatic expressions have to be modified to fit the audience. For example, in *The Incredibles*, when Syndrome meets the Incredibles, he says, "You married the Elastigirl! You got busy! It's a whole family of supers!" The same segment in Portuguese was translated as, "You married the Elastigirl! You've no TV at home! Look at that, a whole super-offspring! It's too good to be true!" spoken with a rural accent.

It is easy to notice that the Brazilian Portuguese text is longer than the original English text, and the joke of having no TV at home and spending time making babies is a Brazilian comment on big families, which makes no sense when spoken in the English text. Because larger families in Brazil live predominantly in rural areas, the use of a specific rural dialect/accent is an especially powerful joke well understood by the Brazilian audience. If we consider that in the U.S. version, the Incredibles is a stressed urban family, it cannot truly correspond to a laid back, baby producing Brazilian type family. So the translation has to include cultural preferences and psychodynamic issues as well. Therefore, localization and not just translation is of paramount import for the dubbing actor to understand and to succeed.

Step 2. Selection of Dubbers

The dubbing director is the professional responsible for the selection of actors, who can be assisted by a voice pathologist. The criteria selection is not always based on matching the original actors' voice. In some cases the dubbed voice fits the character better than the voice of the original actor. As an example, we cite Tom Selleck (whose voice is slightly higher in pitch than the Brazilian ear prefers), who was dubbed into Brazilian Portuguese by an actor with a lower voice fundamental. Interestingly enough, when Mr. Selleck was at the Brazilian Carnival and saw *Magnum P.I.* in a Brazilian version, he commented to the press, "That's the voice I always wanted to have!"

At other times, the actor is selected to match the original vocal characteristics. Bruce Willis is an example whose strong and marked personality prevails on the dubber's choice. Another particular situation is when a character will be repeated in a series, such as Superman; the selected dubber will follow the series to ensure body-voice fidelity in the dubbed language. In this case the dubber is known as the *X-puppet* (Superman's puppet).

The successful dubbing director has seen the film, has checked the translation, and usually knows all the background information about the original material, including actors, characters, history, critics, reviews, and other particulars. The director has an in-depth knowledge of the dubbers' vocal profile and makes a selection on the basis of the original film and on the knowledge of the talents of the dubbing actor. Some dubbers are good at comedies; others can easily disguise their voices and can be used for dubbing several characters in a single movie (which is taken into consideration for lower budgets and practical reasons); some women are skilled at playing children and old ladies, reducing costs and timing, while other actors are not. After casting, the director summarizes the needs to the dubber and guides the interpretation, which is usually done face to face on a single dubber basis. Usually, the dubber has not seen the movie and will have to work with the information given by the director, who explains each scene and gives overview information on the script. The consulting voice pathologist needs to know the vocal profile of the entire film to advise the actor about the techniques to avoid risks.

Step 3. The Actual Dubbing Process

In contrast to what is believed, dubbers whose characters share the scene do not work together in the studio; therefore, the dubbing process is lonely work done by the director and a single dubber at a time. During the actual dubbing process,

the sequence of the original scenes is not followed, which means that a vocally demanding segment can be scheduled for the beginning of the working session, when the voice has not been subjected to vocal load (Izdebski, 1999; 2005). The director explains the scene, the technician plays it on a monitor, the dubber sees the scene on the monitor for the first time, and command is given: "Record." The dubber uses a single-ear headphone to monitor the sentence onset and starts speaking, controlling the sound synchronization (earphone on dominant ear), the image on screen, and his or her own voice through the unaided ear. The actor must assure the match of the dubber's voice with facial and body expressions visible on the screen produced by the original actor. This difficult act requires a smart approach by the dubbing actor. A 100-minute film usually takes a total of 26 dubbing hours. The better the dubber, the lower the number of times he has to repeat the recording scene.

Step 4. Monitoring of Oral Precision and Interpretation

Another task of the director is to verify both articulatory approximation and quality of interpretation. There is a need to match body, personality, social class, ethnicity, gender, and age of characters. Some features are not universal, so the director has to be competent enough to perceive what should be changed to improve understanding in a dubbed version and what has to be kept constant to respect the core of the original material. Although the translation has already been adapted for dubbing, sometimes last moment changes, including word replacement, must be added to match lip movements and give more credibility to the dubbed version.

Step 5. Technical Equalization

The sound technician has the responsibility to carry out crucial sound equalization. A special Dubbing Oscar category for this process reflects the importance of the sound. Furthermore, when needed a musical track can be completely replaced, and new songs and music may be created to fit better the localized character of the foreign soap opera or sitcom series. At times, however, versions of original songs are added and sound effects are modified or even completely changed.

From Disney Classics to Pixar Animations

Dubbing of cartoons and *anime* is of particular interest to voice pathologists, because children constitute a huge market and child actors are not permitted. Dubbers—usually female actors—will have the challenge of lending their voices to a wide range of child characters, while both adult man and women actors become the voices of kings and queens, tea pots, and clocks. Animals and monsters are hard challenges and subjected to hundreds of cultural particularities.

Particularly for children, the vocal psychodynamics of the cartoon character have a fundamental role in understanding and transmitting emotional and psychological features that must appeal to the little viewer. *Vocal psychodynamics* refers to the psychological impact produced by a specific vocal quality, which comprises a wide vocal repertoire and vocal mode selection (from whispering to pressed phonation), to speech rate, prosodic values, and rhythm. The term vocal psychodynamics was proposed by Moses (1948) in association with what he called *creative hearing*, which means the ability of the clinician to consciously use listening to describe the impression transmitted from a vocal set of parameters. This pioneer in our field organized a still valid theory, based on the material from his clinical observations of several types of voices and their impact on the listener (Moses, 1954).

To understand the process of selecting voices for dubbing, which includes several aspects of vocal quality and the psychological impact of the selected options on the viewer, a comparison of 25 characters from eight Disney Classic Films was performed by 20 voice pathologists, at Centro de Estudos da Voz (CEV), Sao Paulo, Brazil (Colnago, 1999; Colnago & Behlau, in press). The vocal parameters were described and a psychodynamic analysis was performed. The selected films were *Cinderella* (1950), *Sleeping Beauty* (1959), *The Little Mermaid* (1989), *Beauty and the Beast* (1991), *Aladdin* (1992), *The Lion King* (1994), *Hercules* (1997), and *Mulan* (1998). After extensive analyses of the scenes, the trained Brazilian listeners concluded that the dubbed voices reflected cultural aspects and limitations of the original spoken text into the target language. Vocal quality, resonance, and vocal psychodynamics were quite different in both versions to achieve a more culturally oriented mood, acceptable by the cultural standards of the Brazilian audience. On the other hand, features such as articulation, pitch, loudness, intonation, glottal attack types, and speech rate were found to be similar, as independent studies of universals by others (Pittam & Scherer, 1993; Scherer, 1995) have suggested that these parameters represent a more fixed physiological set; hence, they were less susceptible to cultural standards.

As an example, in the classic *The Lion King*, the character profile of young Simba can be presented as a curious, naughty, bold, and naïve little lion, while Mufasa, his father, can be presented as a responsible, careful, family and clan oriented leader, yet powerful, strong, upright, bold, and sensitive. The Brazilian voice pathologists analyzed Simba as a spoiled and annoying lion in the original version but as a happy lion in the dubbed version, whereas Mufasa was analyzed as powerful and controlling in English, but less powerful yet serious and controlling in the Brazilian version. This difference underscores the parental relationships differences in father figures between the United States and Brazil. A comparison of some crucial parameters of these two characters, illustrating the differences between the original and dubbed versions, is shown in Figure 16–1.

As another example, in the classic *Beauty and the Beast*, the character profile of Beauty can be presented as a delicate, kind, sweet, optimistic, and unmaterialistic young lady, while the Beast is a conflicted being, full of hurt, lonely, and both threatening and gentle. The Brazilian voice pathologists analyzed Beauty in the original version as fragile and conflicting, and similarly as fragile, but less conflicting and more affectionate in the dubbed version. On the other hand, in the original version the Beast was considered threatening at first, and aggressive with extreme vocal variation throughout the different scenes; meanwhile, the Brazilian Beast was dubbed with the emotions

of sweetness and rigidity but without the extreme vocal variations he demonstrated in the English version. A comparison of some parameters of these two characters in the original and dubbed versions is shown in Figure 16–2.

A new era of animation was launched by Pixar Animation Studios that included many breakthroughs in animated filmmaking (Nelson, 2005; Pixar, 2005; Wikipedia, 2005). For the new movies, Pixar employed three core proprietary software systems, named (a) Marionette: animation software system for modeling, animating, and lighting; (b) Ringmaster: a production management software system for scheduling, coordinating, and tracking a computer animation project; (c) RenderMan: a rendering software system for high-quality, photo-realistic image synthesis. The use of these unique softwares has produced a quality of sound and image never seen before. The top quality of these animations also involves the role of famous Hollywood actors hired for narrating/acting in the original version. This imposed an extra difficulty and a higher responsibility for the Brazilian dubbing industry. In some situations, famous Brazilian actors were also employed, but as said before, not all actors make great dubbers.

At the XV Annual Pacific Voice Conference and First International Pacific Voice & Speech Foundation, Pixar Animation Studios Conference on Voice Quality, analyses of three animations dubbed into Brazilian Portuguese were presented (Behlau, 2005). These included *Monsters Inc.* (2001), *Finding Nemo* (2003), and *The Incredibles* (2004). Analysis of *Monsters Inc.* showed marked differences for all characters except for Boo, who still had an unquestionable baby voice quality. Since Boo is a baby, and babies are under less cultural influence, similar

Young Simba	Original Version	Dubbed Version
Vocal quality	Nasal and strained	Infantile quality
Resonance	Laryngopharyngeal focus	High focus
Articulation	Misarticulated	Neutral
Loudness	Loud	Adequate to loud
Pitch	Adequate	Adequate
Intonation	Rich	Repetitive/rising
Glottal attack	Hard	Adequate
Speech rate	Regular	Regular
Mufasa	**Original Version**	**Dubbed Version**
Vocal quality	Low-pitched	Low-pitched
Resonance	Laryngopharyngeal focus	Laryngopharyngeal focus
Articulation	Precise	Precise
Loudness	Adequate	Adequate
Pitch	Low	Low
Intonation	Variable	Variable
Glottal attack	Adequate	Adequate
Speech rate	Adequate	Slow to adequate

Figure 16–1. Comparison of vocal parameters for Simba (the Lion King as a young animal) and Mufasa (his powerful father) from the Disney classic *The Lion King*, original and Brazilian Portuguese dubbed versions. The results represent 70% or more agreement among 20 trained listeners (voice pathologists).

vocal parameters were identified in both language versions.

In contrast, voices in *Monsters Inc.* are highly influenced by culture and folk tales. The Brazilian monsters showed a more modulated voice range including usage of vocal fry, while the American monsters presented a quasi-normal vocal quality and flat melody. One specific sample showed almost opposite parameters: the Abominable Snowman in the original version presented a normal vocal quality, with low pitch and discrete tension, while in the Brazilian Portuguese

Beauty	Original Version	Dubbed Version
Vocal quality	*Breathy*	*Nasal*
Resonance	Nasal	Nasal
Articulation	Precise	Precise
Loudness	Adequate	Adequate
Pitch	Adequate	Adequate
Intonation	Repetitive	Repetitive
Glottal attack	Soft	Soft
Speech rate	Adequate	Adequate
Beast	**Original Version**	**Dubbed Version**
Vocal quality	*Variable (strained/breathy)*	*Soft*
Resonance	Oral	Balanced
Articulation	Adequate	Adequate
Loudness	Excessive	Loud
Pitch	Low	Low
Intonation	Rich	Rich
Glottal attack	Breathy/hard	Hard
Speech rate	Variable	Adequate

Figure 16–2. Comparison of vocal parameters for Beauty and the Beast from the Disney classic *Beauty and the Beast*, original and Brazilian Portuguese dubbed versions. The results represent 70% or more of agreement among 20 trained listeners (voice pathologists). Different vocal options are marked in *italics*.

version it was played with a range of normal to tense voices, all in higher pitch and with more overall tension.

Analysis of *Finding Nemo* in the original version showed all characters sounding older and more serious than in the dubbed one. When comparing both versions, the breathing sounds of the fish in the ocean were eliminated in the Brazilian Portuguese version. Turtles were regionally dubbed with a *carioca* accent (a dialect of a district of Rio de Janeiro). The voice of Mr. Ray, the teacher, was dysphonic and he had a tired vocal quality in English but a normal and energetic voice in the Brazilian version, which seems to reflect the high prevalence of dysphonia among the teachers in the United States (Roy, Merrill, Thibeault, Gray, & Smith, 2004).

Analysis of *The Incredibles*, which was also a huge success in Brazil (15 million viewers in the first 15 weeks), showed a more marked difference than in *Finding Nemo*, as the characters in this movie represented human beings, and hence a greater cross-cultural diversity between Brazil and the United States was evident. All the elderly characters were very different; the English speaking characters sounded more asthenic than the Brazilian Portuguese, who had higher pitch and volume with instability. The villain Syndrome in the English version shows a hoarse-breathy voice, with an authoritative attitude, while in the Portuguese rendition, there is an excessive vocal modulation, divergent use of register, and an apparent lack of vocal parameters control. The villain in the Portuguese film expressed more openly his sad history and conflict during adulthood, according to the analysis of the Brazilian voice pathologists.

In conclusion, dubbing is a mixture of highly technological skills, talented professionals, and knowledge of cross-cultural features, all blended with art. Voice pathologists can be of profound help both in selecting the best dubbers for the target language and also in finding less risky strategies for vocally challenging situations. Adaptations are often made to appeal to the new audience. Major and original comical elements can be lost in the effort to ensure comprehension. In spite of both the challenges and limitations, the success of animated films is guaranteed.

References

Behlau, M. (2001). Vozes preferidas: Considerações sobre opções vocais nas profissões. *Fono Atual 2001, 4,* 10–14.

Behlau, M. (2005, March). *Comparison of dubbing in Brazilian Portuguese and original voices of characters in children's movies.* Paper presented at the XV Annual Pacific Voice Conference and First International Pacific Voice & Speech Foundation, Pixar Animation Studios Conference on Voice Quality. Emeryville, CA.

Behlau, M., Feijó, D., Madazio, G., Rehder, M. I., Azevedo, R., & Ferreira, A. E. (2005). Voz profissional: Aspectos gerais e atuação fonoaudiológica. In M. Behlau (Ed.), *Voz. O livro do especialista* (Vol. II, pp. 321–323). Rio de Janeiro, Brazil: Revinter.

Colnago, C. (1999). *Psicodinâmica vocal das vozes utilizadas na dublagem de clássicos Disney nas versões originais e dublada.* [Specialization monograph]. São Paulo, Brazil: CEV.

Colnago, C., & Behlau, M. (in press). Uma comparação das versões original e dublada dos clássicos Disney. In M. Behlau (Ed.), *A voz do especialista* (Vol IV, pp. 13–27.). Rio de Janeiro, Brazil: Revinter.

Izdebski, K. (1999, February). *The voice load test.* Paper presented at the 2nd World Voice Congress and 5th International Symposium on Phonosurgery, Sao Paulo, Brazil.

Izdebski, K. (2005, October). *The voice load test. An objective way to assess vocal pain and vocal fatigue.* Paper presented at the 2005 UCSF Voice Conference, San Francisco, CA.

Izdebski, K., Manace, E. D., & Skiljo-Haris, J. (2001). The challenge of determining work-related voice/speech disabilities in California. In P. H. Dejonkere (Ed.), *Occupational voice—Care and cure* (pp. 149–154). The Hague, Netherlands: Kugler.

Leonardo, H. (2004). A história da dublagem. Parte 1. Retrieved September 26, 2005, from http://www2.uol.com.br/ohayo/dublagem/materia_historia1.shtml

Moses, P. (1948). Vocal analysis. *Archives of Otolaryngology*, *48*, 171–186.

Moses, P. (1954). *The voice of neuroses*. New York: Grune & Stratton.

Pittam, J., & Scherer, K. R. (1993). Vocal expression and communication of emotion. In M. Lewis & J. M. Haviland (Eds.), *Handbook of emotions* (pp. 185–198). New York: Guilford.

Pixar. (2005). What is Renderman? Retrieved September 26, 2005, from http://www.pixar.com/

Roy, N., Merrill, R. M., Thibeault, S., Gray, S. D., & Smith, E. M. (2004). Voice disorders in teachers and the general population: Effects on work performance, attendance, and future career choices. *Journal of Speech, Language, and Hearing Research*, *44*, 542–552.

Scherer, K. R. (1995). Expression of emotion in voice and music. *Journal of Voice*, *9*, 235–248.

Yamato Award. (2005). Yamato award: Oscar da dublagem. Retrieved September 26, 2005, from http://www.animefriends.com.br/mini_oscar.shtml

Wikipedia. (2005). Pixar Animation Studios. Retrieved September 26, 2005, from http://en.wikipedia.org/wiki/Pixar

CHAPTER 17

Voice and Emotions in the Philippine Culture

Juliana Sustento Seneriches

Abstract

This chapter discusses how the Philippines' pre-Hispanic/indogenous culture, its history of colonization, and its traditional child-rearing practices affect the people's languages and their vocalization of emotions.

Introduction

The Philippines, an archipelago of 7107 islands in Southeast Asia off the southeast coast of mainland China and north of Indonesia and Malaysia, is rich grounds in which to study more than a hundred languages (Llamson, 1978) and more than a hundred dialects and how they are used by the 75 million Filipinos to communicate with each other and with other people. Their diverse languages belong to the Malayo-Polynesian family of languages. These languages are mutually unintelligible even though there may be grammatical similarities. Attempts at forming a national language mostly derived from the majority language, Tagalog (spoken by 25% of the populace), produced the Filipino language in 1987 (Ignacio, 1991), which is characterized by an openness to borrowing from the other Philippine languages and foreign languages, mainly English and Spanish. This final attempt is characteristic of how this country has absorbed the languages of its Spanish and American colonizers as well as many of their ways and values. Reminiscent of its Spanish colonizers, the Filipino is known to be expressive and demonstrative of his emotions in contrast to the stereotypic reticent Asian. It must be noted that the Philippines is the only Christian (Catholic) nation in Asia and that English is the next most widely used language in the archipelago, making it one of the main English speaking countries in the world, a legacy of their American colonizers (Cheshire, 1991). Filipino and English are taught side by side in schools, and secondary and college textbooks are written in English. The language of public and government documents is English while local movies, popular in the countryside, use Filipino. Most of the population is Catholic and almost everyone understands each other in English.

At present, the number one source of government revenues is the country's overseas foreign workers or OFWs who, like their seafaring forebears, find hopping from one island/country to another in search of livelihood, education, or reunion with families second nature. Most seek foreign jobs because of the country's dire economic state. When they migrate to other countries, they bring with them the six major languages of their native land: Tagalog, Cebuano, Ilocano, Hiligaynon, Bicol, and Waray. Pampango and Pangasinan are also represented in the United States. Most speak English, which is useful when they migrate to English speaking countries.

It is likewise essential to understand how this country's history of colonization and its archipelagic layout affect vocalization of emotions. Traditional child-rearing practices are also important factors.

Influence of Philippine History on the Language and Vocal Expressions

Pre-Hispanic Language and Beliefs

Before 1521, when Magellan discovered the Philippines for Spain, the Negritos were there first, who are believed to have traversed the ancient land bridges from the Asian mainland via Borneo. These stone age, proto-Malay, pygmy cave dwellers came from the jungles of Malaya and Borneo. They probably had their own language, but presently the Negritos speak the languages of the neighboring lowlands, though still preferring to live and hunt in the forested mountains.

After this land migration, seafaring Asians and Pacific Islanders settled on the many islands as they freely traded with the Negritos and each other. Chinese, East Indians, and Arabs were also traders on the archipelagic sea routes. Most Filipinos today are descendants of these early inter-island settlers. They started their own languages, had their own alphabet (Baybayin), and were most probably trying to devise a mutually understandable language when the Spaniards came and put a stop to this process. The Tagalogs, Ilokanos, and Bicolanos of Luzon (the biggest northern island) and the Cebuanos and Hiligaynons of the Visayas (the middle islands), who comprise about 40% of the present Philippine population, are of Young Malay origin. Those with Indonesian and Polynesian ancestry number around 30%. Minority ethnic groups are the Old Malays and aboriginal Negritos (10%), Chinese (10%), and East Indians (5%). The Arabs introduced Islam in the southern part of the Philippines around 1380. Interestingly, the Muslims of the southern Philippines were never subjugated by the Spaniards. Such diversity can only produce multiple and different languages and accents.

Animistic beliefs in spirits occupying the forests, the mountains, the rivers, and seas were predominant. Today it is common for the Filipino, especially the rural population, to invoke *tabi-tabi* (Hiligaynon), often in fear, when they go through forest paths to ask permission from the spirits to traverse the latter's domain.

The Spanish friars, when they came, deftly incorporated these beliefs into the rituals of their churches (Parkes, 1999), thus making particular Catholic saints the spirits of plentiful harvest, good fishing, healers, etc. Philippine practice of Catholicism is distinctly Filipino, with rituals and outward displays, even lavish foot and fluvial processions and fiestas for the saints, the Infant Jesus, "Mama" Mary, the Black Nazarene, the Holy Family, and the Holy Ghost.

Naturalistic beliefs and healing practices believed to be given by higher powers are still widely practiced, frequently side by side with modern medical practices. Basically spiritual, respectful of their elders, and close to nature, the Filipinos, especially those in the rural areas, still invoke the spirits (and later, God) in healing practices, as in the world renowned work of some 80 psychic surgeons. Expressions like the Hiligaynon *gaba* (a punishment for past misdeeds, especially a disrespectful act towards one's elders) and *kulam* and *hiwit* (use of sorcery to express anger, envy, revenge) showcase emotions in these traditional practices. Rituals with incantations are used for healing and to counter spells, with hope and fear.

The Spanish Colonization

In 1521, Magellan discovered the Philippine archipelago for Spain (Agoncillo & Guerrero, 1977). In 1565, Miguel Lopez de Legazpi started Spain's colonization in earnest. It was a zealous effort to subjugate, exploit, divide, and Christianize the Filipinos that persisted for 333 years and left indelible marks. The brown-skinned Filipino *Indios* were subordinate to the white Spaniards; therefore, Spanish was only taught to a few privileged rich landowners and the beginnings of a common language were summarily squashed. Regional languages and differences were encouraged. Even after their independence, the Filipinos mandated that Spanish be taught in secondary and collegiate curricula. At present, speaking or writing Spanish is still viewed as an upper class achievement or vestige of a rich, superior family past. The speaker accordingly flaunts his accent. Social and class stratification has survived in the languages and voice. Accents of those from the interior and provinces away from the (Hispanic) centers or bigger cities and the Muslims or *Moros* are still considered lower in prestige than those in the centers. Glottal stops are more common in the towns farther away from the big cities, as in Iloilo City. At present, English is the common equalizing language. Why, even the national language, Filipino, spoken with a Visayan accent (without the short *e*, with *o* interchangeable with *u*), is derided by the Tagalogs. The speaker is labeled *promdi* or" from the provinces." Superiority and shaming of the lesser privileged have survived, voiced in their languages.

The Filipinos have embraced the Hispanic open expressiveness of emotions in their speech. They have combined their innate childlike playfulness with this expressiveness and come out the most effusive of all Asians in speech, which is invariably embellished with continuing gestures.

This open expressiveness and playfulness accompanied by childlike faith are uniquely evident in the way they practice their Catholic religion. The singing, the novenas, and the mass have varied local translations with distinctive accents and inflections. There is no merrier Mardi Gras, no more effusive fiestas for the many saints, no more profuse and bigger processions on land and on water, and

no more abundant novenas for the saints. Fiestas are an everyday affair in certain months and can occur simultaneously in different towns and baranggays. Effusiveness and merriment are effectively expressed alongside a childlike faith and devotion in their traditions and songs.

The Catholic religion is in the daily expressions of emotions as in the incredulous, surprised or impressed *Susmariosep* ("Jesus, Mary, Joseph!") or *Marya* ("Mary!"). The sign of the cross with the soft or silent "In the name of the Father and of the Son and of the Holy Ghost" is daily invoked to ward away evil or the pre-Hispanic bad spirits and to convey respect and devotion as one passes a church.

Many Spanish words and inflections have become permanent fixtures in Filipino. The original alphabet (Baybayin) was changed to accommodate Spanish vocalization.

The American Colonization

For 45 years after the Spaniards left, the Americans colonized the archipelago with the genuine intent to train them in self-government, with a view towards future independence. English was taught to everyone in a public school system, thus the present situation of the Philippines being one of the largest English speaking countries in the world.

In their emulation of the colonizers, *Taglish* has evolved, Filipino with English words interspersed, in Filipino accent. The *collegialas* or girls in the private or Catholic school and the upper class have their own affected, cloying way of speaking Taglish, again implying superiority (in closer replication of the colonizer) and invoking the emotion of shame in the less privileged.

English is used in a superior way by the urban people who are more exposed to English media and better English pronunciation than their rural counterparts, who in effect become marginalized. A Filipino's native dialect influences his accent. The Tagalog uses short *a* and *e* and can pronounce these better than the Cebuano who only has *i* and *u* when they both speak in English. Some Filipinos also mix up the *p* with the *f* when they speak in English, creating confusion when they migrate to English speaking countries. When a subject is more important or delicate, the speaker switches from his dialect to English, which somehow is less personal and not potentially threatening. In an ordinary transaction between two people, when one addresses the other in English, it may be viewed as an attempt to put down the other. A colonial mentality makes the Filipino sensitive to being made to feel inferior.

American words have also been incorporated into Filipino. American frankness, however, has not replaced the Filipino polite, roundabout way of speaking, with lots of joking around, laughter, and use of familiarization.

Influence of the Islands

Being an archipelago of 7017 islands, the Philippines have pockets of strong regionalism, with regional customs and languages carried on even upon immigration to other countries. The Spaniards emphasized this archipelago effect in their divide and rule policy. Poor transportation and a poor economy reinforce the relative isolation of the different island and regional groups and foster the need for extended families, the emergence of dominant landholding clans, and the hundreds of languages and dialects. The use of *hiya* or shame to curtail unwanted behavior and to underline superiority becomes more potent in places where individual identities are linked to families known by one another (Tompar-Tiu & Sustento Seneriches, 1995). Accents and inflections underline a feeling of superiority to those closer to the big city, Manila, and shame to others who do not use these accents.

In such a setting, familiarization in the mode of greeting and expressions, the tendency not to make waves and therefore to speak in a roundabout way with jokes interspersed, and the need to be indirect when disagreeing are common and indeed necessary. There's a lot of kidding around and laughter when the topic becomes controversial. The Filipino's communication style is predicated on maintaining a hierarchy of respect and making sure relationships are harmonious. They easily communicate through actions, insinuations, euphemisms, and jokes (Sustento Seneriches, 1995).

Influence of Traditional Child-Rearing Practices in Vocal Expressions

The Oral Phase

The first 2 years of life, in the traditional Philippine practice, are centered on the infant, with everyone in the extended family literally caring for all its needs and whims. The mother shares this chore of caring for the infant with other family members, an elderly aunt, the grandparent, the older siblings; and/or a *yaya* or nanny who may be another designated elder or hired help. The infant is rarely left unattended and is often carried around.

There is warm acceptance of his help-lessness and dependency. He is rarely left to cry for a prolonged period (Sustento Seneriches, 1983).

Breastfeeding is encouraged; feeding is by demand and may even be every 10 to 15 minutes. Weaning is a leisurely pro-cess. In the rural areas, it is not unusual to see a toddler still hanging onto the mother's breast in prolonged physical closeness to her.

The languages are replete with endear-ing terms for the infant and younger family members (as in the Hiligaynon *Nene* and *Toto*), often in baby talk if the sibling is a child. In the same token, the elderly are regarded with respect and caring (as in the Tagalog *Lolo* and *Lola*, spoken distinctly to be heard, followed by *po* or *ho*, accompanied by taking the grandparent's hand and pressing it to one's forehead in greeting). The Tagalogs use *po* and *ho* in every sentence to convey respect to parents, the elders, and those in respected positions (Sus-tento Seneriches, 1987). The Hiligaynons compensate for their lack of *ho* and *po* by their gentle, slow, and languorous way of talking.

This tolerance for closeness encourages the later trait of interdependency among family members. It also gives way to seek-ing familiarity in greeting one another and in getting to know one another. It is not unusual to be asked in greeting "*Kamusta*? Where are you going? Who's going with you?" The tone, though most respectful, invokes familiarity.

The Anal Phase

The same leisurely maturation extends into the next two years of life as the infant becomes a toddler and explores his surroundings with new-found skills. The infant is allowed to wean himself by his own interest in other food or is weaned when the new baby comes. The constant cuddling, caring, and overall physical companionship continue. As he takes his first step, there are people around him to protect him from falling down and to pick him up when he does. He is encouraged to communicate ver-bally and to be sociable.

Toilet training is also in a leisurely manner with the caretaker cleaning up after the child. At this point, there is the inculcation of shame to promote toilet training and conformity. There is much teasing by the adults and other children (Sustento Seneriches & Tompar-Tiu, 1995).

The teaching of respect for one's eld-ers is underlined during this phase and respectful language is taught, with the use of teasing and scolding.

The show of anger is curtailed as the family strives for peaceful coexistence. Anger is expressed in euphemisms, round-about ways of expressing oneself, and the use of jokes. Smooth interpersonal relating is striven for and the ability to get along agreeably with others is a greatly desired and awarded skill. The Hiligaynons add their gentle, slow, and languorous way of talking to mask anger as well. To sidetrack delicate negotiations, as in the negotiation of a marriage between two families, verses and metaphors may be used by the two parties in an arranged sitting. The Tagalogs use poetic debates or *balagtasan* as a form of entertainment (Gonzales, 1989).

Because of this leisurely maturation in the beginning of life, and because the child is not given much responsibility for his actions until late preadolescence, there develops a childlike playfulness even in verbalizing disagreements, in the merrymaking of the fiestas, and in relating to one another.

Commonly Used Sounds and Expressions

Across Filipino languages there are some commonly used sounds and expressions:

1. *Psst* (a hissing sound)—familiarization; catching attention in a hidden way
2. *Hoy*!—to accost, maybe in a teasing way
3. *Uyy*— to tease; to emphasize
4. *O*!—to demonstrate; to give
5. *Sus*!—short for Jesus; an exclamation
6. *Susmaryosep*!—short for Jesus-Maria-Joseph; to express surprise and bewilderment
7. *Marya*! (Mary/Mother Mary)—an exclamation or invocation
8. *Diyos ko*!—My God!
9. *Kamusta*—How are you?
10. *Oo* (Tagalog)/*Huo* (Hiligaynon)— Yes
11. *Bye*—Goodbye

References

Agoncillo, T., & Guerrero, M. (1977). *History of the Filipino People*. Quezon City, Philippines: R.P. Garcia.

Cheshire, J. (1991). *English around the world: Sociolinguistic Perspectives*. Cambridge, UK: Cambridge University Press.

Gonzales, A. (1989). Filipino logic: A preliminary analysis. *Karunungan, 6,* (pp. 71–100).

Ignacio, T. (1991). *Tagalog versus Pilipino versus Filipino*. Paper presented at the conference of the C.E. Smith Museum of Anthropology and the Center for Philippine Studies. Hayward, Calif.: California State University.

Lamson, T. (1978). *Handbook of Philippine language groups*. Quezon City, Philippines: Manila University Press.

Parkes, C. (1999). *Philippines handbook* (3rd ed.). Emeryville, CA: Moon Publications.

Sustento Seneriches, J. (1983). *Practical psychiatry in the Philippine setting*. Iloilo, Philippines: West Visayas State University College of Medicine..

Sustento Seneriches, J. (1987). In E. Lee (Ed.), *Working with Asian Americans* (pp. 101–113). New York: Guilford Press.

Tompar-Tiu, A., & Sustento Seneriches, J. (1995). *Depression and other mental health issues: The Filipino-American experience*. San Francisco: Jossey-Bass.

CHAPTER 18

The Strains of the Voice

Steven Connor

Abstract

The voice is often thought of as a spontaneous feature of the human organism, formed out of the force of meanings and utterances pressing for utterance. This essay suggests that the voice is always an effect of strain or duress—always itself in and arising from a state of tension. The voice is the body's capacity to be stretched out, painfully or ecstatically, beyond itself, beyond the condition of body itself. I consider various figures for this stress: architecture, rhythm, and line.

Introduction

What is a voice? It is a straining of the air.

Before Robert Boyle (1658) had demonstrated and measured the "spring of the air," voice had functioned as just this kind of elastic body. For voice is not simply an emission of the body; it is also the imaginary production of a secondary body, a body double: a "voice-body" (Connor, 2000, pp. 35–42). This voice-body is not inert image—specter, wraith, or indolently wreathing smoke. It is tense and braced with a kind of life. Guy Rosolato (1974, p. 76) has spoken of the power of emanation that belongs to the voice, but the seeming naturalness and irrepressibility of the voice's exuberations should not prevent us noticing that voice is produced through a process that necessarily creates stress, as air is directed under pressure through the larynx and then out through the mouth. As it moves it is modified, bent, detained, accelerated. Everything that is said about the exercise of the voice—by coaches, experts, trainers, and voice professionals of all kinds—implies that it should be easy and relaxed, an effortless effect of the breath. The voice must be produced without inordinate stress that will damage or distort it. Coaches and gurus offer exercises and visualizations designed to free your voice from the cramping, vampiric grip of its bad habits. But there is no voice without strain, without the constraining of sound in general by the particular habits and accidents that, taken collectively, constitute a voice, and the constraining of the body to produce voice. The breath is drawn as a bow is drawn, by applying a force against the resistance of the diaphragm and the intercostal muscles. The power of the voice is the release of the kinetic energy stored in these muscles as they return to their resting positions. But the voice's energy is not simply given out. For there to be voice, there must be a secondary resistance, the impedance or thwarting of this outflow. Where the breath simply escapes, there can be no voice. It is on this basis that phonetics distinguishes between "unvoiced" and "voiced" sounds, like the sibilant *s* and the *z*, which comes about through the addition of voice.

Sound, wrote Aristotle, is a kind of pathos, a suffering. The air is battered, stretched, percussed when there is sound. The voice never simply appears, but is expressed, its shape formed out of resistance.

What resists the voice? The heaviness, the reluctant inertia of things, the world's weary wish to hold its peace. The voice must overcome this lethargy deep down in things. It is a striving, and a disturbance: it subjects the world to strain.

Instress

In English, the word *strain* has a double signification. It can signify the physical stress to which an object or material may be subject, up to, but always short of, the breaking point. But it can also mean a form, kind, pedigree, inherited line, genus, or character, most commonly nowadays in references to the differing strains of a virus. The word strain also once meant a musical phrase or measure. All of these usages of the English word have in common the idea of a filtering; of that which is refined, selected, or in some other way distinguished from a background. Perhaps the action of filtering brings together the functions of selection and of physical stress. The filter selects by physically forcing a single or simple substance, or sequence, out of a more complex ensemble.

We conventionally associate the voice with identity (a voice is often synonymous in French, English, and German with a vote). But this identity is a strain, the product of a pressure, as well as the mark of something that is merely distinguished or distinctive; German *Stimme* also signifies a tuning, or pitching

My voice is said to be my own, because nobody else can use my voice, or be in the place of my voice, without theft or deception. But perhaps this is so not because the voice is my property, but because it is, to borrow Gerard Manley Hopkins's term, my *instress*, the power by which my coherence (which Hopkins named *inscape*) is conveyed or borne out. Extending this to nonvocal objects, as Hopkins does, instress becomes the way in which such objects "voice":

> . . . each hung bell's
>
> Bow swung finds tongue to fling out broad its name;
>
> Each mortal thing does one thing and the same:
>
> Deals out that being indoors each one dwells;
>
> Selves—goes itself; *myself* it speaks and spells,
>
> Crying *What I do is me: for that I came*
>
> (Hopkins, 1970, p. 90).

When there is voice, the percussions of the air seem to have formed a determinate shape, a style or signature of duress. In a voice, some syntax organizes the inchoate roar or rattle of pure noise into a dance of opposed internal stresses.

In just the same way, a bridge thrown between two banks can only continue to occupy its space, allowing traffic and communication, because of the patterns of internal stresses that hold it together. What is true of architecture in general—that only that which can support itself, or hold itself together by internal stresses, can stand up—is true of a voice. A voice is a structure of stresses and strains, and is pitched against itself, as well as standing out against the surrounding silence or noise.

Tenor

In the voice, the air is both constrained and stretched out—as, indeed, it is in the cycle of pressure within each individual sound wave. "So I at each sad strain, will strain a tear," says Shakespeare's Lucrece as she listens to the mournful song of Philomel (l. 1131). Lucrece proposes to press a knife to her heart as she listens, matching the thorn against which the nightingale traditionally presses its breast to elicit its song: "These means, as frets upon an instrument, /Shall tune our heart-strings to true languishment" (ll. 1140–1141).

English retains the idea of stretching in the word *tenor*, used to mean the burden or gist of an utterance. The tenor of an utterance is that which, diffused through it, holds it together through time. The idea of holding is there too in what is called the tenor voice, conventionally said to occupy the range from the octave below middle C to the A above it, and so-named because it was the part to which the melody is usually assigned, and which therefore "holds" the tune.

The word *tune* itself is a modification, or screwing up of the word *tone*, which has as its origin the Greek *tenein*, "to stretch," which lies behind the whole family of words signifying modalities of sound and stress: tone, tenor, tune, tension, tendency, tenderness, tenuity, and intent.

Speaking is an action, while the voice-body it precipitates is a quasi-object. And yet the opposite might also be thought to be true. Speech is articulated, broken, or segmented into separate objects. Voice is what reaches across and between these segments, maintaining their continuity. Voice is the tenor and the tensor of speech, what binds or holds it together. More than this, even, we might say that voice is the tone of being. There are many ways of maintaining the tenor of the voice.

The child, enraptured by its new acquisition of the power of voice, will babble, barely pausing for breath. The garrulous aged will similarly keep silence at bay through an unpausing onslaught of voice. There must be no chinks in the continuity through which silence or formless sound could rush. When the mind or body is subject to unbearable stress, the voice may be drawn out into howls and moans, which take the strain all the better for being drawn out, for being, as we say, "inarticulate," unbroken.

What happens, in fact, when the voice breaks, when it is wrenched apart by stammer, terror, hilarity, or grief? The smooth and regularly successive cycles of the breath are breached, by sobs and hiccoughs, say, but the voice survives, in the form, precisely, of the periodic rhythms of the broken voice, that holds together convulsion, holds together in its convulsion. Paradoxically, the voice at breaking point, the voice that appears to give way, is also a tensor, a taut, cohering cuirass.

Though itself formed from tension, voice can also hold or contain stresses that might otherwise tear us apart. Didier Anzieu's *acoustic envelope* or *audio-phonic skin* is an imaginary integument provided by the enclosing, protective touch of the mother's voice (Anzieu, 1989, p. 10). It is an ideal surface tension, neither too slack to maintain coherence and tone, nor too tight to resile from shock and accident.

Hanging on Its Words

Where does the voice come from? The history of ventriloquism provides many examples of voices produced from surprising or illegitimate parts of the body. The ventriloquial voice speaks from the belly, from the sternum, from the armpit, from the genitals, from the nose, from a second throat, or alternative vocal apparatus hidden within or alongside the usual one.

But where does the voice come from in "normal" speech? From the tongue (the tip of the tongue?) The mouth? The throat? The larynx? The lungs? The diaphragm? None and all of these things. The voice depends upon an entire vocal apparatus, a series of way stations, the elements of which are held in tension as long as there is the action of the voice. What joins and holds them together is the straining passage of the air through them. Air joints and articulates the puppet that is voice.

Nor is the production of the voice limited to the physical production of sound or those parts of the body that are capable of producing sound. For the voice also induces and is taken up into the movements of the body. The face is part of the voice's apparatus, as are the hands. The shaping of the air effected by the mouth, hands, and shoulders marks out the lineaments of the voice-body (which is to be distinguished from the voice in the body).

When one clicks one's fingers for emphasis, claps one's hands, or slaps one's thigh, the work of gesture is being taken over into sound, and voice has migrated into the fingers. Strange, that the "unnatural" or artificial production of voice through the classic ventriloquist's dummy should also link hand, fingers, face, mouth, and voice into a single assemblage, though in a different configuration than in ordinary voice production. The ventriloquist's relaying of voice through the speaking figure is a kind of anagram of the organization of elements in ordinary vocalization.

The voice is the body's syntax: its uprightness, its tone, tension, and extension. If it is true of human beings that language enables us to be where we are not, and prevents us from ever being anywhere but beside ourselves, then it is the voice that stretches us out between here and elsewhere. One cannot be fully "here" unless one is silent; one cannot vocalize without being "there" as well as here, without being drawn out into the ambivalence of being here and there at once.

Samuel Beckett gives us in his play *Not I* the image of a speaking mouth, which speaks of "the whole being . . . hanging on its words" (Beckett, 1986, p. 379). In what sense does one hang on another's words, or on one's own? One waits for them, straining to hear, held back until the words come, longing (and when one longs one is elongated, of course). Or one clings by one's fingertips, drawn out tight by one's own strait weight.

Reach

Voice is not just a force of outgoing. It is also often a reaching. Voice is in fact for babies the first grasping, a way of fetching and carrying objects of desire when no other way exists; the baby in the cot brings the world to it by means of voice. The child who has learned how to coordinate eye and hand to grip and carry does not forget that voice can reach further than the fist or fingers.

Perhaps thereafter the voice is identified principally as a mode of extended reach, as a way of stretching towards what one cannot physically reach. The voice reaches out and brings back, like the frog's tongue. The fact that, in Latin and in the Slavonic languages, languages themselves are known as *tongues* allows the sense of spoken languages as protrusions, tastings, attentions, outstretchings.

Freud's account of the *fort/da* game in *Beyond the Pleasure Principle* foregrounds the two modes or states of the voice, excursive and recursive. In staging disappearance, naming what is away and what is there, *fort* and *da*, the voice characterizes, not just the two conditions of its play-object (the cotton-reel as symbol of the mother), but also its own two conditions, as excursive and recursive (Freud, 1955, pp. 14–17). In one phase of the game, the voice is dispatched, sent out, expressed, uncoiled—and Freud characterizes the sound made by the child to accompany and enact it not as the end-stopped *fort*, but as its open, yearning approximation in *o-o-o*. But in the next phase of the game, it is reeled back in, brought back to itself, on the very imaginary elastic employed for its propulsion. The voice is carried in the tension of the cotton, which becomes transformed into a stretched telephone wire, a way of telephoning oneself, calling oneself back. Perhaps the *fort/da* game could be thought of as figuring the hearing-speaking circuit. What the voice gives out, the ear reins back in.

The more complex its utterance, the more the voice may appear to be reaching beyond itself, with the risk that it may be unable to be retrieved. As we come more and more to live in the voice's mode of reach, language proves to be able to reach towards things that can never be retrieved, since they exist only in the reaching for them. "Words, after speech, reach/Into the silence," wrote T. S. Eliot in *Burnt Norton* (1986, p. 8). If language is defined by its units and the rules of their combination (lexis, grammar), then the action of voice seems to be signaled in words that testify to the magically soliciting reach of language: *invocation*; *evocation*; *provocation*; *revocation*.

Of course the voice conceived in this way, as the stream, thread, cable, or wire, is tenuous. But one might also say that it is strengthened by this concentration into the form of the line. The voice is as feeble and as steely as the spider's thread.

Filiation

Though we delight in and are captivated by full, rich, voluminous voices, voices that are full of room and boom and body, the default condition of the voice is as something drawn out or elongated. Voice is one of the principal "extensions" of man, in Marshall MacLuhan's phrase (1964), but extension includes tension, attenuation, as well as enlargement of scope. Voice arises, bubbles up, comes out, is ejaculated, emitted, ejected. But

this emission takes the form of a continuous stream, which we feel remains in contact with its source, as in a jet from a fountain or a geyser. Early graphic depictions of voice represent it not, as contemporary comics, by a speech bubble, a formed and enclosed cloud of utterance hanging complete in the air, but as a scroll, uncurling from the lips. (But even the speech-bubble seems to suggest that the action of the voice may be a kind of lasso or noose.)

The habit of thinking and speaking of ventriloquism as a "throwing of the voice" participates in this tensile conception. The thrown or projectile voice is not dispatched, sent out once and for all, as a cannonball or javelin is, but maintains an unbroken arc through the air. It forms a line, like the line the angler casts, or as though the words one hears were a kite out at the end of a string lodged in the throat of the speaker.

Or like a telephone wire. The telephone actualized the fantasy of the wired voice more palpably and suggestively than any other device. The wired voice of the telephone is much more than a technical prosthesis for the voice; it is an image of the voice itself, considered as prosthesis. In the telephone, the voice is thinned to a filament, a living, thrilling nerve. The fact that wires carried voices, or electrical impulses that were to be converted into sound impulses, suggested that this device had succeeded in compressing sound into a line. Thus we continue to urge each other to "stay in touch." The language of language is full of images of threading and filiation. Somebody who detains you with his speech was once said to be "buttonholing," you, recalling the practice of physically crooking a finger in the buttonhole of one's interlocutor. "I've lost my thread," we may say, when the stream of spoken language fails.

The "voice wars" that raged among French anatomists during the 18th century about whether the voice was a wind, reed, or stringed instrument were eventually resolved during the 1740s by Antoine Ferrein's description of the action of the vocal cords (Connor, 2000, pp. 199–200). This description confirmed the phenomenological intuitions that the voice was a kind of "blown string," an extruded tautening of the air.

Voice was not able to be transmitted through wires until Robert Hooke invented the device that survives in the children's string telephone today and anticipated Bell's electrical telephone. Hooke stretched a silken cord between two diaphragms, and was able to transmit the sound of voices for distances of up to 150 meters; the sound would even go around corners, provided the angles were carefully constructed and the line kept taut. But even before this, there had been an apprehension of the relations between sound, especially the sound of the human voice, and the principles of constraint. Musical instruments, like pipes, trombones, and trumpets, amplified and transformed the voice by forcing it through narrow channels, in what was often understood as a doubling of the voice's own methods of sound production. The use of pipes and speaking tubes to convey voices long distances established an understanding of the energy ratio between power and constraint: the voice that is put under pressure can reach further.

It is not just amplification or increase of reach that involves force. One of the most curious but long-lived beliefs about sound was that, if it could be accelerated, it could also be trapped. Giambattista della

Porta's *Natural Magick* of 1584 devoted a chapter to the topic of "Whether Material Statues May Speak by Any Artificial Way." The chapter begins with the report that, in ancient times,

> there was a colossus of Brass, placed on a mighty high pillar, which in violent tempests of wind from the nether parts, received a great blast, that was carried from the mouth to a trumpet, that it blew strongly, or else sounded some other instrument, which I believe to have been easy, because I have seen the like. (Porta, 1658, p. 385)

Porta goes on to discourse upon the properties of sound upon which both musical instruments and speaking statues depend: "We see that the voice or a sound, will be conveighed entire through the Air, and that not in an instant, but by degrees in time" (Porta, 1658, p. 385). The fact that sounds are preserved and conveyed "entire without interruption, unless they break upon some place" (Porta, 1658, p. 385) makes it possible to convey sounds great distances: "if any man shall make leaden Pipes exceeding long, two or three hundred paces long (as I have tried), and shall speak in them some or many words, they will be carried true through those Pipes and be heard at the other end, as they came from the speaker's mouth" (Porta, 1658, pp. 385–386). This principle of the preservation of sound convinced Porta, as it did others, that cunningly engineered pipeworks might be able also to trap sound, not just conveying it through space, but holding it up in time, thereby adding a phonographic to a telephonic principle:

> wherefore if that voice goes with time, & hold entire, if a man as the words are spoken shall stop the end of the

pipe, and he that is at the other end shall do the like, the voice may be intercepted in the middle, and be shut up as in a prison; and when the mouth is opened, the voice will come forth, as out of his mouth that spake it; but because such long Pipes cannot be made without trouble, they may be bent up and down like a Trumpet, that a long Pipe may be kept in a small place; and when the mouth is open, the words may be understood. I am now upon trial of it. (Porta, 1658, p. 386)

Torsion

Ventriloquism centers around these two strainings of the voice, in extension and compression. The traditional ventriloquist performance has the dummy or speaking figure operated by the ventriloquist's fingers. The voice is out at the finger's ends, the words hovering not on the tip of the tongue, but at the fingertips. In the so-called "distant voice," the voice may be in the air, on the roof, up a chimney, in a basement, or on the end of the telephone line. But the knowledge that the voice really belongs to the one who affects only to hear it keeps us aware of a kind of filament or cord stretching between the apparent and real locations of the voice. The distant voice is also often enclosed, in boxes, suitcases, cupboards, or even underground. When it is thus enclosed, the voice is imagined as coiled upon itself with the kinetic tension of compression. In Edgar Allan Poe's story, "Thou Art the Man," a corpse is stiffened with whalebone and then pushed down into its coffin, so that when the lid is taken off it springs upright, and so that, given a voice by a nearby ventriloquist, it may dramatically denounce its mur-

derer (Poe, 1850, II. pp. 418–432). The voice is either stretched or compressed —but is always elastic, always under pressure.

This means too that there is always a possibility of pain in the voice. Children learn to use their voices first of all to cry, with fear, hurt, or need, before they are able to use language for pleasure. When we cry, with pain or loss, it is as though we used the voice to rid ourselves of an unbearable burden of tension. But the sound that we release can hold the pain, even in its sundering from us. Indeed, the sundering is itself a pain, as though the dissociated voice were haunted, like a phantom limb longing for its tenant body. Philomela, her tongue torn out by her ravisher Tereus, eventually takes the form of a nightingale, the rarely-visible bird whose song takes the place of its physical presence, and will lengthen out our agony into beauty.

Myths, legends, and stories have often imagined the condition of death as being like a voice separated from its body, for example, in the twittering shades who come to drink themselves back into bodily substance from the ditch of blood provided for them by Ulysses in Book XI of the *Odyssey*. The voices of the dead conjoin the two kinds of strain I have been evoking here. They are attenuated, "drawn out" from the body into the most evanescent condition. But they are also, like Echo in Ovid's fable, shriveled down to bones and voice, or like the voices interred in the cave, or grave, or constricted in the tight coils of the gramophone record or the reel of tape, pent in their impalpability. Their contemporary image is to be found in the "electric voice phenomena" allegedly captured on tape by Friedrich Jürgensen in 1959, while recording birdsong. Mere flitters of utterance, the voices seem to be trying to keep themselves entire amid the blizzard of white noise that threatens to obliterate them. We too, apparitions of the voice, hang by a thread, on what continually escapes us.

Conclusions

We can never sit comfortably in our voices, because our voices are our organs of reach, of lengthening, of longing. The voice is always yearning to be elsewhere, to move us elsewhere. But this straining or traction of the voice is not subtractable from it. We can never freely or easily inhabit our voices, nor can our voices fully express what we are. This is because voice is fundamentally expressive of the longing to be otherwise than what, and where, we presently are.

References

Anzieu, D. (1989). *The skin ego*. (C. Turner, Trans.). New Haven, CT: Yale University Press.

Beckett, S. (1986). *Complete dramatic works*. London: Faber and Faber.

Boyle, R. (1660). *New experiments physico-mechanicall, touching the spring of the air, and its effects (Made for the most part, in a new pneumatical engine)*. Oxford, UK: Tho. Robinson.

Connor, S. (2000). *Dumbstruck: A cultural history of ventriloquism*. Oxford, UK: Oxford University Press.

della Porta, G. (1658). *Natural magick by John Baptista Porta, a Neapolitane; in twenty books . . . wherein are set forth all the riches and delights of the natural sciences*. London: Thomas Young and Samuel Speed.

Eliot, T. S. (1986). *Four quartets*. London: Faber and Faber.

Freud, S. (1955). Beyond the pleasure principle. (J. Strachey, Trans.). In *The standard edition of the complete psychological works of Sigmund Freud* (Vol. 18, pp. 1–64). London: Hogarth Press.

Gardner, W. H., & MacKenzie, N. H. (Eds.). (1970). *The poems of Gerard Manley Hopkins* (4th ed.). London: Oxford University Press.

MacLuhan, M. (1964). *Understanding media: The extensions of man*. London: Routledge and Kegan Paul.

Poe, E. A. (1850). *The works of the late Edgar Allan Poe* (Vols. 1–2). New York: J. S. Redfield.

Rosolato, G. (1974). La voix: Entre corps et langage. *Revue française de psychanalyse, 38*, 75–94.

CHAPTER 19

Approaches to Emotional Expressivity in Synthetic Speech

Marc Schröder

Abstract

Attempts to add emotion effects to synthesized speech have existed since the beginning of the 1990s, and have recently gained popularity to the extent that the first commercial synthesizers include emotional or otherwise expressive capabilities. Over the years, several prototypes and fully operational systems have been built based on different synthesis techniques, and quite a number of smaller studies have been conducted. This chapter aims to give an overview of what has been done in this field, pointing out the inherent properties of the various synthesis techniques used, summarizing the prosody rules employed, and taking a look at the evaluation paradigms. Finally, some potentially interesting directions for future development are discussed.

Introduction

With the intelligibility of synthetic speech approaching that of human speech, the need for increased naturalness becomes more palpable. One of the aspects of naturalness most obviously missing in synthetic speech is appropriate emotional expressivity. This observation has been motivating attempts to incorporate the expression of emotions into synthetic speech since the early 1990s, and such attempts have gained popularity in recent years. While advances in other aspects of naturalness of synthetic voices have been made, notably with unit selection techniques, the synthesis of emotional speech still has a long way to go.

In the studies concerned with the expression of emotion in synthetic speech that can be found in the literature,[1] an interesting variety of approaches has been employed. This chapter will try to give an overview of these studies, and work out the differences and similarities in approach, technique, and underlying assumptions. First, the studies are presented in groups according to the type of synthesis technique employed, which coincides in many cases with similarities in the approach. Next, prosody rules employed for expressing emotions are reported, and the paradigms used for evaluation are discussed.

Finally, a number of points will be discussed related to possible directions for future development. Some implications for future research in the synthesis of emotional speech are proposed in the discussion section.

Existing Approaches and Techniques

The modeling of emotion in speech relies on a number of parameters such as fundamental frequency (F0) level and range, duration, voice quality, or articulatory precision (see Emotional Prosody Rules below). Different synthesis techniques provide control over these parameters to very different degrees.

Formant Synthesis

Formant synthesis, also known as rule-based synthesis, is the oldest speech synthesis technique. It creates the acoustic speech data entirely through rules on the acoustic correlates of the various speech sounds. No human speech recordings are involved at run time. The resulting speech sounds relatively unnatural and robotlike compared to state-of-the-art concatenative systems, but a large number of parameters related to both voice source and vocal tract can be varied quite freely. This, of course, is interesting for modeling emotional expressivity in speech.

Several larger undertakings (Burkhardt, 2001; Burkhardt & Sendlmeier, 2000; Cahn, 1989; 1990; Murray, 1989; Murray & Arnott, 1995) have used formant synthesizers because of the high degree of control that they provide. These include the first ones, from 1989: Cahn's Affect Editor (Cahn, 1989; 1990), and Murrays HAMLET (Murray, 1989; Murray & Arnott, 1995). Both used DECtalk as a formant synthesis system, providing dedicated

---

[1]For audio examples, the reader is referred to the excellent collection maintained by Felix Burkhardt at http://emosamples.syntheticspeech.de

processing modules, which adapt their input according to the acoustic properties of a number of emotions. In both cases, the acoustic profile for each emotion category was derived from the literature and manually adapted. While the Affect Editor requires the input to be manually annotated, HAMLET processes its input entirely by rule.

Within the VAESS project (Voices, Attitudes and Emotions in Speech Synthesis), which ran from 1994 to 1996, emotional expressivity was to be added to a formant synthesizer. Montero et al. (1998) report reasonable success for the modeling of three emotions (hot anger, happiness, and sadness) in Spanish using global prosodic and voice quality parameter settings.

Burkhardt (2001; Burkhardt & Sendlmeier, 2000) also chose to use formant synthesis, despite the reduced naturalness, because of the high degree of flexibility and control over acoustic parameters that this technique provides. His systematic, perception-oriented approach to finding good acoustic correlates of emotions for German consisted of two main steps. In a first step, he systematically varied five acoustic parameters known to be related to emotion, without using prior knowledge from the literature about the best parameter values for a given emotion. The resulting stimuli were presented in a perception test, providing perceptually optimal parameter values for each emotion studied. In a second step, these optimal values were taken as the basis for the exploration of a wider set of parameters, inspired from the literature. The resulting variants were presented in another perception test, leading to the formulation of refined prosody rules for the synthesis of the emotions studied.

Diphone Concatenation

In concatenative synthesis, which gained popularity in the early 1990s, recordings of a human speaker are concatenated in order to generate the synthetic speech. The use of diphones, that is, stretches of the speech signal from the middle of one speech sound (*phone*) to the middle of the next, is common. Diphone recordings are usually made on a monotonous pitch. At synthesis time, the required F0 contour is generated through signal processing techniques that introduce a certain amount of distortion, but with a resulting speech quality usually considered more natural than formant synthesis.

In most diphone synthesis systems, only F0 and duration (and possibly intensity) can be controlled. In particular, it is usually impossible to control voice quality.

Fundamental to every attempt to use diphone synthesis for expressing emotions is the question whether F0 and duration are sufficient to express emotion, that is, whether voice quality is indispensable for emotion expression or not. Interestingly, very different results were obtained by different studies. While Vroomen, Collier, & Mozziconacci (1993), Edgington (1997), Montero, Gutiérrez-Arriola, Colás, Enríquez, & Pardo (1999), Schröder (1999), Murray, Edgington, Campion, & Lynn (2000), and Stallo (2000) report that synthesized emotions can be recognized at least reasonably well, Heuft, Portele, & Rauth (1996) and Rank and Pirker (1998) report recognition rates close to chance level. The reason may be that there is no simple general answer: Montero et al. (1999) and Audibert, Vincent, Aubergé, & Rosec (2006) reported that for a given speaker, the relative contribution of prosody and voice quality to emotion recognition depends on the emotion expressed, and Schröder (1999) has found evidence that this may, in addition, be speaker-dependent. In other words, there seem to be speaker strategies relying mostly on F0 and duration for expressing some emotions, and these can be successfully modeled in diphone synthesis. Whether this is true for all types of emotion is not clear yet.

As a first step towards adding control over voice quality to diphone synthesis, Schröder and Grice (2003) have recorded diphone databases with several different voice qualities. This approach, though time and cost intensive, is necessary as long as convincing signal modification techniques are not available that can alter voice quality.

Given the relatively high degree of control over the acoustic parameters, how, then, do researchers determine the parameter settings that should be used for the various emotions? One approach, used by Vroomen et al. (1993), Heuft et al. (1996), Edgington (1997), Montero et al. (1999), Schröder (1999), Boula de Mareüil, Célérier, & Toen (2002), and Bulut, Narayanan, & Syrdal (2002), is copy synthesis: F0 and duration values are measured for each speech sound in a given utterance (usually an actor's portrayal of an emotion), and used for synthesizing the same utterance from diphones. The result is a synthetic utterance with the same F0 and duration values as the actor's speech, but the voice quality determined by the diphones. This technique is suitable for modeling what humans do as closely as possible with the given parameter set. Whether that is the best way to obtain perceptually optimal, believable expressions is open for discussion, though: for example, in the domain of animated characters, it has been observed that fea-

tures occurring in human expression need to be exaggerated in synthetic expression in order to be believable (Bates, 1994; Oudeyer, 2002).

A more ambitious approach is the formulation of prosody rules for emotions (Boula et al., 2002; Iriondo et al., 2000; Mozziconacci, 1998; Mozziconacci & Hermes, 1999; Murray et al., 2000; Rank & Pirker, 1998; Stallo, 2000), which is discussed in Emotional Prosody Rules below.

Unit Selection

The synthesis technique often perceived as being most natural is unit selection, or corpus-based synthesis. It was developed in the second half of the 1990s and now dominates the speech synthesis landscape, particularly for commercial systems. Instead of a minimum speech data inventory as in diphone synthesis, a large inventory (up to several hours of speech from the same speaker) is used. Out of this large database, units of variable size are selected that best approximate a desired target utterance defined by a number of parameters. The criteria used for selecting the units are usually of a symbolic nature, such as the phoneme symbol, stress and accent status, sentence type, or position in the sentence. The actual prosodic parameters, such as phoneme duration and F0, are not directly controlled with this approach, but are considered appropriately set as a consequence of the aforementioned selection criteria. As a consequence, it is very difficult to precisely control prosody in unit selection synthesis. The weights assigned to the selection parameters influence which units are selected. If well-matching units are found in the database, no signal processing is necessary. While this synthesis method often gives very natural results, the results can be very bad when no appropriate units are found.

Limited domain synthesis is a special type of unit selection synthesis in which the speech corpus is especially designed to cover a given limited target domain, such as weather forecasts. Only utterances from the chosen domain can then be generated using that synthesis voice. Careful corpus design can make sure that suitable units for all possible sentences in the domain exist. Therefore, these voices are very natural for the given domain, to the point that they are sometimes perceived as natural human speech.

The feature of unit selection synthesis to preserve the properties of the recorded speech very well has been exploited by Iida and Campbell (2003) for the synthesis of emotional speech. For each of three emotions (anger, joy, and sadness), an entire unit selection database was recorded by the same speaker. In order to synthesize a given emotion, only units from the corresponding database are selected. The emotions in the resulting synthesized speech are well recognized (50–80%).

Johnson et al. (2002) pursued a similar approach. They employed limited domain synthesis for the generation of convincing expressive military speech, in the framework of the Mission Rehearsal Exercise project. The styles, each recorded as an individual limited domain speech database, were shouted commands, shouted conversation, spoken commands, and spoken conversation. In a perception test, the perceived naturalness of the intonation of the synthesized utterances approached that of natural utterances, more so for commands than for conversational speech.

A different, theoretically more demanding approach is to select the material appropriate for the targeted emotion from one database. The equivalent of prosody rules is then used as selection criteria. This has been attempted by Campbell and Marumoto (2000), who used parameters related to voice quality and prosody as emotion-specific selection criteria. The results indicated a partial success: Anger and sadness were recognized with up to 60% accuracy, while joy was not recognized above chance level.

It is also possible to apply signal processing to unit selection, modifying pitch and duration to match emotions (Zovato, Pacchiotti, Quazza, & Sandri, 2004). Even though starting from a higher quality synthetic signal, this approach faces the same limitations as traditional diphone synthesis, the lack of control over voice quality and the introduction of distortions by larger modifications.

The first systems from speech synthesis companies including emotional capabilities (Hamza, Bakis, Eide, Picheny, & Pitrelli, 2004; Loquendo, 2004) are also based on unit selection synthesis. In order to reach high quality output, Loquendo (2004) add emotional speech material to a synthesis corpus, by recording a range of emotional expressions in addition to general corpus recordings. These short emotional recordings can be appended to standard, unemotional synthetic speech. Hamza et al. (2004) follow an approach similar to that of Iida and Campbell (2003) and Johnson et al. (2002): A full corpus is recorded in a given speaking style, here, conveying good vs. bad news.

HMM Synthesis

One synthesis technology that has gained popularity very recently is speech synthesis based on hidden Markov models

(HMMs). These statistical models are trained on a corpus, but similarly to formant synthesis, the audio generation at run time is independent of the original recordings. The HMMs predict spectral parameters that are converted into speech through spectral filters (Yoshimura, Tokuda, Masuko, Kobayashi, & Kitamura, 1999). Limitations of that spectral generation method cause the quality of the resulting speech to be limited.

In the framework of HMM-based synthesis, Miyanaga, Masuko, & Kobayashi (2004) presented a method to control speaking style by training style-specific HMM models and interpolating between them using a "style vector." Experiments were carried out that demonstrated, also for intermediate style values, a gradual effect on perceived style, for models trained on reading joyful, rough, and sad speaking styles.

Even though this approach requires style-specific recordings as in unit selection, the resulting flexibility is greater. Because of the parametric representation, interpolation between the styles is possible, enabling the expression of low-intensity emotions, by interpolating between a neutral speaking style and a high-intensity emotional speaking style. Similarly, blends of emotions can be generated by interpolating between two emotional speaking styles.

Unit Selection and Signal Modification

None of the existing speech synthesis technologies, described above, is able to combine the virtues of all approaches: Unit selection synthesis reaches high naturalness, but the control over acoustic parameters that can be used for flexible expressivity is very low. On the other hand, formant synthesis, diphone synthesis, or HMM-based synthesis can provide various degrees of control over these parameters, but the resulting speech quality is limited.

Attempts are therefore underway to add a certain amount of parametric control to the currently best-sounding technology, unit selection synthesis (Black, 2003). New acoustic target costs are being tried out (Rouibia & Rosec, 2005), which could be more easily extended to emotionally relevant acoustic parameters than traditional linguistic target costs. At the same time, advanced signal processing algorithms are being developed. For example, d'Alessandro and Doval (2003) have proposed a method based on a decomposition of the speech signal into a periodic and an aperiodic part, which can then be separately modified and recombined. In first experiments, the parameters glottal formant and spectral tilt have been modified, which are both related to voice quality. Vincent, Rosec, & Chonavel (2005) have developed a method for the joint estimation of glottal source and vocal tract filter coefficients, automatically from the speech signal. The method has been applied to the analysis of emotional speech (Audibert et al., 2006) and could potentially be used for signal modification.

Voice conversion, transformation, and morphing technologies are also used to convert a speaker's neutral speaking style into an emotional style. Matsui and Kawahara (2003) converted one emotional recording of a speaker into a different emotion uttered by the same speaker. They achieved good recognition rates, but anchor points in the time-frequency plane had to be set manually. Ye and Young (2004) used voice morphing for converting one speaker's voice into another speaker's, by means of linear transformations in a sinusoidal model. The same technology could be used to convert a given speaker's voice expressing one emotion into the same speaker's voice expressing another emotion. Eichner, Wolff, & Hoffmann (2004) used a reverse version of the vocal tract length normalization algorithm usually used in speech recognition to create audibly distinct voices from one database, without adding noticeable distortions to synthetic speech. In general, such voice morphing methods do not model voice quality explicitly, so that the generalizability of results of morphing experiments is limited.

An attempt to specifically control voice quality in a gradual way was made by Turk, Schröder, Bozkurt, & Arslan (2005). Based on diphone voices recorded with the same speaker's voice but different voice qualities (Schröder & Grice, 2003), they created intermediate voice qualities through a spectral interpolation algorithm. If this algorithm could be applied to unit selection synthesis, it could lead to a gradual control over voice quality, if rich unit selection databases with sufficient variation in voice quality were available.

As such approaches mature and become applicable in full-scale unit selection synthesis systems without degrading the resulting speech quality too much, they will make it possible to flexibly change the expression of natural-sounding synthetic voices.

Emotional Prosody Rules

Some of the approaches to expressive speech synthesis described above contain the information about the acoustic realization of different emotions implicitly, because they are based directly or indirectly on emotionally spoken data. The more parametrizable approaches, however, which also have the potential to be very flexibly expressive, require explicit models of how to realize emotions acoustically. The comprehensive acoustic characterization of emotions is already difficult in natural human speech; in synthetic speech, limited speech quality and lack of parametric control make it even more difficult. Nevertheless, several approaches have been proposed and will be presented here exemplarily.

At least in formant and diphone synthesis, prosody rules are at the heart of automatically generated emotional expressivity in synthetic speech. Such rules have been obtained in a number of ways by different authors. Cahn (1990), Murray and Arnott (1995), Rank and Pirker (1998), Murray et al. (2000), and Stallo (2000) have extracted rules from the literature; Montero et al. (1998), Mozziconacci and Hermes (1999), Iriondo et al. (2000), Campbell and Marumoto (2000), and Boula et al. (2002) have carried out their own corpus analysis; and Mozziconacci (1998) and Burkhardt and Sendlmeier (2000) have obtained perceptually optimal values by systematic parameter variation in synthesis.

The types of parameter modeled vary greatly between different studies. All studies agree on the importance of global prosodic settings, such as F0 level and range, speech tempo, and possibly loudness. Some studies try to go into more detail about these global settings, modelling for example steepness of the F0 contour during rises and falls (Cahn, 1990; Iriondo et al., 2000; Murray & Arnott, 1995; Stallo, 2000), distinguishing between articulation rate and the number and duration of pauses (Cahn, 1990; Iriondo et al., 2000; Montero et al., 1999; Murray & Arnott, 1995), or modeling additional phenomena like voice quality (Burkhardt & Sendlmeier, 2000; Cahn, 1990; Campbell & Marumoto, 2000; Iriondo et al., 2000; Murray & Arnott, 1995; Murray et al., 2000; Rank & Pirker, 1998) or articulatory precision (Burkhardt & Sendlmeier, 2000; Cahn, 1990; Murray & Arnott, 1995; Rank & Pirker, 1998). A further step is the consideration of interactions with linguistic categories, like further distinguishing between the speech tempo of vowels and consonants (Murray & Arnott, 1995; Rank & Pirker, 1998; Stallo, 2000), of stressed and unstressed syllables (Burkhardt & Sendlmeier, 2000; Murray & Arnott, 1995; Stallo, 2000), or the placement of pauses within utterances (Cahn, 1990). The influence of linguistic prosodic categories, like F0 contours (Burkhardt & Sendlmeier, 2000; Mozziconacci & Hermes, 1999), is only rarely taken into account, although these have been shown to play an important role in emotion recognition (Burkhardt & Sendlmeier, 2000; Mozziconacci & Hermes, 1999).

Table 19-1 presents a short overview of prosody rules that have been successfully employed to express a number of emotion categories. Instead of a reduced summary of all the rules employed in different studies, one successful modeling example per emotion category is presented in detail, along with the recognition rate obtained. See Schröder (2004) for a more extensive matrix of the prosody rules employed in the listed publications.

Note that in the literature concerned with emotional speech synthesis, global prosodic parameters are often treated as universal, culture-independent cues for emotion. While this is certainly a simplification, there is some support for the assumption of universality (Chung, 1999; Scherer, Banse, & Walbott, 2001; Tickle, 2000), at least as long as the number of

available emotion categories is small. Burkhardt et al. (2006) specifically addressed the question in a diphone synthesis context, comparing the effect of parameter variations taken from the literature on French, German, Greek, and Turkish listeners. They found that general trends were quite consistent accross language groups, but that there were nevertheless differences that may have been caused by cultural differences.

Emotion categories are not the only possible description of emotional states. Schröder (2004) explored modeling expressive speech synthesis using an alternative representation: emotion dimensions. These are continuous scales representing the aspects of emotional states that people consider to be most important: activation (ranging from active to passive), evaluation (ranging from negative to positive), and power (ranging from dominant to submissive).

Table 19-2 presents the rules proposed in Schröder (2004) to express emotions in a speech synthesis system using emotion dimensions. The columns represent the emotion dimensions, while the rows list the acoustic parameters for which emotion effects are modeled. The coefficients were derived from the analysis of a spontaneous database of emotional speech and from the literature.

The numeric data fields represent the linear coefficients quantifying the effect of the given emotion dimension on the acoustic parameter, that is, the change from the neutral default state corresponding to point 0 on every emotion dimension. As an example, the value 0.5% linking Activation to rate means that for an activation level of +50 (on a scale from −100 to +100), rate increases by +25%, while for an activation level of −30, it decreases by −15%.

Table 19–1. Examples of successful prosody rules for emotion expression in synthetic speech

Emotion Study Language Rec. Rate	Parameter settings
Joy Burkhardt and Sendlmeier (2000) German 81% (1/9)	**F0 mean**: +50% **F0 range**: +100% **Tempo**: +30% **Voice Qu.**: modal or tense; lip-spreading feature: F1/F2 +10% **Other**: wave pitch contour model: main stressed syllables are raised (+100%), syllables in between are lowered (−20%)
Sadness Cahn (1990) American English 91% (1/6)	**F0 mean**: 0, reference line −1, less final lowering −5 **F0 range**: −5, steeper accent shape +6 **Tempo**: −10, more fluent pauses +5, hesitation pauses +10 **Loudness**: −5 **Voice Qu.**: breathiness +10, brilliance −9 **Other**: stress frequency +1, precision of articulation −5
Anger Murray and Arnott (1995) British English	**F0 mean**: +10 Hz **F0 range**: +9 s.t. **Tempo**: +30 wpm **Loudness**: +6 dB **Voice Qu.**: laryngealization +78%; F4 frequency −175 Hz **Other**: increase pitch of stressed vowels (secondary: +10% of pitch range; primary: +20%; emphatic: +40%)
Fear Burkhardt and Sendlmeier (2000) German 52% (1/9)	**F0 mean**: +150% **F0 range**: +20% **Tempo**: +30% **Voice Qu.**: falsetto
Surprise Cahn (1990) American English 44% (1/6)	**F0 mean**: 0, reference line −8 **F0 range**: +8, steeply rising contour slope +10, steeper accent shape +5 **Tempo**: +4, less fluent pauses 5, hesitation pauses −10 **Loudness**: +5 **Voice Qu.**: brilliance −3
Boredom Mozziconacci (1998) Dutch 94% (1/7)	**F0 mean**: end frequency 65 Hz (male speech) **F0 range**: excursion size 4 s.t. **Tempo**: duration rel. to neutrality: 150% **Other**: final intonation pattern 3C, avoid final patterns 5&A and 12

Note. Recognition rates are presented with chance level for comparison. Sadness and Surprise: Cahn uses parameter scales from −10 to +10, 0 being neutral; Boredom: Mozziconacci indicates intonation patterns according to a Dutch grammar of intonation; see Mozziconacci (1998) for details.

Table 19–2. Emotion dimension prosody rules from Schröder

	Prosodic parameter	Coefficients Activation	Evaluation	Power
Fundamental frequency	pitch	0.3	0.1	−0.1
	pitch dynamics	0.3%		−0.3%
	range	0.4		
	range dynamics	1.2%		0.4%
	accent prominence	0.5%	−0.5%	
	preferred accent shape		E < 20: falling 20 < E < 40: rising E > 40: alternating	
	accent slope	1%	−0.5%	
	preferred boundary type			P < 0: high P > 0: low
Tempo	rate	0.5%	0.2%	
	number of pauses	0.7%		
	pause duration	−0.2%		
	vowel duration		0.3%	0.3%
	nasal duration		0.3%	0.3%
	liquid duration		0.3%	0.3%
	plosive duration	0.5%	−0.3%	
	fricative duration	0.5%	−0.3%	
	volume	0.33%		

Note. Data are from "Speech and Emotion Research: An Overview of Research Frameworks and a Dimensional Approach to Emotional Speech Synthesis," by M. Schröder, 2004, *Phonus, Research Report of the Institute of Phonetics, Saarland University 7.*

Evaluation Paradigms

The quality of synthetic emotional speech is usually evaluated using perception tests. The most frequently used method is a forced choice perception test including the emotion categories actually modeled, employing a small number of semantically neutral carrier sentences (Burkhardt & Sendlmeier, 2000; Cahn, 1990; Campbell & Marumoto, 2000; Edgington, 1997; Heuft et al., 1996; Iida & Campbell, 2003; Montero et al., 1998; Montero et al., 1999; Mozziconacci & Hermes, 1999; Rank & Pirker, 1998; Schröder, 1999; Vroomen et al., 1993). It can be argued, though (Banse & Scherer, 1996), that this corresponds rather to a discrimination task than an identification task, especially when the number of categories involved is small. The advantages of such a forced choice test are that it is relatively easy to carry out, provides a simple measure of recognition relative to chance level, and allows at least a limited comparability between studies. However, a forced choice test provides no information about the quality of the stimulus in terms of naturalness or believability. Therefore, a number of studies assess the degree of naturalness, believability, or overall preference of the emotion expression in addition to the forced choice rating, often on a five-point scale (Cahn, 1990; Iida & Campbell, 2003; Rank & Pirker, 1998; Schröder, 1999). In addition, the intensity of the emotion (Cahn, 1990) and the synthetic speech intelligibility (Iida & Campbell, 2003) have been assessed.

Another possibility, especially suited for finding phenomena not expected by the experimenter, are free response tests (Murray & Arnott, 1995; Schröder, 1999). A subsequent grouping of the responses into meaningful classes can be performed using validated word lists (Murray & Arnott, 1995).

An interesting alternative evaluation paradigm was employed by Murray and Arnott (1995) and Stallo (2000). First, a number of "distractor" response categories are introduced in the perception test, as well as a category *other*. In addition, semantically neutral as well as semantically emotional texts are used, both synthesized with neutral and emotional prosody. The difference in recognition between the version with neutral prosody and the version with emotional prosody is then taken as the measure for the perceptive impact of the prosody rules. Interestingly, the recognition improvement due to prosody was bigger for emotional texts than for neutral texts.

In an audiovisual context, a talking head visually expressing emotion (Stallo, 2000) was presented with neutral and with emotional synthetic speech. Subjects rated which version they perceived as more natural, more understandable, etc. The version with emotional speech was clearly preferred.

Similarly, Schröder (2004) used situation descriptions and words spoken to define an emotional reference, which was combined with the prosody corresponding to the same and different emotional states. Listeners preferred the combinations where the emotion expressed in the prosody was similar to the emotion expressed in the text. The strongest effect was found for similarity on the activation dimension of emotionality.

Discussion

Emotional speech synthesis is only starting to be applicable in real-life settings. A number of structural problems stand in the way of more widespread application.

First, in many studies, a number of between three and nine discrete, often extreme emotional states are modeled. The implicit assumption that the expression of a few basic or primary emotion categories is most important to model, and that other emotional states can somehow be derived from that, has been questioned by Cowie and Cornelius (2003). They argued that systems should be able to express less intense emotions more suitable for real-life applications. For a perception-oriented task such as the synthesis of emotional speech, emotion dimensions were explored (Schröder, 2004) as a starting point for describing non-extreme emotional states, but only the expression of activation (or arousal) was really successful.

The comprehensive description of acoustic correlates of emotional expression in the human voice is a second missing piece in the puzzle. With more detailed knowledge of the acoustic properties that cause the perception of various emotions, it will become possible to create increasingly natural-sounding emotion portrayals using sophisticated prosody rules. Such descriptions will also need to include new types of parameters. Besides the gradual, global parameter settings such as F0 mean, overall speech tempo, and so on, it is well known in principle that linguistic categories such as F0 contour can have an effect on emotion perception in interaction with other linguistic information like sentence type (Andreeva & Barry, 1999; Scherer, Ladd, & Silverman, 1984). Such effects, most likely language-specific in nature, are not yet appropriately accounted for in the description of human speech, which would be a prerequisite for their realization by rule in emotional speech synthesis systems.

Third, control over acoustic parameters is required for realizing prosody rules. Adding such control to high quality unit selection synthesis is a central technological challenge in this research area today.

Finally, evaluation techniques should be developed that are more suitable for assessing the appropriateness of acoustic parameter settings for a given communication situation. This might be achieved by moving away from forced-choice tests using abstract emotion words towards tests measuring the perceived naturalness of an utterance given an emotion-defining context.

Acknowledgements. Preparation of this chapter was supported by the EU project HUMAINE (IST-507422) and by the DFG project PAVOQUE.

References

Andreeva, B., & Barry, W. J. (1999). Intonation von Checks in der Sofia-Varietät des Bulgarischen (Intonation of Checks in the Sofia variety of Bulgarian). []*Phonus, Research Report of the Institute of Phonetics, University of the Saarland, 4,* 1–13.

Audibert, N., Vincent, D., Aubergé, V., & Rosec, O. (2006). Expressive speech synthesis: Evaluation of a voice quality centered coder on the different acoustic dimensions. In R. Hoffmann & H. Mixdorff (Eds.), *CD-ROM Proceedings of the Third International Conference on Speech Prosody.* Dresden, Germany: TUDpress Verlag der Wissenschaften.

Banse, R., & Scherer, K. R. (1996). Acoustic profiles in vocal emotion expression. *Journal of Personality and Social Psychology, 70*(3), 614–636.

Bates, J. (1994). The role of emotion in believable agents. *Communications of the ACM, 37,* 122–125.

Black, A. W. (2003, September). *Unit selection and emotional speech.* Paper presented at Eurospeech 2003, Geneva, Switzerland.

Boula de Mareüil, P., Célérier, P., & Toen, J. (2002, April). *Generation of emotions by a morphing technique in English, French and Spanish.* Paper presented at First International Conference on Speech Prosody, Aix-en-Provence, France.

Bulut, M., Narayanan, S. S., & Syrdal, A. K. (2002, September). *Expressive speech synthesis using a concatenative synthesiser.* Paper presented at the 7th International Conference on Spoken Language Processing, Denver, CO.

Burkhardt, F. (2001). *Simulation emotionaler Sprechweise mit Sprachsyntheseverfahren (Simulation of emotional manner of speaking with speech synthesis methods).* Unpublished doctoral dissertation, Technical University, Berlin.

Burkhardt, F., Audibert, N., Malatesta, L., Turk, O., Arslan, L., & Aubergé, V. (2006). Emotional prosody—does culture make a difference? In R. Hoffmann and H. Mixdorff (Eds.) *CD-ROM Proceedings of the Third International Conference on Speech Prosody Conference.* Dresden, Germany: TUDpress Verlag der Wissenschaften.

Burkhardt, F., & Sendlmeier, W. F. (2000). Verification of acoustical correlates of emotional speech using formant synthesis. In R. Cowie, E. Douglas-Cowie & M. Schröder (Eds.), *Proceedings of the ISCA Workshop on Speech and Emotion* (pp. 151-156). Belfast, UK: Textflow.

Cahn, J. E. (1989). *Generating expression in synthesized speech.* Unpublished master's thesis, MIT Media Lab, Cambridge, MA.

Cahn, J. E. (1990). The generation of affect in synthesized speech. *Journal of the American Voice I/O Society, 8,* 1-19.

Campbell, N., & Marumoto, T. (2000, October). *Automatic labelling of voice-quality in speech databases for synthesis.* Paper presented at the 6th International Conference on Spoken Language Processing, Beijing, China.

Chung, S.-J. (1999). Vocal expression and perception of emotion in Korean. In J. J. Ohala, Y. Hasegawa, M. Ohala, D. Granville, & A. C. Bailey (Eds.), *Proceedings of the 14th International Congress of Phonetic Sciences* (pp. 969-972). Berkeley, CA: University of California, Berkeley.

Cowie, R., & Cornelius, R. R. (2003). Describing the emotional states that are expressed in speech. *Speech Communication, Special Issue on Speech and Emotion, 40*(1-2), 5-32.

d'Alessandro, C., & Doval, B. (2003, September). *Voice quality modification for emotional speech synthesis.* Paper presented at Eurospeech 2003, Geneva, Switzerland.

Edgington, M. (1997, September). *Investigating the limitations of concatenative synthesis.* Paper presented at Eurospeech 1997, Rhodes, Greece.

Eichner, M., Wolff, M., & Hoffmann, R. (2004). *Voice characteristics conversion for TTS using reverse VTLN.* Paper presented at the ICASSP 2004, Montreal, Canada.

Hamza, W., Bakis, R., Eide, E. M., Picheny, M. A., & Pitrelli, J. F. (2004, October). *The IBM expressive speech synthesis system.* Paper presented at the 8th International Conference on Spoken Language Processing, Jeju, Korea.

Heuft, B., Portele, T., & Rauth, M. (1996, October). *Emotions in time domain synthesis.* Paper presented at the 4th International Conference of Spoken Language Processing, Philadelphia.

Iida, A., & Campbell, N. (2003). Speech database design for a concatenative text-to-speech synthesis system for individuals with communication disorders. *International Journal of Speech Technology, 6,* 379-392.

Iriondo, I., Guaus, R., Rogríguez, A., Lázaro, P., Montoya, N., Blanco, J. M., et al. (2000). Validation of an acoustical modelling of emotional expression in Spanish using speech synthesis techniques. In R. Cowie, E. Douglas-Cowie, & M. Schröder (Eds.), *Proceedings of the ISCA Workshop on Speech and Emotion* (pp. 161-166). Belfast, UK: Textflow.

Johnson, W. L., Narayanan, S. S., Whitney, R., Das, R., Bulut, M., & LaBore, C. (2002, September). *Limited domain synthesis of expressive military speech for animated characters.* Paper presented at the 7th International Conference on Spoken Language Processing, Denver, CO.

Loquendo. (2004). *Loquendo launches expressive TTS.* Retrieved from http://www.loquendo.com/en/news/news_emotional_TTS.htm

Matsui, H., & Kawahara, H. (2003, September). *Investigation of emotionally morphed speech perception and its structure using a high quality speech manipulation system.* Paper presented at Eurospeech 2003, Geneva, Switzerland.

Miyanaga, K., Masuko, T., & Kobayashi, T. (2004, October). *A style control technique for HMM-based speech synthesis.* Paper presented at the 8th International Conference of Spoken Language Processing, Jeju, Korea.

Montero, J. M., Gutiérrez-Arriola, J., Colás, J., Enríquez, E., & Pardo, J. M. (1999). Analysis and modelling of emotional speech in Spanish. In In J. J. Ohala, Y. Hasegawa, M. Ohala, D. Granville, & A. C. Bailey (Eds.), *Proceedings of the 14th International Congress of Phonetic Sciences* (pp. 957–960). Berkeley, CA: University of California, Berkeley.

Montero, J. M., Gutiérrez-Arriola, J., Palazuelos, S., Enríquez, E., Aguilera, S., & Pardo, J. M. (1998). Emotional speech synthesis: From speech database to TTS. In R. Mannell & J. Robert-Ribes (Eds.), *Proceedings of the 5th International Conference of Spoken Language Processing* (Vol. 3, pp. 923–926). Rundle Mall, Australia: Causal Productions.

Mozziconacci, S. J. L. (1998). *Speech variability and emotion: Production and perception.* Unpublished doctoral dissertation, Technical University Eindhoven, Netherlands.

Mozziconacci, S. J. L., & Hermes, D. J. (1999). Role of intonation patterns in conveying emotion in speech. In J. J. Ohala, Y. Hasegawa, M. Ohala, D. Granville, & A. C. Bailey (Eds.), *Proceedings of the 14th International Congress of Phonetic Sciences* (pp. 2001–2004). Berkeley, CA: University of California, Berkeley.

Murray, I. R. (1989). *Simulating emotion in synthetic speech.* Unpublished doctoral dissertation, University of Dundee, UK.

Murray, I. R., & Arnott, J. L. (1995). Implementation and testing of a system for producing emotion-by-rule in synthetic speech. *Speech Communication, 16,* 369–390.

Murray, I. R., Edgington, M. D., Campion, D., & Lynn, J. (2000). Rule-based emotion synthesis using concatenated speech. In R. Cowie, E. Douglas-Cowie, & M. Schröder (Eds.), *Proceedings of the ISCA Workshop on Speech and Emotion* (pp. 173–177). Belfast, UK: Textflow.

Oudeyer, P. (2002, April). *The synthesis of cartoon emotional speech.* Paper presented at Speech Prosody 2002, Aix-en-Provence, France.

Rank, E., & Pirker, H. (1998). Generating emotional speech with a concatenative synthesizer. In R. Mannell & J. Robert-Ribes (Eds.), *Proceedings of the 5th International Conference of Spoken Language Processing* (Vol. 3, pp. 671–674). Rundle Mall, Australia: Causal Productions.

Rouibia, S., & Rosec, O. (2005, September). *Unit selection for speech synthesis based on a new acoustic target cost.* Paper presented at Interspeech 2005, Lisbon, Portugal.

Scherer, K. R., Banse, R., & Wallbott, H. G. (2001). Emotion inferences from vocal expression correlate across languages and cultures. *Journal of Cross-Cultural Psychology, 32*(1), 76–92.

Scherer, K. R., Ladd, D. R., & Silverman, K. (1984). Vocal cues to speaker affect: Testing two models. *Journal of the Acoustic Society of America, 76*(5), 1346–1356.

Schröder, M. (1999). Can emotions be synthesized without controlling voice quality? *Phonus, Research Report of the Institute of Phonetics, University of the Saarland, 4,* 37–55.

Schröder, M. (2004). *Speech and emotion research: An overview of research frameworks and a dimensional approach to emotional speech synthesis. Phonus, Research Report of the Institute of Phonetics, University of the Saarland, 7,.*

Schröder, M., & Grice, M. (2003). Expressing vocal effort in concatenative synthesis. In Sole, M. J., Recasens, D., & Romero, J. (Eds.), *Proceedings of the 15th International Congress of Phonetic Sciences* (pp. 2589-2592). Barcelona, Spain: Causal Productions.

Stallo, J. (2000). *Simulating emotional speech for a talking head.* Unpublished honour's doctoral dissertation, School of Computing, Curtin University of Technology, Australia.

Tickle, A. (2000). English and Japanese speakers' emotion vocalisation and recognition: A comparison highlighting vowel quality. In R. Cowie, E. Douglas-Cowie, & M.

Schröder (Eds.), *Proceedings of the ISCA Workshop on Speech and Emotion* (pp. 104–109). Belfast, UK: Textflow.

Turk, O., Schröder, M., Bozkurt, B., & Arslan, L. (2005, September). *Voice quality interpolation for emotional text-to-speech synthesis*. Paper presented at Interspeech 2005, Lisbon, Portugal.

Vincent, D., Rosec, O., & Chonavel, T. (2005, September). *Estimation of LF glottal source parameters based on an ARX model*. Paper presented at Interspeech 2005, Lisbon, Portugal.

Vroomen, J., Collier, R., & Mozziconacci, S. J. L. (1993, September). *Duration and intonation in emotional speech*. Paper presented at Eurospeech 1993, Berlin, Germany.

Ye, H., & Young, S. (2004, May). *High quality voice morphing*. Paper presented at ICASSP 2004, Montreal, Canada.

Yoshimura, T., Tokuda, K., Masuko, T., Kobayashi, T., & Kitamura, T. (1999). Simultaneous modeling of spectrum, pitch and duration in HMM-based speech synthesis. In EUROSPEEC'H'99, ISCA Archive, 6th European Conference on Speech Communication and Technology (pp. 2347–2350). *Proceedings of Eurospeech 1999*. Budapest, Hungary.

Zovato, E., Pacchiotti, A., Quazza, S., & Sandri, S. (2004). *Towards emotional speech synthesis: A rule based approach*. Paper presented at the 5th ISCA Speech Synthesis Workshop, Pittsburgh, PA.

Index

Wayang (Shadow puppet), vocal
stereotypes in, 268
"Whether Material Statues May Speak by
Any Artificial Way," 303
Wizard-of-Oz scenario, 73
Women
with functional voice disorders, 107–132

case studies, 109–110
"hysterical" personality, 107–108
la belle indifference, 108

Z

Zygomaticus major, 139